CONTEMPORARY FICTION IN FRENCH

Our global literary field is fluid and exists in a state of constant evolution. Contemporary fiction in French has become a polycentric and transnational field of vibrant and varied experimentation; the collapse of the distinction between 'French' and 'Francophone' literature has opened up French writing to a world of new influences and interactions. In this collection, renowned scholars provide thoughtful close readings of a whole range of genres, from graphic novels to crime fiction to the influence of television and film, to analyse modern French fiction in its historical and sociological context. Allowing students of contemporary French literature and culture to situate specific works within broader trends, the volume provides an engaging, global and timely overview of contemporary fiction writing in French, and demonstrates how our modern literary world is more complex and diverse than ever before.

ANNA-LOUISE MILNE is Professor of French and Comparative Literature in the Department of French, International Politics and History at the University of London Institute in Paris. She is also the author of *75* (2016) and the editor of *The Cambridge Companion to the Literature of Paris* (2013), and she has recently co-conceived *The New Internationalists* (2020) on the politics of contemporary solidarity.

RUSSELL WILLIAMS is Associate Professor in the Department of Comparative Literature and English at the American University of Paris. He is the author of *Pathos, Poetry and Politics in Michel Houellebecq's Fiction* (2019), and he writes regularly for publications including the *Times Literary Supplement* and the *Los Angeles Review of Books*.

T0384655

CONTEMPORARY FICTION IN FRENCH

EDITED BY

ANNA-LOUISE MILNE
University of London Institute in Paris

RUSSELL WILLIAMS
American University of Paris

CAMBRIDGE
UNIVERSITY PRESS

CAMBRIDGE
UNIVERSITY PRESS

Shaftesbury Road, Cambridge CB2 8EA, United Kingdom

One Liberty Plaza, 20th Floor, New York, NY 10006, USA

477 Williamstown Road, Port Melbourne, VIC 3207, Australia

314–321, 3rd Floor, Plot 3, Splendor Forum, Jasola District Centre, New Delhi – 110025, India

103 Penang Road, #05–06/07, Visioncrest Commercial, Singapore 238467

Cambridge University Press is part of Cambridge University Press & Assessment, a department of the University of Cambridge.

We share the University's mission to contribute to society through the pursuit of education, learning and research at the highest international levels of excellence.

www.cambridge.org
Information on this title: www.cambridge.org/9781108468916

DOI: 10.1017/9781108570626

First published 2021
First paperback edition 2024

A catalogue record for this publication is available from the British Library

Library of Congress Cataloging-in-Publication data
NAMES: Milne, Anna-Louise, editor. | Williams, Russell, 1977- editor.
TITLE: Contemporary fiction in French / edited by Anna-Louise Milne, Russell Williams.
DESCRIPTION: Cambridge, United Kingdom ; New York, NY : Cambridge University Press, 2020. | Includes bibliographical references and index.
IDENTIFIERS: LCCN 2020040218 (print) | LCCN 2020040219 (ebook) | ISBN 9781108475792 (hardback) | ISBN 9781108468916 (hardback) | ISBN 9781108570626 (epub)
SUBJECTS: LCSH: French fiction–21st century–History and criticism. | French fiction–20th century–History and criticism.
CLASSIFICATION: LCC PQ681 .C66 2020 (print) | LCC PQ681 (ebook) | DDC 843/.909–dc23
LC record available at https://lccn.loc.gov/2020040218
LC ebook record available at https://lccn.loc.gov/2020040219

ISBN   978-1-108-47579-2   Hardback
ISBN   978-1-108-46891-6   Paperback

Cambridge University Press & Assessment has no responsibility for the persistence or accuracy of URLs for external or third-party internet websites referred to in this publication and does not guarantee that any content on such websites is, or will remain, accurate or appropriate.

Contents

List of Figures   *page* vii
Notes on Contributors   viii

Introduction: Mapping the Contemporary   1
Anna-Louise Milne and Russell Williams

1   Mediterranean Francophone Writing   17
    Edwige Tamalet Talbayev

2   After the Experiment   34
    Simon Kemp

3   Getting a Future: Fiction and Social Reproduction   53
    Anna-Louise Milne

4   Contemporary French Fiction and the World: Transnationalism,
    Translingualism and the Limits of Genre   72
    Charles Forsdick

5   The Franco-American Novel   90
    Russell Williams

6   Graphic Novel Revolution(s)   109
    Laurence Grove

7   'Back in the USSR': The Prose of Andreï Makine and
    Antoine Volodine   132
    Helena Duffy

8   Fictions of Self   152
    Shirley Jordan

9   Trauma, Transmission, Repression   167
    Max Silverman

10   Wretched of the Sea: Boat Narratives and Stories
     of Displacement   184
     Subha Xavier

11   Urban Dystopias   199
     Gillian Jein

12   Imagining Civil War in the Contemporary French Novel   219
     Martin Crowley

Notes   236
Select Secondary Bibliography   280
Index   286

Figures

6.1 Fabrice Neaud, *Journal (1)* (Angoulême: Ego comme X, 1996), p. 58. *page* 116

6.2 Dominique Goblet, *Faire semblant c'est mentir* (Paris: L'Association, 2007), n. p. 117

6.3 Chantal Montellier, *Faux sanglant* (Paris: Dargaud, 1992), p. 47. 121

6.4 Marietta Ren, *Phallaina* (2016), at https://phallaina.nouvelles-ecritures.francetv.fr 127

6.5 Pénélope Bagieu, *Les Culottées* (2016) 128

6.6 Fabcaro, *Moins qu'hier (plus que demain)* (Grenoble: Glénat, 2018), p. 6. 129

Notes on Contributors

ANNA-LOUISE MILNE is Professor of French and Comparative Studies and Director of Research at the University of London Institute in Paris. She works between cultural history, multilingualism and urban sociology and also writes more experimentally in French. Recent publications include *75* (Gallimard, 2016) and co-authored or edited volumes *The New Internationalists* (Goldsmiths/MIT, 2020), *The Cambridge Companion to the Literature of Paris* (2013) and *May 68: Rethinking France's Last Revolution* (Palgrave, 2011). She is currently involved in a collective-writing venture with people living in ongoing and forced displacement called the Numimeserian Collection.

RUSSELL WILLIAMS is Associate Professor of Comparative Literature and English at the American University of Paris. He has published widely on the contemporary French novel, including his monograph *Pathos, Poetry and Politics in Michel Houellebecq's Fiction* (Brill, 2019). His research considers the relationships between poetry, literary fiction, popular culture and the attention economy.

EDWIGE TAMALET TALBAYEV is Associate Professor of French and Director of Middle East and North African Studies at Tulane University. A scholar of Maghrebi literature and Mediterranean Studies, she is the author of *The Transcontinental Maghreb: Francophone Literature across the Mediterranean* (Fordham University Press, 2017) and the co-editor of *Critically Mediterranean: Temporalities, Aesthetics, and Deployments of a Sea in Crisis* (Palgrave, 2018) and of the special journal issue 'The Mediterranean Maghreb: Literature and Plurilingualism' (2012). She is currently at work on several projects that examine borders and migration from the standpoint of water as an epistemological site. She is Editor of *Expressions maghrébines*, the peer-reviewed journal of the Coordination Internationale des Chercheurs sur les Littératures Maghrébines.

SIMON KEMP is Associate Professor of French at the University of Oxford and a tutorial fellow of Somerville College. He has published widely on the 20th- and 21st-century French novel, including a monograph, *French Fiction into the Twenty-First Century: The Return to the Story* (University of Wales Press, 2010). His latest book is *Writing the Mind: Representing Consciousness from Proust to the Present* (Routledge, 2017).

CHARLES FORSDICK is James Barrow Professor of French at the University of Liverpool and was, between 2012 and 2020, AHRC Theme Leadership Fellow for Translating Cultures. Recent publications include the co-authored *Toussaint Louverture: A Black Jacobin in the Age of Revolutions* (Pluto, 2017) and a series of co-edited collections: *The Black Jacobins Reader* (Duke University Press, 2016), *Keywords for Travel Writing Studies* (Anthem Press, 2019), *Georges Perec's Geographies: Material, Performative and Textual Spaces* (UCL Press, 2019) and *Postcolonial Realms of Memory: Sites and Symbols in Modern France* (Liverpool University Press, 2020).

LAURENCE GROVE (AKA BILLY) is Professor of French and Text/Image Studies and Director of the Stirling Maxwell Centre at the University of Glasgow. His research focuses on historical text/image forms, and specifically *bande dessinée*. He co-edits *European Comic Art* and has authored twelve books, four exhibitions and approximately sixty chapters.

HELENA DUFFY is Collegium Researcher at the Turku Institute of Advanced Studies, Finland. Previously, she lectured in French at Royal Holloway, University of Queensland in Australia, and Université Blaise-Pascal (Clermont-Ferrand). She has published widely on contemporary French literature and cinema, with a specific focus on postmodernism and cultural figurations of World War II and the Holocaust. Her publications include *World War II in Andreï Makine's Historiographic Metafiction* (Brill, 2018) and *Inventing the Infranovel: The Holocaust in Postmodern French Fiction* (Legenda, forthcoming). Her current research investigates representations of Jewish mothers under Nazi persecution in literature across languages and cultures.

SHIRLEY JORDAN is Professor of French Studies at Newcastle University and Co-Director of the Centre for the Study of Contemporary Women's Writing at London University's School of Advanced Studies. She has published widely on 20th- and 21st-century women's writing in French, on art and art criticism, on photography and on experimental self-narrative across media. Her latest monograph, *Marie NDiaye: Inhospitable Fictions*, was published with Legenda in 2017. Her current projects focus on ageing, ageism and care as expressed in the photographs of Martine Franck, the works of Agnès Varda and a wide range of contemporary self-narrative and theory.

MAX SILVERMAN is Professor of Modern French Studies at the University of Leeds. He works on post-Holocaust culture, postcolonial theory and cultures, and questions of trauma, memory, race and violence. His book *Palimpsestic Memory: The Holocaust and Colonialism in French and Francophone Fiction and Film* (Berghahn, 2013) considers the connections between the Holocaust and colonialism in the French and Francophone cultural imaginary. He has recently published four co-edited books with Griselda Pollock on the theme of the 'concentrationary': *Concentrationary Cinema* (2011), *Concentrationary Memories* (2014), *Concentrationary Imaginaries* (2015) and *Concentrationary Art* (2019).

SUBHA XAVIER is Associate Professor of French at Emory University in Atlanta, Georgia, USA. She is author of *The Migrant Text: Making and Marketing a Global French Literature* (McGill-Queen's University Press, 2016). She is completing a second book, entitled *Transcultural Fantasies: China, France and the History of Sino-French Literary Exchange*, and is beginning a new project on international boat narratives. Her articles, essays and book chapters on the intersections between literature, film and migration appear in journals and edited collections in French and English.

GILLIAN JEIN is Senior Lecturer in French at Newcastle University where she researches in the field of the urban humanities. Her first monograph, *Alternative Modernities in French Travel Writing: Engaging Urban Space in London and New York, 1851–1986* (Anthem, 2016), examined the spatial imaginaries of modernity in urban travel writing. Her recent, AHRC-funded project explores the conflicting visualities of urban regeneration in contemporary Paris, and she is writing a book on this subject, entitled 'Inventing Greater Paris: Visual Culture, Regeneration and the Right to the City'.

MARTIN CROWLEY teaches French at the University of Cambridge, where he is also Anthony L. Lyster Fellow in Modern and Medieval Languages at Queens' College. His current research addresses the question of hybrid or distributed agency, in particular the political possibilities offered by approaches to this question in the work of Bruno Latour, Bernard Stiegler and Catherine Malabou. His recent publications include articles on Jean-Luc Nancy and Michel Houellebecq, and, as co-editor, *Economies of Existence* (Diacritics, 2020). He serves as General Editor of the journal *French Studies*.

Introduction
Mapping the Contemporary
Anna-Louise Milne and Russell Williams

This is a collection of essays about literature. The idea that literature is our first and principle port of call to explore contemporary fiction should not go without saying. If looking for fiction today, we might well turn towards other forms: television and film of course; mangas and video games as well. The corpus convened by this volume reaches in these directions. It includes essays that plot the massive development of graphic novels in the past two decades, that discuss crime fiction, the influence of film, the impact of television series and rock music. It also harbours various more or less fleeting intimations of YouTube and other online landscapes around the edges. One of the primary aims this collection gives itself is to blur the perimeter of the field of literature into the broader mediascape of digitally enabled or enhanced flows.[1] Another is to focus this discussion around writing *in* French, where there is still a tendency in the field to demarcate French and Francophone literature. Our claim is that part of what is signified by 'the contemporary' is a detachment from that prior demarcation. The impetus today must be, in part, to think production in a major world language such as French through polycentric, fluctuating constellations. This does not mean to say that there is now no stake or significance in the places where this contemporary literature is emerging and finding its mechanisms of transmission and distinction, as well as its forms of economic viability. On the contrary. The transformations of the landscape that these chapters collectively assess are very largely conditioned by structures of distribution and translation. So our claim is not that global information technologies have smoothed the factors of differentiation, although they have undoubtedly reduced the lag in connection; but rather that the unevenness of the terrain is more complex today than an opposition between French and Francophone can accommodate. Just as the separation of genres on the basis of high/low, insider/outsider polarities is no longer tenable.

This volume thus puts into effect two significant shifts. Yet it remains within a field broadly delimited by the claim that literature has some specific things to tell us about fiction and the work of the imagination. Or more forcefully, that it is in the work of literature, through the different ways in which it has been carried forward since the mid-1980s, that we can best explore how the French language tradition has grappled with the fictionalization of life. And perhaps more ambitiously still, that it is specifically in literature in French (as opposed to other major or minor world languages) that this exploration has found some of its more experimental forms, in part because of the prior trajectory of that tradition with its long and deeply rooted attachment to the autonomy and universality of the literary text.[2]

The periodicity of this collection reflects and bolsters that claim. Yet it is important to start by considering what founds it. For it is no small claim. On the one hand, it works with the suggestion that 'everything' changed in the course of the 1980s, and that it is difficult to understand the landscape of the contemporary, with the dissolving of demarcations outlined above, without considering a major reconfiguration of 'the literary'. That is, of what literature was thought to be and to do. But on the other hand, it observes how the concept of literature has held out in different ways against fiction, preserving its pre-eminence as an expression of expectation or desire in some contexts, while seeking new forms of critical potential from within that waning pre-eminence in others. So what does literature continue to bring to and to borrow from the broad field of fiction; how does it in turn hold itself apart; and to what extent does the impulse of fiction still remain core to what we understand by literature in an era of accelerated, globalized media? These questions destabilize the previous hierarchy in which literature rose above the particularities of generic distinctions – between the novel, the non-fiction essay and autobiography, for example – but they do not fully dismiss it. For this hierarchy continues to have structural force and to echo across this otherwise radically divergent corpus, as can be noted at the apparently superficial level by the fact that the template of distinction, expressed by the austere seriousness of plain covers and stand-alone titles, characterizes many of the books discussed here. The deeper ramifications of how this 'hautaine beauté' / 'haughty beauty'[3] continues to condition the field are addressed in a number of ways through the following chapters. But by foregrounding fiction we problematize literature, while acknowledging that the notion of literature continues to shape what these chapters ask of fiction. It is from within their uneasy and evolving proximity that this volume is organized, with the objective of considering how it conditions the critical horizons opening up in and for contemporary writing and reading in French.

The scene we will be considering could be said to start with an end, that of an era we can designate by the very different figures of Jean-Paul Sartre and Roland Barthes. Their deaths, barely three weeks apart, coincided almost exactly with a relatively inauspicious new appearance in the form of Pierre Nora's journal, *Le Débat*, published for the first time in May 1980, which we will take here as a different sort of starting point.[4] The aim of Nora's review was to create an alternative intellectual space that was explicitly positioned against the posture of 'engagement' or the pairing of literary and critical force represented at that time most emblematically by Sartre. Oriented more towards the social sciences, *Le Débat* was both the sign of the devaluing of the literary field, and instrumental in the advent of an anti-totalitarian consensus built on the ruins of the long cycle of revolutionary and avant-gardist thinking. Annie Ernaux, a key author in the field this volume explores, detailed the tenor of the moment with characteristically caustic economy:

> Les « nouveaux philosophes » surgissaient sur les plateaux de télévision, ils ferraillaient contre les « idéologies », brandissaient Soljenitsyne et le goulag pour faire rentrer sous terre les rêveurs de révolution. À la différence de Sartre, dit gâteux, et qui refusait toujours d'aller à la télévision, de Beauvoir et son débit de mitraillette, ils étaient jeunes, ils « interpellaient » les consciences en mots compréhensibles par tout le monde, ils rassuraient les gens sur leur intelligence.[5]

> The 'new philosophers' popped up on television and did away with the old 'ideologies.' They waved Solzhenitsyn and the Gulag at the revolutionary dreamers to make them cringe. Unlike Sartre, who was said to be senile and still refused to go on TV, or de Beauvoir with her rapid-fire diction, they were young. They challenged our consciences in words that we could understand and reassured us of our intelligence.[6]

In tandem with this backlash orchestrated most stridently against the 'intellectual' dissidence of May '68 came a newly permissive and exuberant harnessing of 'culture' in all its forms. François Mitterrand's omnipresent Minister of Culture Jack Lang signed off on countless initiatives to boost 'the arts', from the Salon du Livre, founded in 1981, to the 'biggest concert in the world,' launched in 1982 as the Fête de la musique, with a panoply of efforts in between to both protect and extend France's cultural heritage against increasingly international competition. Culture would be abundant, lucrative, democratic and easy-going. Under Lang's watch, there was money for French rap, just as there was for opera via a series of schemes designed to bolster market forces. Included in these efforts was a particular focus on promoting or protecting book sales, which was achieved through the 'prix unique' / 'fixed price' mechanism established under the 1981 'loi Lang'.[7] For some, this newly inclusive or consensual emphasis meant that literature could get back to the business of entertainment and, as a number of chapters here suggest, a 'return to narrative' was part of this tendency.[8] For others, the switching of attention away from 'la situation de l'écriture' / 'the situation of writing', with its capacity to renew subjectivity, towards ever closer relations with media and cinema resulted in a period of 'latence et d'observation' / 'latency and observation', during which there was no measure by which to separate 'le tout venant' / 'the all-comers' from works of importance.[9] Alain Badiou, writing in 2005, argued that the advent of what Marc Fumaroli termed the 'État culturel'[10] had also transformed the critical potential of 'fête' as a 'brutal interruption of the ordinary regime of things' into a 'contre-manifestation' / 'counter-demonstration', a rearguard action to stamp out the last of the political insubordination still hanging around after May '68.[11] Those who, like Badiou, judged that this new 'all-comers' regime of 'culture sans temps mort'[12] / 'non-stop culture' was encroaching ever more into the remaining spaces of opposition were pushed towards new forms or had to draw on marginalized and denigrated antecedents. No one direction emerged, and the result would be a range of discordant developments spanning flamboyant exacerbation of fictional licence through sceptical testing of fictional pitfalls to outright rejection of fiction and narrative. Exploring this map requires abandoning the 'post' that still tethered post-structuralism or postmodernism to a conception of the literary field, whereby a new critical movement would move us beyond now outdated forms.

So this volume invites the reader into a diffracted, polycentric landscape marked by a plurality of forms and modes of emergence and reception, turning towards dispersed and even discontinuous sites of experimentation rather than attempting to identify a hierarchy of significance or a new canon.[13] The field has seen a number of experiments in critical anthology in the past two decades, again reflecting the very strong pre-eminence of traditional forms of anthology in French and the need to displace them.[14] The moment for that sort of exemplary totality is now also past, and as this initial survey of the variable distance between fiction and literature – against the background of the more aggressive meshing of culture, state-led policy and market forces – already suggests, we need more relative perspectives. Before plotting how these perspectives shape the following chapters, however, we also have to consider the other major factor delineating our field, that is, the spread and affirmation of French as a language of literary production across the globe, which accelerated massively from the 1980s on.

Analogous in this respect to the complex entwining of literature and fiction, the medium of French is a constant across this volume but the vectors of interaction between different sites are also variable, resulting in a complex cartography rather than a hierarchy of influence or pre-eminence. Rapidly changing technologies of distribution and publication, new forms of translingualism as well as the structural significance of translation today extend our exploration from Siberia to Haiti, Canada to Morocco, Paris to New York, as well as holding it in a complex dynamic with Anglophone literature and theory. At one level, this significantly enlarges the range of the present collection relative to much other important critical work in French language literary studies. But more fundamentally, as the next two parts of this introductory discussion will show, it also transforms what it means to map the contemporary.

'The French-Speaking World'

Institutional 'francophonie', which aims to promote the use of the French language wherever it is spoken or written globally, was but one arm of the 'état culturel' outlined above, but its impact had particular significance as relations of dependency between metropolitan France and the French-speaking world shifted towards less binding structures of influence and transaction.[15] Driven by France's firmly protective commitment to 'l'exception culturelle' / 'cultural exceptionalism' in the World Trade Organization GATT negotiations of 1993 and coloured by the rhetoric of diversity, what would become known as the International Organisation of La Francophonie gathered momentum through a series of summits that have met biannually since 1986. Its efforts converged with the modalities of the 'fixed-price' law for books, also mentioned above, as the means by which book publishing was protected by state adjustment of market forces. This not only ensured the preservation of 'minority' positions within the literary field, it also promoted networks of bookshops, two key mechanisms that met with similar initiatives in the better endowed areas of 'la Francophonie', notably in Québec, where local publishing took off as a result of equivalently protectionist strategies. The poorer countries of North and Sub-Saharan Africa, as well as the Caribbean, fared less well, however, leaving them largely dependent on France and Paris for much longer, and creating significant disparities in independence from the traditional centre. Authors entering the field from these more persistently 'peripheral' spaces had little choice but to find the right door to knock on in the metropolitan space, while for intermediary players such as the literary magazine *Africultures*, everything hung on developing market share.[16]

Pascale Casanova's major study of the complex processes of entry into the literary field, *La République mondiale des lettres* (1999) / *The World Republic of Letters* (2007), accompanied these years of partial fragmentation and redistribution, appearing at the end of the century as a vast consideration of different phases and places of adjustment by which the space of 'literary freedom' carved itself out new terrain. It was also in itself a reflection of the intermediary situation of French language and Paris-centric production at that time: previously pre-eminent, now waning, still waving.[17] Casanova pointed out this intermediary moment herself in a new preface written for the 2008 reissue of the book in French, in which she responded to the observation that her book, with its totalizing yet critical ambition, could only be French. Developing from this, she differentiated between two modes of reception of its findings: that of dominated language spaces, where her analysis of structural rivalries and modes of traction upon them opened up strategic horizons for 'new players'; and the Anglophone reception. She reserved her comments for the specificities of the strategic or 'dominated' reception. Here, she claims, her hypothesis was confirmed. What the strategic reception showed was how 'the literary' is structurally conditioned by emulation, yet also independent of those conditions in the sense that the 'outsider' can only break in with the joker of formal or stylistic innovation. The importance of borrowing dominant strategies underpins the ambition she expresses in her final remarks: that her work will become 'une sorte d'arme critique au service de tous les excentriques (périphériques, démunis, dominés) littéraires' / 'a critical weapon in the service of all those coming from ex-centric literary spaces (peripheral, impoverished, dominated)'.[18] In this sense, she positions herself as holding out a key to that door in Paris, setting her work in a mimetic relation to the combined 'lucidity' and 'impulse to rebel' of the subaltern writer determined to make her infraction.[19]

The present volume offers the means of reviewing the tight articulation between dominant 'aesthetic invention' and entry into the market that structures Casanova's account. With chapters focusing on writing emerging from the African, American and Asian continents, as well as Europe, it gathers together discussion of multiple 'marginal' spaces, characterized by what Casanova calls 'contiguïté structurale' / 'structural contiguity' in the field.[20] Read together and through the entanglements they reveal, they offer the means of assessing whether we can still identify something like the 'rapprochement [. . .] entre des œuvres' / 'proximity between works' that would underpin a concept of 'the literary' as the essential lever for breaking in.[21] But within the context of this introduction, Casanova's account is also significant for the way in which it binds together the extension of the map and the historicization of literary autonomy. Observing the persistence of 'avant-gardist' distinction within displacement to new territories brings back to the fore our earlier questioning of traditional hierarchies and prompts a broader consideration of what is at stake in our cartographic process.[22]

Literary Geopolitics

Casanova ends her vast study with a return to Barthes, in this respect closing where we also indicated an end before turning our attention towards the questioning of literature's pre-eminence as a starting point for this volume. She also intends to turn away from Barthes, and she will do so with the Irish Francophone writer Samuel Beckett. The Barthes she quotes in conclusion is categorical in his expression of a continental divide between 'the world' and 'literature', between on the one hand, 'le foisonnement de faits, politiques, sociaux, économiques, idéologiques' / 'the profusion of facts, political, social, economic, ideological', and on the other, the remote climes, shrouded in ambiguity, of the literary work or 'l'œuvre'.[23] Casanova's aim through her study has been to contest this incommensurable gulf by showing that what Barthes configured as 'geographical' is better grasped as a temporal disjuncture. Works of literature are historically conditioned forms, caught in the glue of their ideological and social context of emergence. Yet they are dehistoricized, in order to gain entry to the other continent, the continent of literature, which knows only absolute values. The role of the literary critic is, then, to observe how this process happens, plotting the mediation between historically 'extreme' particulars, such as Beckett whose peripheral provenance and 'impoverished' style become the expression of 'the literary' in a gradual becoming of the World Republic of Letters that both absorbs Beckett and is changed by him. What Casanova thus describes can be seen as extensive and dynamic navigation between the two continents that, for Barthes, 'seldom coincide'.[24] But it is also crucial to note that this process happens relative to a further totalizing 'space', the unifying Republic, which absorbs all extremes.

Some fifteen years later, Barthes's two continents again appear in a structuring statement that outlines a new set of horizons for literary studies. The essay in question is the 2014 'manifesto for the social sciences', entitled *L'Histoire est une littérature contemporaine / History is a Contemporary Literature* by the prominent scholar and editor Ivan Jablonka.[25] The shift in terrain is significant, not only because this essay reflects the extent to which the cursor has now switched back towards a valorization of literature from the drift towards 'scientificity' promised by *Le Débat*. Jablonka identifies a problematic proliferation and technicity in historical writing that leaves readers unmoved.[26] In order, he claims, to understand the real better, and to communicate this understanding with affect, we need 'des fictions de méthode' / 'fictions of method' that will find a place for 'les mots justes' / 'the right words' and 'la langue des gens' / 'the way people speak'.[27] His own successful works, *Histoire des grand-parents que je n'ai pas eus* (2012) / *A History of the Grandparents I Never Had* (2017) and *Laëtitia* (2016), which won the literary prize awarded by *Le Monde* newspaper and the Médicis prize for the best novel of 2016, despite also being a work of contemporary history, are examples of a broader trend within the French language canon towards the narrativization of history or what he calls, in English, *creative history*.[28] And their focus on individuals caught in the enormity of the Nazi and collaborationist system, or the tragic fate of a young girl raised under the 'protection' of the social services and victim of systemic abuse before her violent murder, corresponds to the emphasis he places on unveiling the 'la vie des hommes' / 'life of men and women'.[29]

Jablonka's work in this respect is claiming to close the continental divide between the world and literature, and it is characteristic of what a number of critics have referred to as the 'transitive turn' in a finessing of the broader 'return to narrative' already mentioned. If plot and story have made a return in twenty-first-century writing, it is not just in the pursuit of entertainment, but also because they are engaged by the reparative dimension of literature, by its capacity to 'write for' in an effort to heal the wounds of history, both personal and collective.[30] This purposive positioning is inseparable from a significant opening towards the Anglophone academy, as Jablonka's use of the term *creative history* already suggests. His manifesto is peppered with references to James Clifford's *Writing Culture* (1986), to *gender studies, malestream history* and *the linguistic turn*. He carefully insists on a universalist incorporation of postcolonial and gender study paradigms, whose value lies, he writes, in the tools they provide for better understanding of the world, as opposed to the means they might offer 'à chaque groupe de formuler sa « vérité »' / 'to each group to express its own "truth" '. This being said, the final flourish to his own emphatic claim that historical objectivity will always win out over the discourse of identities is a playful sign of a substantial transformation or 'Americanization' of the field: 'C'est un Juif et un féministe qui le dit.' / 'It's a Jew and a feminist who is telling you this.'[31] He is referring to himself.

This complex weaving together of French universalism and Anglo-American categories pulls the map in a different direction to Casanova's concern to think her own positioning in relation to peripheral and excentric spaces. And its articulation of how Barthes's two continents are superseded is equally if differently significant:

> Il y a, sur la carte des écritures, deux continents : la fiction romanesque et le non-texte académique, tous deux nés au XIXe siècle. On peut vivre heureux sur ces deux continents (j'ai moi-même publié un roman et produit un grand nombre d'articles spécialisés), mais on peut aussi estimer que ces espaces sont aujourd'hui bien défrichés, de plus en plus saturés, et qu'il est possible de s'aventurer dans les zones inhabitées du monde. En ce sens, mon *Histoire des grands-parents* et *Laëtitia* sont des explorations. Dipesh Chakrabarty proposait de « provincialiser l'Europe ». Je propose, pour ma part, de sortir du XIXe siècle. C'est un troisième continent qui s'ouvre à nous, celui de la *création en sciences sociales* – une enquête pluridisciplinaire, une hybridation, un texte-recherche, une littérature-vérité, une exaltante aventure intellectuelle.[32]

> There are two continents on the map of writing: novelistic fiction and academic non-textuality, both of which were born in the 19th century. One can live happily on either of these continents (I myself have published a novel and many academic articles), but one can also judge that these spaces are today well-trodden, more and more saturated, and that it is possible to set off on an adventure into uninhabited parts of the world. In this sense, my *History of the Grandparents I Never Had* and *Laëtitia* are explorations. Dipesh Chakrabarty argued that we should 'provincialize Europe.' I suggest that we should get out of the 19th century. There is a third continent ahead of us. It is called *creation in the social sciences* – pluridisciplinary enquiry, hybridization, text-research, truth-literature, an intoxicating intellectual adventure.

Where Casanova's attention was to forms of intrusion into the structures of literary consecration, Jablonka imagines a new continent and reconvenes the old paradigm of the adventure novel setting out into 'uninhabited' territories. This is done in implicit rejection or displacement of the postcolonial reconceptualization of the relations between multiple but finite continents. In contrast to the centripetal force of Casanova's adaptable but self-perpetuating World Republic, Jablonka's emphasis on writerly strategies for defamiliarization, propelled outwards by the avidness of the writer, imagines a fresh start. A new page.

Shifting Coordinates

So how does the mapping undertaken by this volume operate alongside these geopolitical precedents? As previously suggested, it works with a series of relative and overlapping perspectives on a field that is continuous, if structured by different regimes of consecration. There is no one organizing principle such as 'literariness'; no clear vector of movement – from North to South, or outside to inside; no stable generic designations. It starts from an 'in-between' space, that of the Mediterranean, thereby recognizing the importance of destabilizing the organizing process that so often reaffirms the centrality of the European continent and its traditions. Edwige Tamalet Talbayev's exploration in Chapter 1 of Mediterranean Francophone writing begins in the early 1980s, offering a different displacement of our chronological starting point, and draws out the disruption of the ex-colonizer's language in works by Abdelkebir Khatibi and Assia Djebar, before addressing the question of narrative more directly through readings of Colette Fellous and Tahar Ben Jelloun. This displacement of a metropolitan transformation between the demise of Sartre and the rise of Nora also enables a different perspective on Barthes. Tamalet Talbayev quotes his acknowledgement of 'what he owes to Khatibi', thereby situating her chapter in tension with a presumed polarity of metropolitan centre and 'excentric' periphery. This releases cross-currents into the geographies of interaction and redirects the model of belatedness ('les « tard venus »') that still structures Casanova's study.[33] Barthes's attention in this short and peripheral essay within his own sprawling corpus is to how Khatibi positions the complex interculturality of the Maghreb as the space in which 'la compacité terrible [...] de l'*égo* occidental' / 'the terrible compactness of the Western ego' comes apart.[34] In itself, this is a challenge to the cartography of continental divide that has had such structural significance for the mapping of literature. And it is characteristic of how the relative and polycentric approach developed in this volume realigns the temporal and spatial dynamics from within our map of contemporary fiction in French, rather than projecting a world or new continent beyond.

The following chapter also operates across the before/after frontier that delineates a major shift in the literary field in the course of the 1980s with Simon Kemp's 'After the Experiment'. Starting from within the claim that experimentation was now 'over', and therefore also its structuring effect for the consecrated centrality of the French literary novel, Kemp explores multiple expressions of play, ranging across texts of varying editorial profile from the prestigious 'Minuit canon', including Jean Echenoz and Jean-Philippe Toussaint, to the more 'mainstream' publications of Frédéric Beigbeder or Laurent Binet, with a significant focus on Michel Houellebecq. Frequently absent from surveys of contemporary French letters, despite his looming and provocative presence and his prominence in sales (in French and in the numerous translations), Houellebecq appears in a number of chapters here (2, 5, 6 and briefly 12), evidencing the porosity between different clusters of attention and the dynamic approach to the field.

A similar claim can also be made relative to the place of 'banlieue' literature in this volume. Rather than being the focus of one particular chapter, underpinned by a topographical approach, we consider that this work of positioning has now been accomplished with the lasting effect of making the periphery visible.[35] Instead, we are now concerned to consider how this periphery can also be seen within new centralities. This is the case in Chapter 3, where Anna-Louise Milne explores how the novel has accommodated the experience of unremitting social disqualification, particularly in the context of schools. Asking how forms of speech experienced as shameful disrupt the traditional novel form in works that span the 'highbrow' profile of Annie Ernaux or Leslie Kaplan to the 'outsider' position of Faïza Guène or, differently, Edouard Louis, she argues that this disruption contributes to understanding what sort of expectations the novel has of its power and critical potential today. Other works of fiction that also emerge from these or equivalent spaces of social and linguistic relegation, including the detective novel, or *néo-polar*, appear in subsequent chapters (5, 9, 11, 12). And this discontinuous approach to the exploration of an often homogenized social and cultural landscape ('la banlieue') is also characteristic of how literature in French from what is loosely designated as the Maghreb recurs through different chapters (1, 2, 5, 8, 9).

Chapter 4 continues the work of large-scale remapping with Charles Forsdick's discussion of the shifting frontiers between French, Francophone and world literature, which he traces from the early 1990s movement for a new 'travelling' literature through the 2007 manifesto 'Pour une littérature-monde' / 'Toward a "world literature" in French' and on to the more recent developments in translingual and transnational writing, reflected and amplified in the 2017 reworking of the 'littérature-monde' concept in the manifesto 'Nous sommes plus grands que nous' / 'We are larger than ourselves', which opened up 'world literature' to wider debates in France about writing, migration and democracy. In so doing, Forsdick suggests that it is from within a planetary imagination and alive to the new forms that are transforming contemporary literary publishing that we must draw our map.

Following these four opening chapters, which each in their own way seek to reorient or expand the scope of literature in French in relation to the resurgence and the dismissal of fiction, the next three chapters bring the category of fiction back fully to the fore and consider how it has evolved in relation to particular sources of influence or format. In Chapter 5, Russell Williams discusses the emulation and rivalry of Franco-American interchange in the growth and diversity of the *néo-polar*, as well as in the work of Tanguy Viel, Virginie Despentes, Leïla Slimani and Michel Houellebecq. Observing how other genres – cinema, TV series, rock music – brush up against more traditionally literary forms in these works, he reveals how these dynamics cross high/low distinctions to produce new possibilities for the novel. Also keenly attuned to the trans-actions between 'high' literature and the 'low' cultural forms emerging from print media, Laurence Grove's capacious survey of French language *bande dessinée* in Chapter 6 charts a succession of revolutions that it has unleashed within the very heartland of the Republic of Letters. Meanwhile, Helena Duffy's 'Back in the USSR' approaches the prose of Andreï Makine and Antoine Volodine through the paradigm of the prestigious nineteenth-century Russian novel. Having established the marked upsurge in fascination with post-Soviet Russia, and particularly the wild expanses of Siberia within French writing, she shows how two ostensibly very different novelists both choose to dwell within well-established tropes of Russianness.

The next three chapters shift the focus to the ways in which fictional-ization plays a role in the exploration of subjectivity through writing. Shirley Jordan's 'Fictions of Self' addresses the seepage of imaginary material into life writing, revealing the fertility of semi-fictionalization in the work of Jacques Roubaud and Marie NDiaye in particular. This is followed by Chapter 9, in which Max Silverman develops the discussion, opened up by Jordan, of fiction's role in the processing of trauma. Spanning a considerable corpus beginning with Georges Perec and Charlotte Delbo, then Patrick Modiano and Didier Daeninckx, before moving to Boualem Sansal and Nancy Huston, he also explores the complex intersections between European and colonial experiences of trauma and repression. Subha Xavier then brings these questions into a sharply contemporary focus through a discussion of boat narratives and stories of displacement in 'Wretched of the Sea'. Although prompted in part by the current surge in attention to accounts of migration and trauma at sea, particularly in the Mediterranean in the context of the 'migrant crisis' of the past decade, Xavier displaces her focus towards earlier works and other zones of the world through readings of Émile Ollivier, Néhémey Pierre-Dahomey, Kim Thúy and Linda Lê, bringing together a corpus that connects Haiti to Vietnam via Canada, while also observing the time lags and circumnavigations that condition this writing on the frontier between testimony and fiction.

Daeninckx reappears in Gillian Jein's following chapter, 'Urban Dystopias', through a reading of his most recent novel along with texts by Joy Sorman and Lydie Salvayre in a discussion that develops the earlier exploration of social relegation. Here, Jein displaces the centre/periphery dichotomy through attention to how urbanism produces inequality, exploring the different modes adopted by fictionalizing writing to articulate and map the affective impact of this structural violence. This is then followed by Martin Crowley's final chapter, 'Imagining Civil War in the Contemporary French Novel', which brings our volume to a close by returning to the questions opened up by this introduction: what sort of critical effort can the novel encompass today as it continues to evolve in relation to the prerogatives of literature? And how are the new forms of entrenched social and cultural disqualification, unalleviated by the 'democratization' of culture celebrated by Lang and his successors, transforming the novel as we think we know it? In dialogue, across affirmatively literary novels, personal testimony, the subgenre of detective fiction and sociologically inflected prose, through readings of works that explicitly champion their critical intent or camp their evasiveness, these chapters together consider what we might mean by 'committed' literature today.

Quelque chose noir / *Something Black* (Jacques Roubaud)

If, then, our corpus offers the means of identifying a renewed purposiveness for literature, transforming earlier paradigms of 'engagement' while also refusing to operate a de facto delineation between 'serious' literature and 'mainstream' fiction, we can bring this introduction to a close with a final consideration of how this situates this volume in relation to existing accounts of contemporary writing in French, and in particular to that abiding if challenged claim to the 'autonomy' of the literary text. For despite all the reckoning with modes of accountability, this 'literary' literature is still routinely positioned by French critics first and foremost as necessarily in excess of the 'reality' of social relations and what is deemed 'littérature de symptôme, aux effets purement sociologiques' / 'symptomatic literature whose effects are purely sociological'.[36] Described as being pressed against the 'paroi extérieur' / 'outer wall' of the world in one evocative image, it is thus positioned according to the presumption, which it shares with Jablonka, that 'writerliness' can absorb this exteriority and perhaps even redeem it.[37] This is achieved in large part by placing the categories of fiction and the novel under the sign of impossibility, by positioning them as the other against which this renewed effort must wrestle. It is also produced in abstraction of the broader field of writing addressed here, with little or no reference in any of the critical essays referred to in this introduction to writing emerging in French outside of Europe.[38]

In contrast, what our 'scaping' of contemporary literature in French from the range of partially external perspectives collected in this volume aims to produce, is a new cartography constructed between different clusters of attention, excited by variable factors of provenance, construction and dissemination, conditioned in part by processes of translation, but neither defined in opposition to market forces nor simply reflective of them. While the 'World of Letters' for Casanova still implied a centre recognizably indexed against textual invention or a concept of 'literariness' such as Beckett exemplifies, and it is clear that this concept still exerts a strong power of attraction, the recomposition of literary work and its suspicion of its own performative possibilities, as well as the expansion of means and spaces of distribution, have fundamentally deregulated the dynamic. The 'structural contiguity' that Casanova identifies between different works of various 'geographic' emergence is now disrupted by marginalities within dominant spaces which are complexly articulated to a position of literariness. Work has become more difficult to gauge, and its returns are more wildly spiked between unlivable wages and unfathomable fortunes.[39] Contemporary 'literature' is thus also shaped by the need to name its processes, to describe its work, to underscore its effort, while it is also, and perhaps paradoxically, frequently pinned down to the 'default' category of 'fiction' or 'the novel' in a necessary nod to commercial requirements.[40] This is indicative of the sort of contradictions shaping the field. And to engage with them, we need a new sort of map.

It would be possible, at this juncture, to turn back once more to Barthes. Not to the Barthes of *Sur Racine* and the entrenched dichotomy between the imprescriptible work of 'l'œuvre' and the 'foisonnement des faits' / 'profusion of facts', but to the later Barthes, for whom the serious-ness and patience of work was inseparable from a certain *légèreté* or lightness of life; for whom the 'novel' could only be renewed by a vast circumnavigation through critical close reading, through the diary or journal form, through travel writing, through photography, through *haiku*.[41] And the significance of this turn back towards Barthes is evidently to fold back over the putative chronology with which this introduction started, and to recognize in the contemporary a dissolution of vanguardism and an opening in all directions, historically and geographically, to trans-versal movements and alternative spaces and modes of reading.[42]

But rather than turning to Barthes, whose presence in this volume mainly goes no further than its introduction, here we might turn, as Jordan does too, towards Jacques Roubaud. For his *Quelque chose noir* (1986) stands also at the outset of this corpus, marking something of a break at the end of twenty years of formal experimentation within the Oulipo group, and yet is also inseparable from this long trajectory which began in published form in the early 1960s.[43] It bears, too, the trace of painfully felt inadequacy, in the poet's case faced with the tragic death at a young age of his wife Alix Cléo Roubaud. This is poetry defused of its prowess, forced into patterns of repetition, simplified – perhaps – into a slower reckoning with the intractability of loss. It is also closer to prose than his earlier work; to the sort of prose that characterizes certain facets of this corpus; to writing that has been referred to as 'blanche' / 'white', in an extension of Barthes's *Le Degré zéro de l'écriture* (1953) / *Writing Degree Zero* (1967), for its absence of style, its refusal of cultivation, its ignorance of itself, as if the temptations of the literary had to be fought against at all turns, in order to perpetuate its own pre-eminence.

The value of the variable approaches to reading that characterize the chapters gathered here lies in the refractions or density they offer between a polarity of black and white – or the idea that literary effort can redeem or repair the ills of the world. And Roubaud's œuvre stands, too, in that space as an example of long experimentation with the possibilities between genres, in the zone of fiction, contemporary yet ageing, persistent yet unexpected, digitally configured yet attached to its prerogatives, and perhaps above all else: better equipped than many to take itself seriously in a world in which human languages have increasingly to compete with machine rivals and the powers that own them. But for all its monumentality, Roubaud's work is far from alone in that space, as this collection intends to show. The new directions from here are multiple and various, in formal, linguistic and sociological terms, and the map reserves its surprises.

CHAPTER I

Mediterranean Francophone Writing

Edwige Tamalet Talbayev

At the core of this volume stands the proposition that the conjoined forces of globalization and increased transnational mobility are forging new forms of social and cultural transactions which bypass the usual pattern of dominance between France and its ex-colonies. Against the straitjacket of centre/periphery critical models, the recoding of 'French literature' as 'literature in French' favours reading protocols that liberate the production hailing from France's former empire from colonial binaries. This focus on physical mobility and fluid cultural interactions productively upsets the indexing of literary value to predominant metropolitan norms and canonical forms. Instead, through its spatial deployment, this volume's multifarious 'scape' of the contemporary stresses the need to devise critical frameworks cognizant of the diffracted, polycentric reality of our world – particularly models that would rid taxonomies of French-language literature of monolingual, Francocentric perspectives borne of the endless aftermath of colonialism. Drawing from the forces of globalization and its disjunctive methodology, this project brings the Francophone into dialogue with other linguistic and cultural logics – through the adoption of new, diffuse spatial coordinates, and also, as I will argue in the case of the Maghreb, through the examination of the intricate historical entanglements extending far beyond French colonialism that have brought the world's diversity to impact on literary writing in French.

In the Maghrebi postcolonial landscape, the amended literary cartography outlined here yields important insights. It also raises the question of the theoretical assemblages that may be mobilized to account for the full 'scaping' of Maghrebi literature in French in a global perspective. Throwing the spotlight on the rich diversity of French-language writing on a planetary scale, Francophone studies have brought a much needed corrective to the dominance of a Paris-centric literary marketplace.[1] Their thorough engagement with Anglophone postcolonial theory promoted a transnational perspective (what Françoise Lionnet dubbed the "'becoming

transnational" of French Studies'²), which divested French-language literature of the exclusive proprietary claims of the former metropole and
rearticulated it around a more scattered geography. Taking the point
further, this chapter stems from the premise that Francophone studies
themselves, despite the transnational ethos lying at their core, need to be
better attuned to the connective forces of globalization, an endeavour that
can only be performed through a recalibration of our critical methodolo-
gies from what Charles Forsdick and David Murphy have called 'parallel-
ism' (the consideration of Francophone literature from all areas of the
world in relation to the former metropole or, at best, to each other, in a
'transcolonial' perspective resting on the shared experience of colonization)
to 'comparatism' across linguistic traditions and imperial histories.³ In the
case of the Maghreb, the 'comparatism' pursued by Forsdick and Murphy
dons the shape of a sustained investigation into the region's plurilingual,
transcultural literary incarnations in an effort to unearth the multiple
idioms saturating Francophone writing, be they linguistic echoes or
symbolic figures.

The region's longstanding imbrication in a fully globalized order stems,
first and foremost, from its contiguity with the space of the Mediterranean
Sea. A crossroads of languages, histories, religions and cultures for millen-
nia, the Maghreb has endured through history as a space of hybridity and
multifarious contact in the image of its aqueous neighbour. Reverberating
with the multiple waves of conquests and migrations that unfurled on its
shores, the region's embedded narratives etch a multifocal, polycentric
Maghreb, whose full historical deployment is a product of its robust
connection to the Mediterranean. In this continuum between land and
sea, thinkers, artists, texts and concepts have endlessly circulated, forming
new philosophical regimes and aesthetic affinities. The material traces of
these encounters have spelt out a syncretic narrative at odds with the
regimentation performed by colonial and nationalist paradigms. Fostered
as much by trade, religious diasporas and knowledge-seeking travel as it
was by multiple colonizations, this enduring logic of displacement and re-
rooting urges the consideration of cross-Mediterranean contact as a deter-
mining feature of the Maghreb's self-definition. Iain Chambers has drawn
attention to the connective potential of sea-centred paradigms to 'unhook
a particular language and its explanations from the chains of authority,
allowing it to drift toward another shore'.⁴ Adopting the sea as methodology requires focusing our lens on this 'drifting' – on the shore-to-shore
encounters that it enables and, perhaps most importantly, on the reverberating memory of these foundational contacts.

These connections have given shape to a body of texts bearing the mark of multi-site crossings and interactions, a corpus marked by sedimentation and imbrication between mutual imaginaries. Doing justice to the intricacy of these texts implies forging transversal reading protocols that move beyond the strictures of postcolonial form and open the Francophone corpus up to unpredictable textual encounters. It requires paying attention to the spectral presence of interloping idioms within Francophone Maghrebi texts, in order to reveal the process of temporal stratification at work in the corpus. Denying teleological readings and emphasizing multidirectional interactions over time, this strategic shift delineates a more capacious framework for thinking plurality, one informed by the memory of other historical and social collocations that the development of colonial and nationalist modernity has repressed.

To be truly contemporary in the global sense proposed by this volume, then, means to excavate the obfuscated palimpsest of Maghrebi plurality, in order to restore the Mediterranean and its enduring memorial echoes to critical prominence in our dealings with the region. Susan Rubin Suleiman has proposed that to be contemporary means to situate oneself at the intersection of three complementary imperatives – to find one's moorings in a 'contemporary triad' of 'self-recognition, historical awareness, and collective action'.[5] To exist in the contemporary mode is thus to recognize the past and its enduring thrall, to retrospectively find meaning in it while simultaneously embracing 'a process of movement toward an open future'.[6] It is to labour towards the enactment of collective, relational inscriptions, to form new allegiances anchored in this asynchronous model of critical inquiry. In turn, Giorgio Agamben marks out two contrastive understandings of the term 'contemporary', arguing that '[t]hose who are truly contemporary, who truly belong to their time, are those who neither perfectly coincide with it nor adjust themselves to its demands. They are thus in this sense irrelevant [*inattuale*].'[7] Agamben's proclamation of 'irrelevance' should not be construed as an acknowledgement of insignificance. This specific positioning, at a remove from the vicissitudes of one's time, fosters a clearer sense of perspective, as anachronism purveys the necessary distance to gain insight into what may at first seem inscrutable. To these two attributes a third can be adjoined, capitalizing on the polysemy of the Italian original: *inattuale* in a philosophical sense, as that which has not been realized, that which does not conform to the world as it is. For, to quote Agamben further,

> [t]he contemporary is he who firmly holds his gaze on his own time so as to perceive not its light, but rather its darkness [. . .]. The contemporary is

precisely the person who knows how to see this obscurity, who is able to write by dipping his pen in the obscurity of the present [...] it means being able [...] to perceive in this darkness a light.[8]

Cutting through the dense texture of the present, Agamben's proposition reveals time's layered texture, its gaps and overlaps running afoul of teleological visions: 'its backbone is broken and we find ourselves in the exact point of this fracture'.[9]

It is this 'fracture', I argue, that could be held as a figure for the form of contemporaneity that Mediterranean Francophone writing performs. A moment 'in historical time, during which one becomes aware of an interval in time which is entirely determined by things that are no longer and by things that are not yet',[10] Agamben's *frattura* figures a breach in the texture of history through which the depths of time can be glimpsed. Bringing anachronism to life, it lays bare its travails under the surface of teleological meta-narratives of history. From this pressure point, alienated forms of cultural memory surge, layering a counterhistory 'mediated not by recall but by imaginative investment, projection, and creation'.[11] The role of literary writing, considered here in its '*suspended* relation to meaning and reference',[12] is paramount to this imaginative task. Through an examination of literary texts by Abdelkebir Khatibi, Assia Djebar, Colette Fellous and Tahar Ben Jelloun, this chapter thus proposes to explore the resonance of this discrepant, contemporary stance of Francophone writing in relation to the specific context of a Mediterranean Maghreb – a Maghreb cross-cut by the striated, fractal time of the Mediterranean.

A 'wakeful margin'

The publication of Moroccan thinker Abdelkebir Khatibi's *Maghreb pluriel* (1983) / *Plural Maghreb* (2019) effectively invalidated enduring visions of the Maghreb's historicity as the product of two competing forms of *telos,* each supported by a language (Arabic or French) and a transnational, nationalist project (pan-Arabism or French colonialism, respectively). Laying emphasis on the intrinsic heterogeneity of the Maghreb, *Maghreb pluriel* presents a ground-breaking reassessment of the region's layered temporality. Against the grain of Islamic theology and the form of modernity purveyed by the European Enlightenment, Khatibi's concept of postcoloniality in the Maghreb instead advocates for the recognition of 'une pensée-autre, une pensée peut-être inouïe de la différence'[13] / 'an other-thought, maybe an unprecedented way of thinking difference'. The modular vision of identity implied in Khatibi's alternative highlights the intrinsic plurality of the Maghreb and uncouples the process of its decolonization from a deceitful concept of authenticity. Neither Islamic nor the product of European rationality, Khatibi's *pensée-autre* thrives in the gaps between both thought systems, in a rejection of the debilitating quest for 'pure' origins that has animated many national attempts at decolonizing culture. Inscribing the Maghreb on the map of global modernity as a truly decolonized space entails recognizing that it also encompasses intercultural models of identity which cut across religious and identitarian absolutes. Indexing postcoloniality to the acknowledgement and nurturing of difference within the national body, Khatibi's proposition enacts a *double critique* of both colonial hierarchies and Islamic theology:

> Maghreb, ici, désigne le nom de cet écart, de ce non-retour au modèle de sa religion et de sa théologie (si déguisées soient-elles sous des idéologies révolutionnaires) [. . .] d'autre part le nom « arabe » désigne une guerre de nominations et d'idéologies qui mettent au jour la pluralité active du monde arabe [une pluralité comprenant] ses marges spécifiques (berbères, coptes, kurdes . . . et marge des marges : le féminin).[14]

> Here, Maghreb designates this discrepancy, this non-return to the model offered by one's religion and theology (be they disguised as revolutionary ideologies) [. . .] in addition, the term 'Arab' designates a war between labels and ideologies that sheds light onto the active plurality of the Arab world [a plurality comprising] its specific margins (Berbers, Copts, Kurds . . . and margin of margins: the feminine).

The Maghreb's unique positionality on the edge of two geopolitical projects and cultural logics stems from its liminality. A 'marge en éveil'[15] / 'wakeful margin', it keeps totalizing conceptions of identity at bay. It figures a 'site topographique entre l'Orient, l'Occident et l'Afrique, [qui peut] se mondialiser pour son propre compte'[16] / 'topographical site between Orient, Occident and Africa, [a site open to] globaliz[ation] in its own right'. The Maghreb is a space of mediation and connectivity, a 'pluralité (linguistique, culturelle, politique) [qui] repense le dehors d'une manière subversive, décentrée, détournée'[17] / 'plurality (linguistic, cultural, political) [. . .] rethink[ing] its outside through decentring, subversion, deviation'. This 'deviated' deployment builds on the region's contiguous relationship to the nurturing, maritime space of the Mediterranean, a continuum that provides the Maghreb with new coordinates. Rather than relegate it to the fringes of empire, this Mediterranean-centric conception stresses the Maghreb's centrality to the most pressing issues facing Europe and the Arab world. Rid of the burden of monolithic legacies, the Maghreb can lay claim to the order of global modernity on the basis of its own eclectic relevance.

Khatibi's ruminations on the Maghreb's decentring of dominant epistemologies yield unique insights into the literary. In the thinker's subversive vision, literature hinges on the cultivation of linguistic polyphony: 'cette littérature maghrébine dite d'expression française est un récit de traduction. Je ne dis pas qu'elle n'est que traduction, je précise qu'il s'agit d'un récit *qui parle en langues*'[18] / 'this so-called Maghrebi literature of French expression is a narrative of translation. I am not saying that it is only translation, to be precise, it is a narrative *that speaks in tongues*'. Brimming with the multiple, stifled idioms of the Mediterranean, Francophone writing from the Maghreb is to be read in the manner of a palimpsest. The superimposition of languages nevertheless stops short of claiming full semantic legibility. The Maghrebi postcolonial text revels in inscrutability. Nestled deep within the layering of languages lies the *indicible* (unsayable), the point of contact between incommensurable idioms that begets pain and frustration. *Amour Bilingue* (1983) / *Love in Two Languages* (1990), Khatibi's novel of a love story between a Maghrebi man and a French woman, thematizes the tension inherent in any linguistic encounter in colonialism. As the passion for the French woman lures the lover towards an ever-receding, unattainable meeting point, ineffability takes its toll: 'la souffrance de l'indicible. Chaque jour s'écrivait une blessure, chaque jour, de l'irréparable.'[19] / 'the suffering of the unsayable. Every day a wound was written, every day, something irreparable.'[20] However, another concurrent reading of the clash surrounding the colonial situation is possible. Khatibi's reading of *bi-langue* focuses on the 'space between two exteriorities'[21] – a site of *interlangue* (interlanguage), in which various idioms circulate, unsettling untranslatability and the supposed singularity of language. Following the 'lois de l'hospitalité dans le langage'[22] / 'laws of hospitality in language', the act of writing brings plurality to the relation between self and other: 'Dans chaque mot : d'autres mots ; dans chaque langue : le séjour d'autres langues.'[23] / 'In each word: other words; in each language: the sojourn of other languages.' Through this renewed engagement with the world's diversity, the Maghreb rises to the challenge of a global modernity in the making. Recasting the region's awareness of its intrinsic otherness as a historical event, the development of *bi-langue* partakes of the effort 'to take charge of the active plurality of [the Maghreb's] utterances'.[24] In a late essay, 'Paradigmes de civilisation', Khatibi links this self-presence of the Maghreb to its foundational plurality within the 'dispositif à faire de la civilisation'[25] / 'civilization-making apparatus' that is the Mediterranean. This re-inscription into a planetary cartography of interculturality revolves around the Maghreb's ability to forge a 'langue « hétérologique », un « ramassis » de différences, dont le brassage ébranlera un peu la compacité terrible [. . .] de l'*égo* occidental'[26] / '"heterological" language, an "amalgam" of differences whose mixing will further shake the terrible compactness [. . .] of the Western *ego*'.

Assia Djebar's Archaeology

A similar focus on *brassage* animates Algerian *académicienne* Assia Djebar's reflections on her role as a 'Francophone voice' in the literary landscape of the 1990s. In *Ces Voix qui m'assiègent* (1999), Djebar depicts the process through which writing comes to life, 'toujours comme une mise en écho, dans un besoin compulsif de garder trace des voix, tout autour, qui s'envolent et s'assèchent'[27] / 'always as an echoing, a compulsive need to preserve the voices all around that take flight and dry up'. For Djebar, writing emerges as a practice engaged in transmission. Beyond the exiguity of French, its dual movement unfolds as both 'border writing' ('je me place, moi, sur les frontières'[28] / 'I place myself on the borders') and illumination of a pre-linguistic state marked by obscurity and gradual, if violent, emergence ('un amont obscur de la langue'[29] / 'pre-linguistic darkness'). The form of expression that writing begets is tributary to endless displacement ('en constant et irrésistible déplacement'[30] / 'in constant and irresistible displacement'), suturing together disparate languages and accents: 'pour certains un français avec échos d'espagnol, d'italien, de maltais, etc. – pour les autres, les autochtones, [. . .] un français légèrement dévié, puisque entendu avec une oreille arabe ou berbère, écrire tout contre un marmonnement multilingue'[31] / 'for some French with Spanish, Italian, Maltese, and other echoes – for others, the natives, [. . .] French slightly thrown off course since it was heard with an Arab or Berber ear; to write close to a multilingual muttering'. In this Mediterranean-inspired linguistic 'in-between', or rather 'being between languages', this border writing in the making coalesces around a sense of ephemerality, of 'passage' between languages in a 'hors-champ de la langue'[32] / 'what lies beyond language'.

In this space of non-identity, the nurturing obscurity vibrates with the pulse of 'quelque chose d'autre, de signes suspendus, de dessins [. . .] allégés de leur lisibilité'[33] / 'something else, of suspended signs, of drawings [. . .] relieved of their readability'. This interval in the monolith of nationalist monolingualism is the realm of the immemorial Berber language. It sustains the writer's 'extraterritorialité' / 'extraterritoriality',[34] her only accessible form of emplacement. This non-place (utopia in its etymological meaning), which the writing summons, becomes a substitute for the Algerian utopia of political welfare promised in the wake of independence.[35] It morphs into an intuitive, experimental terrain wherein the shortfalls of an unfinished hybridization process, interrupted by the emergence of totalizing discourse, can be scrutinized and remedied. It forms a hospitable site where the echoes of the past are sustained against the tattering power of oblivion, paving the way for other collocations of national identity defined along less restrictive lines. Steeped in the depths of time, it is the domain of myth and, in Djebar's construct, female tradition. Djebar's anamnestic writing aims to resurrect this entombed memory. Djebar's commemorative project must proceed cautiously, '*écrire tout près, non, tout le long de l'abîme*'[36] / '*writing next to, or rather along the abyss*' [of oblivion]. It must cauterize the 'trous de mémoire'[37] / 'memory gaps' that obscure the genealogy of female voices and their transmission of a repressed heritage; it must gaze into the abyss to liberate the occulted secrets from the shroud of silence, the white shroud of Algeria's aphasia. The 'archéologie de [la] généalogie féminine'[38] / 'archaeology of feminine genealogy' revived by Djebar's text sets a template for the decipherment of other interrupted signs, the 'suspended signs and drawings relieved of their readability' ensconced in the darkness, linking female tradition to the dissipating Berber heritage, the historically occluded Numidian roots of Algeria.

Djebar's 1995 novel *Vaste est la prison* / *So Vast the Prison* (1999) highlights the constitutive plurality of the Maghreb through evocations of the early days of Antiquity, when the Maghreb existed only in correlation to other Mediterranean spaces. Djebar engages in a long excursus retracing the strategic alliances between ancient Mediterranean empires, both Numidian and foreign, and their enduring warfare for dominance over North Africa and the broader Mediterranean. This reclaiming of the Maghrebi imperial palimpsest gestures to the temporal fluidity of past and present commingling in layered sites of encounters – the very sites where the destiny of the Maghreb and the Mediterranean came to be decided, through warfare and violence, but also through the multiplicity of accounts that emerged in their wake. Against the grain of historical chronicles and the many orientalist letters and accounts penned by European travellers to the Maghreb,[39] the novel sheds light on another form of writing that had survived the erosion of time – a bilingual inscription on a stele at Dougga, among the ruins of a syncretic mausoleum, 'mi-grecque, mi-orientale'[40] / 'half-Greek, half oriental',[41] celebrating through its very composite form the variegated history whose disappearance its construction was meant to commemorate. The stele was first recovered by chance by Thomas d'Arcos, a seventeenth-century Provençal slave inured to Mediterranean crossings (from Provence to Sardinia and eventually Tunis) and transversal, plurilingual scholarship ('une chronique des mœurs ottomanes, mais écrite en espagnol, ainsi que des commentaires sur la musique des Turcs et des Maures'[42] / 'a project to chronicle Ottoman customs (written in Spanish), as well as commentaries on Turkish and Moorish music'.[43] The narrative will reveal the bilingual formulas to be *punique* and *libyque*, both languages harkening back to an inscrutable, vanishing Berber heritage.

Yet it is only through contact with the ferment of Mediterranean encounters that the long lineage of Algerian women writers within which the narrative voice emerges can come into existence. Nowhere is this as evident as in the rewriting of Cervantes' 'Captive's Tale' that Djebar interpolates at the centre of the novel. The story that Djebar retells is as much the product of cross-Mediterranean intertextuality as it is of inter-cultural dialogue. In Djebar's tale, Algerian noblewoman Zoraidé liberates an enslaved Christian by writing him a letter in Arabic. Zoraidé's betrayal leaves her no choice but to abandon Algiers for Spain, a land whose language will forever remain incomprehensible, prompting her voiceless-ness. The first Algerian woman to have written herself into existence will thus remain mute for the rest of her life – a harbinger of the future of 'expatriation'[44] and aphasia to which Algerian women writers will be condemned. Zoraidé's act of writing assumes an unpredictable outcome, and indeed one might ponder the odds of an Arabic missive being correctly deciphered by a Christian captive were it not for his renegade companion, a Christian converted to Islam, who acts as an intermediary between the two lovers. A catalyst for the plot, the presence of the renegade reverberates with the fluidity of the early modern Mediterranean. Djebar's text suggests a connection between the renegade and another type of transgressive, yet mediating, figure – the *Morisco*[45] or Muslim convert to Christianity, whose ability to navigate distinct linguistic and religious territories embodies the inherent plurality of Al-Andalus, the Muslim rule over Spain and parts of southern Europe that consecrated *convivencia* between the three mono-theistic religions. More than a century after al-Andalus came to an end, Spain's 1609 Expulsion of the *Moriscos* – possibly renegades of another kind – triggered the group's relocation to various Mediterranean sites, among them the home town of the narrator's mother, Cherchell. This cross-Mediterranean ebullition purveys identity narratives predicated on the cherished memory of the Andalusian past: 'brassage des races, des langues et des savoirs [...] lueur vacillante qui traversa les siècles et perpétua la lumière de l'Andalousie des femmes'[46] / 'intermingling of races, languages, and knowledge [...] flickering light from the women's Andalusia that still provided us with a little nourishment across the centuries'.[47] Providing compassionate intercession between languages and religions, the enlightened figure of the renegade helps bring the captive's exile to an end. Zoraidé's exile to Inquisition Spain, however, will be assuaged by no such generous mediation. In a chiasmatic echo of the prisoner's fate (she chooses to liberate the captive only to find herself entrapped in an impenetrable language), Zoraidé will benefit from no translation. The land to which she is exiled is but a remote shadow of its vibrant, plural past; it offers no sanctuary for composite forms of belonging. There, she is forever excluded, reduced to the status of a 'sourde-muette' / 'deaf-mute', her writing both 'illisible' and 'inutile' ('useless' and such that 'no one can read it'): '[il] s'efface' / '[it] is erased'.[48] As the glorious original exchange between the two lovers withers, nothing remains but nostalgia for an earlier moment of true 'entrecroisement des sexes – de langues, puis de regards'[49] / 'intermingling of the sexes – first of languages, then gazes'.[50]

This Andalusian 'mémoire déjà ensablée'[51] / 'memory already covered in sand',[52] ever in danger of disappearance, brings to mind the *lybique* inscriptions recovered from the Dougga mausoleum. Both threatened by disaggregation, they must be the objects of meticulous preservation to contravene the effacement of time. Trans-Mediterranean mobility then conjures a poetic of mediation; it cultivates legibility. It is because of the renegade and his multiple crossings that the original translation at the core of Zoraidé's scriptural destiny – and in her wake, the destiny of all female Algerian writers – was unlocked. Similarly, it was his insatiable curiosity for Mediterranean cross-pollination that spurred the young Provençal scholar to reveal the long-forgotten Berber substrate of Maghrebi expression through his re-discovery of Dougga's alphabet. Spain's cultural depletion under the onslaughts of racist laws,[53] of which the Expulsion of the *Moriscos* is a most striking example, indirectly revived cross-cultural ferment in North Africa. In this perspective, the sea resonates as a diffracting surface bridging the space between conflicting, mutually exclusive cultural stances. On account of its hospitality for the exiled Andalusians, the Maghreb will become heir to the ethos of cohabitation and cross-cultural dialogue that they incarnate. The role of the Francophone writer then is to unearth the legacy of tolerance that the exiles brought along, to reveal the innermost ferment of tolerance that has endured in the Maghreb as a hallmark of Mediterranean hospitality.

Virtual Andalusias

In his now canonical conversation on hospitality with Anne Dufourmantelle, Jacques Derrida reminds us that 'there is no hospitality without memory. A memory that did not recall the dead person and mortality would be no memory. What kind of hospitality would not be ready to offer itself to the dead one, to the revenant?'[54] Tunisian writer Colette Fellous's engagement with the increasingly repressed legacy of the Jewish community in Tunisia offers one such illustration of the kind of retrospective, memorial hospitality that Derrida puts forward. Her 2001 novel *Avenue de France* goes a long way towards amending definitions of belonging in terms of origins and coincidence to ready-made identity narratives.[55] Resurrecting the vanishing memory of the Jewish Tunisian community in the process of being erased from the national narrative, Fellous's text performs the theatrical reconstruction of another Tunisia more heedful of its multi-coloured past. Through the metonym of Avenue de France, the main thoroughfare bisecting the colonial *ville nouvelle* all the way to the old Arab medina, the narrative conjures a motley assortment of memories centred on Mediterranean migrants who have arrived throughout the history of the Protectorate. Basking in peripherality and the liberating potential of estrangement, these resurging ghosts force a revision of the course of national history in light of Tunisia's long-standing diversity.

The fractured structure of the novel reshuffles notions of time through analepses and prolepses, substituting movement for continuity and teleological progress. This destabilization of the narrative finds its most vibrant expression in the insertion of lists distending the text at strategic junctures. Thus, the insertion of a detailed catalogue of the eclectic assortment of objects held in the Piperno store on the Avenue illustrates the full-scale mixity of the early days of the Protectorate. Among these 'Tunisian Curiosities' are objects hailing from the wider Mediterranean cohabitate: 'des vases, des lampes romaines, des lustres de couleur, des amphores, des tapis, des bijoux et quelques meubles damassés [...] une lampe à huile et une tête d'homme en terre cuite'[56] / 'vases, Roman lamps, colourful chandeliers, amphoras, carpets, jewellery and some damask pieces of furniture [...] an oil lamp and a man's head made of terracotta'.

Alongside this hodgepodge collection, Fellous highlights the plasticity of the community's origins:

> Entrez entrez il y a encore de la place. Angelvin, Meyer, Montelateci, Valentin, Cohen, Bortoli, Disegni, Massuque, Fellous, Fourcade, Rondot, Conti, Verzani, Moulin, Licari, Nuée, Achir, Fescheville, Bugui, Ville, Piperno, Borg, Gagliardo, Sangès, Cattan, Teynier, Viola, Licari, Kloth, d'Amico, Ladislas, Saliba, Galano, Saba, Baccouche, Mariani, Zerafa, Cardoso. Un rôle pour chacun. Un spectacle pris en cours l'année 1893.[57]

> Come on in, there is still room. Angelvin, Meyer, Montelateci, Valentin, Cohen, Bortoli, Disegni, Massuque, Fellous, Fourcade, Rondot, Conti, Verzani, Moulin, Licari, Nuée, Achir, Fescheville, Bugui, Ville, Piperno, Borg, Gagliardo, Sangès, Cattan, Teynier, Viola, Licari, Kloth, d'Amico, Ladislas, Saliba, Galano, Saba, Baccouche, Mariani, Zerafa, Cardoso. There is a role for each of you. It is a performance in progress in the year 1893.

The narrator's name figures prominently in the list, nestled amid the foreign patronyms. Redrawing the contours of belonging beyond any adulterated notion of origin, this superlative hospitality facilitates the haunting by the ancestors, the resurgence of their diversity within the self: 'ils bougent tous lentement sous mes paupières'[58] / 'they all move slowly underneath my eyelids'. The leitmotiv 'there is still room' nudges the national community towards more inclusivity for those who have been kept out of the weft of history. The community delineated in the list boasts multi-confessional, plural Mediterranean roots. It recasts the Maghreb as part and parcel of a global landscape of hybridity and encounters. It is reminiscent of the *grana* Jewish community of Livornese origin, a group whose cosmopolitanism anchors the narrative voice (the protagonist is herself half *twansa*, or Jewish from Tunisia, half *grana*). In the wake of the Six-Day War, as anti-Semitism gripped Tunisia, causing riots and the departure of thousands of Jews, the multiple affiliations of the community conjured in the list provide a corrective to the totalitarian rhetoric of Tunisian nationalism.

Fellous's relational ideal shares significant semantic ground with Nadia Khouri-Dagher's concept of 'la Nouvelle Andalousie'. Through this strategic mobilization of the Andalusian heritage, Khouri-Dagher designates writers and thinkers attached to the cultures of the Arab world who, like Colette Fellous, have concurrently formed allegiances to other languages, cultures or conceptions of being. This *mise en relation* of knowledge paradigms and forms of literariness that straddle various cultures and idioms recalibrates modernity not in terms of teleology and hierarchies, but rather as a layering of complementary sensibilities. It outlines a form of modernity receptive to the fluctuations of identity in our global moment. The physical displacement experienced by the *Nouveaux Andalous* is echoed in their itinerant identities. The product of choice rather than birth, affiliations burst forth from encounters: 'j'ai vraiment besoin d'avoir plusieurs appartenances, j'allais dire plusieurs naissances, et je me sens toujours plus vivante lorsque j'entends plusieurs langues autour de moi. Je crois aussi que la modernité se situe précisément là.'[59] / 'I really need multiple affiliations, I almost said multiple births, and I always feel more alive when I hear multiple languages around me. I also believe that this is where modernity comes to life.'

A theatrical world in the making, the swarming Avenue de France becomes a stage where the fate of the Tunisian nation plays out. A virtual site in the Deleuzian sense of the term (in opposition to the actualized rather than to the real),[60] its bustling energy builds up against the backdrop of actualized history. The novel's fictional world substitutes itself for the unfolding nationalist projects in the process of overwriting the centuries-old hybridity suffusing the Avenue. The narrator confesses to a deliberate disinterest in historical circumstances and their traumatic aftermath, be they the colonial conquest or the 'nationalitarianism'[61] that followed it ('je ne crois pas à la vérité des choses présentes'[62] / 'I don't believe in the truth of immanent things'). Deflating the authority of actualized politics, the narrative takes root in a form of estrangement where signification is fractured and words are detached from reality: 'ce sont des phrases qui les ont poussés à faire le voyage vers ce pays d'opérette'[63] / 'it is the power of words that moved them to make the journey towards this make-believe country'. Availing herself of the resistance of the literary to any unambiguous process of reference, Fellous divorces signifiers from historically incarnated meaning and relegates them to the realm of the virtual, laying claim to what Réda Bensmaïa has dubbed an 'experimental nation', that is, 'a nation above all nations that writers have had to imagine or explore as if they were territories to rediscover and stake out step by step, countries to invent and to draw while discovering one's language'.[64]

Relieved of the burden of referentiality, autonomous, unpredictable words are free to follow the course of the narrator's imagination, the itinerary of her wandering. At the core of this perambulation stands Tunisia, both Siren and wound: 'en même temps, je le sais, c'est ma prison'[65] / 'at the same time, I know that it is my prison'. This magnetic pull to the homeland begets its own form of memory, what Fellous calls a 'mémoire aimantée. Le corps battant, vissé dans le présent, mais complètement électrisé, sans le savoir, par toutes les myriades de secondes d'un passé qu'il n'avait même pas connu [. . .] Une gifle assez puissante pour le réveiller et l'illuminer.'[66] / 'magnetic memory. A beating body, bound to the present but completely electrified, without knowing it, by all the myriad seconds from a past that it had not even known [. . .] A slap strong enough to awaken it and illuminate it.' The haunting primum mobile of the narrator's memorial writing, Tunisia remains elusive, an ideal destined never to be realized. The narrator's existence unfurls through perpetual movement in a capacious geography of contacts. Through this displacement, she escapes the exiguous history of Tunisian nationalism, defusing the potential aftermath of the trauma it instigated. This spatial deployment of identity partakes of the 'scaping' at the core of this volume, entwining mobility in both space and time. For the political project underlying Tunisian nationalism Fellous substitutes a decentred, fractal affiliation that only acquires tangible coordinates through its contact with other spaces and histories:

> Tirer le rideau, faire silence sur ce vacarme. Ma prière est ouverte à tous, Arabes, Français, Maltais, Grecs, Italiens, Corses, Berbères, Juifs, Siciliens, Égyptiens, Palestiniens, Portugais, Ouzbeks, Arméniens, Libanais, Chinois, Albanais, Turcs, Afghans, Anglais, Mexicains, Argentins.[67]

> My prayer is open to all, whether Arab, French, Maltese, Greek, Italian, Corsican, Berber, Jewish, Sicilian, Egyptian, Palestinian, Portuguese, Uzbek, Armenian, Lebanese, Chinese, Albanese, Turk, Afghan, English, Mexican, or Argentine.

In this New Andalusian paradigm, Tunisianness is subsumed within a global form of *convivencia*, which, in Fellous's virtual redistribution of identity, constitutes Tunisia's strongest claim to modernity.

Literature as (G)hosting

It would be rehashing a well-known truth to say that the corpus of Francophone literature has by and large coalesced around the experiences of disjunction and mobility relayed by its authors and main protagonists. Chipping away at the integrity of borders and lines of fracture between North and South, the experience of exile in particular has revealed the fundamental fallacy of political discourses advocating for narrow defini-tions of identity and culture. In our dystopian, contemporary times, when migration doubles as a humanitarian crisis bringing to mind the darkest pages of twentieth-century European history, the contact zone of the

Mediterranean has emerged as a space of fracture vitiated by the exclusive political configurations reigning supreme over its two shores. In response to this crisis of hospitality and representation, a corpus of literature devoted to the examination of migrant narratives has emerged. Among those texts, Tahar Ben Jelloun's 2006 novel *Partir / Leaving Tangier* (2009) stands out on account of its subtle reconfiguration of the dynamics of hospitality from the perspective of the clandestine migrant, the 'other' condemned to endless displacement, deprived of any potential re-rooting in the land of his exile.

Unlike many accounts of *hrig* (clandestine migration from the Maghreb to Europe), where attempted crossings eventuate in shipwreck and drowning, *Partir* straddles the line between migrancy and immigration as it considers the lives of the *arrivants* on the foreign soil – as well as their desire to return to their home country, a recurrent trope in literary depictions of immigrant lives in Europe. The story follows the lives of Tangier-born Azel (a truncated, unrealized version of the name *Azz el-Arab*, the glory of the Arabs, in Ben Jelloun's translation) and his sister Kenza in their failed attempts to construct a better life of dignified labour on the other side of the Strait of Gibraltar. The novel demystifies the ethos of happy hybridity that dominates representations of cross-maritime crossings in Maghrebi literature. From the incipit, the sea is indicted for its ambivalence. The Mediterranean is personified as Toutia, 'araignée tantôt dévoreuse de chair humaine, tantôt bienfaitrice parce que transformée en une voix leur apprenant que cette nuit n'est pas la bonne et qu'il faut remettre le voyage à une autre fois' / '[she is a] spider that can feast on human flesh yet will sometimes warn them, in the guise of a beneficent voice, that tonight is not the night, that they must put off their voyage for a while'.[68] Irresistible and treacherous as the unpredictable sea, Toutia is concurrently maternal, symbiotic in her embrace, her benevolent watchfulness eventually guiding the would-be migrants onto the boat of repatriation, also named the 'Toutia', once the migratory experience has proven baleful: 'Elle est là pour ouvrir les bras et souhaiter la bienvenue aux nouveaux passagers.' / 'She is there to welcome the new passengers with open arms.'[69]

Greeting the passengers on the boat, Toutia sings an entrancing Andalusian Arab melody. Undoing the staunch legal and geopolitical dichotomy between the two shores, her song tantalizingly revives the unified history of al-Andalus. Ostensibly dissipating borders through her song, Toutia's echoing voice ushers in a supposed new era of freedom following the announcement of Hassan II's death and the end of his authoritarian reign. It intimates a possible return to an earlier moment of contact and trans-Mediterranean existence. Yet Toutia traffics in both authenticity and deception. Marked with face tattoos in the manner of the Berber women of yore, her supposedly pure tribal origins are no more genuine than the conflicting readings that she induces: she is construed as a 'comtesse' (countess), a 'mannequin venu du Brésil' (fashion model from Brazil) or 'la femme du capitaine' (the captain's wife).[70] Despite her multiple incarnations, Toutia fails to signify both the return to one's country of origin and the opening to a fluid, cosmopolitan world. The site of suspended symbolism and auto-referentiality (Toutia ultimately never signifies anything other than Toutia), her figure invalidates the possibility of belonging on any scale. The Moroccan nation she purports to represent will remain forever out of reach; the boat bearing her name will endlessly float with no hope of mooring.

This representation of return reveals the novel's take on contemporaneity, in both its spatial and temporal dimensions. When considered in lockstep, time and space both crumble under the weight of the unrealized voyage. From the epigraph ('Mon ami camerounais Flaubert dit « j'arrive » pour partir.' / 'My Cameroonian friend Flaubert says "Here I am!" when he's leaving.'), departure is conflated with arrival, collapsing both beginning and end into an indistinct, atemporal unit. Between the two, the voyage at sea is eluded, possibly as a pre-emptive propitiatory gesture meant to ward off a sinister fate. Regardless of its original intention, the formula effectively relegates the crossing to the realm of Agamben's *inattuale* – both on the margins of time and in the parallel dimension of the virtual. In *Partir*, this virtuality doubles as spectrality as the figures of the migrants, eventually bound for their point of origin, are characterized as 'revenants', in the dual polysemy of being home-bound and a ghost. Suspended between space and time, the passengers will dissolve into fictive 'personnage[s] de roman' / 'character[s] in a novel',[71] the boat morphing into a fictive plaint against the cruel fate reserved for those who leave: 'et si ce bateau n'était qu'une fiction, un roman flottant sur les eaux' / 'and what if this ship were just a fiction, a novel cast upon the waters'.[72] This dispersion into the realm of fiction echoes Derrida's proposition that 'an act of hospitality can only be poetic'.[73] Unyoking hospitality from memory, Ben Jelloun's fictional configuration emerges from the darkness of the abyss. To quote Agamben's intuition, it succumbs to the 'obscurity of the present', an endless present of non-presence that engulfs the migrants and seals their suspended fate. Replacing mobility with never-ending errantry, the ethical imperative of hosting yields to the disquieting process of 'ghosting' at work in the novel, emptying the migrant subject from substance and historical realization, condemning him to the non-space of a Mediterranean that has run afoul of its congregating function.

Acting as 'heuristic device'[74] for the global 'scaping' of Maghrebi literature in French, the Mediterranean induces a reconsideration of the Maghreb and its margins, but also of the Maghreb as margin. Whether the product of the palimpsest of colonial conquests in the Maghreb or the outcome of mobility and migration, the deep-reaching diversity of the polyglossic, intercultural corpus of Mediterranean Maghrebi writing points to the latency of other historical inscriptions and aesthetic matrices at the heart of the Francophone text. This consubstantial polyphony gestures towards margin-to-margin trajectories that have loosened the stronghold exerted by the French centre over its former empire. In this ghostly space of hauntings and phantasmatic echoings, a distended thread can be woven between the subject and the collective, in which 'singularities com[e] together [heralding] a non-identificatory community-to-come'.[75] In this interstitial space between processes of nation formation and forms of resistance to it, the Mediterranean, reframed in our contemporary paradigm as a site of dyssynchrony, proposes more inclusive takes on identity. Against the grain of its contemporary instantiation as border and fault line between irreconcilable models, the Mediterranean's repossession of its historic, connective nature alone may foster Maghrebi literature's poetic potential to produce more decentred paradigms. In our times of forceful dichotomies, it is a valuable prospect.

CHAPTER 2

After the Experiment

Simon Kemp

In Frédéric Beigbeder's *Windows on the World* (2003), a blend of personal memoir, factual reporting and imaginative reconstruction around the 9/11 World Trade Centre attacks, the author describes a conversation with Alain Robbe-Grillet in New York during the aftermath of the destruction:

> – Pourquoi venir à New York pour écrire dessus ? me demande le grand écrivain en caressant sa barbe blanche. Moi, quand j'écris un roman qui se passe à Berlin, je ne vais pas à Berlin pour l'écrire.
> – C'est que je fais de l'Ancien Roman. Je laisse la nouveauté aux jeunes comme vous.[1]

> 'Why come to New York to write about it?' the great writer asks, stroking his white beard. 'I'm writing a novel set in Berlin, I'm not going to Berlin to write it.'
> 'Well, I'm writing an *ancien roman*. I leave the *nouveau* to young men like you!'[2]

Three decades before Beigbeder, at the height of his *nouveau roman* experimentalism, Robbe-Grillet, published his own New York-set novel, *Projet pour une révolution à New York* (1970) / *Project for a Revolution in New York*, (1972), a metafictional phantasmagoria of *noir* clichés drawn from pulp American fiction, reassembled into a collage of circular plotting and interchangeable identities, in which the criminals are indistinguishable from the detectives, and police interrogations segue into hostile critiques of the novel's own narrative. Any relation to the real city of its supposed setting is filtered through layers and layers of storytelling, that of the narrators and the author of the novel itself, and those of the myriad influences that gave rise to it. Beigbeider's modest rejection of avant-gardism and espousal of earlier, more traditional forms of the novel is a common attitude among his generation of French writers. His fellow social commentator and literary provocateur, Michel Houellebecq, for instance, similarly distances himself from experimentalism, declaring himself saddened by 'la débauche de techniques mise en œuvre par tel ou tel « formaliste-Minuit » pour un résultat final aussi mince'[3] / 'the riot of techniques mobilized by some "Minuit formalist" or other for such a thin end result'.[4] His own writing he views as a reconnection with older forms, as he told the *Nouvel Observateur* in an interview marking the publication of *La Possibilité d'une île* (2005) / *The Possibility of an Island* (2005): 'Il faut croire que je m'inscris dans la tradition des écrivains français qui posent des questions au monde d'aujourd'hui et ne renient pas la narration balzacienne.'[5] / 'You have to believe that I count myself in the tradition of French writers who ask questions of today's world and do not spurn Balzacian storytelling.' Does the current generation of French literary writers really choose Balzac over Robbe-Grillet, Sand over Sarraute, as its model? And if so, what has become of the postmodern play, the self-conscious critique, the Oulipian system, the theorist-novelist, the writing about writing that so characterized the post-War generation?

Formal experiment, we can say uncontroversially, is neither as widespread nor as culturally dominant now as it was in the second half of the twentieth century. There is nothing on the current French literary scene to match the literary collectives of avant-garde writers and theorists like the Surrealists, the *nouveau roman* or *Tel Quel*, which played such a major role in the literary culture of the last century, while those that continue, such as Oulipo, have lost the profile they once had. We should acknowledge that the importance of these groups may appear somewhat exaggerated with hindsight and reflecting academic preferences; it is not clear that the average French reader of the 1960s would necessarily feel the decade belonged to Claude Simon and Georges Perec, rather than more conventionally realist novelists of the time such as Marguerite Yourcenar, Henri Troyat or Romain Gary. But even granting the continuity of realist fiction and traditional narrative form before, during and after the post-War decades, the flowering of experimental fiction was a real phenomenon of this period. It coalesced around publishing houses, such as *Minuit*, journals like *Tel Quel*, and writers' clubs like Oulipo. It was characterized by a rejection of all assumptions about the fundamentals of narrative form – plot, character, chronology, perspective – and a reinvention of the novel through self-conscious reinvention of these basic elements, accompanied, in the case of the *nouveau roman* especially, by theoretical writings marking the distance travelled from Balzacian realism. The phenomenon lost momentum through the 1980s and 1990s, as authors died and were not replaced by like-minded writers, or as novels outbid each other in experimental extremism and lost readers' interest and good will. By the early twenty-first century, the idea of a *retour au récit* / *return to narrative* in French fiction was commonplace, and it is to this phenomenon that both Houellebecq and Beigbeder are alluding.

However, we do not need to look far to find formal innovation continuing to flourish in contemporary French fiction. It is perhaps less systematic, more modest, less revolutionary in intent than in the heyday of the *nouveau roman*, but it is there. The very 'ancien roman' to which Beigbeder himself was referring, his own *Windows on the World*, is scarcely a work of conformist realism: its fragmented narrative skips between different times and different cities, moving between fact and fiction and discourses from the pornographic to the elegiac. It follows his previous novel, the bestselling marketing satire, *99 francs* (2000), the narrative of which dissolves into a stream of advertising slogans in the final pages. Houellebecq, too, has more tricks and twists in his repertoire than his reference to 'narration balzacienne' / 'Balzacian storytelling' might suggest. The novel he is discussing (*La Possibilité d'une île*) is narrated by a series of clones, each the genetically identical descendant of the present-day protagonist, layering the story as they read and interpret the accounts of their predecessors. Following that novel came the Goncourt-winning *La Carte et le Territoire* (2010) / *The Map and the Territory* (2011), which played disconcerting games with reality and its representation, including introducing as a major character, then brutally murdering, the author himself, and, notoriously, inserting passages copied word for word from Wikipedia into the narrative. When we look more broadly at experimentalism in contemporary French fiction, certain continuities become apparent. The Minuit publishing house, the former home of the *nouveau roman*, remains a nexus of innovative writing, for instance, and the legacy of Oulipo, and Georges Perec in particular, is often acknowledged.

This chapter will focus on one important concept in particular for contemporary French experimental writers, and that is *play*. In his classic study of the play element in culture, Johan Huizinga defines it as 'a free activity standing quite consciously outside "ordinary" life as being "not serious", but at the same time absorbing the player intensely and utterly. It is an activity connected with no material interest, and no profit can be gained by it'.[6] He rejects any understanding of play that assumes it must serve something which is *not* play, arguing that 'the *fun* of playing resists all analysis, all logical interpretation. As a concept, it cannot be reduced to any other mental category'.[7] Activity undertaken in play is thus the opposite of action taken in earnest; it forms an interlude from the serious business of life. True play has an aspect of child-like creativity to it; while it may have rules, the extreme 'systematization and regimentation' found in, say, professional team sports leads to the 'almost complete atrophy' of true play in the mindset and behaviour of the players.[8] Huizinga, writing in the mid-twentieth century, saw the 'play spirit' as widespread in literary culture. Later theorists noted a particular association between play and postmodernism. Jean Baudrillard in the 1980s defined postmodernism as 'playing with the pieces', arguing that experimental modernism had taken literary forms to their extreme limit, and that all that remains to be done in its wake is to rework their remnants in creative and ironic revival.[9] Fredric Jameson developed this idea in the following decade, suggesting that pastiche had become the dominant cultural form in the contemporary Western world. For Jameson, unprecedented pluralism, the commodification of culture and a mania for novelty have eroded the previously shared norms of writer and reader, leading to the 'waning of affect', the loss of personal expression and communicated feeling in an impersonal, consumerist culture.[10] Since the *nouveau roman*, he notes, literature has welcomed the pre-formed content of stereotypes and mass cultural allusions that the much practised cultural consumer can identify at a glance; authors rework and re-present familiar forms and images to readers who can draw on their experience of a lifetime's immersion in the same globalized cultural soup as the writer. While we need not necessarily accept the negative slant of Jameson's assessment, we will find clear echoes of all three theorists' characterizations of contemporary French and francophone literary culture. Two areas in particular are often the focus of the writer's playfulness. One is the narration, the voice and perspective of the narrator, through which the storyteller will often draw as much attention as their tale. The other is genre. The novel has always been a porous literary category, but never more so than today: fiction, memoir, journalism, essays and other modes of writing clash and merge within these texts, as narrative fiction exuberantly appropriates the styles, subject matter and functions of each for its own purposes. Linking both of these kinds of play is a frequent element of reflexivity in the writing. Through the unconventional narration and the transgressive genre-hopping, the construction of the text becomes, at least in part, its subject matter. This is usually not so much as a serious-minded *Verfremdungseffekt*, meant to guard the naïve reader from falling into the illusions of realism, but rather to draw aside the curtain with a wink to reveal how the literary trick is accomplished.

Narratorial play puts the figure of the narrator centre-stage in much recent French fiction, hogging the limelight over the characters and events they are supposedly relating, or drawing the reader's uneasy scrutiny due to their dubious reliability. The Éditions de Minuit publishing house is a hub for such writing, as is its younger rival, Éditions P.O.L., and four of their most prominent authors, Jean-Philippe Toussaint, Éric Chevillard, Christine Montalbetti and Jean Echenoz, are experts in stories about storytelling. Toussaint specializes in first-person narratives by anti-social, sometimes sociopathic narrators, often recounting a relationship with a female companion that is marked by discord, dark humour and an underlying threat of violence. Four of his twenty-first-century novels, *Faire l'amour* (2002) / *Making Love* (2004), *Fuir* (2005) / *Running Away* (2009), *La Vérité sur Marie* (2009) / *The Truth about Marie*, (2011) and *Nue* (2013) / *Naked* (2016), follow the relationship between the unnamed narrator and a woman named Marie. The quartet was published in one volume entitled *M. M. M. M.* or *Marie Madeleine Marguerite de Montalte* in 2017. The anti-hero narrator, who forfeits our trust as a person from the very first line with his admission that he carries around a bottle of hydrochloric acid for the purpose of disfigurement, works to gradually undermine our trust in the strict veracity of his account as the quartet proceeds. After early parts of the narrative, which remain strictly within his first-person perspective, the quartet increasingly includes detailed scenes where the narrator was not present. The storyteller draws attention to his own unreliability: a set piece in the second volume involving a runaway race-horse at an airport includes a moment in which the horse vomits, juxtaposed with the information that horses are physiologically incapable of vomiting. Elsewhere, we learn that the narrator's love-rival, Jean-Christophe, was in fact called Jean-Baptiste, but the narrator continues to misname him as an act of jealous disrespect. Slowly, the theme of truth reveals itself as being a central preoccupation of the series, as in the following extract, in which the narrator muses on the scene of Jean-Christophe's death, which he has just recounted in detail as if an eyewitness, while in fact the account is an imaginative reconstruction from second-hand information:

> Je savais qu'il y avait sans doute une réalité objective des faits – ce qui s'est réellement passé cette nuit-là dans l'appartement de la rue de la Vrillière –, mais que cette réalité me resterait toujours étrangère [...]. Je savais que je n'atteindrais jamais ce qui avait été pendant quelques instants la vie même, mais il m'apparut alors que je pouvais peut-être atteindre une vérité nouvelle, qui s'inspirerait de ce qui avait été la vie et la transcenderait, sans se soucier de vraisemblance ou de véracité, et ne viserait qu'à la quintessence du réel, sa moelle sensible, vivante et sensuelle, une vérité proche de l'invention, ou jumelle du mensonge, la vérité idéale.[11]

I knew that night contained its own objective reality – what had really taken place in the apartment on rue de la Vrillière – but that reality would always be out of my grasp [. . .]. I knew I'd never reach what had been the fleeting life of the night itself, but it seemed to me that I could perhaps reach a new truth, one that would take its inspiration from life and then transcend it, without concern for verisimilitude or veracity, its only aim the quintessence of the real, its tender core, pulsing and vibrant, a truth close to invention, the twin of fabrication, the ideal truth.[12]

What is being described here as 'vérité idéale' sounds very much like fiction. What the narrator is striving for need not be a faithful reconstruction of the actual events of Jean-Christophe's death, nor even a realistic or plausible reimagining. Transcending the facts, he aims for something which replaces literal truth with something figurative, capturing an emotional, psychological or spiritual truth about Jean-Christophe's final moments and his lover's experience of his death which can tell the reader something true about the human condition, if not necessarily anything accurate about the sequence of events in the Rue de la Vrillière that evening. As readers of Toussaint's novel, our understanding of this 'truth' is complicated by our knowledge that the narrator and the entire universe in which he lives are the author's fictional constructs, and there is thus nothing that 'really happened' at the origin of the narrator's account and against which it can be measured. Toussaint's narrator even flirts with the suggestion that the quartet may be non-fiction; facetiously, we assume, given the outlandish and sometimes criminal nature of the events he is involved in. At one point, the narrator emphatically draws our attention to the fact that a minor character's first name is 'Toussaint',[13] without elaboration as to why the name is worthy of comment: is it because the character shares a name with the famous Haitian revolutionary leader, or might it be that he shares it with the narrator himself? We will shortly see other contemporary writers devise much showier incursions of autobiography and other non-fiction discourses into the novel form. For Toussaint, however, his main concern is to explore the boundaries of truth and fiction, testimony and imagination, within the confines of the realist fictional universe inhabited by his narrator.

Among Toussaint's colleagues at Éditions de Minuit, an interest in the playful possibilities of narration and fictionality frequently manifests itself via an *extradiegetic* narrator, a voice which might seem to be that of the author, and which can acknowledge the fictional nature of the story and comment on the processes of its construction. Éric Chevillard, for instance, has his narrator announce in the opening pages of *Le Vaillant*

Petit Tailleur (2003) that the aim of the book is to appropriate the ancient, authorless folk tale and supply it for the first time with a real author: 'Ce sera moi.'[14] / 'That will be me.' After boasting of his own competencies and denigrating the Brothers Grimm and their sources, this intrusive and vainglorious 'author' then leads us along the well-known narrative path of the fairytale, at any moment threatening to head off into an extended digression or to short-circuit the story by peremptorily killing off its hero. Even when the narrator's version coincides with the traditional story, the tale is entirely overwhelmed by commentary on the manner of its telling, explicated to the reader with tongue-in-cheek pedantry, as in the following discussion of the focalization of an episode in which the tailor finds himself unwittingly standing on the head of a giant:

> Déséquilibré, on l'a vu, par le premier hochement, le petit tailleur était néanmoins parvenu à se rétablir en se raccrochant aux branches (car le lecteur sait que ces branches sont les cheveux du géant, mais l'infortuné l'ignorait et la scène est racontée de son point de vue dans un souci de réalisme psychologique qui me paraît primer en l'occurrence l'objectivité scientifique, la vérité étant chose bien relative et qui se mesure plutôt à l'aune de la sensation dans une situation d'urgence ou de catastrophe comme celle-ci).[15]

> Knocked off balance, as we saw, by the first nod of the giant's head, the little tailor nevertheless managed to pull himself back up by holding on to the branches (which, as the reader knows, are strands of the giant's hair, but the unfortunate tailor was unaware of this fact and the scene is being narrated from his point of view out of concern for psychological realism, which seems to me in this case to trump scientific objectivity, truth being a highly relative thing which is better measured with the ruler of the senses in an emergency or catastrophic situation such as this one).

The sentiment expressed is similar to the one we saw expressed by Toussaint earlier: the 'scientifically objective' fact that the hero is grasping at hairs on a giant's head is being discarded by the narrator in favour of the subjective view of the protagonist, who believes himself to be holding on to branches during an earthquake. As with Toussaint, the discussion of truth arises in the clear but unacknowledged context that the story is a fiction, with the difference that here the diegesis is not realist quasi-memoir but a fantastical fairyland that renders the very concept of 'objectivité scientifique' ludicrous. Chevillard's choice of a folk tale as the basic story of his novel is essential to its metafictional aims. He is able to rely on the reader's assumed familiarity with the story, in order to riff on it like a jazz improvisation, such as when the tailor raises his fly-swatter, only

for the narrator to launch unexpectedly into the highly repetitive tale of a
serial killer, who learns with each of his twenty gruesome murders the true
sense of a different turn of phrase, from 'réduire en bouillie' / 'smashed to a
pulp' to 'comme un écorché vif' / 'as if flayed alive'. The serial killer tale
itself, we come to realize, is an extended shaggy-dog story leading us
towards its punchline in the phrase, 'tomber comme des mouches' / 'drop
like flies'.[16] And the familiar, even hackneyed nature of the main tale shifts
the focus of interest to the commentary that is parasitic upon it, sourcing
comedy in the mismatch between the story's childish simplicity and the
sophisticated concepts ('réalisme psychologique' / 'psychological realism')
foisted upon it by the analysis.

Christine Montalbetti is another major advocate of third-person narrators who overwhelm their own narration. Her œuvre, which is published
by P.O.L., makes a particular specialism out of digression. *Western* (2005)
takes a similar approach to Chevillard's *Petit Tailleur*, in that it weaves
narratorial excess around a slight and familiar narrative core, in this case
the clichés of the Hollywood shoot-out:

> Précaution, insistance, ou réduplication, Christopher Whitefield fait feu
> une seconde fois, avant de souffler sur le canon fumant et de rengainer.
> Assez calmement. Il marche lentement vers son cheval, le prend par la bride,
> l'enfourche, et s'éloigne vers le couchant, contre le fond chamarré duquel,
> comment faire autrement, sa silhouette s'amenuise, en un tranquille respect
> des lois de la perspective.[17]

> Whether due to precaution, insistence, or a purely mechanical reflex,
> Christopher fires a second time before blowing on the barrel of his smoking
> gun and putting it back in its holster. Rather calmly. He walks slowly to his
> horse, takes it by the bridle, mounts it, and rides off into the setting sun,
> against which colourful background, how could it be any other way, his
> silhouette grows smaller in peaceful accord with the laws of perspective.[18]

For Montalbetti, however, the familiarity of the story is less important
than its minimalism – short time spans, few events and little character
development – within which her narrator can orchestrate sweeping digressive excursions into the minutiae of the tale and the mechanics of its
telling.[19] As with Chevillard, Montalbetti's excursions come from the
twenty-first century European sensibility that, despite Jameson's more
pessimistic outlook, her narrator is confident that the reader shares. This
sensibility can sometimes be disorientingly at odds with the diegesis, as
when, in *Western*, which draws on twentieth-century popular representations of nineteenth-century rural America, the narrator notes in passing the
chlorophyll content of the foliage around the hero or the molecular

structure of the water he pours. Like Chevillard's narratology, the scientific discourse is comically mismatched with the genre it is supposedly inhabiting, and the clash throws both into relief, drawing attention to our expectations of the story and the norms of discourse.

The godfather of narratorial whimsy and mainstay of Minuit's experimental cohort is Jean Echenoz, who has been playing with narration and genre since the late 1970s, picking up accolades including the Goncourt and Médicis prizes along the way. After a succession of novels pastiching genres of popular fiction through the late twentieth century, Echenoz changed direction in the twenty-first with a trio of novels based on the lives of Maurice Ravel, Emil Zátopek and Nikola Tesla, followed by a historical novel set during the First World War, before returning to his first love with a droll kidnap and espionage thriller (or parody of the same) in 2016, *Envoyée spéciale* / *Special Envoy* (2017). The novel constructs its plot of North Korean assassination out of an implausible mash-up of elements, several of which are recognizably second hand, having been drawn from cult movies, including the Coen brothers' *The Big Lebowski* (1998) and Luc Besson's *Nikita* (1990), the resultant confection then garnished with lively subplots of dubious relevance and unapologetic excursions into topics from wind turbines to elephant pheromones. As is typical in Echenoz's work, the extradiegetic narrator offers a running commentary on the story and characters, often, like Toussaint, playing with the boundaries of reality and fiction. At one point, for instance, he brazens out some unlikely North Korean shenanigans with the comment that the plotting 'peut paraître invraisemblable dans un pays à ce point surveillé, mais je n'y peux rien non plus si les choses se sont ainsi passés' / 'might seem a little implausible in a country with such strict surveillance, but what can I do? That's just how things happened.'[20] Elsewhere, he presents a deliberately contradictory image of his role as both all-knowing and ignorant: 'nous ne comprenons pas non plus, malgré notre omniscience, comment il a pu être informé de ce rendez-vous qui a l'air, ma foi, de se passer pas trop mal' / 'no, we don't really understand either, despite our omniscience, how he could have come to find out about this meeting, which does, it has to be said, seem to be going pretty well'.[21] Much of this play in Echenoz, and indeed in Chevillard and Montalbetti, consists in blurring or swapping the expected codes of narrative. Time of narration switches with narrated time as storytelling is interrupted by events in the story ('Ici nous avions prévu de transcrire le détail de cette conversation. [...] Nous étions sur le point de le faire mais voici que tinte à la porte, en intervalle de tierce majeure descendante, le double gong de la sonnette.' / 'Here, we had planned to transcribe that conversation in detail. [. . .] We were just about to do that when the double gong on the front door rings in a descending major third.'[22]) The impersonal narrator borrows the role of reader, claiming to witness events rather than control them or learn facts only when the characters speak them, borrows the role of a character ('n'ayant rien de mieux à faire et passant dans le quartier, nous nous sommes discrètement introduits chez Lessertisseur' / 'as we had nothing better to do and happened to be in the area, we discreetly slipped into Lessertisseur's apartment'[23]), or foists the same role onto the reader, chiding us, 'Mais cessez de vous prendre pour Constance' / 'But that's enough now. Stop imagining that you're Constance'[24] after a sequence referring to this character in the second person.

This kind of direct engagement with the reader is a common feature of these texts. Chevillard, for instance, includes an extended sequence imagining the reader's frustration and disappointment with his mishandling of the Brave Little Tailor story.[25] The expectation that the reader will be familiar with this intertext, and the reliance on this familiarity to produce many of the narrative effects of his own text, as it follows, spoofs, analyses and undermines its source, is another widespread characteristic of these fictions. Montalbetti and Echenoz play with popular film genres and highlight their different rules from the real world. Other authors take on more specific intertexts. Proust's *À la recherche du temps perdu* / *In Search of Lost Time* becomes the plaything of the narrator in Anne Garréta's *La Décomposition* (1999), in which a serial killer assigns to each potential victim the identity of a character from Proust's novel, then follows up the murder by removing all trace of the character and their story from his copy of the *Recherche*. Garréta, the most prominent of the current generation of Oulipo writers, has been taking their practice of writing under constraint in interesting directions ever since her celebrated debut, *Sphinx* (1986), which recounted in detail the passionate and physical love story between two characters without ever letting slip the gender of either. In *La Décomposition*, she takes us on a dizzying ride through a universe coloured by its evil narrator's reading of Proust, filled with dark humour that can only be appreciated by the act of mentally holding the two stories side by side, as when the relevance of a bright yellow Cadillac to the story becomes apparent through 'Bergotte' fixing his dying eyes on '[un] précieux petit pan de carrosserie jaune' / 'a precious little expanse of yellow bodywork', or when the 'bal de têtes' / 'masked ball' at the end of Proust's novel is replaced by the rather more noirish 'bal[le] dans la tête' / 'bullet in the head' in Garréta's.[26] More pointedly, Kamel Daoud sets his celebrated

2013 novel, *Meursault : contre-enquête* / *The Meursault Investigation* (2015) within Camus's fictional world of *L'Étranger* / *The Stranger*, drawing on and subverting the earlier novel, in order to engage with issues of colonial legacy and the rise of Islamism in present-day Algeria. The premise of *Meursault : contre-enquête* is that Meursault's tale is a non-fiction account, now being investigated by Daoud's narrator, who is the brother of the Arab man Meursault killed. The narrator begins by denouncing Meursault, but as years pass and violence, fundamentalism and religious repression grow in independent Algeria, he finds himself increasingly identifying with his brother's killer. Finally, his own narrative voice merges with Meursault's and they become indistinguishable, as Camus's prison cell scene is replayed with an imam in place of the chaplain. In Garréta's and Daoud's work, the narrator flirts with the status of literary critic even more explicitly than with the genre-deconstructing narrators of Montalbetti, Echenoz and Chevillard, since in Garréta and Daoud's case the text is parasitic on an earlier literary work, which both reader and narrator are assumed to have read.

As this narratorial play lures the novel into liaisons with fairytales, film scenarios or literary criticism, we are already venturing into the territory of the other sort of literary play to be examined here: play with genre. The novel's openness to other discourses is exploited by many contemporary novelists. The genre-hopping and genre blurring in which French literary novels indulge occurs within fictional genres, from short stories and memoirs to popular genre fiction, and going beyond them to other prose discourses like essays, history and journalism, or further still to contemporary media discourses of television and film, marketing and the internet, as we shall see. The infiltration of the short story in the novel form is one example of this phenomenon, which might be viewed as part of this wider tendency to minimalism and fragmentation we have already encountered in contemporary French fiction. Novelists like Emmanuèle Bernheim, Hélène Lenoir and Christian Gailly specialize in tales of limited time frame, few characters, restrained action and reduced word count; Amélie Nothomb's annual bestseller may differ in its often high-concept drama, but frequently takes the structure of an anecdote in its working through of a single striking idea over a brief span of narrative. Many of these writers' texts would be more readily categorized as *contes* or novellas than as novels by the more expansive standards of the nineteenth century. Marie NDiaye's Goncourt-winning *Trois femmes puissantes* (2009) / *Three Strong Women* (2012) is also interesting in this respect, since it is unclear whether it is better seen as a single novel, or as a set of three short stories, which, despite their shared themes and imagery and their minor overlaps of character, are each an essentially self-contained narrative. For instance, the heroine of the third narrative, Khady Demba, is glimpsed as a maid in the childhood home to which the protagonist of the first story returns; both stories end with dreamlike imagery of the protagonists transformed into birds, imagery which also links to the second protagonist in the middle tale. All three protagonists are also linked by their African heritage and the label of 'femme puissante' / 'strong woman' which the text bestows on them. Despite this metaphoric and metonymic interrelation, however, each tale presents us with its own situation, characters, and challenge to be resolved, and can be read in isolation, although doing so would deprive the reader of the resonances echoing between the tales. Fragmentation within the novelistic text is commonplace in recent fiction, ranging from Régis Jauffret's *Microfictions* (2007), collecting together myriad unrelated short stories of two pages or less in length, to François Bon's *Autobiographie des objets* (2012), in which anecdotes relating to sixty-four different objects are linked by the importance of each to Bon's youth and the social history of the periods to which they relate, or to Emmanuelle Pireyre's *Féerie générale* of the same year, a Médicis prize-winning text that is at the nexus of several notable trends in recent French literature. As well as offering fragmented micro-narratives which appear self-contained until their themes and characters recur later in the book, it also mixes fiction and non-fiction, narrative and other prose discourses, exhibits ironic self-consciousness in its presentation of a fictionalized author-narrator, and, subtending many of these characteristics, draws influence from new media of the twenty-first century, most particularly the experience of surfing the internet. *Féerie générale*, like Pireyre's *Comment faire disparaître la terre ?* (2006) before it, has chapters headed with titles which seem like parodies of Google searches or clickbait online articles – 'Le tourisme représente-t-il un danger pour nos filles faciles ?' / 'Is tourism a danger for our girls who sleep around?' or 'Friedrich Nietzsche est-il Halal ?' / 'Is Friedrich Nietzsche Halal?' – within which a comic hotch-potch of stories, analysis and (apparent) personal reminiscence tackle issues of contemporary import, including capitalism, male sexual violence, eco-activism and anxiety. The reader is swept from topic to topic and back again, as if under the control of a distracted internet user, an impression emphasized by the wry sideswipes at bloggers and PowerPoint presentations that keep information technology in the foreground. Two recurring threads recounting kisses experienced and dreams dreamt ground the text in something deeper and more poetic than a simple satire on the information age, and the growing focus on happiness, viewed as elusive and linked to experience of the natural world, leads the novel towards a plangent conclusion.

Writers who join Pireyre in co-opting non-narrative and non-fictional discourses into the novel form are plentiful. Laurent Binet, Olivier Rolin and François Bon are three writers who have brought journalism and literature into contact in different ways. Rolin's *L'Invention du monde* (1993) prefigured the information overload of the dawning internet age with its avalanche of true stories drawn from 500 newspapers from around the world, all of which recounted a single day's events, momentous or trivial, in their corner of the globe. The effect resembles Jauffret's micro-fictions in its unrelenting assault of brief narratives, constantly switching settings, characters and tone, now comic, now tragic, inspiring or disgusting, while the encyclopaedic nature of the project and the growing awareness of linking themes among the disparate particles builds a network of increasing coherence in a manner that has become common in fragmented writing of the years that followed. Binet and Bon engage in writing that brings them close to the role of journalist in their own authorial practice. Binet's *Rien ne se passe comme prévu* (2012) is literally long-form journalism, being a non-fiction account of François Hollande's presidential campaign, in which Binet was an embedded observer. However, his celebrated debut novel, *HHhH* (2010), already owed as much to the styles and structures of contemporary journalism as to the novelistic tradition. At its heart a reconstruction of the assassination of Reinhard Heydrich by Czech freedom fighters during World War II, the novel also recounts Binet's fascination with the story, his research and writing process, his doubts about the project and the incidents of his life at the time of writing. While such prominence given to authorial commentary, facetious and sincere, is common in recent French literature, as we have seen, in Binet the effect is a little different. *HHhH* is of a piece with Binet's account of the presidential campaign. The narrative voice, self-presentation and overlaying of the ostensible subject matter with writerly concerns are to be found in both, and in both create a discourse that is already familiar to us from our experience of investigative journalism and newspaper opinion columnists. It is simply that, in *HHhH* at least, the news story that the narrator is doggedly working to disinter dates from thirty years before the writer was born. Bon takes the hybrid discourse of novelist and journalist in other directions. His *L'Incendie du Hilton* (2009) offers an eyewitness account of the Montreal fire and evacuation in which he was involved, written up from notes taken as the incident unfolded, many of which are included in an appendix to the narrative. It is his *Daewoo* (2004), though, that brings investigative journalism properly into the novel form, transforming both in the process. Through a mixture of interviews and reportage, Bon recounts the closure of three Daewoo factories in eastern France in the early 2000s, and the effect this had on the former factory workers and their community. Bon records what he sees on his visits, and transcribes what he hears from the former factory workers, largely without comment or analysis ('Et laisser toute question ouverte. Ne rien présenter que l'enquête'[27] / 'And leave all questions open. Present nothing but the investigation', he offers within the novel as the guiding principle of its creation). What most clearly distances the novel from straightforward documentary, however, is the aesthetic choice to intersperse eight extracts from a dramatic staging of the story, also by Bon, through the course of the text. The characters in the staging are amalgamations of the people we have seen interviewed, their dialogue sometimes repeats what we have already heard 'at first hand', sometimes prefigures later interviews, and sometimes is either invented or drawn from an unpublished source. The work Bon has carried out, condensing and rearranging his material to create new thematic connections, offers new insights into the human drama sparked by the factory closures, its authenticity vouched for by the presence of the undoctored interview transcripts. Throughout this skipping between genres, the story of Sylvia, an active union member who fought the closures and later, unemployed and alone, committed suicide, acts as the narrative thread which draws the work together, as well as its central indictment of the inhumanity of the capitalist system which destroyed her. Like Rolin, Bon displays a marked interest in language, contrasting the discourses of marketing, management and government with the words of the workers themselves. Unlike Rolin's novel, Bon's is strongly politically committed in purpose, its objective narration a strategy to allow the facts of the injustice perpetrated on the workers to speak for themselves. For neither Rolin nor Bon does the documentary aspect of their work distance them from creative play in their writing, and still less is play at odds with Bon's political commitment. Both pay tribute to arch-Oulipian, Georges Perec, in the works we have been discussing: Bon calls Perec 'un auteur qui m'est cher'[28] / 'an author who is dear to me' in *Daewoo*; Olivier Rolin acknowledges a debt to him in *L'Invention du monde* by slipping in the name of Serge Valène, the artist of *La Vie mode d'emploi* (1978) / *Life, A User's Manual* (1987), among a list of painters in the novel's early pages.[29] Perec was himself often inspired by documentary and encyclopaedic impulses – witness his *Tentative d'épuisement d'un lieu parisien* / *An Attempt at Exhausting a Place in Paris* (1975) – and showed the current generation of writers by his example that documentation and real-world data are in no way incompatible with avant-garde presentation in genre and narration. Binet's journalistic pastiche and Bon's politically committed testimony both bring discourses of the real into the novel form, with striking and disconcerting results. As we saw earlier in Toussaint's uncomfortable autofictions, and as we see here as reportage on manufacturing redundancies morphs into Greek tragedy, textual play along the borderlines between reality and fiction can foreground the notion of truth itself, and interrogate what else truth might encompass beyond the reporting of facts, or the ways in which the creative writer's artistry might engage with it.

Away from journalism, other genre-hoppers in contemporary French fiction include Olivier Cadiot, who mingles fragments of essay and narrative in texts like the two-volume *Histoire de la literature récente* (2016–2017), which belies its title with a tongue-in-cheek self-help guide to aspiring writers, chopped into dozens of 'lessons'. Pascal Quignard is another, whose ten-volume *Dernier Royaume* sequence, from *Les Ombres errantes* (2002) to *L'Enfant d'Ingolstadt* (2018), similarly mixes narrative fragments of fiction or memoir with philosophical or literary musings in essay form. Even Assia Djebar, an author with whom 'play' might not readily be associated, has strong parallels with these writers. Her work as far back as *L'Amour, la fantasia* (1985) / *Fantasia, An Algerian Cavalcade* (1993) has juxtaposed archival research, narrative reconstruction and authorial commentary, which will then give way to female testimony, with the author presented as the interviewer of eyewitnesses. More recently, her engagement with ongoing political and religious violence in Algeria produced an urgent, campaigning tone to her investigations and fictionalized reconstructions of assassinations in *Le Blanc d'Algérie* (1995) / *Algerian White* (2003). For most of these writers, the non-narrative discourses that invade and fragment their storytelling reaches back to established prose traditions, such as history, philosophy and other forms of the essay. Quignard in particular draws on early-modern traditions of essays and maxims, and further back still to the aphorisms of classical East Asian philosophy, to inspire the forms of his writing. His practice was the inspiration for Dominique Viart's concept of the 'fiction critique' / 'critical fiction', which captures the aims of many contemporary writers. For Viart, 'fiction critique' is a form which places itself 'dans l'entre-deux indécidable d'une pratique contemporaine qui fait dialoguer le critique et le fictif / 'in the undecidable in-between space of a contemporary practice that puts critique and fiction in dialogue with one another'.[30] This is a space where narration and reflection can work together in confrontation, collaboration and exchange, creating a hybrid discourse of story and argument through which to interrogate the world, a characterization which fits Bon as well as it fits Quignard, despite their very different aims and methods.

While traditional genres of writing are a major source of innovation and hybridity for contemporary novelists, new media are also important inspirations. Modern television infiltrates the novel in various ways, including the form of Philippe Djian's six-novel *Doggy Bag* series (2005–2008), which presented each novel as a 'season', opening with a cast list and closing with cliff-hangers in homage to the narrative devices of (principally American) television drama. The content too of many novels shows the influence of modern televisual culture, including Nothomb's *Acide sulfurique* (2005) / *Sulphuric Acid* (2008), about the TV reality show as concentration camp, or indeed Toussaint's *La Télévision* (1997) / *Television* (2004), in which blank-eyed channel-hopping becomes a symbol of the protagonist's anomie. Discourses of marketing are equally prominent, notably in Frédéric Beigbeder's advertising satire, *99 francs* / *13.99 Euros* (2001), which, as mentioned earlier, ends in a cascade of familiar slogans, or more subtly and pervasively in Houellebecq, whose impersonal narratorial voice constantly slips into pastiche of other discourses to imitate and undermine, as when *Les Particules élémentaires* (1998) dwells for no urgent reason on the junk mail accumulated by the protagonist:

> Dans leur dernière livraison, les Dernières Nouvelles de Monoprix mettaient plus que jamais l'accent sur la notion d'entreprise citoyenne. Une fois de plus, l'éditorialiste croisait le fer avec cette idée reçue qui voulait que la gastronomie soit incompatible avec la forme. À travers ses lignes de produits, ses marques, le choix scrupuleux de chacune de ses références, toute l'action de Monoprix depuis sa création témoignait d'une conviction exactement inverse. « L'équilibre c'est possible pour tous, et tout de suite » n'hésitait pas à affirmer le rédacteur.[31]

> In the most recent issue of the *Dernières Nouvelles de Monoprix*, the accent was ever more on 'real' food. Once again, the editor took issue with the notion that convenience and gastronomy were incompatible. Their scrupulous choice of ingredients, their range of produce, their own-brand products, everything, in fact, that Monoprix had stood for since the beginning was based on a premise which directly contradicted this. 'It is possible to have gourmet food, a balanced diet, and to have it now' the editor affirmed.[32]

It is this same sardonic parroting of contemporary non-fiction discourses which led to the minor literary scandal mentioned earlier, when passages from *La Carte et le Territoire* on the French town of Beauvais or the life-cycle of the house fly, which appeared to mimic the bland information dump of a Wikipedia entry, turned out to consist of actual Wikipedia entries cut and pasted into the novel. (Houellebecq weathered the scandal without much difficulty; the same could not be said for his next novel, *Soumission / Submission* (2015), which was widely seen as Islamophobic and published on the same day as the *Charlie Hebdo* massacre.) In a similar way, the second-hand factoids about North Korea that make up much of the décor of the later parts of Echenoz's *Envoyée spéciale* – the history and geography of the DMZ, or demilitarized zone, the primary skills of taekwondo, the *kimjongilia* and *kimilsungia* plants in the flowerbeds – serve to derealize the Pyongyang setting they illustrate, since they present themselves so blatantly as the product of web research rather than lived experience. This brings us finally back to Pireyre and the discourses of the internet, which, as her narrator tells us with tongue hopefully in her cheek, promise to definitively overcome narrative as a form, and replace its smooth flow with a new primacy of fragmentation and classification:

> Conclusion, me suis-je dit rassérénée avant d'aller dormir : le classement est finalement plus plaisant, plus opératoire, plus excitant en lui-même que le long déroulement des histoires. Victoire de la taxinomie sur le récit. Victoire du concept et du PowerPoint sur le storytelling, la veillée dans l'étable, la machine à café et la place du marché.[33]

> Conclusion, I told myself before heading to bed, my mind at rest: classification is in the end nicer, more effective and more stimulating in itself than the long unfurling of stories. Victory of taxonomy over narrative. Victory of concepts and PowerPoint over storytelling, late nights in the cowshed, the coffee machine and the market square.

Play with genre and play with narration are thus features of the contemporary French novel that interact with each other as well as being prominent in themselves. There are other genre boundaries that are being traversed which have less of a formal element and which we have not had the space to consider properly here, most obviously the continuing traffic over the borderline between the literary novel and the genres of popular fiction. Just as the twentieth-century avant-gardists like Robbe-Grillet, Perec, or Michel Butor would joyfully exploit the rules and tropes of crime fiction to their own ends, so the current generation of literary experimenters enthusiastically embraces science fiction, as with Antoine Volodine's *Terminus Radieux* (2014) / *Radiant Terminus* (2017) and Marie Darrieussecq's *Notre vie dans les forêts* (2017) / *Our Life in the Forest*, (2018); the thriller in Binet's *La Septième Fonction du langage* (2015) / *The Seventh Function of Language* (2017) and Echenoz's *Envoyée spéciale*, as we have seen, or the crime novel, which continues to haunt the narratives of France's latest Nobel Prize winner, Patrick Modiano. At the same time, the border itself is becoming ever less distinct: Volodine's specialism in what he terms the 'post-exotic' makes him difficult to categorize as a writer of literary fiction or science fiction, while one of France's most celebrated authors of the moment is undoubtedly Fred Vargas, whose subtle characterization and vivid prose garner similar literary acclaim for texts that situate themselves proudly within the *roman policier* / crime novel genre fiction tradition.

I would like, though, to close with a return to one of the important connecting factors between the creative approaches we have seen towards narration and genre in these texts. That is *self-consciousness*, a reflexivity in the text that shows awareness of its own fictional status and co-opts the reader into an embedded critique of the text within its own narrative. As we have seen, the storyteller is often the focus of attention in these novels, as devious and unreliable autodiegetic narrator in Toussaint, as an impersonal voice in Chevillard and Echenoz with plot and characters at the mercy of their whims, or as an authorial persona in Bon and Djebar laying out the process of a real-world inquiry along with its fruits. A fourth mode of storytelling has also come to join these three in recent years: what we might call the authorial auto-libel, in which a narrator or protagonist is given the same name as the author, but exhibits a personality so caricatured or undergoes experiences so improbable that their fictional status becomes obvious. Deriving from the half-true, half-invented *autofictions* of writers like Serge Doubrovsky or Christine Angot, as well, perhaps, as the twenty-first-century fashion for film and television stars to perform as comically warped versions of themselves, recent French literature has seen 'Delphine de Vigan' sidelined from her own writing by a stalkerish imposter in *D'après une histoire vraie* (2015) / *Based on a True Story* (2017), 'Marie Nimier' embarking on a career as a literary pornographer in *La Nouvelle Pornographie* (2000), and both 'Amélie Nothomb' and 'Michel Houellebecq' brutally murdered before the reader reaches the end of their novels, *Le Robert des noms propres* (2002) / *The Book of Proper Names* (2004) and *La Carte et le territoire*. In all these cases, the fake self is used to play games with reality and representation. Vigan's novel, for instance, proposes itself as an account of the real-life aftermath of the publication of her frank and devastating memoir of her mother's experience of abuse and mental illness, in which a backlash against too much candour in that text is countered by her stalker's insistence that modern readers are only interested in narratives which they can believe to be true. As Vigan leads us into doubts about the status of the narrative we are reading, the novel becomes a fictional meditation on the primacy of authentic non-fiction narrative in contemporary culture. These sometimes deeply negative self-portraits in fiction are perhaps the most extreme example of the contemporary novel as auto-critique. They are nevertheless emblematic of a widespread tendency.

Play with genre and with narration does not necessarily require self-consciousness. A novel could tell its story backwards or skip merrily between fact and fiction without offering any commentary on what it was doing or why. Indeed, not all of the texts we have been looking at exhibit self-consciousness. When the uncanny echoes between NDiaye's protagonists and their experiences in *Trois femmes puissantes* leave the reader wondering if the book in their hands is a trio of short stories or a single, coherent whole, the narrating voice is silent as to how the text might best be interpreted. But literature based on play brings with it the temptation to include within the package the rules of the game, and this is a temptation that many contemporary writers have found irresistible. As Montalbetti ignores her cowboys to focus on the ants crawling at their feet or Binet interrupts the story of Heydrich's assassination with the account of his own research into the story, as Toussaint creates fictions within fictions or Pireyre narrates her PowerPoint presentation to us, as Garréta dismantles Proust or Echenoz takes apart the spy novel, all of these writers invite their readers behind the scenes. They gesture us towards their aims, renewing the novel through manipulation of its own conventions of style and structure, or perhaps through opening the door to other discourses foreign to the novel tradition. And they set out, implicitly or explicitly, the means by which they hope to achieve these aims, along with perhaps a preemptive attempt to judge their success or failure, forestalling the reader's own evaluation. In the end, though, it remains up to us as readers to judge. These writers put their faith in our cultural experience, in the fact that we know the conventions of narration and what it means to bend or break them, and in our familiarity with the wide variety of discourses of modernity on which they draw. They have faith that we will use this experience to critique them fairly and empathize with their creative intentions. At best, they hope we will recognize their invitation, whether it be to roam among familiar cultural forms reworked in new ways, as in Baudrillard's and Jameson's characterization, or more broadly to shrug off the regimented, the systematic and the earnest, in order to indulge in an interlude of freedom and creativity, as in Huizinga's, and respond with enthusiastic participation in the game.

CHAPTER 3

Getting a Future
Fiction and Social Reproduction

Anna-Louise Milne

Ainsi, il n'est plus question sans doute des « grands récits » dont parlait Lyotard. Mais il n'est pas plus question de « petits récits », qu'ils soient individuels ou de minorités. Il ne s'agit pas du tout de « récit ». Mais d'une autre phrase, et d'un autre phrasé.

Thus it can no longer be a question of Lyotard's 'grand narratives'. But it is not a question either of 'minor narratives', whether those of individuals or of minorities. It is no longer a question of 'narrative'. But of a different phrase, and a different phrasing.

Jean-Luc Nancy, *La Comparution* (Bourgois, 1991)

If neither 'grand narratives' nor 'micro-histories' were possible as the last decade of the twentieth century began, what was contemporary fiction going to do? The repercussions of a past that would not pass were carving out a broad bay in which historical, non-fictional and literary writing washed in and around one another. But what of a future struggling to begin? A future that felt blocked or stalled by this backwash. That could be neither prophecy nor consequence. Does the writing of fiction have anything specific or constitutive to offer in a context where, as Jean-Luc Nancy suggests, the drive of plot, of narrative or *récit*, appears to lead perpetually to the same impasse, the same foreclosure of the century on its disasters? What sort of new rhythms of writing, new phrasings and propulsions is he calling for as a means of creating lateral movement?

These questions are formulated to strike out from the various modalities of the end, be they apocalyptic, consensual or melancholic. But they point towards a future that lacks confidence; a future that is contemporary in the sense that it is undecided, still lacking direction, bubbling with possibility at the same time as it boils with frustration. We could call this condition one of revolt, which will run like a subterranean possibility under this discussion. And it may not be possible to bring that category to bear without it forcing an articulation with 'revolution', whether that suggests a hackneyed fiction best abandoned to the 'ends' – of history, of modernity, of the avant-garde – that marked the 1990s, or a renewed desire for the coming insurrection.[1] The present discussion will return to revolution in its closing section, but it first takes its focus from that structural moment in a school career within the French education system known as 'orientation', a moment of particularly acute contradiction between apparent openness and effective blockage, which generally occurs at around fifteen years of age when particularly decisive choices about post-sixteen education are made/imposed. Through a series of close analyses of works that start in the last twenty years of the previous century with Annie Ernaux, first read with Faïza Guène, then François Bégaudeau and Edouard Louis, before returning to Ernaux's later work in *Les Années* (2008) / *The Years* (2017), latterly read in relation to Leslie Kaplan's recent work *Mathias et la Revolution* / *Mathias and the Revolution* (2016), the aim is to explore some of the ways in which contemporary fiction has captured the mechanism of orientation. This is not just a question of representation, but more significantly of how literary writing has worked within the unsparing churn of contemporary culture, in which we struggle to imagine that the future belongs to us, to throw up new forms of phrasing, new means of expression. Spanning 'generations' and positions relative to what are dominant poles in the literary field (Gallimard, Le Seuil, P.O.L. and the prominent 'alternative' locations of the 'Incultes' and '*banlieue* fiction'), this corpus shares a critical or reflective relation to the novel form and explicit commitment to the writing of the 'real' as a corrective project. In this respect, it encompasses one of the broad shifts operating within French fiction in the past couple of decades, resulting in what some prefer to call 'prose' in recognition of the problematic status of the novel within it. Within that broad assessment, however, we will find significant variance in the ways in which contemporary writing has entered into the fray of social reproduction by shifting gears within the forms and rhythms of mass-produced and reproduced discourse.

Annie Ernaux and Faïza Guène: 'impasses'

Ernaux's *La Place* (1983) / *Positions*, (1991) begins and ends on a decisive moment of 'passage', which stalls and thereby installs a cyclical temporality figured by the endless return of a supermarket conveyor belt. The opening section concerns the narrator, the 'je' or 'I' whose recounting of a father recently deceased closely resembles the life story of the author's father, although the place names are scrupulously withheld. It describes the final hurdle to becoming a teacher with civil-service status – 'titulaire' – a guarantee of life-long employment and a badge of social status. While waiting to begin her exam, the narrator compares herself to a woman, a teacher, observed working her way with haughty efficiency ('avec hauteur') through a pile of marking: 'Il suffisait de franchir correctement l'heure suivante pour être autorisée à faire comme elle toute ma vie.' / 'All I had to do was sail through the following hour and I would be allowed to do the same as she did for the rest of my life.'[2] The future is imminent, only one hour away, if she is successful. But it is a forbidding future, envisioned as nothing better than more repetition of a different same, in which any illusion of social and intellectual emancipation runs aground on the insistent mechanical undertones that traverse this passage, as if it were all just about going through the motions.

The final scene of *La Place* does something similar, although now the narrator is the teacher, equally capable of 'haughty' indifference to pupils' efforts to advance through the obstacle course of secondary and college education. She has brought her work of recollection of the world that made her father and her in relation to him, to a series of elliptical annotations evocative of cyclical journeys from one 'river-bank' to the other, and then notes that throughout this writing process she was also correcting homework and instructing pupils in how to write essays. Then, with no narrativized motivation for the final anecdote, the text shifts to a supermarket checkout, where the narrator recognizes an ex-pupil from five to six years earlier. She engages the conversation by asking the girl if she likes working there. Her question provokes an embarrassed explanation of a failed post-sixteen pathway, offered as if the narrator/ex-teacher should remember the details of what this particular pupil had aspired to do after she left her class: '« Le CET, ça n'a pas marché. » Elle semblait penser que j'avais encore en mémoire son orientation.' / '"It didn't work out at the technical college." She seemed to think I still remembered what college programme we had sent her towards.'[3] The narrator says goodbye. The text ends with the last vision of the girl moving the next pile of shopping down the conveyor belt.

One successful step up the educational ladder, one failed ascension, neither directly related to the primary focus of the narrator's pained recollection of her father's world and both conjuring the idea that education is dangerously close to the alienation of supermarkets. So what are we to make of this framing?[4] It serves, I suggest, to loosen the focus on the individual drama of displacement and to establish this work entitled *La Place* within a broader distribution of 'places' in which the languages of social conformity, and particularly that of the national educational system, are paramount.[5] Within this system, one particularly freighted element of discourse is the word 'l'orientation', where the usual association with a definite article ('the orientation') expresses the experience of being depersonalized at the very point of crucial affirmation of a singular destiny ('my future'), while the equally frequent verbalized form ('l'école oriente mal' / 'school is a poor decider of destinies' or '« on m'a orienté »' / 'I was directed towards') suggests an even greater sense of passivity in the hands of the institution.[6] The difficult process of laying claim to an active subject position within this discursive and administrative system emerges with sharp clarity in the long written exchange between 'un jeune de la cité' / 'a disadvantaged youth' and the sociologist Stéphane Beaud, published under the title *Pays de Malheur !* / *Country of Misery!* in 2004. Younès Amrani begins by recounting his encounter ('« ma rencontre »') with Pierre Bourdieu, the leading French sociologist whose fundamental analysis of cultural capital and the processes of social reproduction is everywhere apparent in the literature explored in this chapter. Amrani underscores that this encounter was both fraught and improbable, or fraught because improbable, using scare quotes to offset his emphatic possessive form in an expression of this complex positioning. His first reaction to Bourdieu's analysis of the mechanisms of symbolic domination to which he is simultaneously discovering himself to be subject was '« la rage »' / 'rage': 'on nous confrontait à une réalité que l'on ne voulait pas accepter [. . .]. Pour moi, la seule réponse, c'était alors de démentir « ça ».' / 'we were being confronted with a reality we couldn't accept. For me the only possible response was to dispute "it".'[7] The '« ça »' speaks the violence of this subjectivation and the inchoateness of his initial opposition to it. If words such as 'orientation' or 'S' versus 'G' as differently valorized options in the French *baccalauréat* system mean de facto designations of who one will be in the world, then a new vocabulary has to be found, or at least a different way of enunciating it. This is what is at stake in producing his 'récit': the means of reordering social discourse beyond the repulsion of '« ça »' to find some give in the contradiction that is so tightly bound up in the moment of 'orientation'. Amrani pinpoints this contradiction in the role of the very teacher who introduced him to Bourdieu, then let him and his peers down: '[il] n'a absolument rien fait pour nous lors des orientations. Beaucoup d'entre nous ont été expédiés en G. Moi je me suis retrouvé en S . . .' / 'he did nothing for us at the moment of orientation. Lots of us were dispatched into G. I found myself in S . . .'[8] This reconvening of the teacher as (guilty) 'actor' in his destiny is a key element in the 'récit', and in the context of the present discussion it brings the question of narrative form back to the centre of our exploration.

For Ernaux, this question emerges very quickly in *La Place*, where she discounts the 'novel' form with its imperative to 'move' and the memoir with its particular attachments, thus marking a key turning point in her own corpus and arguably in contemporary writing more broadly: 'Depuis peu, je sais que le roman est impossible. [. . .] je n'ai pas le droit de prendre d'abord le parti de l'art, ni de chercher à faire quelque chose de « passionnant » ou d'« émouvant ».' / 'I realize now that the novel is out of the question. [. . .] I have no right to adopt an artistic approach, or attempt to produce something "moving" or "gripping".'[9] Her affirmation corresponds chronologically in the *Atelier noir* (2011) / 'Dark Workshop' of her additional jottings and diaries, which form an essential extension to the more evidently finished literary publications, to a moment of 'désarroi' / 'bewilderment'.[10] In a bid to get out of her 'impasses', she takes up the practice of using loose sheets of scrap paper (bills, unfinished letters, prospectuses). She dates these sheets, approaches them as provisional ('ôter à l'écriture tout caractère solonnel' / 'to remove any solemnity from the process of writing'[11]) and allows them to accumulate unchecked. Reviewing them for publication nearly thirty years later, she discovers that they bear the trace of long periods dominated by the 'sensation de tourner en rond dans un lieu noir' / 'the feeling of going nowhere in a dark place', interspersed by gaps during which the writing of a book takes over and a volume can be released.[12] This rhythm of prevarication, which Ernaux refers to as her 'parcours d'hésitation' / 'path of hesitation',[13] is central to the complex temporality that dominates Ernaux's major body of work, produced over a period of more than forty years (from *Les Armoires vides* in 1974 to most recently *Mémoire de fille* in 2016), and the fundamental role that her unclassifiable texts have had in the transformation of the literary field.[14]

The impossibility of the novel, affirmed so emphatically in *La Place*, expresses a rejection of a traditionally cohesive narrative structure organized around causal connectedness, in which events and characters move the story forward. Instead, the narrator states that the dynamic she is seeking must be one of accumulation, as if of raw evidence, but without a teleology of proof. She likens this process instead to the same factual or 'flat' writing that she used in the regular letters she used to write home, aiming for a mode of recounting that suppresses any distance or reordering. Instead, it is conditioned by a strong centripetal force, reiterating events within a habitual idiom, whose singular force she associates with her parents' disdain for any learnt 'manières' / 'mannerisms'.[15] As she says of the words presented in italics in the text, 'ces phrases disent les limites et la couleur du monde où vécut mon père, où j'ai vécu aussi. Et l'on n'y prenait jamais un mot pour un autre.' / 'these particular words and sentences define the nature and the limits of the world where my father lived and which I too shared. It was a world in which one word was never taken for another.'[16]

'Not taking a word for another' evokes a generalized suspicion of translatability, that is, of exchangeability within or between languages and, by extension, of metaphor. Instead, the value of the words fore-grounded by Ernaux's writing resides in their incontrovertible or unshak-able link to a fund of experience. The risk of detaching her language from this fund is one of betrayal, an abandonment of the 'things' of life to the fragility and arbitrariness of their naming in a regime she characterizes with a reference from Barthes as the 'impérialisme de la langue' / 'imperialism of language'.[17] The effort, therefore, will be to make the circularity of 'play-back' audible within the dominant frame of 'literature' without it becom-ing distortion.[18] From within the exiguity of its range, with its parochial limitations in a world of ever greater mobility, Ernaux's writing from these years depends for its force not so much on the transformations it enables, or the futures it might open up, as on its intransigent attention to where it finds itself, still standing at the supermarket checkout, or engaged in those other small repetitive actions that organize her texts: driving, taking suburban trains, going to the hairdresser's.

Though positioned very differently in the field of contemporary fiction, Faïza Guène's hugely successful first novel, *Kiffe Kiffe Demain* (2004) / *Just Like Tomorrow* (2006), reveals a number of significant points of contact with Ernaux, not least its undiminished attachment to certain forms of language.[19] It is also a text about an unwanted 'orientation' that occurs in the midst of a difficult reckoning with familial and cultural heritage. The particular moment of violence in which the fifteen-year old narrator Doria is dispatched towards a programme she did not choose forms a hole in the narrative continuity of her diary:

> Ah oui, je vous avais pas dit : au lycée, ils ne peuvent plus me redoubler parce qu'il n'y a pas assez de places pour tout le monde. Et dans ce « tout le monde », il y a moi. Alors ils m'ont trouvé une place à la dernière minute dans un lycée professionnel pas trop loin de la maison, en CAP coiffure.

> Yes, I forgot to tell you: I can't repeat the year because there aren't enough places for everybody at school. And that 'everybody' includes me. So they found me a place last minute at this college not so far from home, doing hairdressing.[20]

The painful realization of individuation ('il y a moi' / 'me') in the general and relatively disposable lot of 'tout le monde' / 'everybody' is displaced into an after-thought, repressed momentarily, although the question of this CAP, or certificate d'aptitude professionnelle – about which she will cry her heart out after the first day at the college named ironically Louis Blanc after the revolutionary social reformer – returns as the structuring device that gives the loose diary form its narrative direction. Doria 'gets a future', or at least a belief in one, through this text in the sense that she moves beyond the depression that has been diagnosed, recognizes the strength and character of her mother, and essentially decides to become the language *meister*, if not explicitly the writer, that Guène has become:

> « Du CAP coiffure à l'élection présidentielle, il n'y a qu'un pas . . . ». C'est le genre de phrase qui reste. Faut que je pense à en faire plus des comme ça, comme les citations qu'on peut lire dans les livres d'histoire de quatrième, style ce bouffon de Napoléon qui a dit : « À tout peuple conquis, il faut une révolte. »

> 'From highlights to high office: it's closer than you think . . .' That's a slogan that sticks in your head. I'll have to think up some more along those lines. You know, the kind of quotes you read in history books at school, like that joker Napoleon who said 'Every conquered nation needs a revolution.'[21]

The humiliation of repetition such as her mother has known all her life is dismissed in a moment of exuberance in which she founds the now famous phrase 'kiffe kiffe demain' and announces that she will lead a revolt. The tutelary figure for this revolt is not the rioters of Mathieu Kassovitz's celebrated film *La Haine* (1995), in a reference that reveals the extent to which the periphery of the French nation has now acquired its own lore, but the 'intelligent' and explicitly literary figure of the poet Arthur Rimbaud. In this respect, Guène's novel reads like a manifesto for the renewal of poetic force through the linguistic inventiveness of a postcolonial and multilingual community, even though her own acerbic irony also undercuts this positive thrust towards tomorrow when she ends by mocking her own 'élans républicains' / 'Republican enthusiasms'.[22]

Guène's work thus doubles back on its own optimism, and despite the positive trajectories that it narrates, the future remains undercut by ironic self-disdain. For Ernaux, the passage from blockage to production has none of this teenage plasticity or caustic playfulness. The years between *La Place* (1983) and *Les Années* (2008) reveal a pattern of false starts and obsessive returns, giving rise to a succession of short texts and diary publications, in part intended to 'démystifier la clôture de l'œuvre' / 'demystify the closure of the work', but also, as we learn in the preface to *Atelier noir*, all thought of as extractions from the longer project that would eventually become *Les Années*.[23] In this sense, Ernaux continues to project some complete and future work, beyond all the steps leading towards it, conceived right from the outset of her marginal notes in 1982–1983 as both the 'roman total' / 'the total novel' and simply the 'quoi des images séparées' / 'the what of separate images' in 1982.[24] Yet at the same time, the writing that does get released is thought of as completely disconnected from her own life trajectory. This detachment from prior self is such that she attributes the wave of emotion released by re-reading these long forgotten notes to the writing alone: 'c'était l'écriture qui produisait cette souffrance' / 'it was the writing that was prompting my suffering'.[25] This displacement from interpersonal attachment to the impersonal medium of writing is recognized in countless ways by critics and Ernaux herself as the crucial articulation in her work. Michael Sheringham has dedicated some luminous pages to exploring the different facets of her 'transpersonal' narration and how they reveal 'the indivisibility of the social and the personal in everyday life'.[26] But this indivisibility is complex and testing at the level of a sequence of sentences, and it is here in the dense but fragmentary syntax that we can see better how the pull towards the primal scene – of not taking of one word for another – conditions the shape of the writing, as in the following passage from *La Place*:

> Phrase interdite : « Combien vous avez payé ça ? »
> Je dis souvent « nous » maintenant, parce que j'ai longtemps pensé de cette façon et je ne sais pas quand j'ai cessé de le faire.
> Le patois avait été l'unique langue de mes grands-parents.
> Il se trouve des gens pour apprécier le « pittoresque du patois » et du français populaire. Ainsi Proust relevait avec ravissement les incorrections et les mots anciens de Françoise. Seule l'esthétique lui importe parce que Françoise est sa bonne et non sa mère. Que lui-même n'a jamais senti ces tournures lui venir aux lèvres spontanément.

> The question 'How much did you pay for it?' was taboo.
> Now I often say 'we' because I shared this way of thinking for a long time and I can't remember when I stopped doing so.
> The local dialect was the only language my grandparents spoke.

There will always be people to appreciate the 'picturesque charm' of patois and popular speech. Proust, for instance, took delight in pointing out the mistakes and the old-fashioned words used by Françoise. His concern, however, was purely aesthetic, because Françoise was not his mother but his maid, and because he knew these expressions were not natural to him.[27]

The layering of text that moves through different types of speech is arresting, if only because it comes after a long series of passages written entirely in the third person. Each sentence stands alone, 'comprimée' / 'crushed',[28] resulting in a series of discontinuous advances, cumulatively driving towards the tight but depersonalized comparison between Marcel Proust, author of the vast *À la recherche du temps perdu*, and the narrator/author in the final two sentences: the patois-speaking housekeeper Françoise is Proust's maid, whereas she would be Ernaux's mother; and she, Ernaux, would not be able to quote such 'picturesque' phrases because they would rise unchecked to her lips. This comparison speaks directly to the dilemma Ernaux is wrestling with at this time in her notebooks: how to import the 'mark' of her idiom into literary work modelled on Proust without it becoming an object of fetishistic interest; without writing like Proust.[29] The touchstone for this idiom is the 'body', more explicit in the French reference to the words coming unchecked to her lips. This language is inseparable from the physical life of her childhood, marked by the 'emotion', 'trouble' or 'revolt' that punctuated her daily existence.[30] Contrary to Guène's affirmative malleability that enables her to hold poetry apart from the everyday, signified in 'le rap et le foot' / 'rap and football', and envisage a revolt 'sans aucune violence' / 'without any violence', for Ernaux language and body are locked in step with one another, held in a centripetal embrace to such an extent that there is little space for a projection of self towards an uncharted future.

The risk of impasse for Ernaux is explicitly thematized in the *Journal du dehors* (1993) / *Exteriors* (1996), where she transcribes fragments from the disorienting environment of the 'Ville Nouvelle' / 'New Town' of Cergy-Pontoise on the edge of Paris. She describes a state of limbo in the early years, when she would lose her bearings and drive endlessly along new roads:

[Q]uand j'ai commencé à vivre dans la Ville Nouvelle, je me perdais toujours et je continuais de rouler, trop affolée pour m'arrêter. Dans le centre commercial, j'essayais de bien de rappeler par quelle porte j'étais entrée, A, B, C ou D, afin de retrouver la sortie. [. . .] J'avais peur d'errer jusqu'au soir sans la retrouver sous la dalle de béton. Beaucoup d'enfants se perdaient dans le supermarché.

Rien que le cul, et, dans un coin de mur plus sombre, en rouge, *Il n'y a pas de sous-hommes.*[31]

When I first moved to the New Town, I would invariably lose my way but would go on driving, too panicked to stop. In the shopping mall, I would make sure I knew exactly through which door I had entered – A, B, C, or D – so that I could locate the same exit later on. [. . .] I was afraid of having to wander under the concrete slab until nightfall without ever finding it. So many children got lost in the supermarket.

Only fucking matters, and on a darker part of the wall, in red, *there are no inferior men.*[32]

For Ernaux, in this scene, the only remainders to the marshalled and alienating world of supermarkets and A, B, C or D parking lots are unadorned notations – 'rien que le cul' – dragged up from what she repeatedly figures as underground spaces and left to bristle with their own abrasiveness. As in the extract from *La Place,* where each sentence seems to lurch inchoatively to the next, this places narrative continuity under severe strain, resulting not only in elliptical and fragmentary prose, but in a succession of works that exist in discontinuity, as Ernaux herself acknowledges when she writes in *La Honte* (1997) / *Shame* (1999) that her desire has always been to write books 'dont il me soit ensuite impossible de parler' / 'about which it is subsequently impossible for me to talk'.[33] The least that can be said about this is that it is a radical refusal to articulate past with future.

François Bégaudeau – Edouard Louis: 'for nothing'

For all its internal hesitations and deferrals, Ernaux's work was also unquestionably reshaping the future of contemporary writing through the early years of the twenty-first century, particularly in the progressive blurring of literary and sociological writing. So we will pause within its own discontinuities, in order to consider what it in part made possible in the form of two more recent texts, in which the promise of educational mobility is withdrawn. Both share with Ernaux an attention to the force of particular phrases and their capacity to disqualify. Our question for them will be how they deploy this force within a narrative structure, and what it means for the novel to incorporate its interruptive or rebellious discordances.

François Bégaudeau's hugely successful novel *Entre les murs* (2005) / *The Class* (2009), subsequently adapted by Laurent Cantet into the eponymous film, winner of the Palme d'Or at Cannes in 2008, is characterized by unmarked dialogue, interspersed by fragmentary thoughts from the focalizing point of view of the teacher, whose log of how many days before the next round of holidays organizes the text into five sections. The sparse reproduction of 'ordinary' speech has here become the infrastructure of the text, no longer emerging in terse fragments, but rather carrying the intrigue through a series of scenes of failed transmission. The failure runs both ways: the jumpy vitality of the pupils' interjections easily counters the attempts at humour and the caustic observations that plot the highs and lows of the teacher's discourse. No metatextual commentary is offered. The novel's gambit is that this is the way the world sounds 'within the walls' of the contemporary school in postcolonial Paris. It is discordant, disconnected; the possibility of backfire is ever present, and it is up to the reader to untangle the different voices.

The overall narrative arc of *Entre les murs* plots towards the exclusion of one disruptive pupil, but here I will focus on the tighter scene in which the possible 'orientations' towards post-sixteen education are being discussed by a small assembly of teachers, the U, sitting around a table:

> On passe à Mezut.
> Le U a un soupir unanime. Line a parlé pour les autres.
> – Qu'est-ce qu'on va faire de lui ?
> [. . .]
> – Il demande quoi ?
> – Seconde générale.
> La conseillère d'éducation psychologue a coupé court à la stupeur unanime.
> – Évidemment, en disant ça il ne se rend pas compte, c'est à nous de lui trouver une place plus conforme à ses capacités. Un apprentissage, quelque chose comme ça.
> [. . .]
> – Il y a de la place pour tout le monde en seconde. Un apprentissage dans le commerce, ça existe ?
> – Oui oui ça s'appelle CFA commerce, ou apprentissage unité commerce. En gros c'est s'occuper des rayons dans un Franprix, c'est génial.
> Elle avait dit c'est génial et signifié le contraire par une grimace. Le principal a dit que c'était déjà ça, et qu'il faudrait l'aider pour le remplissage de son dossier d'orientation, et que pour le reste eh bien c'était terriblement triste.[34]

Next is Mezut.
The U gave one unanimous sigh. Lina spoke for the rest of us.

'What are we going to do with him?'

[. . .]

'What is he asking for?'

'A general academic program.'

The guidance counselor interrupted the unanimous astonishment.

'Obviously, when he says that, he doesn't realize – it's up to us to find him a situation more suited to his abilities. An apprenticeship, something like that.'

[. . .]

'There's room for everyone in tenth grade. Is there such a thing as an apprenticeship in business?'

'Oh, yes, it's called a Business Apprenticeship. Roughly speaking it's stocking shelves in a supermarket, wonderful.'

She said Wonderful and indicated the opposite by her grimace. The principal said it was something at least and that Mezut should be helped to fill out the orientation dossier, and that as to the rest, well it was terribly sad.[35]

The scene contains the same fatality of relegation to low-skilled work in a retail environment that we started with, but where Ernaux's sparse consignment of that fact holds like a plug at the end of *La Place*, crushing the revolt into an impermeable form, Bégaudeau's text revolves through its possible permutations, as if trying out different configurations. The grimace worn by the educational counsellor, compounded by the school principal's stuttering, complacent words, operate a deadpan non-response. They reveal nothing that is not known about the world; at best, they slow the text with its onward march towards the 'terribly sad' reproduction of dominant norms, trying out a repertoire of possible attitudes in this stalemate, loosely attached to social positions, but collectively generating a chorus of consensus that Mezut's destiny is low-skilled labour. The novel performs the detachment of words from the world of 'things' with a sort of exuberant plasticity. Hadia's black plastic earrings enter the text on a level with her mistakes in French, the professorial voice's corrections and her Los Angeles 41 sweatshirt.[36] And the teacher Rachel's 'tiny' feet 'in her erotic pink thong sandals' have their place beside Katia's Converse ALL STAR sneakers in a scene in which the boys defend their right to declare their country of origin on the walls of the school yard.[37] Anything goes. Mezut or Djibril. And the novel draws its own ventriloquist vitality from its capacity to span and spin the repertoire.

This abandoning of forms of distinction reflects the persuasions of the broader literary grouping, not conceived so much as a movement as a collective, that gathered around the literary review, *Inculte*, which has proven to be the training ground for a significant number of France's contemporary writers. Bégaudeau was one of its first members to come to public visibility, and his early work lent a strong tonality to the group's emerging literary aesthetic. The amassing of snippets of speech corresponds to their self-characterization as lost without a compass: 'Déboussolés, livrés à nous-mêmes, divagants, à droite à gauche, imprévisibles, déconnants, déviants, déglingués, au sommet de la montagne nous avons perdu le Nord, tout est possible, la volonté est puissante, elle a renoncé au sens. Ces hommes nouveaux sont-ils vraiment en marche ?' / 'Lost, left to our own devices, wandering from left to right, unpredictable and unruly, deviant, messed-up, stuck on top of the mountain without any sense of where north lies, everything is possible, free will rules and has abandoned all meaning. Are these new men really heading anywhere?'[38] But if the collective is founded on the sense that there is no longer a map for the literary field, and that the novelist today is 'n'importe qui' / 'anyone' from whom 'n'importe quoi' is possible ('anything goes'), it is significant to note how some, including Bégaudeau, have reclaimed the novel form so explicitly rejected by Ernaux, and even the notion of 'fable' as the means of playing up the distribution of roles. While this announces the sort of playful revolt 'without any violence' akin to the poetic-republican 'élans' / 'enthusiasms' proclaimed by Guène's Doria in *Entre les murs*, it is the teacher who gets to brandish his Rimbaud, while the pupils claim their attachments via references to football.[39] Asked who Rimbaud is, he replies lightly: 'C'est quelqu'un de ton âge.' / 'A guy your age.' The suggestion is tossed into the mix of this free-for-all, and the book seems to want to suggest that the fact of being young and on the cusp of life, a condition that its own experimentation aims to emulate, might in itself mitigate the symbolic violence it is expressing. But the ironic bite in the text's knowing ellipsis ('a guy') gets the last 'laugh', while the pupils just get left in the dark.

Edouard Louis's *Histoire de la violence* (2016) / *History of Violence* (2019) offers a very different perspective on the latent violence that can accrue around cultural capital. Also billed as a novel, it is closer in self-conscious provenance to Ernaux, with whom it shares a strong intellectual attachment to the work of Bourdieu.[40] The narrative records a rape, the fear of death through strangulation, and the ongoing violence of the subsequent interactions with medical services and the police. The role of reported speech is again essential in this narration, and complex, ranging from the long overheard passages of the author/narrator's sister's re-recounting of the events to short interjections from police and doctors, which we will discuss. But it also includes a scene that suspends the verdict of foreclosed educational promise, marking it up with the performance of disarray, before shifting its ground and opening up a quite different trajectory for the 'novel' to that we have positioned through Bégaudeau's exuberant 'fable'.

As events unfold in the book, Reda's desire for Louis's possessions – his phone and iPad in particular – become the trigger for the switch from erotic encounter to annihilating violence. But in the scene I will discuss, it is the taking up of a book that prompts Reda's confession that school was not his 'trip': 'je préférais faire le con' / 'I was always clowning around'.[41] This sentence later becomes the platform on which Louis tries to develop a story for Reda: 'des explications dans les zones de silence' / 'where there was only silence'.[42] He writes that he told this story in the conditional tense to his friends, positioning the narration we then read within concentric phases of telling, as he does with the use of his sister's version of his rape. Reda becomes his cousin Sylvain in this tale, at the moment when the latter is about to crash out of a failed school career, which is posited as biographically true but known by the author-narrator as part of local lore (he was not yet himself at the same school as his older cousin), of which he himself would become the guardian by later tellings of his own fascinated version of this moment of enviable revolt. Unprompted, Reda/cousin Sylvain suddenly gets up from the desk in a large, silent and sunny classroom, and steps towards the window, which is thrown open, in order to make to climb out. The text gives no indication how big the drop is on the other side. Perhaps the phantasmatic embellishments of silence and sunlight tell us that this classroom, with its polished yellow tables and polished yellow linoleum, was always going to be floating above the world, and Reda/cousin Sylvain's action would throw everyone back down on reality. The text merely says: 'Et l'explosion' / 'And the explosion', before continuing to describe the inevitable gestures of shock and bewilderment provoked by this outburst. The teacher 'pousse un cri' / 'cries out'; so does Reda. And the author-narrator explicitly requests his listeners' imagination at this point:

> « [V]ous imaginez », j'avais dit à Didier et Geoffroy, c'est comme un tableau où elle est debout à droite du cadre, évidemment les mains jointes devant la bouche et les yeux grands ouverts comme cela doit se passer dans cette configuration, quand un corps répond à une situation, impuissante, et à

gauche du cadre Reda, tous les deux presque symmétriques, Reda la jambe par-dessus la fenêtre, hurlant [. . .].[43]

"As you can imagine", I say to Didier and Geoffrey, it's like a tableau with the teacher on the right – hands clasped before her mouth, as well they might be, eyes wide, the only possible response a body can make at a moment of such complete impotence – and Reda on the left, the two of them almost perfectly symmetrical, Reda with his leg out of the window, yelling [. . .].[44]

The power of fiction is strenuously displayed, but not for long. The next chapter section opens with fundamental estrangement from the process of narration: 'je ne reconnaissais plus ce que je disais' / 'I no longer recognized what I was saying'.[45] So while Louis will later claim to his sister that the secret of survival is not to forget the trauma but to reach a new form of memory of the event, the 'tableau' that positions his rapist in his own fantasy of screaming back at school suggests that these efforts to normalize the forces pressing on him are fragile and difficult to hold apart from the versions of events that he finds himself obliged to produce for the police and doctors. The convergence in this scene between cousin Sylvain's holler and the one Louis's 'fictionalisation' lends to Reda also asks what sort of place there is for the language of the 'con' here: '« Je vais me buter, je vais me faire exploser ma race, je vais me faire la gueule. »' / '"I'm fucking going to jump, I'm going to throw myself out of this window."'[46] The text turns the very words that Reda is described as using about Louis back on himself, as the explosion at the heart of this imagined scene becomes a sort of nihilistic performance, powerful only in its ability to control the rhythm of its botched ending: 'c'était pour rien. Il n'avait aucun conflit particulier avec l'enseignante, il voulait juste voir la panique la transformer, la déformer, la défigurer, il voulait faire rire les autres [. . .] c'était lui qui maîtrisait le temps.' / 'he did it for no reason. He didn't have anything against the teacher in particular, he just wanted to see her transformed, deformed, transfigured by panic, he wanted to make the other kids laugh [. . .] he would be the one in control of time.'[47] It hovers close in so doing to the inassimilable remark launched at Louis 'pour rien' / 'for nothing' by the policewoman during his deposition: '« C'est votre truc à vous tout ce qui est arabe ? »' / '"So Arabs are your thing?"'[48] Louis retorts that Reda was Kabyle and offers the evidence of a discussion they had had about a Kabyle proverb in a vain attempt to differentiate and thereby to inscribe his encounter with Reda within a story that could plot towards better understanding between peoples. In the face of this sort of wanton verbal violence, which seems to revel in ways not dissimilar to those displayed in *Entre les murs* in its own capacity to hold the stage and control the timing, Louis clings in his narration to his lover's name, rejecting the cynical belief shared by his friends and the police that he had necessarily given a false one. Referring to 'ces quatre lettres' / 'those four letters' as the gift of truth, they speak the 'real' against the 'scenes' that all those around him paint. In this moment, but perhaps this moment alone, it is evident that 'anything does not go' for Louis. There is no taking another name for this one.

The possibility of inventing a new destiny in part through renaming is central to Louis's literary project, and explicitly so.[49] But it is this explicit thematizing of his reinvention that also undoes its drive, throwing him back into the tangled mess of social relations, as some of the recent controversy has shown.[50] In this sense, Louis's bid for authorship generates more fictional instability than we observe in Ernaux's densely compacted work, and its refusal to give up the 'four letters' of his violator's name crosses this instability as a fragile mediation, suspended between desiring bodies and the momentum of a text that seems to cast in all directions, still unsure about how and whether it should speak out.

Annie Ernaux – Leslie Kaplan: 'but where? It's vast, the *banlieue*.'

There are no names in Ernaux's literary rendering of the life that has been hers, or only names that she receives through the public domain: Simone Signoret, Scarlett O'Hara. Her lovers are P., S. Her mother is 'elle' / 'she', *Une femme* (1988). We learn how her father laps up his soup, not what he was called. In contrast, Leslie Kaplan's fictional world is astir with people with whom we are immediately on first-name terms. Louise, Mathias, Marie. They are often young protagonists, whose relations with other named characters from the city are fluid, sometimes fleeting, sometimes consolidating into groups. Some are students; some work; some drift. Together, they people the scene in ways that are vibrant and specific, without being evidently symptomatic of a deeper social structure. There is no equivalent to the perilous scene of balancing on the sill between inclusion and exclusion. And no scene of 'orientation' as such, although the possibility of looking for something, of seeking the future, generates the work's movement.

Lastingly coloured by the experience of the May 1968 uprisings, Kaplan's work has unfolded over a period comparable to that of Ernaux.[51] There are connections, anchored in shared experiences of changing sexual relations, relayed by antennae finely attuned to the tones and forms of popular culture, and reinforced by a common commitment to literature of the 'real'. But there are important differences too, and they offer a way of closing this chapter's exploration of how narrative writing has responded to and reflected the grinding withdrawal of the promises of social transformation and mobility, promises that continue, in the face of overwhelming evidence, to shape the stories we tell ourselves.

The suppression of names in Ernaux's texts is part of her resistance to the particularizing forces of memoir. It is of a piece with the use of the definite article for *La Place*, a late decision in the composition of that turning-point book. The push towards generality corresponds to the transformation that she defines as the work of her writing, not fictionalization but a process of conceptualization: 'que mon corps, mes sensations et mes pensées deviennent de l'écriture, c'est-à-dire quelque chose d'intelligible et de général' / 'that my body, my feelings and my thoughts become writing, that is to say something intelligible and general'.[52] At the end of *Les Années*, she returns to what had been her desire to find 'un langage inconnu' / 'an unknown language' that would lie ahead of her and offer a way out of 'ce qui la révoltait' / 'what outraged her'.[53] But her realization is that she can only write inside her language, which is everyone's language, resulting in what retrospectively appears as a work of unswerving persistence. This is the achievement of *Les Années*; a mimetic, headlong relation to the present and its discourses, which had left her in such bewilderment and self-abnegation. She describes an opening onto an appeased totality that remediates her place in history, defusing the long wrangling with Proust through the metaphor of immersion in the '*rumeur*' / '*hubbub*' of the past, in order to 'reconstituer un temps commun' / 'reconstitute a common time'.[54] Her own memories become the singular expression of 'une sorte de vaste sensation collective' / 'a kind of vast collective sensation'. When she glides along the motorway, alone in her car, she is no longer terrified that she does not know which direction – which 'orientation' – to take, but is rather 'prise dans la totalité indéfinissable du monde présent, du plus proche au plus lointain' / 'being *taken into* the indefinable whole of the world of now, from the closest to the most remote of things'.[55]

There are plenty of rumblings ('rumeur') in Leslie Kaplan's fictional world too, and perhaps particularly in the latest major novel, *Mathias et la Révolution* (2016). Written against the background of rising social and political unrest since the riots of 2005, the book finds its rhythm in recurrent references to 'émeutes' / 'riots' that are kicking off somewhere, a little remote, in the *banlieue*, but where exactly and why is not clear. This uncertainty is no more a source of anxiety than it is for Ernaux in the final stages of *Les Années*. But where Ernaux achieves a binding of past into present, which holds her within an impersonal succession of years that prompts her to acknowledge that she has lost her sense of the future, Kaplan's writing is stretched towards an outside. She links this in part to her own bicultural and bilingual upbringing, born to Jewish-American parents and raised in France in an expatriate community until she claimed Paris as a permanent home and made French her language of literary expression.[56] The news of imminent unrest circulates as hearsay and on the radio, relayed by the protagonists too, who circulate around the city, on buses, on foot, on errands, and for no specific reason other than the pleasure of wandering. It crosses a dispersed rehearsing of several key facets of the history of the 1789 French Revolution, which becomes a parallel leitmotiv, sounding in a counter-punctual way and creating a cross-current that displaces a fixation either on contemporary events or on the now mythologized past. The café waiter Jérémie breaks into a stirring version of the Battle of Valmy when serving a lemonade to a couple of tourists; Sibylle and Anaïs, two prostitutes taking time off in the city, carry on a conversation that veers from something like #MeToo affirmations to a discussion of the Terror and the guillotine.[57] Emblematic of Kaplan's exhilarant, radiant prose, *Mathias* traverses recognizable places and idioms, and yet is always slightly offbeat or turned towards an unexpected fold in the map. It is this 'orientation' that distinguishes it importantly from Ernaux's centripetal insistence that there can be no taking of one word for another. Kaplan, like all of the other writers discussed here, deploys fragments of speech, certain 'paroles' / 'words of a song', certain brief interjections, as a series of soundings that come unmediated from the world. As in the other books this chapter has explored, these soundings generate interference, speaking the 'realities' of the world through its forms of domination in the very place where the subject is looking to exist on her own terms. For Ernaux, this has meant prose writing that reproduces those forms of domination with unflinching poise; and Louis's work tends too towards this sort of incontrovertibility. For Guène, irony offers a way out of the competing imperatives of rage and desire. Kaplan, however, dismisses irony as a form of cheating.[58] Instead, she holds her words up to scrutiny in fragments that leave the reader suspended, affected yet unsure, in scenes that might just collapse in their own irrelevance but refuse to go away. Then we turn the page and discover we are somewhere else.

This changeability distinguishes Kaplan's work from the harmonious totality of a 'récit glissant, dans un imparfait continu' / 'slippery narrative composed in an unremitting continuous tense', imagined by Ernaux at the end of *Les Années.*[59] *Louise, elle est folle*, declares another of Kaplan's titles, in a pairing that has echoes of the sort of 'double act' that Mathias and the Revolution represent in the later novel. The pairing is unhinged: we do not know if Louise is 'mad', any more than Mathias seems set to launch a revolution. The relation is experimental, neither denied by the corrosive force of irony, nor defused by immersion in an undifferentiated present; a proposition, not a destiny. Maybe it is just a 'way of talking'? No one is really suggesting Louise is mad. Are they? Perhaps the riots are in Gonesse.[60] Or perhaps in Livray-Gargan? Kaplan's work embraces this uncertainty and the cumulative pressure of its non-resolution. Perhaps this is revolution after all? It gives us options, which may remain fictional, and no sense that this looping will stop and narrative composure will be restored. In this, it also reaffirms the potential of fiction to inscribe unlikeliness, and gives the reader the opportunity to lay a claim on some of its excitability, to select from within its soundtrack, and perhaps to grasp that this process is inextricable from getting a future in a ruthlessly reproduced present.

CHAPTER 4

Contemporary French Fiction and the World
Transnationalism, Translingualism and the Limits of Genre

Charles Forsdick

Pour une littérature voyageuse: Travel, Writing and the World

From a twenty-first-century perspective, reading the 1992 *livre-manifeste* produced by authors linked to the *Pour une littérature voyageuse* movement is a reminder of how far and how rapidly French literary culture has evolved since the turn of the millennium.[1] Not strictly a manifesto, the volume draws together essays by writers in the group around Michel Le Bris, who were involved in establishing with him the 'Étonnants voyageurs' festival in Saint-Malo in 1990, and in setting up simultaneously the journal *Gulliver*.[2] Le Bris was a key figure in later twentieth-century literature and thought, progressively reinventing himself as the editor, post-1968, of *La Cause du Peuple* (for which, with the authorities too timorous to arrest Sartre, he was briefly imprisoned), as the structuralist author (under the pseudonym Pierre Cressant) of a 1970 biography of Claude Lévi-Strauss, and – the author of *L'Homme aux semelles de vent* (1977) – as a *nouveau philosophe* or 'new philosopher'. Under Le Bris's steer, the *Pour une littérature voyageuse* authors responded to various crises – literary and political – in fin-de-siècle France, in order to posit a neo-realist form of writing that claimed to respond, somewhat belatedly, to the impact of the *nouveau roman* and its theoretical manifestation, Structuralism. Le Bris himself championed 'une littérature qui dise le monde' / 'a literature which says the world', a reaction to what he saw as the 'mise-en-parenthèses du monde' / 'bracketing-off of the world' that he discerned in the work of writers such as his fellow Breton, Alain Robbe-Grillet. Although those signing up to this project worked across a range of genres, including poetry (in the work, for instance, of the translingual writer of Scottish origin, Kenneth White) and the essay (notably Jacques Meunier), many of them – including Le Bris himself – were novelists with an interest in the intersection of fiction with travel writing. As such, they may be seen as part of two major literary developments in the Mitterrand years: the emergence of an often post-generic 'prose', in which fiction, autobiography and other forms of documentary writing merged; and the reassertion of the narrative as a vehicle for storytelling, in what some critics have dubbed the 'return to the story'.[3]

Part of the function of the *Pour une littérature voyageuse* movement was a retrospective one, seeking to recover, from the shelves of the great unread, books published during the decades following the Second World War that had failed to attract the wider readerships they arguably deserved: texts such as Nicolas Bouvier's *Usage du monde* (1963) / *The Way of the World* (1994) and Jacques Lacarrière's *Chemin faisant* (1974), two travelogues recounting, respectively, their authors' slow, meandering journeys through the rapidly changing landscapes of 1950s Eastern Europe and the Middle East or 1970s France. What is striking in retrospect about *Pour une littérature voyageuse* is the narrow guild identity it represented, and its failure to acknowledge the distinctive subjectivities of those involved in the movement – and the implications of these for their representational practice. Although the work of some women writers was included in the indicative bibliography with which their manifesto concluded, these were primarily figures from earlier generations such as Ella Maillart and Anita Conti, meaning all the contributors to the *livre-manifeste* were exclusively male. At the same time, despite an openness to work in translation (in particular, by contemporary Anglophone travel writers such as Nigel Barley, Bruce Chatwin or Redmond O'Hanlon), the ethnicity of the core writers involved was homogeneously white, failing to integrate any of the Francophone voices increasingly prominent by the early 1990s (Patrick Chamoiseau's *Texaco* was, significantly, awarded the Prix Goncourt in the same year as the *Pour une littérature voyageuse* volume appeared).

The collection of essays seeking to codify the agenda of the *Pour une littérature voyageuse* movement tells, however, only part of the story. The conservative poetics that underpinned the projected 'littérature qui dise le monde', of which these authors sought to be a vehicle, jars with the more complex reality of the literary landscape of which it formed a part. The Saint-Malo literary festival, for instance, while set up as the meeting point for the 'petits enfants de Stevenson et Conrad' / 'grandchildren of Stevenson and Conrad',[4] was a major driver in widening understandings of contemporary French literature in the 1990s, not least in order to include works – most notably comics (*bandes dessinées*) and detective fiction (*polars*) – long dismissed in France as 'paraliterary', and also to celebrate the work of postcolonial authors working in French. *Pour une littérature voyageuse* was criticized by Jean-Didier Urbain and others for its nostalgic attachment to earlier modes of travel writing – solipsistic, Romantic, focused on 'le grand dehors' / 'the great outdoors' – as well as its failure to ally with new ways of engaging with the domestic and endotic in France itself.[5] More diversified representations of France were arguably epitomized by François Maspero's parodic take on late twentieth-century travel, *Les Passagers du Roissy-Express* (1990) / *Roissy Express* (1994), a celebration of contemporary France unfolding against the backcloth of officially endorsed celebrations of the Bicentenary of the French Revolution.[6]

Through the programming of the 'Étonnants voyageurs' festival and the contents of *Gulliver*, however, Le Bris and his fellow authors performed the contradictions of their own self-positioning, nostalgic for earlier modes of articulating the world in literary form, but at the same time intersecting with the new voices and forms that marked the final years of the twentieth century. The 1993 festival was devoted, for instance, to 'world fiction', with Patrick Chamoiseau and Raphaël Confiant prominent among the guests; in 1996, the event's theme was the new literatures of Latin America; and the programme of the 1998 festival was dominated by discussion of the Mediterranean, with a particular focus on North Africa in the work of authors including Rachid Boudjedra and Abdellatif Laâbi. This openness was reflected equally in contributions to *Gulliver*, which devoted two issues – in 1993 and 1999 – to 'world fiction'. This topic was inspired – as the label suggests – by parallel developments in Anglophone literature, not least around the work of Salman Rushdie, but sought at the same time to discern what its French-language equivalent might look like. This activity revealed, therefore, a dual movement: on the one hand, a willingness to accept a variety of alternative voices – available through translation into French – that extended world fiction beyond the limits of a literature defined monolingually or in the light of a single nation; and on the other, a residual commitment to understanding such developments within a frame that remained both French and in French, defined simultaneously in terms of nation and language.

World-Literature in French: Rethinking the Novel and the Nation

The shift from a limited understanding of 'littérature qui dise le monde' in the *Pour une littérature voyageuse* collection from 1992 to these potentially more expansive definitions underpins a wider trajectory that would lead to a second manifesto in 2007. Advocating 'une « littérature-monde » en français', this intervention was similarly coordinated by Michel Le Bris and included several signatories from among the 1992 contributors.[7] This call for a 'world-literature in French' was ostensibly a reaction to a literary phenomenon, the award in autumn 2006 of a cluster of the main literary prizes in France to novelists of origins other than French, dubbed in the manifesto itself as 'écrivains d'outre-France' / 'writers from beyond-France'. The authors represented in this group were eclectic, including Jonathan Littel, a writer whose childhood was split between France and the United States, awarded the Prix Goncourt and the Grand Prix du roman de l'Académie française for *Les Bienveillantes* (2006) / *The Kindly Ones* (2009); Alain Mabanckou, a French citizen born in the Republic of the Congo, who won the Renaudot for *Mémoires de porc-épic* (2006) / *Memoirs of a Porcupine* (2012); Nancy Huston, a Canadian author who writes primarily in French but also self-translates into English, awarded the Femina for *Lignes de faille* (2006) / *Fault Lines* (2007); and Léonora Miano, a writer born in Cameroon but resident in France since 1991, winner of the Goncourt des lycéens for *Contours du jour qui vient* (2006). The diversity of this group – mixing translingual authors with those whose trajectory was more conventionally postcolonial – actively challenged any residual understanding of the 'French' in 'French literature' along exclusively national lines. The manifesto presents the impact of such a shift in terms of a 'Copernican revolution', a paradigm shift in which a heliocentric understanding of the solar system inverts centre and periphery, and causes the world to be viewed in new ways. The deployment of such a metaphor from astronomy permits a radical reordering of French literary constellations:

> [L]e centre, ce point depuis lequel était supposée rayonner une littérature franco-française, n'est plus le centre. Le centre jusqu'ici, même si de moins en moins, avait eu cette capacité d'absorption qui contraignait les auteurs venus d'ailleurs à se dépouiller de leurs bagages avant de se fondre dans le creuset de la langue et de son histoire nationale : le centre, nous disent les prix d'automne, est désormais partout, aux quatre coins du monde. Fin de la francophonie. Et naissance d'une littérature-monde en français.

> The center, from which supposedly radiated a franco-French literature, is no longer the center. Until now, the center, albeit less and less frequently, had this absorptive capacity that forced authors who came from elsewhere to rid themselves of their foreign trappings before melting in the crucible of the French language and its national history: the center, these fall prizes tell us, is henceforth everywhere, at the four corners of the world. The result? The end of 'francophone' literature – and the birth of a world literature in French.[8]

Under scrutiny here was the division of literary production in French, according to a logic of ethnolinguistic nationalism, into 'French' and 'Francophone' writing – a division as evident in the publishing, marketing and retailing of novels as it was in the ways in which those texts were studied in formal educational environments in France. Although these claims, most notably about the death of Francophonie, caused consternation in certain quarters (the former Senegalese president Abdou Diouf, then Secretary-General of the Organisation internationale de la Francophonie, was among those who protested vociferously), the manifesto does not proceed to develop them in detail, but instead wearily reiterates – in sections of the text rarely subject to critical scrutiny – some of the material first included fifteen years previously in the *Pour une littérature voyageuse* collection: 'The world is returning – and it's the best of news. Wasn't the world always conspicuous by its absence in French literature? [. . .] The novel was too serious an affair to be left to the novelists alone, who were guilty of a "naïve use of language" and encouraged to repeat themselves in complaisant linguistic exercises.'[9] From the bold claim that the term describes a post-national literature, disrupting conventional understandings of French literature and positing something approximating more to a transnational, even post-national literature in French, 'littérature-monde' is then drawn into the orbit of an earlier tradition. This is in part indebted to the detective fiction of *néo-polar* authors such as Jean-Patrick Manchette and to the comics of Hugo Pratt or Moebius, in part to the work of those whom Salman Rushdie dubbed in the 1980s 'translated men', such as Kazuo Ishiguro, Ben Okri, Hanif Kureishi and Michael Ondaatje.

The manifesto returns nevertheless in its final two paragraphs to a focus on the French/Francophone divide, describing a sprawling corpus of postcolonial and translingual fiction of global dimensions: 'à l'évidence multiples, diverses, sont aujourd'hui les littératures de langue françaises de par le monde, formant un vaste ensemble dont les ramifications enlacent plusieurs continents' / 'literatures in French around the world today are demonstrably multiple, diverse, forming a vast ensemble, the ramifications of which link together several continents'.[10] The suggestion is that the 'world' in 'world-literature' is double-edged, in part reflecting the object of representation of a neo-realist attention to the everyday, in part suggesting the transnational reach of twenty-first-century novelistic production. Unlike *littérature voyageuse*, which had helpfully provided an indicative biography in its own manifesto to signal the emerging corpus towards which it gestured, *littérature-monde* promised instead a future apparatus by

which it be would defined (two 'world-literature' prizes were launched in
2017, one for a novel in French, another for a text in translation; an
anticipated periodical has not yet materialized). Understanding of the term
is as a result largely implicit in the manifesto itself, which refers to a new
generation of authors who would seize 'sans complexe des ingrédients de la
fiction pour ouvrir de nouvelles voies romanesques' / 'without hesitation
the ingredients of fiction in order to open up new novelistic paths'.[11] The
identity of *littérature-monde* may be discerned in the light of the work of
those who feature in its varied list of forty-four signatories, but it is also
projected in the concluding sentences of the manifesto: we are witnessing
'la formation d'une constellation que nous assistons, où la langue libérée de
son pacte exclusif avec la nation, libre désormais de tout pouvoir autre que
ceux de la poésie et de l'imaginaire, n'aura pour frontières que celles de
l'esprit' / 'the birth of a new constellation, in which language freed from its
exclusive pact with the nation, free from every other power hereafter but
the powers of poetry and the imaginary, will have no other frontiers but
those of the spirit'.[12]

In their enthusiasm for the concept of a literature transcending the
boundaries of the nation as set out in the first part of this definition, a
number of critics have skirted round the haziness otherwise implicit in this
outline. Such abstract commitment to poetry, to the imaginary and to the
power of the 'spirit' lacks distinctiveness and does little to indicate what
such an intervention might ultimately reveal about twenty-first-century
fiction. At the same time, *littérature-monde* fails to question the apparatus
of contemporary literature in French which contributes to the perpetuation of Gallocentric tendencies and acts as a brake to any further diversification by discouraging more polycentric or devolved publishing practices.
As has been acknowledged already, the movement unquestioningly
adopted the predominantly conservative mechanisms of literary prize
culture as its initial justification; it also relied on dissemination through
the pages of *Le Monde* and – as a follow-up to the manifesto – via a
collection of essays published by Gallimard (a publisher responsible for the
perpetuation of the French/Francophone divide through its books series,
most notably 'Continents Noirs', in which is included the work of African
and Afro-European authors who rarely make their way into the prestigious
'Collection Blanche'). *Littérature-monde* operates therefore as a paradoxically suggestive category, arguably raising key questions about the nature of
the contemporary novel in French and the current trajectories of the genre,
but at the same time failing in itself to demonstrate the difference it
purports to champion.

Central to such questions is the relationship of literature to the world as privileged in evocations in 'world-literature'. It is clear that the 'monde' in 'littérature-monde' overlaps in certain ways with the earlier aspiration to a 'littérature qui dise le monde' associated with the *littérature voyageuse* of the early 1990s. This was, however, constructed in exclusive ways linked in part to nostalgic views of the function of writing, whereas world literature deploys a more expansive rhetoric of inclusion that claims to respond to the challenges of representation in the twenty-first century. Emily Apter explores the genealogy of the term, seeing 'littérature-monde' as a 'reserve of philosophical untranslatability and conceptual density'.[13] Her focus is in particular on the semantic divergence between the French 'monde' and the German 'Welt', suggesting that close attention to the variations of the 'world' in the terms' linguistic and cultural niches provides access to 'reimagining what in the world the "world" in literature might be'.[14] On the one hand, to evoke the world is to raise the risks of 'worlding' identified by Gayatri Spivak, mistaking the particular for the general (as is the case with French republican universalism), imposing a European version of reality for the understanding of non-Western social worlds. At the same time, however, reference to the world encourages engagement with another early concept of postcolonial criticism, Edward Said's 'world-liness', a recognition that the literary text is of the world and has the potential to impact on that world – in Jonathan Arac's terms: 'For Said, the world of world literature requires a vividly concrete sense of geography and an acknowledgement both of large-scale relationships of political power and also of human-scale circumstances of individual lives.'[15] What might it mean to explore 'littérature-monde' in the light of these terms, and to read the contemporary French novel both macroscopically and microscopically in the context of the challenges they raise? The response to such questions may be seen to emerge – as the subtitle of this chapter suggests – along three intersecting axes, relating to literature and the nation-state, to literature and language, and to the new forms and genres emerging in the twenty-first century. Such developments address the contemporary demands of cultural representation and consumption (not least in urgent response to the politics of globalization). 'Littérature-monde' thus operates more as a project to be realized than as a fully functioning school or movement. Its component parts merit scrutiny. The foregrounding of 'literature' links contemporary writing to a longer tradition, and seems to posit a certain set of cultural values while retaining the possibility that this form of creative expression has the potential to evolve constantly in response to the context of its production. As such, to speak of 'literature' raises questions not only of form but also of voice, and demands the adoption of a position in relation to a phenomenon that is perceived to be – in the terms of Tzvetan Todorov's 2007 essay – 'in peril'.[16] Todorov's argument relating to the latest iteration of this crisis, published in the same year as the *littérature-monde* manifesto, was a surprising intervention from a critic who had been largely responsible for championing the role of Structuralism in literary criticism. His focus was, however, on what would manifest itself as the hyphen in 'world-literature', that is, the link between these two elements – in short, the place of literature in the world as well as that of the world in literature.

Translingualism, or *Language Freed from Its Exclusive Pact with the Nation*

Central to the manifesto is the idea that French has become – or has the potential to become – a 'language freed from its exclusive pact with the nation'.[17] One of the clear legacies of the *littérature-monde* manifesto relates to a destabilization of the yoking, in the French context, of the novel and the nation, even if its catalytic role in this process remains moot. It might be argued that, with the rise of a specifically Francophone postcolonial novel, especially from the 1970s onwards, this process had long been in train. As has already been shown, however, the emergence of a 'Francophone' tradition, itself often compartmentalized along the national lines of, for example, the 'Algerian novel', or at least along the regional lines of the 'Sub-Saharan African novel', lent itself to a binary manoeuvre whereby French (national) literature maintained, according to a protectionist logic and through the eclectic apparatus of literature culture (prizes, publishers' collections, institutions, academic curricula), its distinctiveness in relation to the emergence of these new voices. Contemporary writing in French reveals the extent to which – in the literary Francosphere – things are falling apart while the centre somehow continues to hold. The progression erosion of the French/Francophone is evident in the visibility in French literary culture of authors of African and Caribbean heritage, who have negotiated the pitfalls of what Graham Huggan called the 'postcolonial exotic' to assert themselves in terms of poetic confidence as well as institutional presence.[18] Authors of substantial œuvres that are widely taught and translated include Haitian writer Dany Laferrière, elected to the Académie française in 2013, and novelist Alain Mabanckou, who was appointed in 2016 to a chair of 'création artistique' at the Collège de France. In some ways, this follows the logic of the institutions of French language and culture, sensing themselves under siege from Anglocentric globalization, and seeking to extend their power base while maintaining control of the (predominantly French national) infrastructures on which they depend.

The link in France between French literature and national identity is a close one, epitomized by the ways in which Pierre Nora, in his resolutely Hexagonal *Les Lieux de mémoire* (1984–1992) / *Realms of Memory* (1996–1997), integrates literary culture (including, in an essay by Antoine Compagnon, the seven parts of Proust's *À la recherche du temps perdu*) into these realms of national memory. This process culminates in Marc Fumaroli's exploration of 'the genius of the French language' in the concluding contribution to the seven volumes of the collection. The *littérature-monde* manifesto is an attempt to claim that such reification of these national institutions (as well as the proprietorial approach with which this is associated) is increasingly ineffective, as there is an increasing sense of the commonality of the French language as a marker of literary belonging. As such, it is arguable that – just as postcolonialism has become, after several decades of resistance, an item of critical currency in France – a more polycentric literary landscape has emerged for which the prefix 'post-', with its overtones of historic succession allied to the persistent legacies of the past, is less relevant than that of 'trans-'. José Saldívar has proposed a concept of 'trans-Americanity' that encourages a shift from 'acting and thinking from the nation-state level' towards 'thinking and acting at the planetary and world-systems level'.[19] What might be seen as a 'trans-Francophone' approach could similarly nurture a productive engagement ranging from macro to micro levels, allowing what Arthur Goldhammer – in a different context – has called a 'reflective equilibrium between the local and the global, in which even more intimate knowledge of the part fosters deeper insight into the workings of the whole'.[20]

Evidence of these post-postcolonial shifts may be seen in the consolidation and growing visibility of the translingual or exophonic novel in French. The production of French fiction by authors who have acquired the language later in life, often but not exclusively as a result of physical migration and exile, is not a new phenomenon. The leading French symbolist poets Jean Moréas and Francis Vielé-Griffin were, respectively, born in Greece and the United States; and a survey published in *Les Nouvelles littéraires* in 1940, motivated in part by the award of the Prix Goncourt to the Russian-born novelist Henri Troyat in 1938, sought to identify a 'French Conrad'.[21] Recent manifestations of exophonic writing came to prominence in 1995, when Andrei Makine and Vassilis Alexakis –

authors of Russian and Greek origin, respectively – were awarded major literary prizes for their novels *Le Testament français* and *La Langue maternelle*. Fictional production in French by writers operating translingually has since expanded exponentially, with the language operating as a site of hospitality for those, such as Atiq Rahimi (of Afghanistani origin) or Chahdortt Djavann (born in Iran), who have fled oppressive regimes, or as a place of personal renewal for authors such as Akira Mizubayashi or Aki Shimazaki (both of Japanese origin), who seek an alternative space of self-expression.

The dynamics of translingual creativity remain complex, with some authors – including Alexakis himself, the Mauritian author Ananda Devi and the Canadian writer Nancy Huston – operating ambilingually, either composing their works in two languages or engaging in self-translation, with the result that any distinction between notions of original and copy become increasingly blurred.[22] For many exophonic writers, however, writing and achieving recognition in French are part of paying homage to France, French culture and the universalist values with which they are associated. As a result, translingual novels are often drawn inexorably into a sphere of Frenchness. Some focus on the processes of language acquisition, as is the case in Akira Mizubayashi's *Une langue venue d'ailleurs* (2011) or Chahdortt Djavann's *Comment peut-on être français ?* (2006). Others enter into dialogue with classic French literary texts, as is the case in Dai Sijie's *Balzac et la petite tailleuse chinoise* (2000) / *Balzac and the Little Chinese Seamstress* (2001), a coming of age narrative that unfolds against a backdrop of the Chinese cultural revolution, in which the two protagonists undergoing re-education steal a suitcase of translated forbidden Western texts and use them to seduce and educate the eponymous little seamstress, eventually providing her with the tools to leave her rural environment.

These emphases on French language and culture reveal the extent to which, while translingual writing may indeed reveal an opening up of literature to a wider world of reference, there is nevertheless evidence of a conditioning of this practice within certain Francocentric parameters. These wider dynamics may be integral to the capacity of the French literary establishment to recuperate and capitalize on contributions seen as potentially disruptive, not least in terms of the decoupling of literature and nation. The presence of translingual writers in the contemporary French literary canon serves a dual purpose, at once radical and conservative, challenging the ethnolinguistic nationalism of any equation of a single nation with a single language, but at the same time perpetuating the distinctiveness of French as a language that seeks to project and protect

its status in a global frame. Exophonic writers now figure notably among
the members of the Académie française: Eugène Ionesco was elected in
1970, and current *immortels* include François Cheng (elected in 2002),
Michael Edwards (2013) and most recently Andrei Makine (2015).
Whereas Cheng's relationship with France and French has always been
dialogic, foregrounding bilingualism as well as transnational connections
between cultures of origin and adoption, Makine illustrates an alternative
position of responsibility and even indebtedness. In works such as *Cette
France qu'on oublie d'aimer* (2006), the latter has adopted the rhetoric of
déclinisme to evoke 'this impalpable French quintessence that interested me
above all', while regretting the disappearance of any such essence from
contemporary literary production.[23] Identifying such tendencies is not to
deny the role of the translingual novel, in much the same way as
'Francophone' writing introduced readers in France to a range of colonial
and postcolonial topics, operating as a vehicle for the radical diversification
of the subject matter of French fiction. Ranging from the Greece recovering from the regime of the colonels in Vassilis Alexakis's *La Langue
maternelle* (1995) / *Mother Tongue* (2017), to the Maoist China of
François Cheng's *Le Dit de Tianyi* (1998) / *The River Below* (2001), from
war-torn Afghanistan in Atiq Rahimi's *Syngue sabour : pierre de patience*
(2008) / *The Patience Stone* (2010) to Second World War Japan in the two
pentalogies of Aki Shimazaki's fiction, exophonic fiction can be seen to
fulfil a quasi-ethnographic function, as if the subjects its authors can
address are themselves policed according to what may be seen – by analogy
with Graham Huggan's notion of the 'postcolonial exotic' as mentioned
above – as a translingual exoticism. There is nevertheless an eclecticism to
this body of fiction that makes any such formulaic reduction, even if we
may discern particular tendencies in contemporary novelistic production,
ultimately unhelpful. Translingual writing retains the potential to disrupt
and defamiliarize, often in unexpected ways. Engaging, for instance, with
the common form of the fictionalized language memoir, Alexakis's *Les
Mots étrangers* (2002) / *Foreign Words* (2006) describes the acquisition by
its narrator of an additional language, Sango, spoken by around 400,000
people in the Central African Republic. An interest in Greek and French
continues in the novel, as elsewhere in Alexakis's œuvre, but the impact of
learning Sango on the narrator's existing linguistic competence is radical:
'Apprendre une langue étrangère oblige à s'interroger sur la sienne propre.
Je songe aussi bien au grec qu'au français : je les vois différemment depuis
que j'ai entrepris de m'éloigner d'eux, la distance les rapproche, par
moments j'ai l'illusion qu'ils ne forment qu'une seule langue.'[24] /

'Learning a foreign language requires questioning one's own. I am thinking of Greek as well as French: I see them differently since I have started to move away from them, the distance brings them closer, sometimes I have the illusion that they form only one language.' The identification of a linguistic third space allows a reassessment, outside the normative expectations of dominant French literary culture, of the dynamic linking his two customary languages of expression, French and Greek.

Transcending the Monolingual: From Creolization to Experimentation

The work of Alexakis – not a signatory of the 'littérature-monde' manifesto, but a contributor nevertheless to the Étonnants voyageurs festival associated with it – raises key questions about literature, language and the world. The qualifying and singularizing 'en français' appended to 'littérature-monde' imposes a monolingualism that sits uneasily with the global ambitions of any such literary designation. Much translingual writing in French fails to display the linguistic and creative experimentation evident in the Anglophone translingual novel, a leading practitioner of which, the US-based author Junot Diaz, draws on his Hispanophone origins in the Dominican Republic to disruptive linguistic effect. The result is a literary version of what sociolinguists dub translanguaging, a melding of different languages into new forms of expression fit for the twenty-first century. Largely absent from translingual writing in French, such innovation was evident in the creolized French – or more accurately, in the terms of Milan Kundera, 'Chamoisified French' – of an early novel by Patrick Chamoiseau, *Texaco*, awarded the Prix Goncourt in 1992.[25] Published in the wake of the bilingual manifesto *Éloge de la créolité/In Praise of Creoleness* (1989), *Texaco* offers a literary manifestation of the cultural and linguistic heterogeneity of the French Antilles, and of the Caribbean more generally. An account of Texaco, a shanty town on the outskirts of the capital of Martinique, Fort-de-France, the novel's principal narrator is Marie-Sophie Laborieux, daughter of once enslaved parents, who tells her family history through the nineteenth to the late twentieth century. Her voice is complemented and contested by those of Christ, the urban planner sent by the authorities to develop Texaco, and the authorial Oiseau-de-Cham, whose role is to track Marie-Sophie's oral testimony. As Stanka Radovic has noted, 'Chamoiseau's novel explores the dynamic interplay between Creole and French languages and social spaces as they encounter one another in a colonial and postcolonial context, revealing the

conflicting histories and the productive potential of their relation.'²⁶ The
duality of Creole and French ultimately destabilizes the relationship
between the two languages in the text through varied processes, including
the citation of Creole, its partial integration in French and, on occasion,
the active creolization of language.²⁷ These languages interact on a number
of levels, most notably lexical and syntactical, but also through an innovative use of paratextual and typographical features of the novel, to the
extent that *Texaco* points, in this French-language context, towards the
possibility of a multilingual poetics of the novel.

Despite the prominence of the novel, *Texaco*'s illustration of this new
diglossic practice has had few emulators, as if readability by a French
audience has remained a principal criterion for success. In Martinique,
such an approach has continued not in fiction but in the poetry of
Monchoachi (pen name of André Pierre-Louis), an author and translator
who works in French and Creole, but whose writing – in collections such
as *Lémistè* (2012) – turns the page into a linguistic contact zone where the
writer performs what Kavita Ashana Singh has called 'complicated cura-
tions between Creoles and standardized European languages'.²⁸ In a rare
intervention on Monchoachi's poetics, Chamoiseau has commented, 'Le
langage-Monchoachi ne relève plus d'un rapport entre écriture et oralité,
entre langue créole et langue française (petits débats aujourd'hui vains)
mais véritablement d'une vision singulière, incandescente, extrême tout
autant que totale, confrontée à ce que nous sommes individuellement et
collectivement dans les mutation du monde et du vivant.'²⁹ /
'Monchoachi-language no longer relates to a relationship between writing
and orality, between Creole language and the French language (little
debates that today are largely irrelevant) but truly to a singular vision,
incandescent, as extreme as it is total, confronted with what we are
individually and collectively in the mutations of the world.' He points
here to the need for literary responses to the transformations of the twenty-
first-century world, supplementing thematic concerns with radical linguistic innovation, a tendency largely absent from the translingual, transnational shifts underpinning 'littérature-monde'. This is not to say that such
a quest for alternative poetics reflecting new intralingual and interlingual
configurations is absent. Such potential is visible in the *polar*, for instance,
as well as – as the work of Gemma King on multilingual cinema makes
clear – in film.³⁰ Karim Miské's *Arab Jazz* (2012) is a work of detective
fiction set in a multilingual area to the northeast of Paris, populated by
Hassidic Jews, Muslims 'of all shades' and evangelical Christians from all
around the world.³¹ The novel's originality lies in its observation of the

interactions between these various communities, illustrating the ways in which a transnational environment is inevitably a translingual one.

At the same time, there is evidence of an associated linguistic diversification in the work of French-language publishers: Éditions Zulma has, for instance, in collaboration with the Quebecois publisher Mémoire d'encrier, recently launched a new imprint called Céytu, in which major Francophone postcolonial texts (by authors such as Mariama Bâ, Aimé Césaire and Jean-Marie Le Clézio) are to be translated into Wolof. The progressive loosening of the ties of the 'genius of the French language' is also evident in the more experimental work of translingual writers in French, a tendency exemplified by the work of Katalin Molnár, an author of Hungarian origin, who writes in a French that is actively, in the author's terms, 'fôtif' / 'faulty'. In prose texts such as *Quant à je (kantaje)* (1996), Molnar's work harnesses the challenges of learning French, in order to write in a way that disrupts literary and linguistic norms. Literary composition is no longer the reverential restitution of a debt by a grateful author paying homage to the national literature that has graciously granted them access to its ranks. Instead, Molnár eschews the lexical borrowing and occasional idiomatic interference evident in other translingual writers, in order actively to inscribe her exophonic condition into a phonetically transcribed language. The elaboration of such a poetics is inevitably political, reflecting not least the difficulty of immigrants in France to integrate linguistically as well as socially. Translingual production becomes for Molnár a form of self-positioning that is not only interlingual (Molnár's French is, as is the case with a number of exophonic writers, 'déranjé par unn lang apriz avan' / 'disrupted by a language learned previously',[32] but also intralingual. French is no longer stable, homogeneous, singularized and monolingual, but deregulated in a way that echoes both with writers of the early modern period such as Rabelais, but also contemporary Caribbean writers such as Edouard Glissant and Patrick Chamoiseau himself.

Nous sommes plus grands que nous: Rethinking the World in 'World-Literature'

Miské and Molnár are very different types of novelist, deploying fiction in distinctive ways that encompass, respectively, the popular culture of the *polar* and the avant-garde potential of experimental writing. What links their works, however, is a commitment to reflecting on how the contemporary French novel might innovate in its engagement with the rapidly changing circumstances – cultural, linguistic and political – of both twenty-first-century France and the wider world. There is growing evidence that the authors associated with 'littérature-monde' are increasingly engaging in such a reflection. To mark the tenth anniversary of the original manifesto and in the wake of the 2017 French presidential elections, Le Bris drafted a new document, co-signed by fifty-nine other authors, entitled 'Nous sommes plus grands que nous' / 'We are larger than ourselves', opening up 'world-literature' to wider debates in France about writing, migration and democracy. This intervention is linked to a wider reaction among creative writers to the rise of populist extremism and to a sense of growing weariness with Western democratic institutions. At the heart of the document is a reflection on the meaning of being human, with this definition linked to the systematic dehumanization associated with the representation of, and political response to, trans-Mediterranean migration. Unlike the earlier manifestos of 1992 and 2007 discussed above, this text locates literary production overtly in a political context and gestures towards forms of *engagement* associated with French literature of the post-War period. It is less interested in the politics of language as they manifest themselves in a French and Francophone context than in finding a language within literature to talk about the political. The focus is on the correlation between writing (and the freedom of literary expression) and democracy, foregrounding a Glissantian concept of culture based on openness and relation:

> Sans échange, sans ouverture, la culture est une asphyxie lente et inexorable. Nous devons, pour notre survie, ouvrir notre esprit aux autres cultures : loin de nous menacer, elles nous apportent sang neuf et respiration. Il ne suffira plus désormais de voisiner avec les cultures entrantes, nous devons changer en échangeant, devenir autres, éduquer nos enfants dans cette pluralité relationnelle.[33]

> Without exchange, without openness, culture becomes a slow and inexorable asphyxiation. We must, for our survival, open our minds to other cultures: far from threatening us, they bring us new blood and breath. It will no longer be enough to exist alongside incoming cultures, we must change by exchanging, become others, educate our children in this relational plurality.

The engagement implicit in the manifesto is developed further in Patrick Chamoiseau's *Frères migrants* (2017) / *Migrant Brothers* (2018), a text that responds directly to the European crisis of hospitality and political will relating to trans-Mediterranean migration. Structured around a conversation between two people bringing everyday humanitarian assistance to those, in Calais and elsewhere, struggling precariously to survive, Chamoiseau creates parallels between the Mediterranean and the Atlantic, both transformed at certain points in history into *gouffres*, gulfs into which those crossing them disappear. The links between Atlantic slavery and contemporary economic migration are not straightforward, but Chamoiseau's interest is in ethical deficit, in discerning the locations of what he calls 'barbarie nouvelle' / 'neo-barbarism', and in the differential dynamics of mobility afforded to those in the Global North and Global South. *Frères migrants* repeats its author's previous critiques of the globalized economy, and foregrounds the importance of *mondialité* as opposed to *mondialisation*, with the former Glissantian term resonating clearly with the manifesto with which it appeared contemporaneously, especially in terms of its commitment to 'multi-trans-cultural encounters' and privileging of mobility as a mode of cultural dynamism. In the 1990s, *Littérature voyageuse* had posited elite, solipsistic forms of travel associated primarily with a self-policing guild of travel writers in France. *Littérature-monde* opened up these emphases to a wide range of non-metropolitan voices, but still retained a Francophone monolingualism that limited any possible openness to the multilingual worldliness of the twenty-first century. The more recent interventions, however, moving beyond the original emphases of French-language debates on world literature, stress an interconnectedness and even an interdependence that reflect urgent transnational, postnational concerns. Chamoiseau concludes his own manifesto, his 'déclaration des poètes' / 'poets' declaration', with a critique of differential regimes of mobility, an indictment of the dehumanization inherent in the increased securitization of frontiers, a call for radical hospitality and a reimagination of the nation-state: 'Les poètes déclarent que toute Nation est Nation-Relation, souveraine mais solidaire, offerte au soin de tous et responsable de tous sur le tapis de ses frontières.'[34] / 'The poets declare that every Nation is a Nation-Relation, sovereign but in solidarity, offering care to all and responsible for all on the carpet of its borders.'

Underpinning these recent developments is a wider corpus of prose writings, semi-fictional and semi-documentary, that focuses on spaces around the Mediterranean. These texts, recounting stories of contemporary migration, blur the lines between novel and travelogue to questions regarding the 'travel-liar', apparent since the emergence of travel writing in a recognizably modern form. The hopes, fears and often disastrous endings of clandestine itineraries undertaken by sub-Saharan African migrants are fictionalized by the Senegalese novelist Abasse Ndione in *Mbëkë mi* (2008), a text whose subtitle – 'à l'assaut des vagues de l'Atlantique' /

'out to conquer the Atlantic waves' – underlines the precarious nature of the journeys they undertake.[35] Ndione's work opens with a brief, neutral account in his preface of an inaugural journey, from Senegal to the Canary Islands, of fifteen Senegalese fisherman 'en pirogue' / 'in a canoe'. Their arrival in Tenerife and transfer to Madrid are reported to their parents, who thought them lost at sea. Their achievement is then transformed into the myth that *Mbëkë mi* explores: 'La voie de l'extraordinaire immigration de milliers de jeunes Africains fuyant leur pays en temps de paix, à la recherche d'un avenir meilleur en Europe, était ainsi ouverte ...'[36] / 'The route of the extraordinary immigration of thousands of young African men, fleeing their country in peacetime and seeking a better future in Europe, had been opened ...'

Ndione's narrative has been supplemented, over the past decade, by a number of other accounts that recount attempted journeys from the Global South to Europe. Central to the reception of these have been questions of authorship. Some, such as Mahmoud Traoré's *'Dem ak xabaar', partir et raconter* (2012), have been co-written.[37] The journey recounted in this text lasts three years, and follows an itinerary using multiple modes of transport across Mali, Burkina Faso and Niger, up through Libya and across the Maghreb, finally gaining access to Spain via the Moroccan enclave of Ceuta. Given co-author Bruno Le Dantec's paratextual additions and his overall (re)writing of Traoré's account, the authenticity of the text has been called into question, but the strategy of ghost-writing migrant journeys is not uncommon, as Olivier Favier's *Chroniques d'exil et d'hospitalité* (2016), a collection of narratives recounted orally and then retold, makes clear. At the same time, the rise of the graphic novel in France has provided another forum in which authors increasingly present these narratives of migration. The *bande dessinée* artist Jean-Philippe Stassen produced, for instance, *I Comb Jesus et autres reportages africains* (2015), a series of reportage-cum-travelogues in the format of the *carnet de voyages* that recount the transcontinental and intercontinental itineraries of sub-Saharan African migrants. Jérôme Rullier's graphic novel *L'Étrange* (2016), a follow-up to his earlier album *Les Mohamed* (2011), portrays human migrants as animals in an exploration of a hostile environment of prejudice, exclusion and exploitation. Striking in the work is the use of an invented language, markedly different in terms even of the written characters it uses, that further estranges the eponymous figure – the 'strange one' – seeking integration into the work's Francophone environment. Such works seek to re-humanize narratives from which personal dimensions are often evacuated in political and journalistic discourse.

Shifts evident among authors associated with the *littérature-monde* movement are increasingly apparent. The 2018 Prix Littérature-monde was awarded to the Senegalese author Mohamed Mbougar Sarr for his *Silence du chœur*, a long novel about a group of migrants in a small Sicilian town seeking regularization of their status. The focus is on the relationship between the new arrivals and the local population, with Sarr exploring the tensions between those hostile to the new arrivals and those seeking to support their integration, and also focusing on the individual narratives and itineraries of his characters. Although the task of elaborating and extending a genealogy of such texts – illustrating a very different form of *littérature-monde en français* from that originally imagined in the 2007 manifesto – is an urgent one, it is equally important to explore the ways in which such a tradition continues to co-exist with, interrogate and ultimately challenge many assumptions about language, culture and nation that persist in French metropolitan literature. For too long, non-metropolitan figures have been denied voice, agency and mobility in this tradition, and the emergence of these new works illustrates the clear creative repercussions of interventions such as 'Nous sommes plus grands que nous'. Moving beyond the ultimately limited and limiting concept of *littérature-monde*, they illustrate new forms of writing, of and in the world, but also suggest the emergence of innovative forms of creativity and political engagement with which studies of any world-literature – whether worlded or worldly – must urgently engage.

CHAPTER 5

The Franco-American Novel

Russell Williams

France has a long, complicated and often fraught relationship with the United States, a relationship that is arguably more difficult than the one it sustains with its nearer English-speaking neighbour. This, of course, stretches back particularly to the dialogues instigated during the two countries' founding revolutions and through two world wars. The complexity of this relationship is exemplified by the awkwardness of the relationship between their current presidents. Deep tensions were acutely evident at the first meeting between Donald Trump and Emmanuel Macron in front of the world's press in 2017, crystallized in the symbolic handshake they were expected to share. President Trump, as was his habit in the opening months of his presidency, appeared to try to outmuscle his younger counterpart in a display of swaggering machismo and political dominance. President Macron, however, was not to be intimidated and, likewise, tried to strong-arm the American premier in an uncomfortably physical display of French exceptionalism. The pair were left temporarily joined in a state of anxious tension, neither wishing to be seen to be the first to drop hands and concede to the other.

The persistent, underlying tension of the Franco-American relationship has also contaminated contemporary literary production in France, which similarly has an anxious link to that produced in the United States. Much contemporary writing in French ostensibly embraces the United States. Bestsellers by the likes of Marc Levy, Guillaume Musso and (the Swiss) Joël Dicker frequently speak to a mainstream cultural fascination with American characters and settings, usually New York, the most Parisian of American cities. The appeal of the United States to the contemporary literary imagination is also illustrated by the 2017 launch by high-profile literary journalist François Busnel of *America*, a quarterly 'Mook', an ugly anglicized portmanteau of 'magazine' and 'book', dedicated to celebrating American writing in French translation. However, the attitude is not only one of happy acceptance. Jean Rolin's *Le Ravissement de Britney Spears*

(2011), for example, initially appears to be a celebration of the spectacle of American celebrity, but soon amounts to a bemused exploration of the absurdity of it all, as its increasingly cynical narrator strolls the Los Angeles streets. This chapter strives to demonstrate how contemporary French writing serves as a site for an ambiguous – but perhaps above all creatively stimulating – combination of embrace, anxiety and critique of the United States. The contemporary French novel acts in this way by exploiting and interrogating notions of America and Americanness, bringing them into dialogue with tropes about France and Frenchness. This takes place through a sometimes unsteady, sometimes playful embrace of American forms, or at least forms perceived as American: genre fiction, cinema, rock music and television series. What follows maps moments in the extensive corpus of French fiction that responds to and, perhaps in some small way, identifies sites of resistance to American cultural dominance. As examples, it considers in particular work by Jean-Patrick Manchette, Tanguy Viel, Michel Houellebecq, Virginie Despentes and Leïla Slimani.

In articulating a relationship with the United States in this way, French literature is also, of course, situating itself in relation to corporate-led globalization. Fredric Jameson argues that 'this whole global, yet American, postmodern culture is the internal and superstructural expression of a whole new wave of military and economic domination throughout the world: in this sense, as throughout class history, the underside of culture is blood, torture, death and terror'.[1] In interrogating such domination by literary means, the French novel speaks to the power of capital and concurrently reveals insecurities, perhaps in a similar way to Macron's handshake, about its own waning influence on the global stage. The arrival, to a fanfare amid a storm of criticism, of Disneyland Paris in 1992, just outside the French capital, is also a crucial symbol for the uneasy cohabitation between French and global American cultures, a significant marker within a contemporary France that consistently adopts, adapts and interrogates dominant Anglo-Saxon forms, as tired and often precariously employed French workers strive to embody American cultural myths for overseas tourists.

One route to exploring Franco-American tension from the Liberation to the present day is through genre fiction, with Gallimard's Série Noire imprint existing as a principal conduit for the American crime novel form, its language shaped by the stylish swagger of American street slang, frequently approximated in a new French vernacular. The Série Noire was established in September 1945 by its first director, Marcel Duhamel, a figure close to the Surrealists, and a translator of Steinbeck and

Hemingway into French. The imprint's initial focus was British and American crime fiction in translation, capitalizing on a post–World War II French fashion for the English-speaking world. Early published writers include Peter Cheyney, James Hadley Chase and, most notably, Raymond Chandler. These early translations, however, were far from straightforward. They were, rather, frequently acts of creative reinterpretation for the French market; notably, Boris Vian's 1948 translation of *The Big Sleep* famously involved considerable cuts to the original text.[2] Home-grown French writers slowly made their way into the collection, but crime writing was so entrenched as an American genre that writers such as Serge Arcouët and Jean Meckert were encouraged to adopt pseudonyms – Terry Stewart and John Amila, respectively – in order to be taken seriously by readers of the collection.

The French reinvention of crime fiction gathered pace after 1968, as a generation of writers had their political consciousnesses awakened, with a radical critique of the growing cultural and political hegemony of the United States being one of the ambient preoccupations of the period. Writers who had been raised on a cultural diet of movies, pulp fiction and rock music, all of which were shaped to a large extent by implicit and explicit American dominance, chief among them Jean-Patrick Manchette, began to question the literary and political implications of Frenchifying American forms against the background of the Vietnam War (and with France's own colonial war with Algeria a recent memory). What did it mean when the crusading detectives prowled the cafés and villages of *la France profonde* rather than the dive bars of Los Angeles' mean streets, speaking French yet brandishing a quintessentially American .45 Smith & Wesson? Manchette's *Le petit bleu de la côte Ouest* (1976) / *Three to Kill* (2007), for example, sees Georges Gerfaut, an average *cadre* / 'executive' with a penchant for American jazz unwittingly caught up in a murder case and pursued across France by mysterious hitmen. Manchette saw his novels as spaces to assert writing as political commitment, famously describing the crime novel form as a 'roman d'intervention sociale très violent'[3] / 'novel of very violent social intervention'. Manchette's protagonists find themselves at odds with a society saturated with the trappings and mentalities of an American-led globalized world. Aimée, the heroine of *Fatale* (1977), for example, arrives in the financially corrupt Bléville as a moral force, righting wrongs throughout the town. A dramatic highlight of *Ô dingos, ô châteaux !* (1972) / *The Mad and the Bad* (2014) sees a bloody shoot-out at a provincial French supermarket; as the protagonists dodge bullets, the consumer products detonate in a radical deconstruction of the shopping experience in a scene that also gives a nod to the explosive end of Michelangelo Antonioni's *Zabriskie Point* (1970), as Manchette, a passionate movie-goer, gestures to his twin Hollywood and anti-capitalist influences.

Manchette was not alone in asserting the critical possibilities of genre fiction, becoming the reluctant figurehead of a literary moment of polit-ically committed crime writers, loosely grouped under the *néo-polar* / 'new crime novel' epithet. These are writers who sought to use the form of the crime novel to interrogate French cultural history as well as social and cultural questions, and whose legacy continues to the present day. Most notably, these include Thierry Jonquet and Didier Daeninckx, and novels such as *Les Orpailleurs* (1993) and *Le der des ders* (1984) / *A Very Profitable War* (2012). Jean-Bernard Pouy, billed *papy polar* / 'grandpa crime' by *Libération* in 2018, continues to use his novels, anthologized by the Série Noire in *Tout Doit Disparaître* (2015), to subvert formal stereotypes and explore what Christophe Guilluy has termed, 'la France périphérique'[4] / 'peripheral France', outside the Parisian metropolis, embodying his asser-tion that 'le succès du polar français est [. . .] dû au fait qu'il n'est pas du tout parisien'[5] / 'the success of the French crime novel can be attributed to the fact that the genre is not at all Parisian'. Pouy's *Ma ZAD* (2018) uses the setting of a regional 'zone à défendre' / 'zone of militant occupation', for example, as a counterpoint to the metropolitan literary circles. Alongside Pouy, the Série Noire, which celebrated its seventieth birthday in 2017, continues to publish politically conscious fiction, including work such as *Pukhtu* (2015–2016), DOA's two-volume novel critiquing the American-led Afghanistan war and its legacies, and *Or Noir* (2015), Dominique Manotti's novelistic exposé of shadowy forces at work in the global oil industry.

As Simon Kemp has argued, the crime genre has stimulated the exper-imental or avant-garde imagination in addition to the more popular mainstream.[6] This has provided impetus throughout the *fin de millénaire* to the purveyors of literary fiction by writers from Alain Robbe-Grillet to Jean Echenoz and Patrick Modiano. Most recently, Bertrand Schefer, whose *Série noire* (2018) is a stylish meta-interrogation of a real-life kidnapping itself inspired by a novel from the Gallimard imprint, and Julia Deck's *Sigma* (2017), which brushes up against the spy fiction subgenre to provide a biting satire of the world of contemporary visual art, continue in this vein. Contemporary writing in French and – as Kemp demonstrates – the Minuit publishing house (home to Echenoz and Deck) have shown an ongoing French avant-garde preoccupation with work that adopts and interrogates the forms of the *roman policier* / 'crime novel' over which the American shadow still looms large.

The work of Brittany-born Tanguy Viel, another writer to have found a home at Minuit, firmly situates itself within this current. Since his debut, *Le Black Note* (1998), Viel has become one of the most consistent explorers of the implicit cultural politics of the *polar* / 'crime form', his novels being the most pre-eminent literary avant-garde continuation of the preoccupations of the Série Noire. As Ari J. Blatt argues, his stories are 'indebted in various ways to the classic thriller genre'.[7] Viel uses these American forms in a similar way to Pouy, demonstrating a fidelity to the French regions, particularly his Breton heritage, in taut, suspenseful yet stylish novels such as *Paris-Brest* (2009), which evoke the light, misty mornings and unique personality of the Finistère coast. Viel diverges from this project to fascinating effect in *La Disparition de Jim Sullivan* (2013) / *The Disappearance of Jim Sullivan* (2020). *La Disparition* can be read in terms of how it engages the tropes of *noir*; there is a murder, a shady underground crime, a whisky-soaked central protagonist, a *femme fatale*. More precisely, the novel recounts its narrator's writing of 'un roman américain' / 'an American novel'. This novel, the reader learns, has been written; the novel the reader has in his hands is a compelling metafictional consideration of that text and the textual strategies the narrator engaged while writing it. Since he opted to write an American novel, there are certain conventions the writer felt he needed to adopt to recreate a transatlantic literary experience. In terms of setting, it should take place 'dans une cabane au bord d'un grand lac ou bien dans un motel sur l'autoroute 75'[8] / 'in a cabin on the shore of a lake or even in a motel on highway 75'. He opts for blue-collar Detroit to situate his characters, drawn from generic character types:

> Mes personnages habitent une grande ville complexe et internationale, une ville pleine de promesses et de surfaces vitrées. C'est même à ce genre de détails, me suis-je encore dit, qu'on pourra apprendre à connaître Dwayne Koster, qui est le nom de mon personnage principal, de même qu'on pourrait apprendre à connaître Susan Fraser, l'ex-femme de Dwayne Koster, puisque j'ai remarqué cela dans les romans américains, que le personnage principal, en général, est divorcé. Du moins, c'est souvent à ce moment-là qu'on le découvre, en général autour des cinquante ans, après que sa vie sentimentale s'est un peu compliquée.[9]

> My characters live in a big, complicated international town, a town filled with promises and shiny surfaces. It's through this type of detail, I told myself, that we can get to know Dwayne Koster, which is the name of my

main character, the same way we can get to know Susan Fraser, Dwayne
Koster's ex-wife, since, as I've noticed in American novels, the main
character is generally divorced. At least we meet them, generally, when they
are fiftyish, when their emotional life tends to be a bit complicated.

The reason for the divorce is Milly, a waitress and another stock character
type, 'j'ai toujours pensé que toutes les serveuses d'Amérique s'appelaient
Milly, qu'elles portaient une jupe noire et un chemisier blanc, qu'elles
avaient forcément une vie sentimentale un peu houleuse avec le type
désœuvré qu'on pouvait voir à l'autre bout du comptoir'[10] / 'I always
thought that all the waitresses in America were called Milly, that they all
wore black skirts and white blouses, that they definitely all had stormy
relationships with the lazy bloke you could see at the end of the bar'. Style,
too, is deliberately and self-consciously 'American', not least since swear
words 'sonnent mieux en américain'[11] / 'sound better in American', as he
notes:

> [J]'ai remarqué qu'on n'écrit pas un roman américain sans un sens aiguisé
> du détail, que la saleté de la douche ou le ressort grinçant du matelas ou
> bien la lumière de la lune qui tombait sur le visage inquiet de Dwayne, ce
> devait faire comme des flèches que j'aurais lancées dans le cœur du
> lecteur.[12]

> I noticed that you don't write an American novel without an acute sensi-
> tivity to detail, that the filth of the shower or the squeaky mattress springs
> or even the moonlight falling on Dwayne's troubled face, should act like
> arrows fired into the heart of the reader.

As well as such pathos-evoking details, the American novel's treatment
of historical time is another distinctive characteristic that the narrator seeks
to exploit in his novel. He notes that American fiction is inseparable from
the major cultural events that take place around it. The novel references
memorable moments in US history: the assassination of JFK, 9/11 and the
first Gulf War – all American events, yet with a collective impact on the
global cultural imagination. He notes, 'Ce sont des choses qui doivent faire
comme une onde de choc sur les personnages, de sorte que même un
Américain comme Dwayne Koster, à un moment ou à un autre, devait être
concerné par la guerre en Irak, pas directement, bien sûr, mais disons,
indirectement.'[13] / 'These are things that should act like a shockwave on
the characters, so that even an American like Dwayne Koster, from one
moment to another, should be concerned by the Iraq war, not directly, of
course, but, let's say, indirectly.' All of these events, however, are experienced vicariously, at a distance through television, experienced as memory,
then refracted through the American novel.

We learn, though, that the narrator, in writing his novel, did not completely adhere to the codes and conventions of the American realist novel. Indeed, *La Disparition*, by using the idea of the American novel as a point of reference, tells us much about what it means to write a contemporary French novel. In an essay, 'Quelques remarques sur la littérature américaine' (2013) / 'Notes on American literature', Viel notes a self-referentiality in French, writing, 'l'horizon d'un roman français [...] c'est la littérature'[14] / 'the horizon of a French novel [...] is literature itself'. This contrasts with a broader preoccupation with historical referentiality in American fiction: 'il est impossible de lire un roman américain sans être sensiblement orienté vers une lecture référentielle'[15] / 'it is impossible to read an American novel without being gently guided towards a referential reading'. As Sylvie Cadinot-Romerio notes of Viel's text, 'l'auteur fictif ne réfute pas la pertinence du modèle romanesque américain, ni sa fonction de déclencheur d'écriture ; mais il lui faut en reconnaître le faible poids par rapport à son identité littéraire française'[16] / 'the fictional author doesn't refute the pertinence of the American novelistic model, nor its function as a trigger for writing; but he needs to recognize the weakness of his identification with it compared to French literature'. This introduces a significant tension between the Frenchness and Americanness in Viel's work; as much as he seeks to embrace the American novel, his writing continues to resist it. He is 'pas trop pour décrire physiquement les personnages'[17] / 'not much of a fan of physically describing his characters', and he expresses his dislike of flashbacks, both hallmarks of the American novel. The narrator remains, however, committed to his Frenchness: 'après tout, même si j'ai regardé vers l'Amérique tout le temps de mon travail, je suis quand même resté un écrivain français'[18] / 'after everything, even if I've looked towards America throughout my work, I've stayed, all the same, a French writer'.

There are, too, larger implications for the narrator's aesthetic choices. Although he pledges allegiance to his homeland, he can't escape American influence. As Alice Richir argues, 'Viel insiste régulièrement sur la manière dont le modèle du « roman américain » dicte au narrateur ses choix formels, ce qui a pour effet de remettre en question la toute-puissance de son autorité.'[19] / 'Viel regularly insists on how the model of the "American novel" dictates formal choices to the narrator, which effectively calls into question the all-powerful nature of his authority.' It is significant that our narrator is a university professor specializing in Herman Melville – at least at the start of the novel. The nods towards *Moby Dick* (1851) that pepper the text are more, however, than just signs of the French novel's literary self-reflexivity. If, as Viel argues, 'l'Amérique ressemble un peu à une baleine'[20] / 'America looks a bit like a whale', then it seems that one of his narrator's objectives, in writing his novel, is to resist being swallowed up by it. Metaphorically, then, the embrace and rejection of the formal and stylistic characteristics he considers are attempts to assert – again like Macron's handshake – French identity in the face of ravenous capitalist forces.

An interesting precedent to this approach is Viel's more explicitly experimental *Cinéma* (1999), another metafictional narrative, where the narrator recounts his repeated viewings of Joseph L. Mankiewicz's film *Sleuth* (1972). Mankiewicz's film is a British production, although the director himself is American, but the movie spectacle is frequently synonymous with overwhelming American cultural dominance. Here, as in *La Disparition*, Viel's narrator is attempting to articulate his own distinctive French voice concurrently with, yet also against, a dominant cultural form. In the same way as Viel's work displays an acute sensitivity to cinematic forms, character types, settings and tropes, a generation of contemporary French writers have been directly – and knowingly – inspired by cinema. In particular, the work of writers such as Frédéric Beigbeder, Michel Houellebecq and Marie Darrieussecq have at least to some extent been inspired by – and in turn inspired – a form of French film-making contemporaneous with their literary debuts in the 1990s that knowingly acts as a point of creative resistance to dominant American culture by means of a violently transgressive aesthetic. Indeed, the film and literature output of the directors and writers concerned can be read as an explicit attempt, by means of adopting and working through American forms, to articulate the 'underside' of postmodern culture, which is, according to Jameson as noted above, 'blood, torture, death and terror'.

The 1990s saw the emergence of the 'New French Extremity' style in cinema, a term used to describe the work of directors that included, among others, Gaspar Noé, Claire Denis and Bruno Dumont. The term was coined by film writer James Quandt, who noted the 'recent tendency to the willfully transgressive' in film-makers such as the above, which amounts to a commitment to 'break every taboo, to wade in rivers of viscera and spumes of sperm, to fill each frame with flesh, nubile or gnarled, and subject it to all manner of penetration, mutilation, and defilement'.[21] This embracing of the transgressive in film has its corollary in contemporary French fiction of the same period; the direct expression of violent acts has been highlighted as a key stylistic trope of what Alain-Philippe Durand and Naomi Mandel have described as novels of the 'contemporary extreme', which 'do not merely reflect on violence, they seek it out, engage it and, in a variety of imaginative ways, perform it'.[22] Quandt also speculates that the New French Extremity in film can be associated with 'a short-lived resurgence of the violational tradition of French culture [. . .] reflected in contemporaneous literature (e.g. Michel Houellebecq, Catherine Millet, Marie Darrieussecq, Jonathan Littell)'.[23] In addition to the French transgressive tradition,[24] another key point of reference for both the writing of the 'contemporary extreme' and the New French Extremity film-makers is the work of American novelist Bret Easton Ellis, particularly his notorious *American Psycho* (1991), which, as Viel has argued, is a novel 'qui parle de l'Amérique'[25] / 'that speaks of America', and which has set a precedent for the broader sphere of contemporary writing in terms of its visceral qualities and what Mandel has described as its 'notorious' and 'extensive descriptions of racism, sexism, rape, torture, murder, mutilation and cannibalism'.[26] Ellis's novel is indeed a significantly influential text with regard to contemporary French writing, and Martin Crowley and Victoria Best argue that *American Psycho* has had a 'considerable' impact on 'the generation of French writers publishing from the mid-1990s' in terms of its graphic representations of sex and violence.[27]

The anxious influence of Ellis's novel and, closer to home, the films of the New French Extremity can be observed throughout the novels of the contemporary extreme, as Durand and Mandel's description suggests, bringing the reader into confrontation with some deeply unsettling material. Nicolas Jones-Gorlin's notorious *Rose bonbon* (2002), for example, narrated from the first-person perspective of an unrepentant paedophile, is symptomatic of the contemporary cultural impulse to unsettle and, accordingly, provoked a modest literary scandal in the Left Bank publishing world on its publication. Other notorious novels of the period include Christine Angot's autofictional *L'Inceste* (1999) / *Incest* (2017) and Beigbeder's *99F* (2000) / *13.99 Euros* (2001), itself a Debord-lite satire of the Parisian advertising industry. The novel, which led to Beigbeder's resignation from the same advertising agency he was apparently attacking in the novel, is peppered with scenes of cinematic sex and spectacular violence. The same novel also resonates with Ellis, since a subplot of the novel can be read as a miniature *relooking* of his follow-up to *American Psycho*, *Glamorama* (1998). Michel Houellebecq, too, formerly a student of film and also a keen admirer of Bret Easton Ellis, similarly makes use of profoundly unsettling and frequently visceral images throughout his work, but notably in his early poetry and his debut novel *Extension du domaine de la lutte* (1994) / *Whatever* (1998) as a way of giving voice to acute, apparently authorial, depression. Another contemporaneous debut, Darrieussecq's *Truismes* (1996) / *Pig Tales* (1998) similarly uses viscerally alarming body transformations to describe and explore contemporary urban female identities. Other writers of the same generation have a less problematic relationship with America and its cinematic culture, which they embrace more enthusiastically, if more darkly. Of particular interest, for example, is Simon Liberati, whose novels are in thrall to the murky Kenneth Anger-inspired myths of the golden age of Hollywood.[28] *Jayne Mansfield, 1967* (2011), for example, is a stylish interrogation of the actress's infamous car crash, exploring her much rumoured dalliances with Anton LaVey's Church of Satan, while *California Girls* (2016) is a similar revisiting of the late 1960s Manson murders.

In addition to cinema, music – in particular loud, noisy, electric guitar-based rock – has been a consistent aesthetic inspiration for the contemporary novel. Viel's debut, *Le Black Note*, has its roots in a story about a wannabe rock band, while the protagonists of *La Disparition* met at an early Iggy Pop gig; Dwayne drives around with one of the singer's albums in his car boot. There is, in the novels of the 'contemporary extreme', a preoccupation with music and musicians. Such a state of affairs was noted in 2011 by bestselling novelist Amélie Nothomb, who claimed that the 'roman rock' / 'rock novel' was a burgeoning subgenre, fostered by reviews in the influential cultural weekly *Les Inrockuptibles*, her observation perhaps tinged by a recognition that her own novels weren't 'cool' enough to be included. This prompted the magazine's literary editor, Nelly Kaprièlian, to respond via an acerbic column, claiming that the 'roman rock' indeed existed, but that it was based on a different definition, 'toute la littérature transgressive, révoltée, en opposition avec l'ordre et la convention ou les consensus, est « rock » et nous intéresse, parce qu'il ne peut s'agir, par essence, que de vraie littérature'[29] / 'all transgressive literature, writing as revolt, writing in opposition to order, convention and consensus is "rock" and interests us, because it is what real literature is all about'. As examples, Kaprièlian cites work by Ellis, Angot, Bataille and Pierre Guyotat, all of them provocative, none of them obviously 'rock', in musical terms at least. That said, there is perhaps a grain of truth in Nothomb's statement, since *Les Inrockuptibles*, its name a nod both to musical forms and an appreciation for 'true' cultural forms, has indeed consistently championed novels that appear to align with its Anglo-Saxon rock-inspired sensibility.

Les Inrocks was also an early supporter of Michel Houellebecq, positively reviewing all of his novels from his debut, *Extension du domaine de la lutte*

(1994), regularly including him as cover star and even giving him a column, 'Temps morts', for a period in 1997. As contemporary French fiction's bestselling, highest profile and most notorious export, a veritable industry of criticism has blossomed around both the man and his work. Many critics have more or less successfully situated Houellebecq within the context of French literary tradition. For some he is a contemporary naturalist, renewing Zola's work for the twenty-first century. For others, he is reconnecting with the provocative work of Céline, and even – perhaps less convincingly – Proust. Critics of the enfant terrible of contemporary French writing agree on the idea that seems to underpin all of Houellebecq's work: a critique of the way in which market-based liberalism, encouraged rather than rejected by the post-68 generation, has extended its reach over its human subjects, infiltrating and undermining the traditional Western bastions of unity, most notably the family. In contrast to the rather soft-focus nostalgia Houellebecq retains for the mythical solidarity of the *trentes glorieuses*, contemporary market society leaves the majority of its members lonely, alienated and resentful. Often overlooked by critical readings of Houellebecq, a former film student at the renowned Luis Lumière film school, is the fact that his work sustains a dialogue with artifacts from contemporary popular culture, with music existing as a particularly frequent point of reference. Houellebecq's œuvre would certainly qualify as a 'roman rock' according to both Nothomb's and Kaprièlian's definitions.[30] A chapter in his debut novel opens with a quote from the grizzled Canadian rocker Neil Young, while his most recent novel, *Sérotonine* (2019) / *Serotonin* (2019), sees the narrator eulogize about late-1960s, early-1970s rock. At one point, the narrator spends 'esthétiquement [. . .] peut-être le plus beau moment de ma vie' / 'perhaps the most aesthetically beautiful moment of my life' drunkenly listening to an obscure Deep Purple track on repeat.[31]

What is perhaps most interesting about Houellebecq's engagement with popular culture is how it can be seen to further his critique on the incessant march of market liberalism. In particular, Houellebecq's work is particularly suspicious of the pernicious American influence on contemporary experience. Seth Armus has described the 'American menace' in Houellebecq's work, arguing that 'anti-Americanism provides the glue that gives his [anti-liberal] thesis cohesion'.[32] While critics regularly, and rightly, highlight that Houellebecq is a vicious critic of contemporary France, his writing is also a site of resistance to American cultural hegemony. As Armus underlines, 'he hates France primarily for having become Americanized'.[33] This line of critique, implicit throughout Houellebecq's œuvre, is closest to the surface in *Les Particules élémentaires* (1998) / *Atomised* (2001). Here, the two main protagonists, brothers Bruno and Michel, have both seen their adulthood damaged by the parental neglect they suffered as children. Michel was damaged because his mother placed him in the care of his grandparents when she followed the 1960s hippy (read 'American') dream of loud rock and free love. Bruno grew up hating his father, a plastic surgeon responsible for importing the latest techniques (including penis enlargement). The novel's most explicit anti-American thesis, however, is articulated by Bruno, who lengthily recounts the fictional story of David Di Meola, a product of the idealistic 1960s, whose enthusiastic embrace of the logic of liberalism sees him slide from promising rock musician to snuff movie star and serial killer. The narrator notes:

> [L]a destruction progressive des valeurs morales au cours des années soixante, soixante-dix, quatre-vingt puis quatre-vingt-dix était un processus logique et inéluctable. Après avoir épuisé les jouissances sexuelles, il était normal que les individus libérés des contraintes morales ordinaires se tournent vers les jouissances plus larges de la cruauté ; deux siècles auparavant, Sade avait suivi un parcours analogue. En ce sens, les serial killers des années quatre-vingt-dix étaient les enfants naturels des hippies des années soixante.[34]

> The destruction of moral values in the sixties, seventies, eighties and nineties was a logical, almost inevitable process. Having exhausted the possibilities of sexual pleasure, it was reasonable that individuals, liberated from the constraints of ordinary morality, should turn their attentions to the wider pleasures of cruelty. Two hundred years earlier, de Sade had done precisely the same thing. In a sense, the serial killers of the 1990s were the spiritual children of the hippies of the sixties.[35]

Revealing the damaging dark side of personal freedom, the philosophy of individualism and the global reach of the American dream in this way is a current that runs deep throughout Houellebecq's work.

As well as this current of anti-Americanism, there is also a more implicit, and perhaps less intolerant, dialogue with the United States which occurs throughout Houellebecq's work and positions him more line with Viel and Manchette. His prix Goncourt-winning *La Carte et le territoire* (2010) / *The Map and the Territory* (2011), ostensibly a novel that bemoans the touristification of the French regions, adopts many of the codes and conventions of the *polar* in the final third of the book after the gruesome murder of Michel Houellebecq, here making a postmodern intervention in his own text. In fact, it is possible to argue that in turning his novel into a police procedural, Houellebecq is paying literary homage to the novels of the *néo-polar*, particularly the work of Thierry Jonquet.[36] In adopting the 'American' codes and conventions, as reimagined by the writers of the *néo-polar*, it is possible to read here how Houellebecq is situating himself in their critical tradition. It is perhaps most notable, however, that the most dependable trope of crime fiction, the dramatic reveal of the criminal (a trope sustained in the *néo-polar*'s reinvigoration of the genre), is disappointingly absent from the novel, resulting in a dissatisfying narrative closure. In withholding closure, Houellebecq is denying the reader satisfaction and frustrating the reading experience – a critical protest against literature as a satisfying or marketable consumer product. Any gesture of this sort is drenched in irony, however, since the unavoidable marketing of Houellebecq's work has led to him being derided in French literary circles as an Anglo-Saxon 'rock star'.

Another significant contemporary voice whose work navigates the tensions of the Franco-American relationship in ways that reflect, yet significantly deviate from, the authors considered so far in this chapter is Virginie Despentes. Despentes is a fascinating example because, since her relative acceptance by the hierarchical Left Bank literary establishment (above all, since her Prix Goncourt shortlisting for *Apocalypse Bébé* in 2010, and her membership of the judging committee since 2016), her work sustains a consistent dialogue with the globalized, Anglo-Saxon-led cultural mainstream. Even though the work has tended, in the years subsequent to her notoriously violent debut *Baise-Moi* (1993) / *Baise-Moi* (2003), away from the shock, 'trash' impact of her early work, her most recent work, the *Vernon Subutex* trilogy (2015–2017) continues to consistently interrogate both cultural forms and the politics of American-led cultural dominance. Indeed, her position of critical opposition is articulated in the polemical *King Kong Théorie* (2006) / *King Kong Theory* (2009): 'J'écris de chez les moches, pour les moches, les vieilles, les camionneuses, les frigides, les mal baisées, les imbaisables, les hystériques, les tarées, toutes les exclues du grand marché à la bonne meuf.' / 'I am writing as an ugly one for the ugly ones: the old hags, the dykes, the frigid, the unfucked, the unfuckables, the neurotics, the psychos, for all those girls that don't get a look-in in the universal market of the consumable chick.'[37]

While it has since been republished in a more mainstream collection, firstly by Grasset, then in the J'ai Lu 'Nouvelle Génération' paperback edition, it is significant that *Baise-Moi* was initially marketed as a *polar*, in the 'Poche Revolver' imprint of Despentes's first publishers, Florent Massot. Indeed, the fast-paced plot, which outlines Nadine and Manu's bloody rape and revenge rampage across France (from Paris to Brittany), described in a sparse, stripped down and glacial prose, recalls the work of Manchette and could conceivably have existed in the contemporary Série Noire. The novel resonates particularly with Manchette's *Fatale* and *Ô dingos, ô châteaux !* which also dramatize feminist protagonists seeking violent vengeance against the structures of patriarchy. Stylistically, Despentes shares Manchette's preference for consumer brand names: the characters down bottles of Four Roses Whiskey and pop Dinintel tablets while Nadine is constantly plugged into her Walkman. In its evocation of two outsider females – one a recent rape victim, the other working as a prostitute – and their systematic revolt against the symbols of sexual and class-based domination (shopkeepers, the bourgeoisie and sleazy, predatory males), the novel can be read as a continuation of Manchette's efforts to use the crime novel as a tool of 'violent social intervention', turning the implicit American machismo of the crime novel against itself in a knowingly empowering, feminist gesture. As with Manchette, the cinematic blockbuster is an important point of reference. Nadine and Manu's feminist reinterpretation of the clichéd Hollywood male road trip also explicitly and specifically recalls, as Jacinthe Dupuis has demonstrated, Ridley Scott's 1991 film *Thelma and Louise*.[38] The cinematic is also a key stylistic influence as the protagonists take pleasure in the spectacle of their violence. After an early slaying, Manu notes that, 'c'est moins spectacle qu'au cinéma' / 'it's less spectacular than it is in the movies'.[39] As she becomes more comfortable handling a gun, the more cinematic the slaughter looks: 'D'un point de vie strictement visuel, c'est plus probant que la première fois. Plus de couleurs.' / 'From a strictly visual point of view, this is more convincing than the last time. More colours.'[40] There is also a stereotypically comic book element to the violence here: 'Cette formidable détonation, la ligne du menton est partie en bouillie. La femme entière est partie en purée.' / 'That amazing explosion, the jawline turning into gruel. The whole woman becoming puree.'[41]

Despentes's text can also be situated in what Crowley and Best suggest is the slipstream of Bret Easton Ellis's *American Psycho*. This is not only because the text celebrates visceral violence, but also in terms of a distinct stylistic echo due to the manner in which Despentes uses lyrics drawn from English and American rock music, in order to suggest Nadine's inner life. Ellis's novel famously intersperses details of Patrick Bateman's murders and torture with long considerations of the musical merits of artists including Whitney Houston, Phil Collins and Huey Lewis and the News. In *Baise-Moi*, Nadine is constantly connected to her Walkman, the narrative presenting lyrics in their untranslated (sometimes misheard)

English form from the likes of contemporary 1990s noise rock bands such as Suicidal Tendencies, Mudhoney, Sonic Youth and L7. There is more at stake than characterization here and the fact that Nadine (and her author) like the music of the American counterculture. In using italicized, untranslated quotes ('*It's going down in my dark side. It's an emotional wave*'[42]), which are disappointingly absent from Bruce Benderson's English translation, Despentes's text provides tacit recognition of the inescapable dominance of American culture (and, of course, tacit American-ness of the *polar* form), but also the linguistic markers which motivate Nadine's rebellion. In appropriating loud, American noise rock in the context of her violent revolt, she is self-consciously reimagining her own contemporary version of the myth of the American hero: here, she is female, French, alienated and intensely pissed off. This Franco-American knife edge is also, notably, articulated in more traditional literary forms. The second part of the novel features epigraphs from both Charles Baudelaire and crime writer James Ellroy, establishing the extreme limits of the space inhabited by the text, and acknowledging both the French transgressive tradition and the more popular contemporary forms it gestures towards.[43]

Despentes's taste for gory violence may have been tempered over time, but her texts' dialogue with the American world, particularly in terms of how it manifests in pop culture, persists. Her *Vernon Subutex* trilogy, a sprawling panorama of contemporary Parisian life, continues in this manner, particularly in terms of how it interrogates pop and rock music. Despentes described the trilogy as 'un livre qui s'écoute'[44] / 'a book that should be listened to', and its soundtrack spans from Gainsbourg to Die Antwoord. The narrative, among other sprawling plot lines, largely focuses on the eponymous Vernon, a former record store owner whose Revolver records was a centrepiece of the East Parisian alternative music scene in the 1980s and 1990s. The shop was a meeting point for the underground Parisian community, all of them aficionados of English language rock music: Iggy, Leonard Cohen, Nirvana. Vernon is, in many ways, an old school rocker, and as such his fortunes are linked to music's physical format. The growth of downloading and streaming (products, lest we forget, of the rise of technology steered by American tech behemoths) has led to the collapse of his business and the closure of his shop, leading to him drifting from sofa to sofa before finally joining the Parisian homeless community. Despentes continues her exploration of the paradoxical Franco-American condition first sketched in *Baise Moi*. The community of music fans that revolved around Vernon's shop were initially brought together by their love of music but – over time – the increasingly visible capitalist machine behind the music industry has ultimately led to their alienation. In *Vernon Subutex*, Despentes sketches a bleaker contemporary vision than in her earlier work. There is no redemption or release through emancipatory violence; after the virtualization of the music industry, and the incessant march of social media, her protagonists find themselves increasingly atomized (at home, connected). It is only in the final volume of the trilogy that, through Vernon and through music, the alienated protagonists are again able to realize a sense of community.

Indeed, these changing physical forms of the industry of contemporary culture are providing fresh impetus for contemporary French writing. In particular, these include the form – and indeed the tropes – of the contemporary television series. One character in Despentes's novel is defined by box sets in a similar way to how Nadine in *Baise Moi* is inspired by her musical soundtrack: 'Elle regardait la télé sans arrêt, elle se faisait offrir des coffrets de séries et elle s'enfermait dedans. *Ally McBeal, Sex and the City, Buffy* étaient davantage sa réalité que le collège. Une fois assise devant son écran, elle était une mince Américaine élégante.' / 'She spent the whole time watching television, she would get presents of box sets and retreat into another world. *Ally McBeal, Sex and the City, Buffy* were closer to her reality than school. Sitting in front of the TV screen she was a slim, elegant American girl.'[45] As in the English-speaking world, the box set of the TV series, as physical DVD or via streaming services, is more or less replacing the channel for escapist immersive entertainment previously provided by music, big-screen movies and, of course, the classic realist novel. It is significant, and not without irony, that the roots of the logic of the serialization of cultural products can be traced back to the nineteenth-century French *feuilleton* and, of course, to the serialization of such landmark works as Flaubert's *Madame Bovary* (1857). In the domain of world literature, and most notably literature in English (in translation or otherwise), the most significant publishing phenomena of the last decade have been serials – from the trashy pseudo-erotica of E.L. James's *Fifty Shades of Grey* (2011–2012) trilogy to the more interesting sprawling autofiction of the Italian Elena Ferrante and the Norwegian Karl Ove Knausgård. While all have been translated into French, they have not yet attained the same phenomenal status as elsewhere in the world. That's not to say that serialized novels are not read in France (outside of the world of the *bande dessinée*); there is a growing corpus of serialized fiction – in addition to *Vernon Subutex* – that has adopted the tropes of the American TV series. A significant early example of this was Philippe Djian's *Doggy Bag* (2005–2008) series, each volume representing a 'season', mobilizing character types, tropes and settings from the clichéd *Dallas* and *Dynasty* era US soap opera. More recently, the Swiss writers Bruno Pellegrino, Aude Seigne and Daniel Vuataz have collaborated on the *Stand-by* (2018) quartet, an episodic literary series that aims to straddle the techniques of the *feuilleton* as well as 'la nervosité scénaristique'[46] / 'lively screenwriting' of *Les Revenants / The Returned*, *Breaking Bad* and *Black Mirror*. *Vernon Subutex*, too, transposes some of the formal constraints of the US TV series onto the gritty streets of northeastern Paris, with a cast of outsider characters that challenge stereotypes rather than being drawn from the sun-drenched west coast: homeless, transgender people, working-class right-wingers, teenage Muslim misfits. In a similar, and perhaps even more explicit way, Sabri Louatah's quartet, *Les Sauvages* (2012–2014) / *Savages* (2018) is a political thriller spread over four novels, which interrogates the French political landscape in a manner that takes its cue from gritty American TV series, with its most obvious antecedent being HBO's landmark *The Wire* (2002–2008). Louatah's novel, in a similar way to Despentes, juxtaposes US TV form, cliff-hangers, tightly drawn and fast-moving (yet often dubiously credible) plot foregrounded at the expense of characterization with an acutely French setting. Louatah's novel, in a way that pre-empts Houellebecq's notorious *Soumission* (2015) / *Submission* (2015), imagines the coming to power of a moderate Islamic president in France. Unlike in Houellebecq's text, the incoming president is – almost immediately after election – the victim of a debilitating yet unsuccessful assassination attempt. Louatah's text is interesting for the way in which it explores the tensions between secular France and its Muslim communities within the unconventional framework of the TV-inspired novel. *Les Sauvages* also gives voice to a young, disaffected French-Kabyle youth, whose points of cultural reference are more likely to be North American than those of their native France. It is notable, too, that French television has adapted both *Vernon Subutex* and *Les Sauvages* for the small screen.

Another contemporary writer alongside Despentes, who uses what amounts to a Franco-American novel form to interrogate social class, is the Franco-Moroccan writer Leïla Slimani. Slimani's prix Goncourt-winning novel, *Chanson Douce* (2016) / *Lullaby* (2018), in addition to adopting the intrigue and pace of a cinematic thriller, has an American *fait divers* as its starting point, the highly mediatized 2012 murder of two young children by their nanny in New York.[47] Transposing the facts of the case to Paris from Manhattan, Slimani additionally uses the novel to provide an astute critique of white bourgeois Parisian conventions and morality. Like Despentes, Slimani's text seems to strive to articulate a tension between working-class and bourgeois class divisions in contemporary Parisian society, with Louise the nanny, although ostensibly invited into Myriam's home and this social sphere to take care of her two young children, remains effectively excluded from it. At a family party to which she is invited, 'Elle est nerveuse comme une étrangère, une exilée qui ne comprend pas la langue parlée autour d'elle.' / 'She is as nervous as a foreigner, an exile who doesn't understand the language being spoken around her.'[48] Rather than continuing a sustained critique of Louise's alienation, however, the novel ultimately abandons this avenue of exploration, suggesting instead that her horrific crime is the result of a pre-existing medical condition, 'mélancolie délirante' / 'delirious melancholia',[49] rather than any specific class pressures. *Chanson Douce* is ultimately perhaps most interesting in the way it articulates what it highlights as contemporary middle-class hypocrisy. While Myriam and her husband belong to the 'progressive', liberal and professional classes (her a lawyer, him in the music industry), they replicate broader contemporary prejudices, above all when selecting their new nanny:

> Pas de sans-papiers, on est d'accord ? Pour la femme de ménage ou le peintre, ça ne me dérange pas. Il faut bien que ces gens travaillent, mais pour garder les petits, c'est trop dangereux. Je ne veux pas de quelqu'un qui aurait peur d'appeler la police ou d'aller à l'hôpital en cas de problème.

> No illegal immigrants, agreed? For a cleaning lady or a decorator, it doesn't bother me. Those people have to work, after all. But to look after the little ones, it's too dangerous. I don't want someone who'd be afraid to call the police or go to the hospital if there was a problem.[50]

Later in the novel, Louise concludes: 'Elle ne veut pas engager une Maghrébine pour garder les petits. [...] Elle s'est toujours méfiée de ce qu'elle appelle la solidarité d'immigrés.' / 'She does not want to hire a North African to look after the children. [...] She has always been wary of what she calls immigrant solidarity.'[51]

For all its perhaps ultimately stuttering attempts to explore contemporary class and middle-class morality, the novel serves up its narrative in a distinctly Franco-American form, one that despite its publication in the prestigious Gallimard blanche imprint shares, in fact, many characteristics with the Série Noire. It is, of course, centred around a crime and even has a walk-on part from Nina Dorval, an investigating detective, an emblematic figure – of course – of a crime novel. Perhaps more precisely, *Chanson Douce*'s closest literary peers come from within the emerging Anglo-Saxon subgenre of the so-called domestic thriller. These are texts, which, in addition to their domestic setting, create a suspenseful criminal narrative around the testimony of the 'flawed, scorned, disbelieved, misjudged, and underestimated female witness'.[52] Gillian Flynn's novel *Gone Girl* (2012) / *Les Apparances* (2013) is emerging as the archetype of this subgenre, which is increasingly taking its place as a model within contemporary mainstream French writing. In addition to English language bestsellers such as *The Woman in the Window* (2018) by Daniel Mallory and Paula Hawkins's *The Girl on the Train* (2015) in French translation, this subgenre increasingly includes home-grown texts such as the novels of Delphine de Vigan, including *D'après une histoire vraie* (2015). While Slimani's novel proffers a degree of social insight, it is the bestseller logic, the grisly yet taut and ultimately satisfyingly *lisible* / *readerly* reading experience that wins out.

Outside of the domain of fiction, Slimani serves as a resonant example of French cultural exceptionalism, or indeed what remains of it in the face of continued American cultural dominance. She is an example of a figure – increasingly rare in France, exceedingly so in the English-speaking world – of the novelist as public intellectual, whose writing and influence spills over from the field of literature, as she writes, comments and indeed is asked for comment on a variety of real-life political issues. Her *Sexe et mensonges* (2017) / *Sex and Lies* (2020), for example, is an essay-length consideration of sexual mores in contemporary Morocco. Notably, Slimani's influence has moved towards the more directly political, having been selected by President Macron as a spokesperson to represent his office in discussions of subjects relating to Francophonie.[53] If Slimani's novels are motivated by the implicitly American logic of the bestseller, what does this mean for the way in which the diversity of Francophonie is set to be represented at the highest level of government? Will it nudge towards the conservative mainstream rather than the periphery? Macron's government has been criticized for its insistence on a neoliberal and hence implicitly Americanized agenda, mirroring the movement of the Trump handshake or weakening in response to its force rather than resisting it. Slimani, too, has been criticized for her complicity with power by taking up the role, which perhaps suggests that the Franco-American relationship as expressed through literature, like its political counterpart, is less one of contestation than one of quieter resignation. It would be harder, even slightly absurd, to imagine a Tanguy Viel – or a Virginie Despentes – advising the French president on global diplomacy, but their writing shows a deep strand of informed resistance that could yet, perhaps, provide an inspiration.

CHAPTER 6

Graphic Novel Revolution(s)

Laurence Grove

In the early pages of Michel Houellebecq's *Les Particules élémentaires* (1998) / *Atomised* (2001), the theme of the novel's denouement – the artificial propagation of life – is presented to the reader, albeit unknowingly, through the leading character's love for comics; Michel is fascinated by the free gift that comes with *Pif* magazine, a *poudre de vie*, whereby the powder in question can be mixed with water so as eventually to create living crustaceans. Michel, ironically, finds them so disgusting that he throws them into the river, but the same issue of *Pif* provides him with the backstory to a key character, Rahan, the prehistoric warrior. Rahan is given a necklace decorated with three claws, each representing an attribute. It is by these attributes – *loyauté, courage* and *bonté* / *loyalty, courage* and *kindness* – that Rahan tries to lead his life, the implication being that the same will be true of Michel.[1]

As well as being a reminder of Jean-Paul Sartre's reference to his love for a previous generation of comics – *Cri-Cri* and *L'Épatant* – in *Les Mots* (1963) / *The Words* (1964), Houllebecq's inclusion of *bande dessinée* (BD) as a prescient literary trope underlines the extent to which BD is now an integral part of cultural production in French. Ironically, at the very moment when French comics tragically took centre stage worldwide on 7 January 2015 with the *Charlie Hebdo* massacres, Houellebecq was featured on the cover of the then current issue on the occasion of the publication of his latest novel *Soumission* / *Submission* (2015), a coincidence that prompted the author to withdraw from all media interviews and which became a factor in the runaway sales of his novel.[2]

What I have designated here as the *Graphic Novel Revolution* is defined therefore in terms not only of production, but also of social integration and mainstream relevance. But the term itself needs to be broken down into multiple frames, for while the concept of the *graphic novel* is a useful tag for a form that interacts with recognizably literary work such as that of Houellebecq and points towards the sorts of self-contained narratives that

109

receive critical acclaim in themselves, the field we will be considering here is more varied and also encompasses *comics*, which emerged from a very different editorial context. The place of *bande dessinée* in contemporary cultural production has been shaped by complex and sustained attachments as well as rapid, unexpected innovations, and it is a combination of progressive expansion and sudden successes that generates this revolution in the field of contemporary fiction which this chapter describes.

Historically, the modern *bande dessinée* developed in the 1800s from strips in periodical publications, which enjoyed large-scale popular distribution, but whose authors, even if credited, would not have been thought of in terms of cultural creativity. A further BD revolution took place in the years following the creation of *Pilote* magazine in 1959, which saw new levels of institutionalization – exhibitions, festivals and national centres – alongside critical acclaim, diversity of subject matter, tone and format, and, eventually, recognition of BD authors and artists as household names.[3]

Contemporary *bande dessinée*, which can be assigned to the post-1984 period (a marker date for a period of social, economic and scientific change, coinciding, for example, with the first Apple Mac), has seen further consolidation of the form's status at an institutional level, together with increased formal diversity in line with new technologies. Whereas the coming-of-age period favoured the switch to the novel format – for economic reasons, but also in terms of perceived cultural legitimacy – now legitimacy is increasingly bestowed upon hybrid and hi-tech culture, moving away from the unity of the book towards a *métissage* of formats of expression, both through the multiplicity of themes and the authors themselves. *Bande dessinée* now incubates superstars, be they bloggers or broadcasters, metropolitan or postcolonial, with a variety of backgrounds, production formats and outlets which increasingly create and redefine the nature of the form itself, perhaps more than is the case for other channels of contemporary fiction.

Content

One of the markers of the *bande dessinée*'s grown-up status was the evolution towards 'adult' content, with Jean-Claude Forest's *Barbarella*, which first appeared in 1962, often cited as a watershed. In the twenty-first century, the notion that comics can address themes not suitable for children is no longer noteworthy, but it is interesting that in the contemporary context 'adult' is not simply a byword for 'erotic', even if eroticism in comics still sustains its forward thrust.

Mainstream comics continue to cover the themes that have proved successful throughout the post-War BD boom, and in particular those that came to the fore in the 1980s, when BD switched from being largely aimed at children via weekly periodicals to the album format – generally with forty-eight bound A4 colour pages – which represented a larger one-off financial commitment.[4] Reasons for the change can be sought in the decline in appeal of the deferral expressed in the ending tag 'to be continued', a decline we can attribute to the immediacy of television, or simply to the fact that the journals' audience had grown up into adults with disposable incomes and a taste for purchases with permanency.

Bestselling content includes album versions of previously serialized household favourites such as *Lucky Luke*, *Gaston Lagaffe*, *Blake et Mortimer* and *Largo Winch*. It is by no coincidence that these are the very titles that have starred in English translations; for example, those distributed by Cinebook, 'The 9th Art Publisher' (www.cinebook.co.uk), founded by Olivier Cadic in 2005 and operating from Canterbury, but with worldwide sales. In general, popular BD fiction can be divided into adventure strips or knockabout fiction.

In terms of the former, *XIII*, originally by Jean Van Hamme (script) and William Vance (artwork), represents a leading example of formulaic success: an all-action hero, identified only by his 'XIII' tattoo, tries to discover his past while battling a conspiracy to assassinate the US president. The appeal is that of a recognizable fantasy hero – XIII is good looking, enigmatic, iconoclastic and rich – with evolving cliff-hanger narrative. The clear line artwork provides instant visual appeal, which interacts enticingly with the mystery of linear page turning.

High-profile comedy fiction likewise tends to develop expectations via a main character with individual episodes providing variations on a theme. Zep's *Titeuf*, the school-based adventures of a lovable but cheeky eight-year-old, involves a series of stock individuals – Manu, Titeuf's best friend; Titeuf's parents and sister; Nadia, the love interest – who bring out different aspects of the eponymous star. The reader is drawn in by Zep's friendly pastel style caricaturing daily life, while awaiting each episode's punchline; for example, when Titeuf equates taking out a girl with taking out a dog and comes equipped with a clean-up bag.[5]

Examples such as these tend to have print runs in the hundreds of thousands, but also, and increasingly, a range of spin-off products, such as a top-selling video game for *XIII* and a series of sex education exhibitions for *Titeuf*. We will touch on the array of these when we look specifically at the diversity of format within the BD world, a phenomenon that includes the role of smaller publishing houses producing experimental works in contrast to the bestsellers of the market leaders.

One example of bestselling BD fiction is worth a slightly closer look on account of its unique status worldwide and the iconic nature of its content. The *Astérix* series – founded in 1959 in *Pilote* magazine by René Goscinny (script) and Albert Uderzo (artwork), continued by Uderzo alone after Goscinny's death in 1979, and since 2013 further continued by Jean-Yves Ferri (script) and Didier Conrad (artwork) with Uderzo's blessing – is by far the bestselling comic-book series in the world, and by some accounts the bestselling book series.

To a certain extent, *Astérix* follows the same formula that creates success across the mainstream BD range: a text/image mixture of stock situations and characters are applied to a new dilemma, the resolution of which provides the intrigue. Indeed, the system can be compared with that outlined by Vladimir Propp,[6] with the key addition being the visual-textual interplay.

In the case of *Astérix*, certain now hallmark added extras can be regarded as giving the series its edge. The formula itself operates on the level of each individual album, or indeed the series as a whole, as 'home' adventures centred largely around the Gauls' village (e.g. *Astérix le Gaul, Le Domaine des Dieux, Le Papyrus de César*) alternate with travels 'away', where the key characters journey worldwide (*Le Tour de Gaulle, La Grande Traversée, Astérix chez les Pictes*). Within each album, a number of ploys have become household favourites: the characters' names, with the '-ix' endings for Gauls and '-us' endings for Romans, providing constant challenges for translators; anachronisms, such as Astérix posing as the Statue of Liberty, or the reference to motorway service stations in *Astérix chez les Helvètes*; and above all the array of both verbal and visual plays, for example, quotes from Victor Hugo in *Astérix chez les Belges* (translated to Shakespeare for the English version) or pictorial cameos from the Beatles to Tintin.

Of particular interest in the context of how contemporary literature functions is the policy behind, and the success of, the continuation of the series by Ferri and Conrad. In all four post-Uderzo albums (up to 2019) – *Astérix chez les Pictes* (2013), *Le Papyrus de César* (2015), *Astérix et la Transitalique* (2017) and *Astérix et la fille de Vercingétorix* (2019)[7] – the authors have aimed as far as is possible to reproduce the style of Uderzo and Goscinny based on a perceived *Astérix* golden age of the 1970s. Conrad's style to an untrained eye might seem indistinguishable from that of Uderzo, and the script continues to concentrate on an adventure plot with humour via anachronistic societal references avoiding scatology or innuendo. However, the references have been updated, for example, to the 2014 Scottish referendum, WikiLeaks, or big-money sports sponsorship. The success of the new volumes points to an interesting and perhaps unusual literary phenomenon, that of contemporary fiction which calques the past while remaining up to date and without being bland.

Beyond the mainstream bestsellers, contemporary BD is marked by the diversity of its content – as is much fiction – although certain trends remain discernible, of which two are literary adaptations and autobiography.

Literary adaptations in *bande dessinée* form have long thrived, from series such as *Alice in Wonderland*, which appeared in weekly episodes in *Fillette* in the 1950s, to single volume versions of the classics from the early days of the album boom, undoubtedly influenced by Albert Kantner's *Classics Illustrated* series, originally published from New York, that ran from 1941 until 1971.[8] The trend continues with the Glénat series, *Les Grands Classiques de la littérature en bande dessinée*, a collection of over thirty volumes marketed via *Le Monde* newspaper. A similar series, including works by Molière, Racine and Shakespeare, is retailed by the Comédie française. The corresponding website describes the albums as:

> Une collection, à la fois ludique et pédagogique – une façon originale de donner le goût de la lecture aux plus jeunes, et aux plus âgés de revisiter leurs classiques en texte intégral.[9]

> This fun but informative collection offers an original way to hook the young reader into reading, while giving older readers the chance to revisit their classics.

Indeed, such a strategy corresponds to the view of the *bande dessinée* as akin to illustrated books for children or hesitant learners; an accessible second-rate version that nonetheless allows those who might not be able to cope with the full text a way in to works they would not otherwise read.

Alternative developments, whereby literary adaptations play to the uniqueness of the *bande dessinée* form and create challenging works in their own right (as transmedial form rather than bland adaptation[10]), stand as a microcosm of BD's evolving sophistication. This notwithstanding, one of the markers in this area is generally classed as an illustrated text rather than a BD proper, namely Jacques Tardi's 1988 version of Louis-Ferdinand Céline's *Voyage au bout de la nuit* (1932) / *Journey to the End of the Night* (1934).[11] The large format volume, with the two authors' names given equal prominence on the front cover, reproduces the full text over 380 pages, interspersed with illustrations by Tardi. By dint of their number (at least one, but often several per page), the variety of placings within the text and Tardi's ability starkly to capture key places and moments, the text is transformed, with the images providing a counter-balance in the reader's mind. The effect is that of the interaction of text and image akin to the working of a *bande dessinée*, where the two are formally mingled.

The case of Enrique Corominas's 2011 *Dorian Gray d'après Oscar Wilde* exemplifies *bande dessinée* as a transnational form – a Spanish author creating a French version (as of 2020, the book is not available in English) of a novel by an Irish writer first published in the United States and then England – while raising many of the issues relating to the specificity of BD.[12] As Corominas puts it in the postface that is 'disguised' as an issue of the *The Illustrated London News*, 'Comment reproduire le style emphatique et théâtral, plein d'aphorismes, de la littérature de Wilde dans un genre où l'information visuelle est primordiale ?' / 'How to reproduce the emphatic, theatrical style that characterizes Wilde's writing, with its abundance of aphorisms, in a genre in which visual information is primordial?'[13]

The solution comes with an arrangement in five acts, each of which has a frontispiece showing a version of Basil Hallward's portrait as it advances towards its grotesque climax. More generally, Corominas uses colour, going from naïve pastels to harsher expression, to capture Dorian's moral development. The exotic atmosphere of Victorian repression is evoked visually by reference to Leighton, Beardsley and Whistler, with *planches* befitting Daniel Maghen, the volume's high-end publisher specializing in the sale of original artwork.

In his 2013 version of *L'Étranger* / *The Stranger* (1942), Jacques Ferrandez uses the visual to evoke aspects of Albert Camus's text that are implied but not explicit.[14] As with other adaptations of *L'Étranger*, such as the 1967 Luchino Visconti film starring Marcello Mastroianni, the pictorial representation of a first-person narrative that allows Meursault, the protagonist, the possible role of everyman, inevitably sells short a key aspect of the novel. Where Ferrandez does succeed, and thereby vaunts BD's potential, is in the visual *clins d'œil*, such as the inclusion of the role of the prosecutor Jacques Brochier, a member of the intelligentsia who had questioned the depth of Camus's work, or Jean-Paul Sartre as an antipathetic journalist. In particular, Ferrandez plays on the fact that the film Meursault and Marie go to see features Fernandel, who is known for his scene in Marcel Pagnol's *Le Schpountz* (1938), in which he acts outs the phrase 'tout condamné à mort aura la tête tranchée' / 'every condemned man will have his head cut off' with a variety of dictions. Camus's text is not explicit, but Ferrandez adds haunting images of Fernandel at the moment when the sentence of execution is read out, emphasizing the absurdity of the link between the seemingly banal events of the first half of the novel and Meursault's eventual condemnation.

To return to Michel Houellebecq, his prominent standing in contemporary French fiction, and the visual nature of many of his descriptive scenes, would seem to make him a clear target for adaptation. However, the question of the nature of love, and the interaction between cerebral tenderness and sexual compatibility, are key to Houellebecq's fiction, with explicit eroticism playing a part, but within broader considerations. As such, cinema versions become problematic due to the need to include potentially pornographic scenes that could limit the target audience. The *bande dessinée* version of *Plateforme* (2014), signed by Houellebecq and Alain Dual,[15] allows for such scenes to be intermingled with the overall narrative and philosophical outlook, without submitting the work to restrictive censorship.

More generally, however, Dual's version borders on the illustrated story, choosing a succession of key scenes from the original novel and presenting them alongside Houellebecq's text. A consistent use of frame size conveys the mundane, passive outlook that characterizes the main protagonist, but the impression is of a spin-off rather than of a transmedial stand-alone creation.

The rise and format of literary adaptations is indicative of BD's accessibility and popularity, but also, potentially, of its sophistication. However, it is interesting to note that even if BD itself has embraced diversity, most of the adaptations are of works by metropolitan white males.

Autobiography as an increasingly prominent format in BD productions is also an indication of comics embracing the role of a self-reflexive, and thereby credible, form of expression.[16] Autobiography in BD can be traced back to the early post-War period in mainstream productions and often has a playful touch,[17] but more recently, often but not exclusively via arthouse publishers such as L'Association (more on this later), self-narratives have given a direct voice to contemporary diversity.

A ground-breaking forerunner was Fabrice Neaud's daringly open account of gay life in small-town France as presented in his four-volume *Journal*, covering 1992–1996 and published between 1996 and 2002.[18] Neaud mixes everyday incidents that together build up a picture of the different facets of his personal and professional life, with musings on the nature of friendship, love and art. He uses differences in frame size and structure to underline important elements – the set-up of his studio, which takes a full page – or key contrasts, such as an embrace, with a void, and the anatomy of a heart.

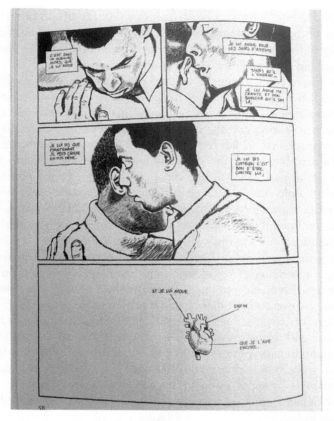

Figure 6.1   Fabrice Neaud, *Journal (1)* (Angoulême: Ego comme X, 1996), p. 58.

Neaud mixes graphic styles, from realism-based portraiture to caricature, scientific diagram and cartography, creating visual juxtapositions that
would be hard to achieve in other media.

Dominique Goblet also emphasizes the unique potential of the BD
form by playing on contrasting visual styles. Her *Faire semblant c'est mentir*
(2007) / *Pretending Is Lying* (2017) was written over a twelve-year period,[19]
and consists of four chapters, of which 1 and 3 echo each other as both deal
with traumatic family memories of childhood, while 2 and 4, co-written
with Guy Marc Hinant, concern Dominique's love relationship with Guy
Marc, and his inability to commit to her exclusively. The evolution in time
of creation produces an evolution in style, moving to less naïve expression
as events, or memories of events, move on. The specifics of the BD form

Figure 6.2 Dominique Goblet, *Faire semblant c'est mentir*
(Paris: L'Association, 2007), n. p.

allow Goblet to intersperse key moments with full-page expressionist artwork, and to use the text as image, for instance, as her father's drunken words become increasingly scrawled.

One incident in the book is pivotal, in which a stroppy rainy-day Dominique exasperates her mother to the point that she ties the child up in the attic. Dominique's father, meanwhile, is distracted by the television coverage of a fatal Formula 1 collision. The text of the mother's anger and Dominique's supplications are played out against images of the crash, so that the personal inflicted violence spills onto and overrides the televised horror of the accident.

The scene is key for Dominique's re-evaluation of her father's passive role in the domestic scene, to be contrasted with his claims that as a firefighter he would have saved the racing driver. Goblet's text/image juxtapositions allow us to live the reconstructed memories of trauma, and underline autobiography as, inevitably, personal fiction.[20]

This is evident in another non-French (Goblet is Belgian) autobiographical BD, Julie Doucet's *Ciboire de Criss* (2004),[21] her episodic account of her daily 1990s life in her home town of Montreal. The use of black and white, often a prerequisite for publications by L'Association, points to an art-house style production, with subject matter that is provocative and direct, including masturbation and menstruation. The mixture of daily banality, such as a trip to the 'centre d'achat', with fantasy dream sequences – Julie imagines herself waking up to find she has had a penis transplanted – allows the BD form to counter reader expectations, be they of a literature aimed at children, or indeed of the role expected of women. Here, and perhaps in general, *bande dessinée* is at its strongest when used to create and express ambiguities, formally by the imagining of events that happen 'in the gutters',[22] or through the expression of subject matter that can be seen directly – unlike text-only works – but with a flexibility of artistic expression difficult to achieve on film.

Authors

As already mentioned, BD has had a strong pull towards the white male author, reinforced by the legitimacy that the development of literary adaptations has offered. This gave it a relatively limited and often conservative base. But I have also already suggested that the form has increasingly become an incubator of new talent, with the promise of major notoriety and high sales drawing authors from a wide range of horizons and increasingly from the previously marginal spaces of the *banlieue*, as well as from the feminist movement. This diversification has opened BD up to wildly different horizons, generating much greater eclecticism, a process that is reinforced by the spread of BD publication well beyond its European bases. At the same time, it has also seen a process of institutionalization through a number of mechanisms, including the now famous Angoulême Festival, as I will discuss, and this too has had an impact on the changing profile of BD authors.

The fledgling modern *bande dessinée* grew in the twentieth century through the distribution of strips in weeklies for children, generally with the lead character taking pride of place and the author or authors remaining anonymous, to the extent that modern scholars studying 1950s weeklies for girls – *Bernadette, Lisette, Fillette*, for example – will be hard pushed to ascertain what percentage of the content, if any, was created by women. Going against the grain was the 1955 New Year issue of *Cœurs Vaillants*, in which selected star characters from the journal present their authors – Noël Gloesner, Robert Rigot, F. A. Breysse, Erik and Pierre Brochard – photo-montaged into a scene from their strips. The first presentation, showing adventurer character Yann Le Vaillant in a jeep, is an indication of the status of the artist at the time:

> Vous avez évidemment reconnu le personnage de gauche : notre grand ami Yann . . . mais qui donc est [l]e compagnon qui attire son attention ? C'est une vieille connaissance de notre héros et de la rédaction *Cœurs Vaillants*. Ce monsieur en veston n'est autre que notre ami Noël Gloesner, l'illustrateur de Yann.[23]

> Reader, you will obviously have recognized the character on the left as our great friend Yann . . . but who is the companion trying to get his attention? He's an old acquaintance of our hero and of the editors at *Cœurs Vaillants*. The man in a jacket is none other than our friend Noël Gloesner, Yann's illustrator.

It is the magazine *Pilote*, founded in 1959 by a team based around René Goscinny, that is often credited with taking the *bande dessinée* into culturally recognized maturity.[24] From the early issues, artists and scriptwriters were credited, generally with their names on the strip header next to the title. By the early 1970s, the role of the creators was newly emphasized by a caricature portrait, an initial step, therefore, towards iconic status. Nevertheless, the vignetted stars – Tabary, Chakir, Bilal et al – remained uniformly white and male, with the glaring exception of Claire Bretécher.

Indeed, from 1974 to 2019 the forty-five winners of the Grand Prix de la Ville d'Angoulême, a lifetime achievement award that is the culmination of the town's festival (see below for more on this) and is often considered to be the highest accolade in the world of French comics, has included only two women, Florence Cestac, winner in 2000, and Rumiko Takahashi, in 2019. Indeed, of the forty-five men (2008 was won by the partnership of Philippe Dupuy and Charles Berbérian), all are over fifty years of age (most considerably so), and none is of colour.

Angoulême's statistics drew widespread attention in 2016, when the long-list of thirty candidates for the main award did not include any women. Boycotts followed, and the situation was further exacerbated by the official response, posted on the Festival's website.[25] In short, the Festival's organizers replied that the omission of female candidates was no more than a faithful reflection of the lack of *auteures* throughout the growth of the *bande dessinée*, and that 'Le Festival ne peut pas refaire l'histoire de la bande dessinée.' / 'The Festival cannot remake the history of BD.' A counter-argument, as shall be discussed below, is that acceptance and canonization is a key part of cultural development, and as such Le Festival, and what it represents, does contribute to BD history.

The lack of such institutional recognition does not, however, mean that female BD artists have been entirely absent. Of note in the struggle to bring feminist issues to the *bande dessinée* is Chantal Montellier (b. 1947), one of the founding contributors to *Ah ! Nana*, the first BD journal for women and largely by women and dealing with female issues. Although not exclusively feminist in content, *Ah ! Nana* brought together female creators from the United States and from France, and raised gender issues that were not being addressed elsewhere. The journal was, however, short lived, lasting only nine issues from October 1976 to September 1978, before folding as a result of economic pressures that ensued from the censorship imposed due to its adult thematics (e.g. sex and young girls, incest). In the final issue, Montellier has drawn a woman proclaiming 'Ah ! Nana. Le seul journal de bandes dessinées fait par des femmes !' / 'Ah! Nana. The only cartoon strip made by women!', to be countered by five men proclaiming 'Interdit par des hommes !!!!' / 'Banned by men!!!!'[26]

Montellier's career covers a broad span of works and styles, including illustrated books and prose fiction, but it is marked by its left-leaning political engagement and pro-feminist stance. One of her most charismatic characters, Julie Bristol, is a globe-trotting private detective, whose travels are imbued with meta-references to the world of comics – Tintin, Malto Cortese, and above all Disneyfication – while exploring through visualization a complex braiding of eroticism, pornography and feminism.[27] Julie's adventures draw upon historical references, such as to Artemisia Gentileschi and Camille Claudel, with the life of the protagonist and those of feminist icons from the past intertwining, perhaps to suggest that the role of woman is such that her actions often amount to little more than fiction.

Just as Montellier was on the list of women drafted in at the initial attempt to rectify the 2016 Angoulême omission, so does one of the figures leading the boycott by the long-list nominees, Riad Sattouf (b. 1974), provide an example of how *bande dessinée* has potentially evolved with respect to creators from minority ethnic upbringings. Sattouf gives a frank

Figure 6.3   Chantal Montellier, *Faux sanglant* (Paris: Dargaud, 1992), p. 47.

portrayal of his family background with his Syrian father and travels in the Middle East (*L'Arabe du futur*, four volumes from 2014 to 2018),[28] as well as *tranche de vie* snapshots of the Parisian youth culture of those of non-metropolitan descent (*La Vie secrète des jeunes*, two volumes from 2007 and 2010, but serialized in *Charlie Hebdo* from 2004).[29]

In the case of *La Vie secrète des jeunes*, the original format was one-off single page strips, portraying 'vu et entendu' scenes, such as conversations overheard in the Paris Métro. The accessibility of the everydayness, matched by a caricatural style, means that the format integrates rather than differentiates minorities, although the visible aspect of the *bande dessinée* inevitably forefronts the characters' physiognomy. Sattouf further feeds in to a notion of youth culture that is coupled with ethnic culture by drawing on a diverse range of expressive media, as befits the world of soundbites and memes: initial one-pagers, album versions, then a series for Canal+ made up of sketches of under five minutes, as well a related César-winning feature film, *Les Beaux Gosses* (2009).[30]

Whereas Sattouf champions postcolonial culture without postcolonial culture necessarily defining his outputs, other artists draw primarily on the representation and underlining of difference. Of these, Marjane Satrapi's *Persopolis*, the four-volume series (2000 to 2003) and critically acclaimed animated film (2007), is probably the best known.[31] Satrapi's autobiographical BD presents her passage to adulthood against the backcloth of her upbringing in Iran during the Islamic Revolution, and the cultural differences between lifestyles as a woman in France and in the Islamic Middle East. For Jacques Ferrandez, his *Carnets d'Orient* series (1986–2009, published by Casterman) recounts the colonial history of the Algeria of his childhood. In *Morts pour la France* (2018), Pat Perna and Nicola Otero use the BD form to commemorate a largely overlooked episode of Senegal's history, the Thiaroye massacre of 1944.[32]

Aya Marguerite Abouet and Clément Oubrerie's six-volume *Aya de Yopougon*, set in the 1970s, tells the story of a nineteen-year-old woman's life in Abidjan, her Ivory Coast home town.[33] Particularly striking is the use of bright pastel colours, thereby evoking the warmth of the setting. The traditions of the Ivory Coast are brought to us through the array of local clothing, but the background details of neon advertisements and multinational hoardings convey the omnipresence of Western commercialism. The volumes themselves reflect inherent transnational globalism: although Abouet is Ivorian, Oubrerie is French, both live in or near Paris, and the production is by Gallimard, so mainstream metropolitan. In many ways, *Aya* allows the reader to journey to the Ivory Coast, while remaining within the known traditions.[34]

Sattouf, Satrapi et al. are undoubtedly mainstream authors, be it in terms of public visibility and acclaim, or simply sales figures, and as such they point to a widening of the creative base to include authors from minority backgrounds. However, it could be argued that their outputs, and maybe the authors themselves, are sanitized portrayals of the Other, presenting difference but in a way that conforms to metropolitan expectations, perhaps akin to the films of Ken Loach or Spike Lee. Here and as elsewhere, a contrast is to be made with the vibrant BD community of North African creators – Farid Boudjellal, Fawzi Brachemi and Benyoucef Abbas Kebir are just a few names – to be sourced at festivals, BD markets or online postings. One movement (among many) of interest is the creation of manga-influenced Algerian strips, or Dz-Manga,[35] which brings together the cultures of Asia and North Africa, applied to a European, or possibly North American, tradition.

It is obvious in this respect that *bande dessinée* is no longer produced only by French authors, indeed French-language comics have perhaps always been decentred from the dominant frame of France as a result of the key Belgian dimension. But now more than ever, BD extends beyond European authors, and as such this discussion could easily produce further chapters on Canadian, Caribbean, Polynesian or African literature.[36]

Overall, the role of the BD author has evolved markedly, from anonymity, or a cog in a studio production – the Studio Hergé being probably the best-known example – to the status of individual creator as *BD d'auteur*. Indeed, authors have become very high profile, in some cases – such as Albert Uderzo or Marjane Satrapi – reaching media stardom comparable with Cannes. With prominence has come diversity, and *bande dessinée* now boasts a growing range of artists with respect to geographic origins and ethnicity, gender and sexuality. As such, BD is on a par with other forms of creative expression, while at the same time representing a popular psyche in a way that 'academy forms' – those discussed in other chapters of this volume – might not. However, the conclusion is not that BD is breaking boundaries of inclusion: most authors continue to be white, male, straight and of metropolitan origin and outlook; however, the trajectory is nonetheless one of increasing movement towards eclecticism.

Institutionalization

The relationship between *bande dessinée* and 'academy forms' raises questions as to the status of the graphic novel today, but it is also a marker that moulds that status. The evolution of such status has now been documented critically, a fact that in itself suggests institutionalization.[37] Selected landmarks on the pathway to becoming the *Neuvième Art* might be summarized as follows.

- 1962: Foundation of the Club des Bandes Dessinées (CBD), largely fan-based but with prominent contributors including Edgar Morin, Umberto Eco, Alain Resnais and Raymond Queneau.
- 1967: Exhibition *Bande dessinée et figuration narrative* at the Musée des Arts Décoratifs in Paris.

- 1974: The inaugural Salon International de la Bande Dessinée d'Angoulême took place. In 1975, Luc Boltanski's 'La Constitution du champ de la bande dessinée' overviewed BD for the first issue of Pierre Bourdieu's *Actes de la Recherche en Sciences Sociales*.[38] From the early 1980s onwards, critical engagement was marked by the works of Thierry Groensteen, including his editorship of *Cahiers de la Bande Dessinée* from 1984.
- 1989: Inauguration of the Centre Belge de la Bande Dessinée (CBBD) in Brussels, then in 1990 of Angoulême's Centre National de la Bande Dessinée et de l'Image (CNBDI). This had followed on from Jack Lang's 1982 'Quinze mesures pour la bande dessinée', the initial government-backed statement of the intention to promote BD's cultural value.
- 1999: The first International *Bande Dessinée* conference took place in Glasgow, with just over twenty scholars from a variety of French studies backgrounds – literature, cinema, linguistics, postcolonialism – applying knowledge gained elsewhere to the fledgling field of BD. At the follow-up conference in 2001, plans were put in place for the creation of the International *Bande Dessinée* Society (IBDS). Although at this time BD was still largely absent from university activities in France, in 2000 the Bibliothèque nationale de France opened a major exhibition, *Maîtres de la bande dessinée européenne*.
- 2020: The inclusion by Cambridge University Press of *bande dessinée* as a chapter in a volume outlining and exploring contemporary literature in French serves *de facto* as a new marker.

In short, a transformative period towards the end of the 1980s has seen *bande dessinée* lauded as a subject of academic worth, with widespread acceptance in universities in the English-speaking world from the 1990s onwards. It would now be unusual to find a university syllabus in French studies that at some stage does not make reference to BD, be it *Tintin* and colonialism, *Astérix* and '68, or indeed the study of individual authors per se. In France, the change can be pinpointed more to the twenty-first century, with the strict subject boundaries of the Centre national de la recherche scientifique and of the *comités de recruitment*, or academic recruitment system, for a long time acting against the inherent interdisciplinary nature of BD studies. But in the final years of the first quarter of this century, *thèses de doctorat*, conferences and university publications – one such example being the Paris 7-based online journal *Comicalités*[39] – are becoming increasingly frequent in the field.

One viewpoint is that institutionalization leads to conservative tendencies, as the Angoulême debate might seem to indicate. But whether conservative tendencies mean a conservative canon, or rather a conflict that contradicts the move away from a traditional canon, is a further debate. Again, by its interdisciplinary and transmedial nature, *bande dessinée* is potentially central to such a debate, but here the question of institutionalization becomes intertwined with that of technology-inspired evolution of format.

Format

Inevitably, format is linked to both economics and technology. The recession of the 1980s saw the folding of the vast majority of BD journals, with the notable exceptions of *Le Journal de Mickey*, *L'Echo des Savanes* (which largely switched format to soft eroticism and current affairs) and *Charlie Hebdo*, which likewise had been faltering prior to the attacks of 2015. Economic imperatives meant it made more sense to target those with disposable incomes who could afford the pricier but more solid album format.

Despite the seemingly inherent oneness of the album production, a more recent shift has been towards disintegration, with publications at the popular end of the market, such as *Titeuf*, *Les Blondes* or *Joe Bar Team*, relying largely on collections of short stories rather than a single extended narrative. In addition, albums are increasingly part of a multimedia phenomenon that might include spin-off products, films and exhibitions. *Titeuf* is again a leading example, with its television series, full-length film and exhibitions tying the teenager's exploits in to science-based sex education displays.[40] More generally, the current trend for cinema adaptations of *bande dessinée* material – *Les Beaux Gosses* is mentioned above, but versions of *Astérix*, *Tintin*, *Bécassine* and *Valérian* are also some of the offerings – underlines the transmedial nature of culture in general and BD in particular, but perhaps could be the subject for an entire chapter in an updated volume of this kind.

Diversity is nonetheless encouraged by an evolving range of publishing strategies. Initially, L'Association, founded in 1990, challenged the hegemony of the '48CC/HF/KK', or the standard format mainstream album ('48 pages, couleur cartonné/héroïc-fantasy/kaka'), as the publishing house's founder and main driver, Jean-Christophe Menu, was to explain in his credo publication *Plates-bandes* (2005).[41] L'Association championed *BD d'auteur* at a time when this was still not the norm, showcasing its difference through divergence of format: albums exclusively in black and white, but also of difference sizes and length.[42] A key point of principle was the refusal by Menu to print a bar code on publications for aesthetic reasons, although this led to conflict among colleagues, and a less than satisfactory resolution via costly bar code stickers.

L'Association led the way in alternative publishing, a leading example of which is the Montpellier-based 6 Pieds Sous Terre.[43] Rather than asserting a credo – the website, for example, does not include a tab giving an overview of the house's history or guiding principles – the distinguishing feature is that of an eclectic and culturally diverse set of authors whose styles range from social coming-of-age narratives to the possibility of female solidarity in a patriarchal system. In terms of format, the *Poulpe* collection is of particular note. The series adapts the detective novels of the same name, where the adventures of the shared leading character – the eponymous Poulpe, aka Gabriel Lecouvreur – are penned by different authors. In the BD update, the changing of artists leads to a variety of styles but retains the cohesion of the shared story-world, thereby requiring the reader to suspend belief regarding the physical aspects of Lecouvreur, while acknowledging implicitly the richness of the medium's artistic possibilities.

The *bande dessinée*'s seeming ability to evolve format while keeping its identity is currently reflected in the extent to which digital outputs are being embraced. One could argue that all artistic forms are developing in this way, and in particular the visual arts; however, the hybrid immediacy of online productions is particularly suited to graphic narrative and befits a form that has embraced technology from lithography onwards.

One digital example of many is Marietta Ren's *Phallaina* (2016), described on the Apple App Store site as:

> Ta première 'bande défilée', une bande dessinée numérique originale et entièrement gratuite de Marietta Ren. [...] Phallaina est le récit intime d'une transformation personnelle, mêlant sciences cognitives et mythologie.

> The first 'rolling strip', an original digital comic strip entirely free of charge by Mariette Ren. [...] Phallaina is the intimate story of a personal trans-formation blending cognitive science and mythology.

The story is that of Audrey's hallucinations of whales, linked to a neuro-logical condition allowing her to remain underwater for sustained periods, and to the (fictional) myth of Phallainas, or hybrids between humans and whales. Frames are replaced by the scrolling effect as the reader swipes the tablet so as to advance the story, with progress matched by changes in

Figure 6.4   Marietta Ren, *Phallaina* (2016), at https://phallaina.nouvelles-ecritures
.francetv.fr

viewing angles – a parallax effect – and accompanied by an interactive soundtrack. It is perhaps the experimental nature of the work that strikes the viewer of 2020 above all else, but the work nonetheless places a marker for what is possible.

A household BD name as a result of online output is now that of Pénélope Bagieu (b. 1982), a blogger recognized increasingly for her web-comics. Archived from February 2007, *Ma Vie est toute à fait fascinante* (www.penelope-jolicoeur.com) is the blog of Bagieu's daily life and various travels,[44] presented largely as an informal handwritten illustrated diary giving an overview of the author's preoccupations, projects and tourist tips. Potential criticisms of Bagieu's Bridget Jones style, on the grounds that in this blog and elsewhere she equates female philosophy with shopping and the hunt for male partners, are overridden by her *Culottées* project. Published between January and October 2016 on a site hosted by *Le Monde*, each weekly update presents the *bande dessinée* account of the life, struggles and achievement of a woman who, according to the site, 'ne fait que ce qu'elle veut' / 'only does what she wants', again in Bagieu's distinctive informal handwritten style. This modern-day update of the seventeenth-century notion of *femmes fortes* includes such examples as Peggy Guggenheim, Joséphine Baker, Margaret Hamilton or Cheryl Bridges.

Figure 6.5   Pénélope Bagieu, *Les Culottées* (2016)

In formal terms, Bagieu is of note as an artist whose web blogs might initially have been subservient to a professional promotional platform – as is often the case for personal pages – but rather her creations have become of note per se and valid well beyond their function as a tool for her illustration work.

It is fitting to end the main section of this chapter with a glimpse of the success of digital *bandes dessinées* as, at the time of writing, this is the most swiftly developing platform for the form and, it might seem, the way forward. But one caveat should be that this is no more than a glimpse via two examples, as any *bédéphile* with a keyboard would attest. The second caveat is that like video and the radio star, digital comics have definitely not killed the print medium. Pénélope Bagieu's blogs have gone on to print success; in general, transfers between media, and transmedia interaction, are increasingly common, and, above all, the traditional book format continues to thrive. The revolutions in the graphic novel, like the form itself, remain hybrid.

'Dans ta conclusion': Fabcaro

'où sont les clés du garage : dans ton cul' / 'where are the keys to the garage: in your arsehole'

Figure 6.6   Fabcaro, *Moins qu'hier (plus que demain)* (Grenoble: Glénat, 2018), p. 6.

Fabcaro's *Moins qu'hier (plus que demain)* (Glénat, 2018) consists of fifty-nine single-page strips, each showing a couple's daily interaction and a time of day, as the album progresses from dawn to night. At 7h46 for 'Anne et Grégoire', we see three elongated static frames arranged vertically, with the protagonist on a living-room couch. The only movement is facial, as a voice-off asks 'Chéri, tu sais où sont les clés du garage ?'/ 'Darling, do you know where the garage keys are?', which is met with the impassive reply 'dans ton cul' / 'in your arsehole'. The second frame remains silent, before the crescendo of the third: 'Ah mais oui, c'est vrai, j'avais complètement oublié que je les avais mises là . . . Allez je file ! Bonne journée mon chéri,' 'Bonne journée, mon amour.' / 'Oh yeah, right, I'd completely forgotten

I'd put them there . . . Right, I'm off! Have a great day sweetheart.' – 'You too, sweetheart.'

Fabcaro's iconoclastic slice of everyday life might appear to be a flippant conclusion to an overview of the Graphic Novel Revolution. But viewed more closely (the work of Fabcaro, not the present location of the garage keys), in many ways it exemplifies the current direction of *bande dessinée*. An initial wry reaction would be to say that BD is 'up itself'. As the up-and-coming trendy form, BD has taken over from cinema, while awaiting the hegemony of YouTubing. But a closer look at the phenomenal rise of Fabcaro – despite publications dating from the 1990s, he only received widespread recognition in 2015 following *Zaï, zaï, zaï*[45] – points to a form that succeeds through simplicity and accessibility; here, it is irreverent scatology, while nonetheless offering a deeper social message for those who want it. Fabcaro and *bande dessinée* is to 2020 what Monty Python's *Meaning of Life* was to 1983.

For those looking for something deeper in the tale of Anne and Grégoire (tale, not tail), one could point to the portrayal of a consumer society marked by ritual and boredom. Stylistically, we are reminded of the retro-realism of post-War romance stories, perhaps an indication that the social revolutions of the 1960s have not really changed anything, or, on a meta-level, that the *bande dessinée* is now an established form that can look back ironically on its own history.

In terms of inclusivity, could it be argued that Fabcaro is not the best example to represent the Graphic Novel Revolution? He is white, male, straight and from metropolitan France (although not Paris), and born in 1973, approaching 'establishment' age. Alternatively, and in the style of the irony that marks Fabcaro's work, one could point to a self-assured form that no longer needs to justify itself or display its inclusiveness. And despite the move towards inclusiveness, not to finish on a straight white male would be a misrepresentation, but nonetheless Fabcaro is an open-minded socially aware white male.

Fabcaro's output is prolific, with an interdisciplinarity and intermediality that fits the current form, including work for the established *Achille Talon* series, two novels, musical recordings and a strong online video presence. The album that brought him prominent recognition, *Zaï, zaï, zaï*, with its title taken from a Joe Dassin song, is the road movie of an unassuming *bande dessinée* artist who is forced to flee for having flaunted society's rules by getting caught in a supermarket without a loyalty card. Two years later, *Et si l'amour c'était aimer* (6 Pieds Sous Terre, 2017) parodies the love romances of the *roman photo*, telling of the steamy forbidden relationship between Sandrine and Michel, the *salade macédoine* delivery boy.

Here and elsewhere, Fabcaro pokes irreverent and often surreal fun at the foibles of modern society, be it the expectations of family life, the tendency to be defined by one's employment title, or the farcical manipulations of mainstream media. The works can be introspective, voicing everyday *angoisse* about health or the fear of death, or quite simply given to reflection on banality, essentially what happens when nothing happens. By their very nature, Fabcaro's *bandes dessinées* give us a metatextual view of the BD form, creating humour from the disparity between mood and subject matter, or indeed between what is written and what is drawn (cf. 'dans ton cul'). Fabcaro mixes tones to include pathos, social comment and comedy.

The nature of Fabcaro's rise to prominence gives us pause to reflect on the shift in the canon, but also on the process of canonization. Fabcaro's success has essentially been as a word-of-mouth cult figure, a freelancer rising via small presses and blogs, without big business contracts or advertising, but nonetheless increasingly now the subject of mainstream journalism – *France Inter, France Culture, Télérama, Le Monde* – and, since 2015, cultural prizes. As such, he is a microcosm of the canonization of the BD, matched also by the format he chooses: that of the traditional book, but with twists, such as the paratextual reference to the promotional yellow band used to envelop the album,[46] the accumulation of one-pagers within a work that nonetheless has overall coherence, a story that is not really a story, the backup by technology to create an online presence, and references to the retro of the past while deconstructing the developments of the future.

While all such elements draw upon the specifics of the *bande dessinée* form, much could also be compared to the work and persona of Michel Houellebecq, with whom we opened our discussion. It is a discussion that is inevitably a subjective snapshot of 2020 – a marker date twenty-one years on from the first IBDS gathering – but perhaps will be seen, in this case via the example of Fabcaro, as a period of both static conciliation and movement. Like the keys to the garage.

CHAPTER 7

'Back in the USSR'
The Prose of Andreï Makine and Antoine Volodine
Helena Duffy

The 'Russian Novel' Then and Now

Speaking in 2018 of his longstanding enthrallment with Russia, French writer Olivier Rolin extols the Russians' effusiveness and hospitality, and marvels about their country's immense spaces, extreme weather, dramatic history and literature or, more specifically, 'le grand roman russe' / 'the great Russian novel'.[1] Reciprocally, Rolin is flattered by the Russians' enduring interest in French culture, as manifest in the large turnout to a reading of Claude Simon's reputedly inaccessible novel, *L'Acacia*.[2] Rolin's engrossment with Russia's exotic charm and incongruities illustrates what literary journalist Grégoire Leménager recognises as the rebirth of the Russophile French writer, a rebirth that he finds incongruous with Putin's recent handling of home and international affairs. To substantiate his point, Leménager lists Russia's annexation of Crimea, invasion of eastern Ukraine, support for Bashar al-Assad and shooting down of the Malaysia Airlines flight MH17, as well as the assassination of Boris Nemcov and persecution of opposition figures.[3]

Yet, the contemporary French novel about Russia hardly touches upon these contemporary events, instead revisiting the country's past or engaging in speculations about its future. To support this claim, the present chapter will examine the prose of two present-day writers: Andreï Makine, who, though born and raised in Russia, since 1992 has been writing exclusively in French, and Antoine Volodine, whose self-theorising *œuvre* vehemently rebukes contemporary Western politico-economic realities and traditional literary criticism. While mobilizing stereotypes that have accompanied France's centuries-old fascination with Russia, which I will survey later in this chapter, the two novelists nevertheless succeed at engaging with contemporary issues, such as global capitalist expansion, the collapse of political idealism, ecological catastrophe or unremitting sexual violence. In so doing, they deploy, I will show, characteristically postmodern narrative techniques and tropes. However, contrary to the widespread attachment of postmodernism to the questioning of dominant historiographies and advocating progressive politics, the two writers enlist these postmodern strategies in support of nostalgic or even reactionary agendas. My discussion will therefore be underpinned by questions regarding, on the one hand, the capacity of the French Russocentric novel to tackle current sociopolitical concerns, including Russia's renewed appetite for superpower status, and, on the other, its continuity with eighteenth- and nineteenth-century Russia-themed literature.

Before attending to Makine and Volodine's prose, a few words must be said about other contemporary Russophile French writers. The most prominent of them is undoubtedly Emmanuel Carrère, whose newly found interest in his grandfather's homeland has informed his recently published autobiographical novel, *Un roman russe* (2007) / *A Russian Novel* (2010), and fictionalized biography of a Russian writer and politician, *Limonov* (2011).[4] The former opens with the authorial narrator's erotic fantasy staged on a train bound for Kotelnich, a town located 500 miles northeast of Moscow. The reason for Carrère's journey is his documentary about András Toma, a Hungarian prisoner of war, who spent over fifty years in a mental asylum, forgotten by all and unable to communicate with his carers.[5] During his trip, Carrère embarks on a short-lived affair with a journalist called Galia, while his admittedly exploitative crew are told by the indignant locals: 'nous vivons comme des chiens, vous vous vivez au paradis, vous êtes de beaux salauds de venir nous filmer' / 'we live like dogs while you, you live in Paradise; you're real bastards to come and film us'.[6] He also relearns Russian, which his mother Hélène Carrère d'Encausse – a prominent political historian of Georgian origin – transmitted to him through nursery rhymes. The quest for Toma becomes one for Carrère's own origins, and in particular for the truth about his grandfather, a déclassé intellectual whose wartime collaboration with the Germans most likely cost him his life on France's liberation. Even if *Un roman russe* was bound to cause Carrère's rift with his mother, the memoir-cum-fiction becomes an opportunity for the writer to confront the shady aspects of his family history, but, disappointingly, not the questions arising from present-day Russian politics.

Beside Carrère, several other contemporary French writers, including Frédéric Beigbeder and Patrick Deville,[7] have produced narratives with a Russian flavour. So whence this sudden revival of interest in a country that the French once saw as their main cultural Other?[8] Part of the answer to this question may lie in the trans-Siberian journey fourteen French writers undertook in 2010 as part of the celebrations of the Year of France in

Russia.[9] Commemorating the near-centenary of the publication of Blaise Cendrars's *La Prose du Transsibérien et de la petite Jehanne de France*, the voyage resulted in works by Dominique Fernandez, Maylis de Kerangal, Jean Rolin, Mathias Enard, Danièle Sallenave and Sylvie Germain.[10] The question that such a journey inevitably begs concerns the ethics of an undertaking that potentially legitimates Russia's problematic foreign and home policy. Yet, when challenged by journalists, Germain defensively insisted on the absolute spontaneity of her and her fellow travellers' exchanges with Russian readers. Likewise, while underscoring his own political detachment, Rolin voiced his understanding for Putin's popularity at home by praising the leader's capacity for restoring both order at home and his country's international reputation.[11]

Considering that French fascination with things Russian dates back to the eighteenth century, it is tempting to see the work of present-day Russophile authors as a continuation – or revival – of a longstanding literary tradition. According to a contemporary literary critic, Jean-Claude Fizaine, 'Tout écrivain qui prétend accéder au premier rang est donc requis de prendre position à un moment ou un autre de sa carrière sur la place qu'il donne à la Russie dans sa représentation du monde.' / 'Any writer aspiring to prominence must at some point in his/her career make a stand on the place s/he accords Russia in his/her representation of the world.'[12] Fizaine's view is validated by studies of French novels that have taken Russia as their subject, and that include works by both canonical writers such as Balzac, Zola, Stendhal, Jules Verne, Alexandre Dumas, George Sand and Alphonse Daudet, and less well-known novelists.[13] Among the latter are André Theuriet, Augusta Coupey, Alexandre de Lamothe and two writerly duos: Émile Erckmann and Alexandre Chatrian, and Victor Tissot and Constant Améro.[14] That French authors have been significantly more interested in Russia than their counterparts in Germany, Italy, England, China or Japan is confirmed by Janine Neboit-Mombet's survey of nineteenth-century Russia-themed novels.[15] Charlotte Krauss frames this phenomenon with the vacillating history of Franco-Russian relations that date back to Catherine II and her intellectual engagement with (and generous patronage of) French philosophers of the Enlightenment.[16] Of significance is also Napoleon's Russian campaign of 1812, which familiarized ordinary Frenchmen with the country of the tsars, or Astolphe de Custine's book *La Russie en 1839*, which propagated a highly negative portrait of Russia.[17]

Yet, according to Krauss, the nineteenth-century literary image of Russia is largely stereotypical.[18] This means that novelists regularly portray

Russia as a country of extremes, emphasize its vastness and represent it in monochrome which is only here and there splashed with the golden onion domes of Moscow or the garishly dressed crowds of Nizhny Novgorod.[19] Other standard ingredients of a Russian-themed French novel are snow-covered expanses crossed by sleds and roamed by wolves, tigers and bears.[20] This inhospitable landscape is punctuated with wooden dwellings (*izbas*) that house archetypal objects such as icons and samovars.[21] Russians themselves are cast as barbarians or as character types such as the capricious prince, the cold-hearted seductress and the long-suffering woman.[22] To this collection of archetypes Neboit-Mombet adds the tsar and the superstitious, devout and hospitable peasant, who drinks a lot but speaks little.[23] Although, according to Krauss, the French writers' preoccupation with Russia waned after the October Revolution, little has changed in its literary representation: 'l'univers imaginaire russe, construit au XIXe siècle, reste d'actualité pour la fiction française du XXIe siècle' / 'the imaginary Russian universe of the nineteenth century stays unchanged in twenty-first-century French fiction'.[24] In order to ascertain whether, as Krauss has it, the present-day Russocentric novel barely does more than continue to inscribe the well-worn paradigm of Russianness or also manages to address more contemporary issues, I will now turn to the prose of Makine and Volodine, with particular focus on *L'Archipel d'une autre vie* (2016) / *Archipelago of Another Life* (2019), henceforth *L'Archipel*, and *Terminus radieux* (2014) / *Radiant Terminus* (2017), henceforth *Terminus*.

Andreï Makine

Among today's French Russophile authors, Makine has certainly the strongest connection to the country he writes about. Born in Siberia, the author of the award-winning *Le Testament français* (1995) lived in the Soviet Union until he was thirty.[25] While little information is available about his Russian years and Makine himself disputes the few established facts, interviews and biographical notes systematically mention a childhood spent in an orphanage, the influence of an older French/Francophile woman, and a degree from the Moscow State University followed by an academic career in French studies at the Pedagogical Institute of Novgorod.[26] In Paris, where he arrived in 1987 as a political refugee, Makine completed his second doctorate and taught Russian at the École Polytechnique. In 1992, he made his novelistic debut, which, however, he managed only thanks to a subterfuge; desperate to break the string of publishers' refusals, he submitted his first two manuscripts as translations from the Russian, although in reality he had written them directly in French.[27] These texts, as well as *Au temps du fleuve Amour* (1994) / *Once Upon the River Love* (1999), met with little enthusiasm from Parisian critics. Recognition came only with *Le Testament français*, which, presented as autobiographical and staging a Russian adolescent inculcated with love of France by his (adoptive) grandmother, legitimated Makine's claim to a place among French writers and, according to some, contributed to his long-awaited naturalization as a French citizen.[28] Since then, Makine has been publishing with exemplary regularity and has won many literary prizes.[29] These were topped in 2016 with his election to the prestigious Académie française,[30] an honour that, shockingly, the writer used to accuse recent French presidents of ignorance and to blame NATO and, more specifically, France for the civil war in Ukraine.[31]

Despite having lived in France for over three decades and targeting mainly Western readers, Makine has written about little else than Russia. Beside the novels he published as Gabriel Osmonde,[32] all Makine's works are set in Russia, or at least have Russian themes and characters. His works have also been consistent in confirming some Western *idées reçues* concerning Russian history, geography and people, at the same time dislodging our other preconceptions. Broadly, Makine likes to return to the moments of national triumph, such as the tsars' conquest of Eastern Siberia,[33] the reign of Catherine II[34] and, more frequently, Russia's heroic albeit costly victory over Hitler. In so doing, the novelist foregrounds the courage and sufferings of individual Russians, yet glosses over the violence committed by the Russian state towards its own citizens and other nations. In the novels that revisit the Eastern Front, Makine posits his homeland as a country-martyr which sacrificed thirty million lives at the altar of Europe's freedom from fascism. As for the Russians themselves, Makinean protagonists are invariably characterized by generosity, altruism, self-denial, humility, predisposition to suffering (*priterpelost*), anti-materialism and communality (*sobornost*). Perpetually oppressed by the violent yet seemingly anonymous state, or ruthlessly mistreated by the crass elites of today's savagely capitalist society, they patiently bear their lot without ever contemplating dissent or escape. This is one reason why Russia emerges out of Makine's œuvre as France's incomprehensible other. Other reasons include the country's vastness, position between eastern and western cultures, and history that Makine figures as 'une monotone suite de guerres, un interminable pansement de plaies toujours ouvertes' / 'a monotonous succession of wars, an interminable dressing of ever-open wounds'.[35]

L'Archipel d'une autre vie

Makine's most recent novel at the time of writing largely reiterates these ideas. It also reproduces the structure of the author's earlier works, where the story of an individual persecuted by the Soviet system is embedded in that of the narrator's own marginalization by mainstream society. As anticipated by its title's unmistakable allusion to *The Gulag Archipelago*, the novel is set in northeastern Siberia, a region notorious for the forced labour camps, which Solzhenitsyn branded 'that pole of cold and cruelty'.[36] More straightforwardly, the title refers to the Shantar Islands, where the protagonist, Pavel Gartsev, and his female companion, Elken, find safe haven after the woman's escape from a gulag and Pavel's desertion from his military detachment which unfairly charged him with treason. The bulk of the novel is set in the taiga and taken up by the hunt for the fugitive woman by Gartsev's military unit. Having become separated from his comrades, the protagonist embarks on a solitary pursuit of the escapee and then wanders through marshy forests, first trying to return to his detachment and then, having been brutalized by his superiors, to rejoin Elken. Gartsev's story is framed, *matrioshka*-like, by that of the narrator, an orphan who briefly met Gartsev in the 1970s while undergoing an apprenticeship in Russia's Far East. Years later, the news of Gartsev and Elken's violent death prompts him to relate their story.

Gartsev's tale begins in 1952 in Leningrad, where he lived with his fiancée, Sveta, and was studying the Marxist conception of the legitimacy of revolutionary violence. His academic interests stemmed from his personal loss; in 1932, the dam that his parents had been overseeing was sabotaged, flooding their office. As confirmed by their successors' tragic fate, had they not died in the accident, Gartsev's father and mother would have been purged, and Gartsev himself would have been stigmatized as a child of the 'enemies of the people'.[37] Reminiscent of an episode from *Requiem pour l'Est* (2000) / *Requiem for the East* (2001), whose narrator's home is destroyed as part of some grandiose engineering project and whose parents are murdered by Stalin's henchmen, the deluge simultaneously symbolizes and problematically disembodies the crushing power of political forces. More specifically, Gartsev, whose scholarly research has failed to illuminate his experience of loss, rationalizes his parents' murder as caused by two interlinked primordial forces: sexual desire and pursuit of power.

By making Leningrad the locus of Gartsev's epiphany, Makine articulates his consistently disparaging attitude towards large cities.[38] As in the author's earlier works, in *L'Archipel* the former Russian capital is associated with artifice, materialism and *poshlost*, a culturally untranslatable term combining 'vulgarity, sexual promiscuity, and lack of spirituality', and opposed to spiritual life, self-sacrifice and communality.[39] Indeed, Sveta proves to be a fraud and their relationship based on an illusion. Soon afterwards, the arrivisme, pettiness, egoism and vengefulness of the protagonist's army superiors further expose the fallacy of the political theories Gartsev was studying. As the ultimate manifestation of violence, the nuclear war for which the protagonist is training in the Far East will be the upshot of the pursuit of material gain and sexual satisfaction, a pursuit the novel fleshes out with the image of two drunks fighting over a woman. This quest for domination is facilitated, as Gartsev realizes, by the survival instinct which transforms men like himself into immoral cowards and which, consequently, perpetuates the repressive sociopolitical order.

Structured by the dichotomy between metropolitan and provincial Russia, Makine's œuvre repeatedly idealizes the latter as a space where traditional values have been preserved from the onslaught of moral decadence and consumerism. *La Femme qui attendait* (2004) / *The Woman Who Waited* (2006), for example, is set in Mirnoe, a fictional village near Archangelsk, whose name invokes the *mir*, as was called the pre-1920s self-governing peasant commune designed to 'hel[p] the sick and old, g[ive] mutual aid to the needy, t[ake] care of all its members, and provi[de] a warm and supportive atmosphere'.[40] In contrast to the sex-crazed and rebellious Leningrad, the isolated and depopulated village is a model of *sobornost*, a religious term which, secularized by the Slavophile philosophers, designates a common bond uniting a community. Likewise, in *La Terre et le ciel de Jacques Dorme* (2003) / *The Earth and the Sky of Jacques Dorme* (2005), Makine opposes an unnamed city on the Volga, which teems with prostitutes, including a young girl being pimped by her own grandmother, with a remote corner of northeastern Siberia.[41] There, in a cosy *izba*, strong alcohol flows as freely as crude jokes are told. That minds have not yet been infected by Western values, including those of feminism, is illustrated by the silent and stout woman who, having served the men their meal, retires to her bedroom to pour over voluminous socialist-realist novels.

Northeastern Siberia is also the setting of *L'Archipel*. Seemingly infinite, roamed by wolves and bears, and home to both remedial and poisonous plants, the taiga is imagined as an ambiguous space that either protects or brings doom upon people.[42] Overall, the coniferous forests are endowed with positive significance through allowing Gartsev to escape persecution and, ultimately, liberating him from his past fears and aspirations.

Paradoxically, by reducing him to animal status, the taiga not only renders the protagonist free and happy, but also restores his humanity. As the soldiers trail the escapee, Gartsev notes the forests' conciliatory potential: 'La beauté de la taïga nous immergeait dans son lent ondoiement vert, loin de la hargne de petites pensées qui nous opposaient les uns aux autres.'[43] / 'The beauty of the taiga absorbed us into its slow undulations, far away from the hostile little thoughts that had been setting us against each other.' The forests' liberating power is amplified by the proximity of the coast that in Makine's writings routinely connotes freedom.[44]

Gartsev's metamorphosis from an intellectual, ambitious and pleasure-seeking man about town into a hermit living in utmost simplicity in internal exile, is fostered not only by his exposure to natural beauty but also by his near-death experience. Notwithstanding the resolute godless-ness of Makine's novelistic universe, both here and elsewhere the novelist styles his protagonists' transformation on Christ's resurrection. Such imag-ery appears to be rooted in Christian Orthodoxy, where humility, simplic-ity, poverty, patience, silence and self-denial have been regarded as 'a genuine expression of the human communion with Christ'.[45] Among characters who live through a resurrection-like experience is Alyosha (*Le Testament français*), who, after a sojourn at a Parisian cemetery, becomes determined to renew morally contemporary France,[46] or Alexei Berg (*La Musique d'une vie*, (2001) / *A Life's Music*, (2003)), whose stay in a coffin-like hideout in Ukraine transforms him from being a member of Moscow's Jewish cultural elite into an ordinary Soviet citizen resigned to a life marked by destitution and political terror.[47] Likewise, *La Vie d'un homme inconnu* (2009) / *The Life of an Unknown Man* (2012) features a pietà-like scene showing its central character, Volsky, faint in the arms of a maternal woman. Having come to, the protagonist renounces his ambition to pursue an operatic career in Leningrad and becomes an anti-materialistic anti-individualist dedicated to helping disabled orphans.

Like his predecessors, Gartsev emerges from his twenty-four-hour imprisonment thoroughly altered; after nearly suffocating in an under-ground shelter, where he was additionally tormented by thirst and insects, the protagonist grasps the banality or – to use the Russian term – *poshlost* of his former concerns: 'La percée s'ouvrait sur une vie face à laquelle tout ce que j'avais vécu et appris perdait importance. Mes déboires sentimen-taux et les doctrines qui prétendaient englober le sens de l'univers, tout cela n'avait plus aucun écho dans la vérité que je venais d'approcher.'[48] / 'The opening was giving on to a life wherein everything that I had lived and learnt was losing significance. My romantic setbacks and the doctrines that pretended to capture the meaning of the universe, all this had little relevance for the truth I had just now reached.' The protagonist's meta-morphosis is completed, however, only by his trek through the taiga, which transforms him from the prospective aggressor of the woman he is pursuing into her ally and partner. One day, on waking up, Gartsev feels not only free from the male predatory drive towards sex, but also 'loin de ce corps qui s'accrochait à la survie, loin de mon passé, du monde des autres où je n'avais plus de rôle à jouer'[49] / 'distanced from my body that was clinging on to life, far from my past, from the others' world where I no longer had a role to play'. Correlatedly, he feels no longer capable of hating others or seeking revenge, or even of forgiveness, which he now considers to be symptomatic of self-righteousness and pride. Nor does Gartsev ever complain about the regime's brutality or the absurdity of history. Instead, like his novelistic avatars, he emerges from his transformative experience at peace with himself and the world.

With Gartsev and Elken's escape to the uninhabited island of Belichy, where, like *La Musique's* Volsky and his sweetheart Mila who foster orphans, they re-educate a delinquent, Makine revisits one of his favourite themes, which is the individual's isolation from a world ruled by political oppression and conventional preoccupations. By fancying Belichy as an island off the hypothesized pre-historical super-continent Rodina and surrounded by the super-ocean Mirovia, Gartsev reinvents it as the Garden of Eden or perhaps as the revival of the already mentioned *mir*. In this sense, he and Elken follow in the footsteps of other defiant couples populating Makine's œuvre, such as Olga Arbélina and her teenage son, whose incestuous relationship flourishes as rising waters protect their dwelling from their neighbours' ill-founded curiosity.[50] It is also floodwa-ters that shelter Volsky and Mila from the post-War revival of *poshlost*, which the couple recognize in the sound of a tango played on a gramo-phone, a token of the bourgeois lifestyle.[51] Yet, as in Makine's earlier novels, the world eventually catches up with the rebellious couple, even if in *L'Archipel* it is not the Soviet state but the post-1991 introduction of tourism to Belichy which wrecks the pair's happiness. In this way, Makine's latest narrative contributes to the writer's ongoing critique of Russia's opening to the Western way of life and of its linked abandonment of its traditional solidarity, generosity and resignation to one's fate. More generally, like Makine's other texts, *L'Archipel* promotes a utopian vision of a minimalist existence away from the materialist, debauched and violent world.

Antoine Volodine

Although very different in texture, the works of the writer using as his main pseudonym the name 'Antoine Volodine' echo many of Makine's own ideas, while his split writerly self brings to mind the Franco-Russian novelist's doubling as Gabriel Osmonde. Indeed, in 2010 Volodine published three texts, each time taking on a different identity.[52] Then, posing in turn as Antoine Volodine, Lutz Bassman and Manuela Draeger, and talking of himself in the plural but claiming to be of sound mind,[53] he gave three separate interviews to *Le Nouvel Observateur*.[54] This bifurcation, which Volodine implicitly frames with the Barthesian conception of the text that exists independently of its creator, is meant to be a hallmark of 'post-exoticism', as the novelist dubs the literary movement constituted by himself and his homonyms: '[p]our un narrateur post-exotique [. . .] il n'y a pas l'épaisseur d'une feuille de papier à cigarette entre la première personne et les autres' / '[f]or a post-exotic narrator [. . .] there is not a thickness of a piece of cigarette paper between the first-person and others'.[55]

If Volodine's strategy has been ascribed to his nostalgia for egalitarian and proletarian literature, the nationally ambiguous character of the novelist's five pen-names has been identified as his ambition to create 'une littérature étrangère écrite en français' / 'a foreign literature written in French'.[56] This ambition stems from the writer's rejection of the purported link between a language and the cultural tradition created in it, a link in which Volodine recognizes a sign of misplaced patriotism. An alternative to a national literature is 'post-exotic' fiction that, although created in French, is transnational, as illustrated by the oblique spatiotemporal settings of Volodine's novels or by his characters' names. Vaguely defined spaces such as Central Asia (*Nuit blanche en Balkhyrie*, (1997); *Terminus*) or Amazonia (*Le Nom des singes*, (1994) / *Naming the Jungle*, (1996))[57] are populated by characters bearing names that, as instantiated by Julio Sternhagen or Petra Kim, resist association with any one given national culture. Another manifestation of, to quote David Bellos, Volodine's 'internationalist militantism'[58] is his tendency to pepper his texts with neologisms and archaic or obscure words,[59] and to unsettle French syntax with calques from the Russian.[60]

In line with the erasure of the authorial figure underpinning Volodine's novelistic enterprise, little paratextual information is available concerning the author himself.[61] Presumably of Russian origin, Volodine was born and educated in Lyons, where he studied Russian and then, working as a teacher, translated into French works by Limonov and the Strugatsky Brothers. Volodine, who now lives in Orléans, made his novelistic debut with *Biographie comparée de Jorian Murgrave* (1985). Setting the tone for his later fiction, the novel casts an alien, who, having suffered persecution on his now devastated planet, is being hounded again on Earth. Since then, Volodine has been exceptionally prolific, creating an œuvre whose scope Bellos compares to Balzac's *Comédie humaine*, and whose originality and constructedness the critic equates with those of Perec's novelistic puzzles. The cycle of texts that Bellos calls 'one of the strangest and most compelling literary projects of modern times', and that, in Jean-Didier Wagneur's words, has shown 'exceptional narrative genius',[62] comprises over forty titles published under five different pen-names.[63] Further aliases are still to come, promises Volodine, who, like the character Lutz Bassmann in *Le Post-exotisme en dix leçons, leçon onze* (1998), considers himself to be a mere spokesman transmitting stories of captive revolutionaries. Having lost their battle against capitalism, these prisoners-writers keep on fighting for their cause, even if it is only with words.

Possibly responding to the original (mis)construction of his writing as science-fiction or as a revival of the *nouveau roman* or Oulipo,[64] Volodine has used both interviews and his metafiction to formulate a theory of what he conceives of as a distinct and cohesive body of work. With the paradoxically entitled and self-theorizing novel, *Le Post-exotisme en dix leçons, leçon onze* (1998), which parodies manuals in the style of Jean-François Lyotard's *Postmodernisme expliqué aux enfants* (1985) / *The Postmodern Explained to Children* (1985) or Alain Badiou's *Thèses sur l'art contemporain* (2003) / *Fifteen Theses on Contemporary Art* (2003), Volodine deters traditional critical approaches to his writing. The novel stages two journalists, Blotno and Niouki,[65] who interrogate imprisoned authors with a view to reporting on the movement of post-exoticism that these authors represent. The resistance to the external attempts to 'domesticate' post-exoticism or, in Wagneur's terms, to 'appropriate a "marginalised" literature in order to falsify it as a "cultural object" ',[66] finds expression in Yasar Tarchalski's reply to Blotno: 'Nous sommes ailleurs, nous ne vous parlons pas, vous m'entendez, Blotno [...] Nul d'entre nous ne communique avec vous !' / 'We are elsewhere, we don't want to talk to you, do you hear me, Blotno? [...] None of us is speaking with you!'[67] That Tarchalski's position is also Volodine's is confirmed by the novel's following metatextual passage: 'il est hasardeux d'analyser production post-exotique quand on emploie les termes que la critique littéraire officielle a conçus pour autopsier les cadavres textuels dont elle peuple ses morgues' / 'it is hazardous to analyse the post-exotic production with terms conceived by official literary critics, made for performing autopsies on the textual cadavers that riddle their morgues'.[68] While here, Volodine defines his writing as alien literature coming from elsewhere, in an interview he calls 'post-exoticism' 'une étiquette fantaisiste qui a l'avantage d'être vide et de pouvoir être remplie par des textes qui vont lui donner un sens' / 'a fanciful label that has the advantage of being empty and of being able to be filled with texts that will give it its meaning'.[69] Dissecting 'post-exoticism', Magdalena Mancas points to the inappropriateness of the prefix 'post-', which, in Lionel Ruffel's view, suggests an end that is simultaneously a beginning. Conversely, as imagined by Volodine, 'l'histoire récente est située dans un avenir lointain, et ne laisse nullement entrevoir les possibilités d'un début' / 'recent history is situated in a distant future and does not in any way envisage the possibility of a beginning'.[70] As for the term's other component, Dominique Viart considers it equally unfitting, 'exotic' denoting what is unfamiliar to Western civilization. Consequently, as Viart convincingly conjectures, 'post-exotic' designates a time when 'la géographie exotique ne le serait plus [. . .]. C'est un monde sans aucune altérité possible [. . .] : un monde entièrement globalisé, réduit à la domination totale, totalitaire du même.' / 'exotic geography will no longer be such [. . .]. It is a world deprived of the possibility of any alterity [. . .]: an entirely globalised world, reduced to total, that is, to totalitarian domination.'[71]

Terminus radieux

The suggestion that 'post-exotic' signifies the erasure of all diversity is strongly invited by *Terminus*, a novel set in a post-apocalyptic universe described as '[l]e même monde en continu' / 'the same world throughout'.[72] Having been largely colonized by the *Second* Soviet Union, this world has now been recaptured by those who are interchangeably named 'fascistes' / 'fascists', 'les ennemis à tête de chien' / 'dog-headed enemies', 'barbares' / 'barbarians' or 'capitalistes agressifs' / 'aggressive capitalists'.[73] Volodine's award-winning novel, which the author himself regards as the apotheosis of his literary achievement,[74] shows – and this is in keeping with the rest of his œuvre – a world that, having reached the end of history, is lying in ruin. After the failure of the nuclear reactors that ensured the self-sufficiency of the Second Soviet Union's towns and villages, kolkhozes have been left to disintegrate, abandoned gulags are melting into what used to be 'l'extérieur concentrationnaire' / 'concentrationary exterior' and, wearing rags, people themselves have been rendered lethargic by both radiation and the despair caused by the revolution's failure.[75] After the enemy captured the Orbise, the remaining defenders of this last stronghold of the egalitarian world have been dissipated into the irradiated steppes, where, though safe from their adversaries, they face lethal gamma rays. Weakened by radiation, Kronauer, Ilyushenko and their dying female companion, Vassilissa Marachvili,[76] break their journey where the steppes meet the taiga, by a deserted *sovkhoz* 'Red Star'. From this vantage point, they observe a stationary train and its passengers, possibly prisoners and their guards. The uncertainty as to the travellers' identity stems from their uniform appearance; all dressed in tattered clothing, the soldiers and the *zeks* seem equally exhausted by their circuitous journey in quest of the gulag where, paradoxically, they hope to be looked after and feel free. Or rather, just like the novel's other characters, these men may already be dead and in the state of *bardo* 'où l'on est soi-même étranger [. . .], ni vivant ni mort, dans un rêve sans issue et sans durée' / 'where you are a foreigner to yourself, [. . .] neither living nor dead, in an unending, endless dream'.[77]

While Ilyushenko joins the search for the hypothetical camp, Kronauer reaches the novel's other key location: a defunct kolkhoz separated from 'Red Star' by a strip of enchanted taiga and named 'Radiant Terminus'. Opposed to the train's shuddering movement is the stagnation of the collective farm, whose inhabitants have achieved immortality through their prolonged exposure to high-level radiation and/or the sorcery of the kolkhoz's shamanic chief, Solovyei, and his common-law-wife, the Grandma Udgul. The collective farm's name is undoubtedly an ironic allusion to the dream of *svetloe budushchee* (radiant future) promised by communist demagogues to Soviet citizens in recompense for the everyday deprivations they endured, and satirized by Alexander Zinovev's novel *The Radiant Future* (1978). In Volodine's book, instead of 'glory' or 'brightness', 'radiant' denotes contamination by deadly atoms, while 'terminus' signifies, as we will see shortly, a dead end where humanity's forward progression stalled or took a backward leap to a horde ruled by a violent and incestuous father. That 'Radiant Terminus' is meant to be a microcosm of the real-life Soviet Union can be deduced from the *kolkhozniks'* references to class warfare, the proletariat and egalitarianism. The USSR's ailing economy and exploitative attitude towards its satellite states are in turn reflected in the fact that 'Radiant Terminus', which no longer produces anything, procures its supplies through theft: Solovyei, whose character alludes to the fabulous figure of *Solovyei Razboynik* (Nightingale the Robber) steals from merchant caravans passing through the taiga.[78]

Finally, as in the actual USSR, where literature was subject to censorship, at 'Radiant Terminus' books considered to be 'counter-revolutionary' or of little ideological import are consigned to the nuclear core now sunk into a two kilometre deep pit.

Watched over by the Grandma Udgul, a veteran liquidator of the Second Soviet Union's exploded nuclear plants, the insatiable core consumes irradiated objects, human and animal cadavers, and, finally, its tireless guardian herself. It is through the trajectories of the Grandma Udgul and Solovyei that Volodine paints a sarcastic picture of the Second Soviet Union, which in fact uncannily resembles the USSR as we remember it. Despite her self-sacrificial dedication to the decontamination of irradiated territories, the Grandma Udgul was constantly troubled by the paranoiac authorities puzzled by her astonishing resistance to radioactivity:

> [E]lle devait [...] se plier à des procédures humiliantes, réécrire son autobiographie pour la millième fois, reprendre à zéro ses autocritiques et [...] se rendre à l'Académie de médecine, justifier son état organique et idéologique devant des commissions ouvrières spéciales [...] qui n'hésitaient pas à l'accuser d'individualisme petit-bourgeois.[79]

> The Grandma Udgul was forced to [...] undergo humiliating procedures, rewrite her autobiography for the thousandth time, do her self-criticism over again, and [...] had to appear at the Medical Academy's meetings [...], in front of special work councils that didn't hesitate to accuse her of petit-bourgeois individualism.[80]

Equally suspect in the eyes of the Party was Solovyei, who, together with his common-law wife, then worked at a school for deaf-mutes. Due to his rebellious poetry and generally defiant attitude, Solovyei languished for many years in camps and prisons, before, ninety years later, becoming the self-appointed president of 'Radiant Terminus'. There, he was reunited with the Grandma Udgul, who became a reluctant curator of Solovyei's 'counter-revolutionary' literary œuvre. The other *kolkhozniks* are the president's three beautiful daughters – Myriam Umarik, Hannko Vogulian and Samiya Schmidt – whose disparate names are the legacy of their three different and 'unknown' mothers. Beside some barely surviving liquidators, the kolkhoz is also home to Solovyei's three emasculated sons-in-law – the tractor driver, Morgovian; the one-armed demobilized soldier, Abazayev; and the engineer Barguzin.

No satire of the real Soviet Union could be complete without a tyrannical ruler. Inspired by the already mentioned half-man half-bird

Solovyei Razboynik, who lives in a forest and stuns strangers with his deafening whistle, the collective farm's president torments his community with ear-splitting shrieks and psychedelic poems broadcast over the kol-khoz's loudspeaker system. While being a reference to the *bylina* 'Ilya Muromets and Nightingale the Robber',[81] Solovyei's ability to enter people's minds and corrode their thoughts and dreams with his hallucina-tory texts is a hyperbole of both the Soviet authorities' unrelenting invig-ilation of citizens' lives and Soviet propaganda, which is indeed closely bound up with the image of loudspeakers.[82] In addition, the sound of a woodpecker resounding in the taiga over which Solovyei reigns may be a playful allusion to the 'Russian Woodpecker', the nickname for the USSR radar system used to disrupt communications and television signals all over the world.

Solovyei's intended timelessness is confirmed by his representation as an enormous *muzhik* straight out of 'un conte de Tolstoï mettant en scène des paysans dont l'apparence et le style de vie n'avaient pas changé depuis mille ans' / 'a Tolstoy novella describing peasants whose appearance and lifestyle had not changed for a thousand years'.[83] As well as figuring him as someone who '[a] échappé à l'écoulement des siècles et à leurs soubresauts, [...] l'invasion mongole, le servage et la collectivisation' / '[has] escaped the course of the centuries and their jolts, [...] the Mongolian invasion, serfdom, collectivization', Volodine inscribes Solovyei into the tradition of taiga shamanism that for centuries resisted religious and ideological pressures.[84] His mythical quality manifests itself equally in his affinity with the despotic ruler of the primal horde famously conceptualized by Freud in *Totem and Taboo* (1913).[85] Like the head of the hypothetical primitive tribe, Solovyei monopolizes access to the community's women, including his own daughters, and condemns the other males to celibacy. But society's course traced by *Terminus* inverts that outlined by *Totem and Taboo*, where, after the sons slay and eat their tyrannical father, the horde metamorphoses into a fraternal clan cemented by a shared sense of guilt and periodic re-enactments of the original murder. Here, conversely, the Second Soviet Union's egali-tarian society has reverted to autocracy, as it did in the actual USSR, which, after a brief spell of democracy, saw a succession of repressive dictators. Thus contextualized, 'le paisible quoique incestueux enfer post-nucléaire' / 'the peaceful albeit incestuous post-nuclear hell' satirizes Stalin's Russia, where mass terror was accompanied by personality cult.[86] Additionally, mirroring Stalin's infamous jealousy of his daughter, Svetlana, the kolkhoz's despotic chief enters into Oedipal rivalry with Kronauer, murders Samiya's husband, Morgovian, and exiles Hannko's husband, Aldolay Schulhoff. With

Schulhoff closely fitting the Jewish stereotype of a dark-haired, wandering and musically talented polyglot, Solovyei's banishment of him closely echoes Stalin's incarceration of Svetlana's Jewish suitor, the film-maker Alexei Kapler.

As well as painting a scathing portrait of the Second Soviet Union and its aberration in the shape of 'Radiant Terminus', Volodine redeploys communist newspeak with palpable irony. For instance, to evidence Ilyushenko's level-headedness, he states that 'il préférait expliquer les bizarreries du monde par le matérialisme dialectique, les manigances criminelles des ennemis du peuple ou les divagations imprévues des plans quinquennaux' / 'he preferred to explain the world's oddities through dialectical materialism, evil plots hatched by enemies of the people, or the unexpected detours of the five-year plan'.[87] Likewise, the absurd-sounding awards that the Grandma Udgul receives – 'Valeureuse Combattante de l'atome' / 'Valiant Combatant of the Atom', 'Glorieuse Liquidatrice' / 'Glorious Liquidator', 'Héroïne rouge' / 'Red Heroine', 'Doyene rouge intrépide' / 'Intrepid Red Doyenne'[88] – playfully mimic the Soviet honour system that, having developed under Lenin, assumed immense proportions under Stalin.[89] All this suggests that, like his defeated protagonists, Volodine himself harbours no illusions as to the potential fulfilment of the revolutionary dream. Yet, like Ilyushenko, Kronauer, or the commander of the unit searching for a welcoming gulag, Umrug Batuyshin, who all uphold communist values despite having lost their struggle, Volodine uses his novels to rekindle the egalitarian dream. His writing can therefore be likened to the rusting red star, which, suspended over the entrance to the *sovkhoz*

> allait persister longtemps là-haut [. . .], pendant plusieurs décennies [. . .], indifférente aux vilenies et aux défaites qui allaient accabler les métropoles, les continents tachés de capitalisme et de sang. Elle va continuer à nous éclairer [. . .], elle va briller encore et encore dans les endroits où nous sommes.[90]

> would remain there [. . .] for several decades [. . .] indifferent to the vileness and defeats overwhelming the metropolises and continents filthy with capitalism and blood. It will keep shining on us [. . .], and on and on over the places where we are.[91]

Conclusions: A Requiem for the Revolution?

The cursory presentation of *L'Archipel* and *Terminus* suggests that the two novelists' writings have few commonalities, at least on the formal level.

For, even if their works are postmodern in terms of their narrative components and sensibilities, Volodine and Makine deploy the narrative strategies of historiographic metafiction, as Linda Hutcheon terms the postmodern novel, in different ways.[92] Despite the typically postmodern metafictionality of Makine's prose and its equally emblematic commitment to the 'losers of history',[93] that is, to those marginalized by mainstream historiography, his novels remain free from postmodern doubt and unseriousness, while only occasionally reaching for the characteristic use of irony, pastiche and parody. Conversely, Volodine's intensely self-reflexive writings are not only populated by 'ex-centrics',[94] as Hutcheon calls those excluded from the history written from the victors' perspective, but are both paradoxical and parodic, in the sense of simultaneously inscribing and playfully destabilizing existing literary conventions. This is evidenced by *Terminus*, which fuses and travesties narrative traditions as diverse as socialist realism, dystopia, science-fiction and the *bylina* into a singular and unexpectedly cohesive and engaging narrative style.

These formal divergences are not, however, necessarily accompanied by a disparity between the values communicated by the two authors' prose. Their most recent novels are, for instance, driven by nostalgia for non-metropolitan spaces, where humans can become reintegrated into their erstwhile living environment and lead a non-violent existence built on the ideals that once motivated the revolutionary struggle for non-hierarchical societies. Incidentally, both authors stage man's return to nature in Russia's coniferous forests, which, like their nineteenth-century predecessors, they portray as an immeasurable space roamed by wild animals. Also, by simultaneously associating it with mortal danger and showing it to be capable of providing men with food and shelter, both texts cast the taiga in a traditionally ambiguous light.[95] In *L'Archipel*, boreal forests are Elken's, and later Gartsev's, ally, while being their pursuers' enemy. Likewise, although in *Terminus* the taiga may temporarily protect Batuyshin's fugitive mother or Myriam Umarik and Barguzin, for Kronauer, whose parents perished during their escape from a gulag, 'la taïga, ça peut pas être un refuge, une alternative à la mort, ou aux camps. C'est des immensités où l'humain a rien à faire. Il y a que des ombres et des mauvaises rencontres.' / '[t]he taiga can't be a refuge, an alternative to death or the camps. It's vastness where man has no place. There is only shadows and bad encounters.'[96] Aligning his representation of the forest with its fairytale figuration as an enchanted space inhabited by fantastic creatures, Volodine paints it as planted with '[d]es arbres hostiles' / 'menacing trees' and 'de[s] traquenards étranges' / 'strange traps' where one wanders in circles, 'comme empoisonné, comme drogué [. . .], comme dans un cauchemar où l'on s'entend ronfler et gémir mais où le réveil n'advient pas' / 'as if poisoned, as if drugged [. . .], as in a nightmare where you can hear your own snoring and moaning, but where wakefulness never comes'.[97] The taiga thus stands in for the state between death and resurrection, a realm where god-like Solovyei is an absolute master. This means that, ultimately, the taiga has a more positive investment in Makine's novel, where it conforms to its customary construction as a place where 'inner darkness' can be confronted, uncertainty resolved and people become once again in touch with themselves.[98]

This restorative process is, in both texts, related to man's efforts to tame his violent instincts, including his sexual impulses, which both authors construe as destructive. If Makine generally depicts sex as non-consensual,[99] L'Archipel openly identifies predisposition to sexual violence as man's primordial and driving force: 'ce violeur logeait en nous, tel un virus, et aucune société idéale n'aurait pu nous guérir' / 'this rapist was in us, like a virus, and no ideal society would have been capable of curing us'.[100] The question of endemic sexual abuse in women's labour camps, which Makine illustrates with a *mise en abyme* description of the extremely brutal gang rape and murder of a female *zek*, comes up in the context of the soldiers' pursuit of Elken. With rape being among its objectives, their hunt acts as synecdoche for man's urge to dominate and possess, an urge that L'Archipel passionately denounces.

The message carried by Makine's novel is reiterated in *Terminus*, where Kronauer recognizes that it is, after all, 'le langage de queue' / 'language of the cock' speaking through him: 'ce qui remontait des profondeurs [. . .] avait beaucoup plus avoir avec des images de copulation inscrites en lui depuis des millions d'années, avec des fantasmes immémoriaux, des envies de viol, de secousses animales et de tripotages ou de prise impérieuse de vulves' / 'what came from the depths [. . .] had more to do with the images of copulation embedded within himself over millions of years, with immemorial fantasies, urges to rape, animal tremors, and groping or dominating vulvas'.[101] The efforts to curb man's predatory nature undertaken in the Second Soviet Union have proven futile, sexual desire being the common denominator of all men, 'camarades et ennemis confondus, mélangés dans la même boue, les égalitaristes modèles comme les partisans du capitalisme et de l'esclavage' / 'comrades and enemies alike, commingled in the same sludge, egalitarian prigs as well as partisans of capitalism and slavery'.[102] To support this thesis, the novel abounds in scenes of rape and women fearing abuse,[103] all this despite the narrator's belief that relating sexual violence makes one its accomplice. Volodine's novelistic world therefore justifies the incendiary feminist writings produced under the Second Soviet Union and studied by Solovyei's daughters. In Dominique Soulès's view, by construing sex in this way, Volodine derides radical feminists such as Andrea Dworkin or Annie Le Brun, whose work the critic herself judges 'simplificateur, guerrier et sans nuance' / 'simplistic, militant and unnuanced', as well as corrosive for consensual sex.[104] Soulès's interpretation becomes debatable if we remember that, while systematically denoting sex using expressions such as 'faire le rut' / 'to rut' or 'faire du mal' / 'to hurt', and linking it to the woman's death,[105] Volodine's novel – as does indeed *L'Archipel* – valorizes positively only platonic relationships like that between Kronauer and Vassilissa. Rather than as a condemnation of radical feminism, I therefore decipher *Terminus* as a feminist take on the story narrated by *Totem and Taboo*, where, as corroborated by Samiya's deranged attack on Solovyei, the daughters – and not the sons – rebel against their sexually abusive father, so that they may live with another man or by themselves. Volodine's sympathy for the sexually oppressed female is further manifest in his identification with Hannko Vogulian, who sublimates her sister's gang rape through her writing. Having chosen solitude in the taiga, Hannko dedicates herself to reconstituting the radical feminists' texts which nourished her adolescent imagination. In transcribing from memory Maria Kwoll's (fictional) novel, *Chiens dans la taïga*, Hannko invents forgotten episodes or replaces them with personal experiences, as she does when substituting a generic rape scene with the violence suffered by Myriam. Such an ending of *Terminus* challenges Soulès's reading and implies that Volodine shares Makine's conception of sexuality as the utmost expression of man's desire to oppress the Other.

The two authors' representation of sex is consistent with their evident yearning for a by now extinct sociopolitical reality, which was premised on the erasure of domination, including sexual domination, and which provided a counterforce to capitalism. Having said that, the two writers are, as we have seen, far from idealizing the actual USRR. In *Terminus*, the latter's absurdities are derided through Volodine's caustic depiction of both the Second Soviet Union and its splinter version, 'Radiant Terminus', whose demonic president fervently protects his daughters from male attention while systematically raping them himself. To remove Kronauer or Schulhoff, Solovyei fabricates ludicrous accusations, puts the men on trial in Stalinist style, and tortures, interrogates, banishes or incarcerates them. Likewise, *L'Archipel* foregrounds the Stalinist authorities' brutal treatment of nonconformist individuals, even if the novel ends by blaming the persecutions suffered by Gartsev and Elken on the inherent evil of human nature. Ultimately, however, it is the market economy that engenders the couple's demise, just as in *Terminus* the capitalists are held responsible for the collapse of a value system cherished by the novel's main protagonists, and more specifically, for the rape and assassination of Kronauer's wife. In brief, what the two novels bemoan is the post-exotic – to use the term in Viart's sense – homogeneity of today's sociopolitical reality, without, however, losing sight of the limitations of communism, which was once its alternative. Crucially, in their criticism of the global expansion of liberal democracy, neither writer specifically confronts the vagaries of today's Russia. Instead, the two novelists prefer to dwell in a historical space that, despite its inanities and cruelties, Makine visibly considers preferable to a Westernized Russia, and that Volodine regards as superior to a generalized post-Soviet end-of-history realm.

CHAPTER 8

Fictions of Self

Shirley Jordan

Que l'autobiographie est fiction : of course. Il ne saurait en
être autrement.

Of course autobiography is fiction. It could not be otherwise.

Jacques Roubaud, *Peut-être ou la nuit de dimanche* (2018)[1]

Debates about the fictional nature of self-narrative and the relationship
between materials of very different factual status within autobiography or
memoir are far from new. This chapter explores the reach and role of
fiction within contemporary life-writing in French, where practices of and
controversy about *autofiction* have assumed a distinctive cast and particular
intensity in recent years. My title, 'fictions of self', gestures towards an
emerging consensus among practitioners and consumers of self-narrative
alike that imagination and fact are not opposites; no longer, as Mary
Cappello puts it in a recent study of creative non-fiction, 'weary binaries',[2]
but mutually supportive, differently legitimate routes to self-investigation.
Indeed, it is precisely the seepage of imaginary material into life-writing in
French that renders it such rich terrain, exciting the imagination of writers
and readers alike.

There are two obligatory stopping-off points in any account of the
evolution and stakes of contemporary life-writing in French. The first is
Philippe Lejeune's now famous statement on the 'autobiographical pact',
which focuses on reader-writer relations and roots life-writing within an
ethical framework of truth-telling.[3] The second is Serge Doubrovsky's
coining of the term *autofiction* to characterize his psychoanalytically driven
self-narrative *Fils* of 1977.[4] *Fils* threw into question the premise of the
autobiographical pact, posited alternative modes of authorial integrity, and
paved the way for what is currently a vast spectrum of experimental
practices, generating an array of labels: *autobiografiction, autobiofiction,
phautofiction, témoignages fictionnels* and the somewhat disparaging *auto-
friction* are just some examples.[5] *Autofiction* and its associated debates have

become a hallmark of the French literary scene, foregrounding with particular intensity philosophical and epistemological propositions about knowledge, self-knowledge and the discontinuous self in life-writing,[6] and probing what undoubtedly remains the special kind of investment required of both author and reader of such works. If Lejeune's 'pact' has been thrown into question and readers have been re-educated to engage with self-narrative on less stable terms, the production and reception of such texts remain nonetheless potentially fraught with all manner of discomfort, doubt and mistrust. Special kinds of betrayal and indignation still linger (productively) around the writing of lives, as some of the examples elaborated in this chapter will discuss.

Semi-fictionalization has proved especially fertile in the case of experience that is hard to express and that challenges ordered articulation. Its communicative power is recognized by authors who write as 'shattered subjects'[7] struggling in the wake of trauma. Accounts of a discontinuous self, which confuse fiction and fact in response to traumatic memory, have a precedent in Georges Perec's *W ou le souvenir d'enfance* (1975) / *W or The Memory of Childhood* (1988), one of the foremost examples of a 'fiction of self'.[8] Perec's multi-layered self-narrative problematizes (Holocaust) memory, resorts to conspicuous fictionalization as compensation, and invites readers to locate in his story's fictional strand screen memories that steer us towards a psychoanalytic reading. More recently, Philippe Forest resorts to *autofiction*, in order to write about the death of his child, demonstrating like Perec that what a writer invents can be as revealing of the self as what they record as 'fact'.[9] Contemporary French literature is particularly notable for a high concentration of women's experimental self-fiction,[10] much of which explores traumatic material, and I shall briefly focus on this important trend for the remainder of my introduction.

Consigning to history the fragility of their earlier position within autobiography demarcated as a male pursuit, women writers have claimed ownership of the genre with singular energy, and have helped to bring about and to feminize the recent 'return to the subject' in French literature. Key female practitioners whose corpus is entirely constructed around the problems of self-fiction include Chloé Delaume, Christine Angot and Sophie Calle, who is perhaps known primarily for her work as a visual artist. All three seek, in different modes, to convey traumatic or disturbing material. Delaume's writings shunt the reader-writer relationship into new spaces, offering a succession of self-reinventions through the use of avatars in response to witnessing the brutal death of her parents. Angot's interconnecting texts progressively create a splintered life-narrative, caught on the cusp between fact and invention, which is shot through with the trauma of father-daughter incest, and which records and produces relationships fraught with doubt and betrayal.[11] Calle's more playful works take the form of intimate installation exhibitions and phototexts that are poised between fact and fiction, often curating (rather than narrating) deeply felt and troubling episodes from her private life, and playing sophisticated games of hide-and-seek with her 'consumer'. We might also cite Camille Laurens, whose shift from the writing of fiction to the writing of *autofiction* was prompted by the death of her newborn son, giving rise to *Philippe* (1995). Long-established women writers whose literary achievements are not first and foremost associated with *autofiction* also experiment with its possibilities. Thus, Hélène Cixous's forays into life-writing are described by Mairéad Hanrahan as 'semi-fictions', snagged between fact and imaginative elaboration.[12] It is also worth noting that Cixous's work draws intensively on material from dreams, and we might well ask what the status of dream material is within a life narrative: is the elusive life of the mind during sleep, with its allusive relationship to waking life and its surreal characteristics, 'truth' or a 'fiction' of the self? Finally, self-fiction is relevant even in the case of Annie Ernaux, France's most canonical experimental female life-writer, who sees her pursuit in terms of the social sciences and determinedly resists the label of *autofiction*. In Ernaux's most recent work, *Mémoire de fille* (2016), it is nonetheless clear that the author's writing about her awkward younger selves is predicated on a discontinuous view of selfhood, and is a process of discovery driven by the imagination as much as by memory, which brings the self into being in new ways.[13]

Two recent studies of women's life-writing in French explore in particular the powerful connections between self-fictionalization and apprehensions of risk.[14] If owning intimate experience feels risky for women, then the production of doubt may be a useful sidestep, releasing it from private ownership and allowing the author to achieve some distance from it while retaining the intensity of a deeply felt first-person account. To pause on one example, in Angot's writing truth and fiction are not necessarily agonists, but often pull in the same direction in the interests of expressing something vital about the inner world of the autobiographical subject. When, in *Léonore, toujours* (1994), Angot describes how her infant daughter Léonore falls off a chair and dies while her mother is absorbed in her writing, we freeze in horror.[15] The incident turns out to be 'untrue' on a literal level, although it has truth value in terms of Angot's early experience of mothering (and trying to write). This fiction of self, a rehearsal of every mother's worst nightmare, gives sharp insight into the intractable meld of love, responsibility, guilt and fear that are a part of becoming a mother.

While Cappello describes creative non-fiction in American life-writing as 'by and large a white, middle-class genre',[16] French-language writing boasts more culturally diverse practitioners. Women's life-writing composed in Algeria during the *décennie noire* of the 1990s, a period of civil war marked by the escalation of Islamic fundamentalism and the widespread abuse, torture, rape and murder of women, is produced in a specifically risky context, since a writing woman, deemed ideologically aberrant, writes at the risk of her life. Névine El Nossery explores how writers such as Assia Djebar, Latifa Ben Mansour, Leïla Marouane and Malika Mokeddem produce 'fictionalized testimonial', inventing stories that are generated by real-life experience, and that constitute counter-histories addressing the period's violent excesses.[17] Here, the delicate points of slippage between lived experience and invention serve to establish truths about what is particularly unspeakable in a culture and political climate where women are intensively silenced. The violent writing of Marouane in *Le Châtiment des hypocrites* (2001) and *La jeune fille et la mère* (2007), for example, forges powerful accounts of rape from the point of view of the victim, harnessing allegory, metaphor and the fantastic, while Mansour incorporates within fictional frameworks factual material, political analysis, psychoanalytic introspection and journalistic reporting.

The remainder of this chapter moves away from a focus on gendered identity and trauma, turning instead to examine two recent fictions of self whose starting point, rationale and status are quite different from those already discussed. Here, fiction is seized upon not as a way of navigating hard-to-express experience which resists narrative, but rather in order to sharpen our focus – sometimes playfully, sometimes caustically – on the production of knowledge about the writing subject. My chosen texts, one by celebrated Oulipian writer Jacques Roubaud, one by the notoriously private writer of fiction Marie NDiaye, prod persistently at the very idea of the textual construction of a life and deploy self-fiction as a provocation through which the author's traces are not only revealed but also insistently covered. Both reflect, and bring us to reflect, upon the complexity of what American life-writing theorist Paul John Eakin regards as everyday self-invention;[18] both highlight the fictional dimension of their accounts by drawing on the novel and declaring this generic affiliation in their title; both engage overtly with a range of conventions of life-writing, including autobiography, memoir, biography and hagiography, and enjoy troubling the lines between them. Finally, both raise the question of what we think 'fiction' in life-writing is, and where its outer limits might be.

Jacques Roubaud's Little Fires

Jacques Roubaud, poet, mathematician, member of Oulipo and prolific writer of generically indeterminate texts in prose, has produced several complex works that take on the challenge of, but are not confined by and cannot entirely be defined as, autobiography. His forays into life-writing include the multi-volume *Le grand incendie de Londres* (1985–1987) / *The Great Fire of London* (1991), an ambitious project published over a twenty-year period, which foregrounds repeatedly the relationship between truth-telling and artifice and elaborates, according to Alison James, 'a new kind of autobiographical contract', wherein 'Roubaud's explicitly stated principle of truth-telling (*véridicité*) generates a complex and paradoxical strategy, based on a form of sincerity that foregrounds itself as artifice and constraint.'[19] In the current chapter, I explore some of the ways in which Roubaud's latest contribution to life-writing, *Peut-être ou la nuit de dimanche* (Brouillon de prose) *Autobiographie romanesque*[20] (*Perhaps or the Night of Sunday* (Draft in Prose) *A Novelized Autobiography*; henceforth *Peut-être*), builds on and furthers such preoccupations.

Peut-être concerns the author's life and self, his attempt to set down in writing something about them while taking account of his conviction that 'toute autobiographie est en grande partie fictive'[21] / 'any autobiography is largely fictional', and his experimentation with possible models for so doing. The work is an extraordinarily good fit with the description of creative non-fiction provided by Cappello: 'a laboratory for testing the boundaries that divide spheres, modes, and genres of living, thinking and writing', which is in formal terms 'more often assembled, collaged, combined, and improvised'[22] than arranged as linear narrative. *Peut-être* selects only one or two aspects of Roubaud's past with which to experiment, and is in no sense a complete life story. It elides, for instance, the painful material related to the mourning of his first wife Alix, with which he grapples throughout *Le grand incendie de Londres*. It is in addition and very conspicuously a late-life work: the writer's ill-health and vulnerability are foregrounded throughout, both thematically and formally, and, given the challenges posed by his failing memory, in terms of a compensatory recourse to invention. Performative and playful, this is the self-reflexive record of a writer creating a work which is deeply concerned with the dynamics of self-narrative, which is littered with acknowledgement of notable practitioners (from Montaigne to Christine Angot), which has an autobiographical cast to it, yet which attacks autobiography's conventions even as it adopts them. Alluding to Roubaud's metaphor of the self-destructive text in *Le grand incendie de Londres*, James notes that this work 'bears the intended title [...] of an unrealized novel that would have tied together a vast project of mathematics and poetry', and that what Roubaud ultimately produces is 'simultaneously a metatextual reflection and a destruction' of that projected work.[23] My analysis of *Peut-être* pursues the idea of incendiary intent, not by considering any great conflagration of traditional autobiography, but by tracing the ways in which Roubaud sets multiple little fires throughout his text, repeatedly requiring us to watch him damage, or even destroy, the fragments of autobiographical narrative that he has bundled together to constitute his 'life story'. In order to demonstrate the tension between the production and the loss of narrative in *Peut-être* and the ways in which it repeatedly tests the elasticity of truth and fiction in life writing, I will focus on just a few telling features: the establishing and typographical material (the title, preface and fonts); accounts of the distant past; self-portraiture in the present; and the psychoanalytic thread uncovered by Roubaud as he writes, which raises the notion of a 'core' self.

The title as set out on the book's front cover, and reproduced approx-imately here, already demonstrates that the author struggles with commit-ment to the traditional conventions of autobiography, yet does not want to stop [us] thinking with them:

PEUT-ÊTRE
OU
LA NUIT DE DIMANCHE
(Brouillon de prose)
AUTOBIOGRAPHIE ROMANESQUE

With this opening gambit, Roubaud performs a delicious micro-drama of feigned indecisiveness, clearly setting out not an 'either/or' but an 'and/ and' approach. The first three lines, printed in red, express a perception of urgency, proposing one title then another, pointing us first towards a meta-autobiographical treatise on doubt (perhaps), then towards the author's particular memories of Sunday night(s) when, it turns out, he had romantic trysts with a girl called Esperliette during his youth. Next, and as if further to trouble any of our coalescing assumptions, we learn that the work is to be ragged, a (very drafty) draft or '*brouillon*' (we later read that Roubaud also considered as alternatives 'esquisses' / 'sketches';

'ébauches' / 'rough drafts'; and 'embrouillamini' / 'muddle').[24] The formal choice is to be prose, although the text to come is often poetic and includes many references to poems and meditations on the merits and properties of both prose and poetry. Finally comes the generic denomination 'autobiographie' (so this *is* an autobiography), once more in capitals (but in black because maybe not so urgent?), with the qualifying 'romanesque' (so fictional, or like a novel in nature). Roubaud's performative title, then, carries out a thoroughgoing destabilization of bounded genres and practices even before we open his book.

The following two-page preface begins with the self-conscious deployment of a classic autobiographical trope, as the author, aware of his advancing years, resolves to look back over his life: 'je décidai d'essayer de m'exercer à l'autobiographie. À mon âge (quatre-vingt-quatre ans), et dans mon état (plutôt précaire), il était temps.'[25] / 'I decided to try my hand at autobiography. At my age (eighty-four), and in my state of health (rather precarious), it was about time.' Roubaud's tongue is firmly in his cheek here, for as we have seen, this is far from his first foray into autobiography. Thus, his text begins on a fiction of self, an ironic position vis-à-vis the genre and its conventions. Next comes affirmation of the writer's conviction that autobiography is fictional. Finally, we are introduced to the complicated array of fonts used to distinguish the various '« modes biographiques »'[26] / '"biographical modes"' adopted. Times Roman is used for the first 'fragment romancé'[27] / 'fictionalized fragment' of his life, up to 1966, and Times Semibold for accounts of the remaining years. Gill sans Light denotes the exploration of conscious memories and elaborates a psychoanalytic strand revealed little by little, which lends the project a dimension of suspense. For the author's writing diary – probably the most factual and certainly the most immediate portrait of Roubaud – the font is Archer; and for ongoing meditations about the status of the unfolding work, the layers and degrees of truth that it harbours, the complexity of time and tenses, 'le New Baskerville'.[28]

What elements of *Peut-être* ask us to consider it as a fiction of self? While the formative episodes that we expect of autobiography, the account of how the mature individual has become what he is, are included, they are so undercut with irony, parody or doubt that they cannot be taken at face value. Thus, chapters 1 and 2, which present material from the author's schooldays – the Sunday night love trysts with *Esperliette* and a decisive encounter with his father, which set him on course for a career as a mathematician (both Times Roman) – are so heavily interrupted by reflections on memory, on factual veracity, on the author's (lack of) authority to talk with any degree of certainty about past incarnations of the self – that they in fact approach the function of the final (New Baskerville) font. Sensitive to the contingency and phenomenology of the writing present, they emphasize lack of knowledge and a necessarily speculative and hesitating bent. While a convincing scene is painted of a young man sitting on a bench at 139, avenue Jean-Jaurès in Paris's nineteenth *arrondissement* on a warm summer evening in the 1950s, the account is factually fuzzy:

> Juillet, août. Plutôt août. Une nuit d'août de l'année 1952. 1952 ? Pourquoi pas ? Qui décide ? Qui objecterait ? Personne. Tels sont les droits imprescriptibles de la fiction romanesque.[29]

> July, August. Let's say August. An August night in 1952. 1952? Why not? Who decides? Who would object? Nobody. Such are the imprescriptible rights of fiction.

It is unmoored, too, in terms of pronoun and tense: 'Derrière ton dos il y a un hôtel. Derrière moi, il y avait un hôtel [. . .] Je suis là, j'étais là.'[30] / 'Behind your back there is a hotel. Behind me there was a hotel [. . .] I am there, I was there.' Should the author plump for first-person immediacy or investigative self-distancing (both in any case forms of artifice)? Further, since he cannot reconstitute in memory the staircase, which after all must have been there to lead him back to the street after his tryst, Roubaud decides 'Je [. . .] sautais les deux étages'[31] / 'I leapt down two storeys'. This is a move reminiscent of Marguerite Duras's elaboration of the fictionalized photographic self-portrait in *L'Amant* / *The Lover*, where, unable to remember which shoes she might have been wearing, she determines that it must have been the gold lamé high-heeled ones.[32] Here, Roubaud raises the issue not of truth but of truth value. After all, such a leap is entirely consistent with the excitement of a young man about to walk home reciting poetry after a summer evening love tryst. Some such certainties are, while completely unverifiable or even obviously fabricated, unshakeable: 'je n'en sais rien, mais j'en suis sûr'[33] / 'I don't have a clue, but I'm sure of it'. Ultimately, however, the romance plot with which Roubaud launches his self-narrative and kindles our interest in his younger self is abandoned, undercut by the declaration of its fictional status. Of the hotel and bench, Roubaud writes: 'leur existence n'est qu'une existence de narration, qui seule la garantit'[34] / 'their existence is no more than a narrative existence, which is their sole guarantee'.

Roubaud's unrelenting exposure of autobiography's artifice surfaces, too, in his elaboration of a (fictional) psychoanalytic thread, an enduring subliminal motivation which takes root in childhood, accounts for his behaviour and choices in adult life, and is discovered only as he writes. This relates to the birth of his brother and the sense that he was no longer his mother's favourite. The realization that there are advantages to being the youngest of a group gives rise to a 'compulsion benjaminienne persistente'[35] / 'a persistent compulsion to be the youngster', and the replication of this position in friendship groups and even in his recruitment to the Oulipo collective. After congratulating himself on this find, Roubaud at once recasts it not as an illuminating self-discovery, but as (merely?) 'un bon moteur fictionnel'[36] / 'a good fictional device' that will help to hold his fabricated self together on the page in what is after all 'qu'un roman, que brouillon d'un roman même'[37] / 'only a novel, indeed only a rough draft of a novel'.

The sole dimension of *Peut-être* that remains untroubled by the vagaries of memory and that has the stamp of directness is the life-writing subject's current world, the phenomenology of which is vividly present. Roubaud creates a powerfully embodied self-portrait, that of a weak, physically vulnerable old man just out of hospital following one of a series of operations. We understand that fragmentation, sketchiness, muddle and recourse to invention are determined in part by his failing body, unreliable memory and sense that time is short. Thus, fictions of self emerge as an important dimension of late-life self-narrative, privileging the pleasures of reimagining what has been and relishing the inevitable malleability of the life lived. Such fictions have, in addition, demonstratively compensatory or restorative functions. If this frail, elderly man records the banal, even bathetic details of everyday life in his now restricted world (pacing the small apartment to keep his circulation going; taking short walks in the dangerously bustling city streets; stopping off at Marks and Spencer's to buy Cumberland sausages), he nonetheless does so with a fictional flourish. Now the self becomes a great explorer, an urban hero of twenty-first-century Paris or even, given the endurance needed for the repeated indignities and struggles of old age and sickness, a legendary character such as Sisyphus.[38] In this case, as elsewhere in *Peut-être*, we are brought to consider the truth value and the worth of self-fictional strategies. The final fiction that Roubaud sustains is that of the very possibility of a total, definitive life narrative: should he manage to avoid further surgery, he informs us in his last chapter, he will take up the gauntlet once more, only this time 'je peignerai le tout'[39] / 'I will paint the whole thing'. Roubaud and his reader alike know such a feat to be impossible.

Roubaud's *Peut-être*, then, rather than narrating a life, illustrates how we invent ourselves on a daily basis, always pressing forward in a trajectory that combines verifiable, imagined and projected images of the self, including the self we have been or would like to be, and the self we imagine others think we are. The life-writing subject, splintered, fragmented, changeable and elusive, asserts with every line not only the ungraspable complexity of life, but also the value of artifice in arriving at something approaching 'truth'. And, to return to the metaphor of destruction by fire, if Roubaud systematically kindles doubt, imperilling autobiography's reliability at every turn, the little fires that he repeatedly sets illuminate with singular intensity the dynamics of life-writing as a fiction of self.

Marie NDiaye's Autofictional Fragments

Like Roubaud's *Peut-être*, NDiaye's *La Cheffe, roman d'une cuisinière* / *The Cheffe, A Cook's Novel* (henceforth *La Cheffe*) explores life-writing as fiction, but with a particular focus on the self that is created by others against the author's will, and as an ironic response to the way in which literary celebrity makes commodities of writers, not only of their books.[40] The tension between engaging with the mechanisms of fame and keeping them at bay has been pronounced throughout NDiaye's career. Unlike Roubaud, she has sought persistently to dismiss autobiographical recuperation of her work, remained tight-lipped in interviews and succumbed only reluctantly to the economy of visibility that is required nowadays of major writers. Nonetheless, the legend of the shy mixed-race girl from a modest background who left school one day to find the editor of a major publishing house waiting for her, contract in hand, and went on to win the *Prix Goncourt* – France's most prestigious literary award – has taken root in the public imaginary. The author's private self has repeatedly been sought and 'found' within her fantastical fictional œuvre, as critics have attributed to her a range of experiences lived out by her protagonists, notably those related to social class, gender, family relations, motherhood, and especially race and belonging in the universalist, colour-blind French Republic.

Considering concealment and performance as negotiated by major writers, Margaret Atwood proposes wryly a 'cloak of visibility' (a sly twist on the 'cloak of invisibility' from the Harry Potter universe).[41] NDiaye first dons this cloak in the experimental phototext, *Autoportrait en vert* (2005), whose intricate fictionalization of aspects of her life and richly uncanny mode direct the reader teasingly and conspicuously along the axes between autobiography and fiction, not least via the text's perplexing visual material, which is composed of photographs of (white) strangers entirely unrelated to the author's life.[42] Noelle Giguere analyses *Autoportrait en vert* as NDiaye's response to the risks of self-definition and as a dilution, fragmentation and unsettling rather than a stabilizing of identity: in short, a self-portrait that undermines its own declared purpose.[43] If Doubrovsky considers *autofiction* as offering a deeper understanding of self, NDiaye seizes upon it instead to direct us away from the figure of the author. A decade later, with *La Cheffe*, her fiction of self is resumed from a very different angle.

At once an oblique self-portrait, a sophisticated and nuanced consideration of how celebrities become public property and projections of various kinds of desire, and an elaboration of NDiaye's poetic art, *La Cheffe* takes the form of a biography – or would-be hagiography – in the making: 'Je voudrais tracer une Vie de la Cheffe comme on écrit une Vie de Saint' / 'I should like to map the Life of the Cheffe as one writes a Saint's Life', says the narrator, adding regretfully that the *Cheffe* would have found this ridiculous.[44] The novel stages an attempt to reconstruct, posthumously, the life of a female chef, whose lowly beginnings in a family of poor agricultural workers seem an unlikely springboard for her extraordinary success – not least in the gender-unbalanced world of *haute cuisine*. Sent to be a maid in a bourgeois household, the girl discovers a passion for cooking that becomes a vocation, and goes on to own a restaurant in Bordeaux, *La Bonne Heure*, which is ultimately awarded a Michelin star. The unnamed male narrator, a commis chef both devoted to and enamoured of her, is now self-appointed spokesperson and custodian of her public image. His interlocutors, whose voices we never hear but intuit, are the avid interviewers whose probing propels the narrative along, drawing out the *Cheffe*'s life story from this key witness and seeking to unearth marketable nuggets. The novel opens in medias res with the narrator's response to an implied question about the secret of the *Cheffe*'s success: 'Oh oui, bien sûr, c'est une question qu'on lui a souvent posée'[45] / 'Oh yes, of course, she was often asked that question', and continues throughout in the same vein, its focalization and structure clearly essential elements in NDiaye's mature consideration of the stakes of celebrity.

La Cheffe is notable for its conjoining of a range of biographical acts and invites various readings. One might, for instance, pick over the self-narrative of the commis chef, for although this is not his purpose, his own life story is constructed gradually and obliquely as he fabricates a portrait of his idol. Or one might trace the dilemmas of biography: the narrator affirms and depicts, speculates and invents, questions the validity of his observations and occasionally agonizes over the ethics of his position as he divulges for imminent public consumption (and presumably for a fee) the life of a woman whose reclusiveness and privacy he claims, paradoxically, to value. The kinds of meta-consideration present in Roubaud concerning layers and levels of knowledge and the problem of reliability are thus also prominent in this novel. Finally, *La Cheffe* implicitly invites us to read it as a fiction of self that narrates NDiaye's own rise, and attitude, to fame. Its title, like Roubaud's *Peut-être*, is a clue to the reading contract that will emerge. It lays claim explicitly to fictional status as a novel (*La Cheffe*), whose author is a cook (*une cuisinière*). As the latter term is in the feminine, it directs us to NDiaye and not to the (fictional) biographer/narrator. The title, then, refers us twice to NDiaye: first, through grandiloquent confirmation of her public status (we note the capitalized 'C' of *Cheffe* throughout the text); second, through quieter reference to her creative activity (a *cuisinière* is simply a person who cooks for a living). A ludic, double self-narrative is thus created, in which the reader's appetite for information about the author is, as in NDiaye's other works, at once whetted and diverted. Here, I focus briefly on shared characteristics between NDiaye and her fictional avatar; her allusions to literary creation and reader-writer relations; and finally, what appear to be references to specific books and their reception.

Ambitious, ascetic and devoted to her art, the *Cheffe* is unmovable in her privacy, clinging to her worktop with both hands rather than be paraded before diners or food critics. She intends the encounters in her restaurant to be not with her but with the dishes that she prepares, delicate offerings intended to nourish and even to change those who consume them, and is ready to struggle 'pour empêcher qu'on lui desserre les dents par la force'[46] / 'to prevent anyone forcing her to open her mouth'. This fiction of self, then, reveals NDiaye's awareness of her reputation as a puzzlingly recalcitrant interviewee. It also evokes her evolving poetic art. If the youthful author was prone to syntactical pyrotechnics, even producing a novel that consisted in a single, unbroken sentence,[47] so the *Cheffe*'s first dish was a needlessly complicated, pretentious set piece: a chicken first emptied of, then stuffed with its own flesh. Does NDiaye, like the *Cheffe*, feel a lingering regret about this early desire to dazzle? The later creations of both, while unusual, are instead sober and subtle. We note the *Cheffe*'s ambition to modify her clients' taste and seduce them into appreciating her particular kind of difficulty; her distaste for a cuisine that is easy on the

palate; her disgust for extravagance; her struggle with the 'vieux et profond
désir pour un dénouement sucré'[48] / 'ancient and deep desire for a sugary
ending'; and her determination to engender new relationships with food
and its combinations, such that her restaurant would be remembered by
clients as a place where 'une énigme leur avait été posée'[49] / 'they had been
faced with an enigma'.

Reader-writer relations are also alluded to via the novel's persistent
contrast of two levels of lexis: on the one hand, hyperbolic praise and
rarefied analyses, which the *Cheffe* despises as 'indécents and superflus'[50] /
'indecent and superfluous'; on the other, terms that promote an ethics of
modesty, related to the inflexible 'état de sincérité'[51] / 'state of sincerity'
that the *Cheffe* requires of herself. Here, NDiaye carves out an opportunity
to pass somewhat acid comment on the vagaries of critical reception: while
the *Cheffe*'s 'gigot d'agneau en habit vert'[52] / 'leg of lamb dressed in green'
is her most talked about creation – a signature dish deemed emblematic of
her style – she does not value it so highly herself and is resentful of public
opinion about it. It is hard not to see here a reference to the aforementioned *Autoportrait en vert*, a work which has attracted much critical
attention, yet which is undeniably less challenging than the author's much
meatier novels, implicitly referred to here as '[des] plats qui exigeaient
d'elle plus de travail et de talent'[53] / 'dishes that demanded of her more
work and talent'.

If we are to read *La Cheffe* as a self-fiction about literary celebrity, an
especially telling insight is the heroine's negative reaction to being awarded
a Michelin star:

> Elle joua le jeu [...], répondant à quelques journalistes, remerciant *le
> Guide*, bien que, toujours, ce fût à sa façon, élusive, contractée, à la fois
> équivoque et brève, qui a fait croire à beaucoup qu'elle n'était pas intelli-
> gente, que sa pensée remuait lentement, qu'elle n'avait pas de vocabulaire.
> Personne n'a su qu'elle était ravagée de honte.[54]

> She played along [...], replying to a few journalists, thanking the *Guide*,
> although still in her own elusive, tense manner, at once equivocal and brief,
> which led many people to think that she was unintelligent, not a quick
> thinker, and with no vocabulary.
> Nobody knew she was consumed with shame

Is this culinary accolade an allusion to the Goncourt prize? Was NDiaye's
reaction to her national consecration one of dismay? Scant possibility now
of eluding the prurient public gaze, even if the very Frenchness of the

award was the acme of praise for an author whose classically chiselled prose has been seen as a strenuous bid on the part of a young mixed-race female writer for belonging in a largely white, male national canon. If the *Cheffe* finds the terms of popular enthusiasm for her work debasing and compromising, then might winning the *étoile* represent a personal failure, a tipping-over into the mainstream? The author clearly holds out such an interpretation to her readers.

In *La Cheffe*, then, NDiaye devises a fiction of self, in order to explore explicitly for the first time the unreliable construction of a life narrative, and to satirize the production of her own public persona by competing voices within an intrusive, rapacious media machine. This unusual text encourages us to identify its protagonist as an avatar of NDiaye, yet at the same time to think about the fragility of the exercise in which we are involved: after all, we learn very early in the text that the *Cheffe* 'aimait qu'on fasse fausse route à son sujet'[55] / 'liked people to get the wrong end of the stick about her' and 's'ingéniait à brouiller les pistes'[56] / 'did her utmost to cover her traces'. Ultimately, however, one cannot help but feel that NDiaye's peculiarly ingenious take here on the writing of lives allows her to have her cake and eat it. If, as the ever-bedazzled narrator affirms, the *Cheffe* was disinclined to 'travailler à former sa légende'[57] / 'work at crafting her legend', her real-life counterpart appears on the contrary deliberately to undertake – and indeed to relish – such crafty crafting in her novel.

Conclusion

In a much cited study of French women's autobiography entitled *Autobiographical Tightropes*, Leah Hewitt asks what it means to write on the perilous 'mobile borderline' where fact and fiction interweave, and explores the writing subject's need for a fictional self.[58] In the current chapter, written some thirty years later, I have referred to women's life-writing in French as a field where this need for self-fictionalization is still more pervasive and urgent, and have located one of its most specific functions in recent decades: the exploration of trauma. I have also made the more general point that the truth/fiction binary inherent in Hewitt's key trope has lost some of its critical purchase, both in the case of women writers and in this (sprawling) field as a whole. The various writer/reader pacts constructed by French postmodern life-writing from both male and female authors have sensitized readers to the truth value of the imaginary and fostered reading habits that cling less determinedly to the binary divide. I have argued that Roubaud's *Peut-être* and NDiaye's *La Cheffe* draw these developments forcefully to the reader's attention, their restless experimentation offering knowing dramatizations of the status and range of life-writing projects in French literature at the current moment.[59]

CHAPTER 9

Trauma, Transmission, Repression

Max Silverman

In recent decades, contemporary fiction in French has been reinvigorated by works that deal with questions of violence, trauma and memory. These works – many of which relate to the Holocaust, but also to other sites of extreme violence, such as the Algerian War of Independence, slavery and the Rwandan genocide – have often been influenced by the broader theoretical debates about art, catastrophe, trauma and the telling of history.[1] How can fiction respond to traumatic events, what is the relationship between history and memory, who gets to define the past, and how does a fiction of trauma deal with questions of complicity, guilt and justice? Recent literary responses to these questions show fiction's complex engagement with histories of violence, and demonstrate the ongoing relevance of literature to our encounter with pasts that have not passed. This chapter will approach this complexity and range through a consideration of seven works by Charlotte Delbo, Georges Perec, Patrick Modiano, Didier Daeninckx, Thierry Jonquet, Nancy Huston and Boualem Sansal. It is organized in four sections, each one addressing a range of the above issues: testimony, fiction and writing; spectral memory and the city; crime fiction; and interconnected memories.

Testimony, Fiction and Writing

Charlotte Delbo's Aucun de nous ne reviendra *(1970)* / None of Us Will Return *(1995)* and *Georges Perec's* W ou le souvenir d'enfance *(1975)* / W or the Memory of Childhood *(1988)*

The French historian Annette Wieviorka named the post-War period 'l'ère du témoin' / 'the era of the witness'.[2] She was referring to the role of testimony of those who survived the camps of the Second World War in shaping our collective understanding of the Holocaust. From the liberation of the camps onwards, however, the need to bear witness to atrocity by

167

survivors was never far removed from the question of how to transmit testimony. In the preface to the most famous of French survivor testimonies, *L'Espèce humaine* (1947) / *The Human Race* (1992), Robert Antelme is acutely aware of the gap between experience and language, and between what is felt in the body and explanation:

> Et dès les premiers jours cependant, il nous paraissait impossible de combler la distance que nous découvrions entre le langage dont nous disposions et cette expérience que, pour la plupart, nous étions encore en train de poursuivre dans notre corps. Comment nous résigner à ne pas tenter d'expliquer comment nous en étions venus là ? Nous y étions encore. Et cependant c'était impossible. À peine commencions-nous à raconter, que nous suffoquions. À nous-mêmes, ce que nous avions à dire commençait alors à nous paraître *inimaginable*.[3]

> From those very first days, however, it seemed impossible to bridge the gap we discovered between the words at our disposal and that experience which, for most of us, we were still living through in our bodies. How could we resign ourselves to not trying to explain how we had got to the state we were in? For we were still in that state. And even so it was impossible. As soon as we began to tell our story we choked over it. Even to us, what we had to tell then started to seem *unimaginable*.[4]

The dilemma highlighted by Antelme immediately after the end of the Second World War becomes the crucial question for survivors of the camps (and, as we shall see in the case of Perec and others, for the children of survivors or those who did not survive): how can language represent a traumatic experience faithfully when language is, as Cathy Caruth observes, 'always somehow literary'?[5] It took Charlotte Delbo twenty years before she could address this question publicly when she published her trilogy *Auschwitz et après* (1970) / *Auschwitz and After* (1995) on her experience as a political prisoner in Auschwitz and Ravensbruck and its aftermath.[6] In the epigraph to the first volume in the trilogy, *Aucun de nous ne reviendra* / *None of Us Will Return*, which I will discuss here (henceforth *Aucun de nous*), Delbo presents this dilemma in paradoxical terms: 'Aujourd'hui, je ne suis pas sûre que ce que j'ai écrit soit vrai. Je suis sûre que c'est véridique.' / 'Today, I am not sure that what I wrote is true. I am certain it is truthful.'[7] Through subtle shifts in tense and degrees of certainty, and a play on words ('vrai'/'véridique'), she acknowledges both the need to be truthful and the problematic nature of telling the truth.

There are other moments in the text when the narrator steps back from her narration to comment on the writing of the narrative in the present, and the consequent dangers of transforming Antelme's '*inimaginable*' into fiction: 'Et maintenant je suis dans un café à écrire cette histoire – car cela devient une histoire.' / 'And now I am sitting in a café, writing this story – because it is turning into a story.'[8] Here, the past of experience (the 'énoncé') and the present of writing (the 'énonciation') are confounded, and the lines between testimony and fiction become blurred. Chronological time dissolves into something more indistinct ('Nous avons perdu le sentiment du temps.' / 'We have lost all notion of time.').[9] Almost a third of the thirty-three short sections which comprise the text as a whole are related to time: 'Un jour' / 'A Day', 'Le lendemain' / 'The Next Day', 'Le même jour' / 'The Same Day', 'Le matin' / 'The Morning', 'Dimanche' / 'Sunday', 'Le printemps' / 'Spring'. Yet the repetition of the same elements across the different sections has the effect of disrupting the distinctions of linear time and questioning the categories themselves as reliable markers in the organization of reality. The particularity of 'place' is subject to the same challenge as that of time. In the example of writing in the café, Auschwitz and Paris are confounded at the same time as past and present. Elsewhere, dead bodies laid out in the snow at Auschwitz remind the narrator of a tailor's dummies seen on a hot summer's day in Paris, and the spring foliage in Paris of the narrator's youth is confused, ironically, with the season of rebirth in the camp.[10] The opening section of the book, 'Rue de l'arrivée, rue de départ' / 'Arrivals, Departures', describes a place – 'the station' at Auschwitz – where the familiar opposition between 'arrival' and 'departure' is incommensurable with the reality of that site, as this is a place where 'ceux-là qui arrivent sont justement ceux-là qui partent' / 'those who arrive are those who are leaving', where 'on n'arrive pas' / 'there is no arriving', where '[l]a gare n'est pas une gare. C'est la fin d'un rail' / '[t]he station is not a railroad station. It is the end of the line', and where '[c]'est une gare qui n'a pas de nom' / '[t]his is a station that has no name'.[11]

Delbo's fear that the 'inimaginable' will simply be distilled into a familiar narrative leads her, then, to reject the narrative conventions of realism and, instead, adopt modernist devices to create what Michael Rothberg has called a 'traumatic realism', as if trauma has permeated the familiar and the known and shocked language out of its representational mode.[12] Words are stretched and float uncannily between the known and the unknown as dichotomies fail to fix them in their familiar place. Hence, distinctions between life and death, dream and reality, women and men, Jew and non-Jew, speech and silence, and prose and poetry are destabilized, and the reader is immersed in a strange third space. Let us look at just two examples of this practice: the everyday and the extreme, and the singular and the plural.

The disturbances of time and place mentioned above mean that here and there (Paris and Auschwitz), and then and now (the time of the camps and the time of the present of writing) are no longer clearly delineated. The portrayal of the camps that emerges from these ambiguities is, thus, not simply one of a hellish other world, but that of a strangeness produced by an overlapping of the commonplace and the extreme. The resemblance between a dead body in the camp and a tailor's dummy on the streets of Paris is perplexing: they are not the same, but neither are they completely different. In fact, they occupy a realm between sameness and difference, the realm, that is, of the uncanny. This could be said of all other aspects of camp life: a leg (but detached from a body), thirst (but not the sort we know in everyday life), a tulip (but in the garden of a member of the SS), fertilizer (but made up of the ashes of human remains).[13] Delbo's writing is informed by surrealism's strange juxtapositions and its defamiliarization of the everyday; by David Rousset's seminal work *L'Univers concentration-naire* (1946) / *The Other Kingdom* (1982), itself informed by the proto-surrealism of Alfred Jarry, in which the camps and society are not two separate worlds but profoundly connected;[14] by the work of the poet, novelist and survivor of Mauthausen concentration camp, Jean Cayrol, whose screenplay for Alain Resnais's film on the camps *Nuit et brouillard* / *Night and Fog* (1955) opens with the lines, '[m]ême un paysage tranquille [. . .] [peut] conduire tout simplement à un camp de concentration' / [e]ven a peaceful countryside [. . .] can lead quite simply to a concentration camp',[15] and whose theory of concentrationary, or Lazarean, art defines the strange place 'between two worlds' of the 'rêve éveillé' / 'waking dream';[16] by the work of the Frankfurt School of political philosophy, for whom the Holocaust is not an aberration in the Enlightenment version of progress and civilization in modern Europe but a product of it.[17] Delbo's text is disturbing because it refuses to separate the Holocaust from everyday life and makes us think about similarity and difference, and distance and proximity, in challenging ways.

Delbo uses Brechtian alienation devices to establish a dialogue between the everyday and the extreme. She finds in the practices of the 'nouveaux romanciers' / 'new novelists' of the time (Alain Robbe-Grillet, Claude Simon, Marguerite Duras, Michel Butor) the radical tools of narration for challenging the dichotomy between inside and outside the camps. She applies these tools especially to the narrating voice of her text. Slippages between pronouns in the text shatter the stable ego and render fluid the distinctions between the singular and the plural ('je'/'nous') and the personal and the impersonal ('je'/'nous'/'il y a'). In similar fashion, the identity of the addressee slides between a personalized but unspecified 'nous' and 'vous' and an impersonal reader. Hence, just as the frontiers between testimony and fiction and the everyday and the extreme are blurred, so the line between a singular and collective voice is ambiguous, and the intended recipient of the text is both particularized and universalized at the same time. The fragmented and floating nature of the voice forestalls all attempts to answer definitively the question, 'whose story is being told and who is the "nous" in the title?' The last lines of the text – 'Aucun de nous ne reviendra. Aucun de nous n'aurait dû revenir' / 'None of us will return. None of us should have returned' – contain, in microcosm, the repetitions, slippages in time, paradoxes and ambiguities that characterize the text as a whole.[18]

Georges Perec writes not as a survivor but as the child of those who did not survive the war (his mother was murdered at Auschwitz and his father died as a soldier during the war itself). His response is therefore that of the next generation, those for whom the Holocaust has not been experienced directly but transmitted through family ties and other means, the generation that Susan Suleiman calls the 1.5 generation and that Marianne Hirsch has described in terms of 'postmemory'.[19] Perec's work is, however, just as ambiguous as regards the relationships between testimony, fiction and writing as that of Delbo. In *La Disparition* (1969) / *A Void* (1995), a 300-page novel that Perec wrote without using the letter 'e', the most common letter in the French alphabet, the missing vowel is, paradoxically, only made visible as an absence. What cannot be spoken – the 'e' whose French pronunciation resembles 'eux' / 'them', the parents who disappeared during the war – thus contaminates the writing as a whole, a metaphorical gesture to the absent presence of the parents that writing is made to embody. In *W ou le souvenir d'enfance* / *W or the Memory of Childhood*) (henceforth *W*), Perec reworks the theme of the absent presence through the epigraph 'pour e' / 'for E' at the beginning of the text, and also by placing, on a blank page at the centre of the text, the typographical mark of an ellipsis, '(...)', a visible textual sign which references what is missing.[20] In this 'elliptical' way, the unbearable wound and trauma of the missing parents is registered as an absence – what cannot be spoken directly but is always allusively and obliquely present. Language is made to play a paradoxical double role: it cannot show what has disappeared (no full testimony is possible), yet it must bear the imprint left by the disappeared on its figurations.

Doubling features prominently throughout *W* in this Janus-like way. Neither of the two narrative strands of the text – the 'autobiographical' first-person narrative and the 'fictional' third-person narrative – is sufficient in itself to tell the whole truth (that is, neither is 'self-sufficient'), as each has left its invisible mark on the other. The 'fiction' of the island of W, where athletes compete for glory, turns into the 'real-life' horror of the camps, while the 'real-life' accounts of the narrator's youth grow more and more 'fictional'. If 'impersonal' history ('Histoire avec sa grande H' / 'History with a capital H')[21] is incapable of telling the truth, because of its inevitable gaps and silences, 'personal' memory is equally as unreliable, as it cannot help falsifying the past. It is only in what Perec calls the 'fragile intersection' between the two narratives[22] that we are able to read a writing that, in Michael Sheringham's words, 'is attuned to the reality of loss', as it embodies its own gaps, and gestures allusively to what it cannot say.[23] Two narratives, two Gaspard Wincklers, two mothers called Cécile, the doubled quest for identity itself (Gaspard on a mission to rediscover the original Gaspard, whose name he has taken, and the narrator in search of his past), the two 'v's which make a 'w', and so on, all problematize the binary opposition of 'the double' by playing on similarity and difference. The title of the novel is itself the prime example of this: is the 'ou' / 'or' to be read as the choice between different stories, or does it signify the same story being told in different ways? This is an oxymoronic text, in which apparent opposites are reconfigured in a composite, yet ambiguous, form. Allegory, too, is Perec's modus operandi, as its founding principle is that one story can only be told through another.[24]

As with Delbo's work, Perec's text explores the difficult encounter between writing, trauma and loss. Trauma and loss are figured symptomatically in the text as a wound on the body, whose source and location are constantly displaced from one part of the body to another, and from one body to another: a broken arm, a cut hand, a hernia, a broken scapula, the deformities of athletes on W, being hit as a child with the tip of a ski, a bee sting, a bobsleigh accident. The scars that these have left on the body are like the marks of writing, as both constitute the visible traces of an open wound. Perec writes, '[J]'écris parce qu'ils ont laissé en moi leur marque indélébile et que la trace en est l'écriture; leur souvenir est mort à l'écriture; l'écriture est le souvenir de leur mort et l'affirmation de ma vie.' / 'I write because they left in me their indelible mark, whose trace is writing. Their memory is dead in writing; writing is the memory of their death and the assertion of my life.'[25] Here, Perec notes the double function of writing: it is both the mark of the open wound and of loss and, like the scar on the body, the mark of the healed wound and support in the face of loss. Hence, the arm in a sling, the post-hernia truss and the braces which act as a parachute in the Charlie Chaplin comic book are, like writing itself, a prosthetic means of suspension from the void.[26] The ellipsis at the centre of the text is, thus, not simply a sign of what is missing but also a support against that loss as, in French, the ellipsis is known as 'points de suspension' / (literally) 'suspension points'. Although writing cannot resolve grief or bring about closure, it can provide temporary support, in the way that Freud describes the child's necessary negotiation of separation from the mother through the presence and absence of an object in the game of 'fort/ da'.[27] Writing – as 'ressassement sans issue' / 'reiteration [...] leading nowhere'[28] – becomes the site of mourning and tomb for the dead mother who died at Auschwitz and for whom there is no grave.[29] It is, as suggested by Perec through another play on words, an anchoring (ancrage) of self, effected by the graphic inscriptions (encrage) on the page.[30] Like Delbo, Perec finds a language which references pain and loss obliquely, while recognizing, at the same time, that it is an imperfect substitute for both.[31]

Spectral Memory and the City

Patrick Modiano's Dora Bruder *(1997)* / Dora Bruder *(1999)*

Patrick Modiano's *Dora Bruder* also deals with the paradox of writing an absence. The narrator's quest for traces of a young Jewish girl, Dora, whose brief life was ended in Auschwitz in 1942, yields little factual information. There are very few mentions of Dora in the official archives; history seems to have written out victims of the genocide, in the same way that, in *W*, History 'avec sa grande hache' / 'with its capital H' is responsible as much for forgetting as remembering the past.

The city of Paris, in which Dora lived, is as implacable as history when it comes to yielding its secret past, in that no traces of Dora's life are visible in the present. Paris has forgotten; nobody knows today that 'ce quartier paisible [...] est aussi le quartier des départs' / 'this peaceful quarter [...] is also a point of departure'.[32] So, if the narrator must act like a detective investigating a crime that has been covered up, he will need something other than logic and the powers of deduction to succeed, as reliable information is simply not available. His method is, instead, to walk the streets of Paris and revisit the sites where Dora and her family lived before the war. Marcel Proust will be the narrator's mnemonic guide: as with the epiphanic experience of the 'madeleine' in *À la Recherche du temps perdu*, the past is to be sought not in voluntary memory, but in the sensations and associations related to involuntary memory triggered by place and objects (what Delbo calls 'la mémoire profonde' / 'deep memory'). Or, like a Baudelairean *flâneur*, the narrator will open up normalized city space to the 'echoes' of Dora's presence.[33] André Breton's classic surrealist text *Nadja* (1928) is reworked, so that the sites and objects encountered on the narrator's perambulations are re-enchanted with absent voices and figures, and the city is transformed into a space of spectral presences:

> On se dit qu'au moins les lieux gardent une légère empreinte des personnes qui les ont habités. Empreinte : marque en creux ou en relief. Pour Ernest et Cécile Bruder, pour Dora, je dirais : en creux. J'ai ressenti une impression d'absence et de vide, chaque fois que je me suis trouvé dans un endroit où ils avaient vécu.[34]

> It is said that premises retain some stamp, however faint, of their previous inhabitants. Stamp: an imprint, hollow or in relief. Hollow, I should say, in the case of Ernest and Cécile Bruder, of Dora. I have a sense of absence, of emptiness, whenever I find myself in a place where they have lived.[35]

Ultimately, as this quote shows – and with Proust as guide once again – the imaginative act of writing is the performative process by which the past can be made to return. The surface of the city becomes a palimpsest in which hidden traces re-emerge beneath, or are inscribed on, the visible surface. The palimpsestic writing of the city[36] is referenced here by the same play on words used by Perec in *W*; if, on one level, the 'marque en creux' refers to a site 'hollowed out' by traces of the past, as a pun ('marque encre -ux' / '"inky" mark') it also refers to the capacity of words themselves, of writing, to conjure up what is hidden.

In *Dora Bruder*, walking and writing the city are therefore interconnected processes in the overlaying of past and present. As the past is brought into the present, so a profound connection is established between the narrator and Dora. The sites that the narrator visits in Paris are not only the places inhabited and visited by Dora and her family before the war, but also where he grew up after the war, so that the personal (and historical) memories they evoke are entwined with the reverberating echoes of the Bruder family. The quest for Dora is, thus, also a search for the narrator's own past (especially, as in so many of Modiano's novels, the tortuous relationship with his father), so that the lives of Dora and the narrator intersect on a number of levels.

Just as, in *W*, the writing gives a voice to the silenced and voiceless victim (the mother) while, simultaneously, acknowledging the unbridgeable gap between mother and son, so, in *Dora Bruder*, Modiano creates an ambivalent hybrid relationship between the narrator and Dora, and between autobiography and biography. At times, he must place himself, imaginatively, in her position. At other times, most notably those when Dora disappears, he refuses to fill in the gaps. The narrator is neither the victim nor absolutely different from the victim, but occupies a place between proximity and distance, between identification and separation. Dora's story cannot be told as testimony (she has perished) and yet depends on the narrator as ventriloquist to be told at all: '[S]i je n'étais pas là pour l'écrire, il n'y aurait plus aucune trace de la présence de cette inconnue.' / 'Were I not here to record it, there would be no trace of this unidentified girl's presence.'[37] Similarly, without the reading process, there would also be no trace of the presence of Dora. The text thus constructs a space for empathy for the narrator and reader – that is, those who come after the event – which is not dependent on the binary opposition of sameness and difference. Dora is the spectral other who 'hollows out' the bland exterior of the city in the present, and who estranges the self-presence of narrator and reader, without ever becoming assimilated into either.[38]

Crime Fiction

Didier Daeninckx's Meurtres pour mémoire *(1983)* / Murder in Memoriam *(1991) and Thierry Jonquet's* Les Orpailleurs *(1993)*

One of the genres that Modiano exploits in *Dora Bruder* is that of crime fiction. Crime fiction lends itself particularly well to an investigation into traumatic moments forgotten or repressed by official history. Just as the task of the fictional investigator in a classic *roman policier* is to unearth hidden connections in the quest for truth, so the model can be applied to history to shed new light on the past and its relation to the present. Furthermore, as crime fiction's stock-in-trade is questions of responsibility, guilt and justice, when applied to crimes against humanity that may not have been dealt with adequately (or at all) by the law and the judicial structures of the state, it can reshape our understanding of justice and the law.[39]

Didier Daeninckx's *Meurtres pour mémoire* / *Murder in Memoriam* uses a fictional investigation into the murders of Roger Thiraud and, twenty years later, his son Bernard as a means of exposing the extraordinary career of Maurice Papon (André Veillut in the novel). As the official in charge of Jewish affairs in the Bordeaux region under the Vichy government during the war, Papon collaborated with the Nazis and was directly responsible for the deportation of over 1,500 Jews to the internment camp at Drancy, to the north of Paris, and then to Auschwitz and other extermination camps in the East. In the late 1950s, he was appointed Prefect of police in Paris and, in that post, was responsible for the massacre on 17 October 1961 of over 120 Algerians peacefully protesting in the streets of Paris against the introduction of a curfew for Muslims at the height of the Algerian War of Independence.[40]

The text opens on the day of the massacre with short portraits of Said Milache, Roger Thiraud and Kaira Guelanine. Said and Roger are killed (although for different reasons), and Kaira is injured and then arrested by the police. The police bulletin the next day mentions three dead, sixty-four wounded and 11,538 arrests. Although the narration is in the third person, the perspective is that of the characters, thus giving the impression of a personal testimony by unarmed civilians in the face of a brutal attack by the forces of the state. The juxtaposition of horrific force on unarmed protestors and the bland police statement the next day highlights the falsification of historical events by the state. Daeninckx uses this structure throughout the novel to expose the gap between a violent reality and its official representations. During the course of his investigation into the deaths of Roger and Bernard Thiraud, Inspector Cadin becomes aware of the silences and euphemisms in the official records. As in *Dora Bruder*, the archive is not the guardian of objective history but an official means of dissimulating the truth.[41] Cadin must read beyond the formal apparatus of the state to piece together a reality that has been suppressed. Bureaucracy is not neutral; it is, instead, shown to be a systemic form of violence. Veillut's role in the deportation of Jews to the transit camp of Drancy was as 'un simple fonctionnaire' / 'a simple civil servant', who acted '[n]i par conviction politique, ni par antisémitisme, mais tout simplement en obéissant aux règlements et en exécutant les ordres de la hiérarchie' / 'neither by political conviction, nor by anti-Semitism but, quite simply, by obeying the rules and carrying out the orders passed down to him'.[42] As Hannah Arendt said of the leading Nazi Adolf Eichmann at the time of his trial in Jerusalem in 1961, evil can be banal, simply a question of making sure the trains run on time.[43]

Daeninckx uses a subgenre of crime fiction ('roman noir' – *noir* fiction) as a way of writing history 'from below' (of the sort pioneered by the British 'new left' historians E. P. Thompson and Raphael Samuel in the

1960s), a counterhistory which reveals a past that has been written out of official versions of history and a violence that has been performed on voiceless minorities. Daeninckx's method for constructing a counterhistory is twofold: either personal memory is pitted against the state's official history (as in the opening section of the novel), casting doubt on the conventional distinction between the two;[44] or the historian must engage in the sort of detailed critical research that Roger Thiraud undertakes on Drancy, unearthing (like an archaeologist) layers of time to reveal how the housing estate constructed on the site in the late 1930s ('la cité de la Muette') was, under the Occupation, transformed into a detention centre and concentration camp for Jews from 1942 to 1944.[45] Not only does this use of the 'roman noir' create a counterhistory; it can also play a part in the future direction of history. In a remarkable example of life imitating art, the detail revealed in the novel became instrumental in bringing Papon to justice in the 1990s and tried for crimes against humanity (1997–1998). It was also one of the early works to draw attention to the true import of the events of 17 October 1961.

Thierry Jonquet also uses the 'roman noir' as a counterhistory to official history and a means to retrieve buried memories of the past. In *Les Orpailleurs* – or 'The Gold Panners' – Nadia Lintz and Rovère, respectively, the 'juge d'instruction' / 'examining magistrate' and the senior policeman investigating a series of murders in which the victim's hand has been severed, are taken on a journey through the Parisian underworld and, ultimately, back to Auschwitz-Birkenau. The ruby ring that has passed from one of the eventual victims to another is the major device that drives the intrigue and its historical contextualization; it is a clue that will help piece together the jigsaw of the different murders and the means to draw the plot back to the Holocaust.

The hidden history that unfolds in this way represents a challenge to conventional histories of the Holocaust and questions of complicity and justice. Regarding the first of these, the transfers of the ring from one hand to another establish a series of links between crime in contemporary Paris and the genocide almost fifty years before, the effects of which are to draw the past into the present and overlay one space with another. As suggested by Modiano's spectral memory or Delbo's uncanny superimpositions of the everyday and the extreme, not only are our concepts of linear time and compartmentalized space disturbed in this way, but also our understanding of the history of the Holocaust. By displacing the protagonists from the centre of Paris to the desolate site of Birkenau, and by showing the connections between the Parisian drug and imported meat trades and the gold digging by Polish peasants at the former camp (those who are seeking to profit from the abandoned possessions of the victims of the genocide), our concepts of the temporal and spatial parameters of the Holocaust are problematized. None of this is apparent in the museum at Auschwitz, which presents a simplified narrative of the Holocaust, just as the archive in *Meurtres pour mémoire* falsifies the past. Nadia and Rovère have to go to the unmanaged and non-museified site of the adjacent Birkenau for a more complex historical network to emerge.

The same disturbing connections between apparently separate spaces, times and actions affect our understanding of complicity and justice. Who are the 'orpailleurs' of the title? Are they only those Poles at Birkenau who seek to profit from the genocide, or is the term to be applied to all those who, through their association with objects like the ring, have profited in more indirect ways? The peripeteias of the plot broaden out notions of complicity and guilt by spreading the dark history of genocide across the landscape of Europe. How can a formal sense of justice deal with this expanded notion of complicity? The novel does not provide an easy answer to this question. It does, however, point out the shortcomings of a blinkered legal framework and emphasizes the importance of the affective approach, which official justice (like official history) must repress. Nadia's interest in the murders is not simply a professional one, but also a personal one, prompted by the discovery of her father's complicity in the round-up of Jews for deportation and the appropriation of their belongings. This remains a family secret (at least for Nadia; her husband and mother have known about it for years), thus paralleling the larger collective secret of the extent of collaboration and complicity in France, first revealed by Marcel Ophuls's documentary *Le Chagrin et la pitié / The Sorrow and the Pity* (1969). Nadia's parents can clearly be placed in the same category of 'orpailleurs' as the Poles around Birkenau. Significantly, Nadia only tells this personal story after the visit that she and Rovère make to the museum at Auschwitz, so that the staged piety of the official commemoration is juxtaposed with the emotional intensity of the personal recollection.[46] It is also Nadia's personal friendship with her neighbour and Auschwitz survivor, Isy Szalcman, and her empathy with his memories of the past, that shape her sensibility towards the crimes she is investigating. The personal retribution that lies behind the murders committed is not completely endorsed in the novel; yet it does highlight a sense of justice that cannot be satisfied by the law itself.

Interconnected Memories

Nancy Huston's L'Empreinte de l'ange / The Mark of the Angel *(1998)* and
Boualem Sansal's Le Village de l'Allemand, ou le journal des frères Schiller
(2007) / The German Mujahid *(2008)*

By fictionally retracing the career trajectory of Maurice Papon from complicity in the Holocaust to responsibility for the brutal assassination of Algerians in Paris in 1961, Daeninckx's *Meurtres pour mémoire* reveals hidden connections between the Holocaust and colonialism. In the epilogue to the novel, Daeninckx condenses this process in a metaphor in which adverts on a wall at the Paris Métro station Bonne Nouvelle are being removed by Algerian workmen to reveal parts of a notice pasted by the Nazis at the time of the Occupation.[47] Daeninckx's palimpsestic image has profound consequences for the reading of history and memory across temporal, national and ethnocultural boundaries.[48]

In the 1950s, many French left-wing intellectuals who supported the Algerian struggle for independence compared the brutality of French forces in Algeria, especially their use of torture, to the practices of the Gestapo during the Second World War. Jean-Paul Sartre, for example, famously pronounced 'Colonialisme là-bas, fascisme ici : une seule et même chose.' / 'Colonialism there, fascism here: one and the same thing.'[49] Yet this was also the refrain of many victims of colonialism. In his critique of colonialism *Discours sur le colonialisme* (1950) / *Discourse on Colonialism* (1972), the Martinican poet and politician Aimé Césaire said that Hitler's real crime was to apply to Europe 'des procédés colonialistes dont ne relevaient jusqu'ici que les arabes d'Algérie, les coolies de l'Inde et les nègres d'Afrique' / 'colonialist procedures which until then had been reserved exclusively for the Arabs of Algeria, the "coolies" of India and the "negroes" of Africa'.[50]

In recent decades, the relationship between different moments of extreme violence has been hotly debated, especially centring on the unique or comparable nature of the Holocaust.[51] Those who oppose the 'connective' mode believe that analogies dilute the singularity and, hence, import of the event itself. Some suggest that to view the Algerian War of Independence through the prism of the Holocaust is a form of what Freud called 'screen memory', whereby one memory (in this case, the Algerian War of Independence) is a proxy for another (the Holocaust), thus diminishing the specificity of the substitute in relation to the more painful memory that it hides.[52]

Beyond the analogical mode, however, there is another way of seeing histories of violence not as distinct and discrete but profoundly interconnected. The case of Papon, who learnt his trade first in Vichy France during the war, then in colonial North Africa after the war and, finally, back in Paris in the late 1950s and 1960s, seems to suggest that, in historical terms, the links between the genocide of the Jews and colonialism (what Hannah Arendt called 'the subterranean stream of Western history')[53] are, indeed, there to be made. In terms of cultural memory, these connections are, perhaps, clearer still. Cultural memory studies today invariably describes the transnational, transcultural and multidirectional nature of memory in an age of globalization and the ceaseless movement of capital, culture and communications.[54] Two works that can be approached in this way are Nancy Huston's *L'Empreinte de l'ange* / *The Mark of the Angel* and Boualem Sansal's *Le Village de l'Allemand, ou le journal des frères Schiller* / *The German Mujahid*.

In *L'Empreinte de l'ange*, the interconnections between different traumatic events are effected through the relationship between Saffie, a twenty-year-old German woman whose father was complicit in the Final Solution during the war, and Andràs, a Hungarian Jew who lost most of his family to the Nazis, and then had to flee Hungary in 1956 at the time of the Russian invasion of his country. The action in the narrative traces their affair in Paris through the late 1950s up to the events of 17 October 1961. How are connections between different moments of extreme violence treated? Andràs seems to have a cyclical view of history, in which the same violence repeats itself in different contexts:

> Je sais ce qui se passe ! Autour de Paris, déjà, les camps de concentration pour les musulmans ! [. . .] *Ça continue !* Les rafles, les ratonnades, c'est les mêmes Scheisskopfe qui les font ! Les gens qui torturent à l'Algérie, ils ont appris leur métier ici, avec la Gestapo ![55]

> I know what's going on! Already, near to Paris, there are concentration camps for Muslims! [. . .] *It's still happening!* The people who arrest the Muslims now, they're the same Scheisskopfe that deport the Jews in '42! The French generals who torture in Algeria now, they learn their job here – with the Gestapo![56]

At times, Huston presents this endless cycle in terms of a fairly static model of victims and perpetrators, as for example in the contrast between the family backgrounds of the two men in Saffie's life: the French lineage of her husband Raphael, and his family link to colonial exploitation in Algeria, in opposition to Andràs's foreign and Jewish heritage, with his family link to victim-hood of Nazism and communism. This dichotomy is rather crudely underpinned by Raphael's love of the pure and affect-less lines of classical music in contrast to Andràs's passion for the syncopations and fusions of jazz.

At other times, however, the connections between different sites of racialized violence suggest a more disturbing relationality. So, for example, the curfew (for Jews in the war and Algerians in Paris in October 1961) is interrupted as simple repetition by Saffie's memory of the curfew that she experienced as a young girl in Germany during the war.[57] Rather than a simple repetition of the same event across history, this treatment shows that the stories relating to the different characters and their sites of trauma tend to intersect on multiple, and often contradictory, levels. This indeterminate relationality cannot simply be captured by a model of the repetitive struggle between victims and perpetrators, or by the analogy between different histories of violence.

The final encounter between Raphael and Andràs, when they are both old men, metaphorically captures this condensation of different planes, similar, in a way, to the final image of the superimposed posters in *Meurtres pour mémoire*. The two men catch sight of each other by chance in a bar at the Gare du Nord. During this momentary glance – which, paradoxically, is held for eternity – Andràs is 'reflété dans le mur de miroirs, de sorte que Raphael le voit à la fois de face et de dos' / 'reflected in the wall of mirrors, so that Raphael sees him simultaneously from the front and from the back'.[58] This image, and the title of the novel, recalls Walter Benjamin's famous commentary on Paul Klee's painting 'Angelus Novus', which Benjamin called the 'Angel of History', where the angel is caught in a moment of apparent movement, its face turned to the past while being propelled into the future by the storm blowing from Paradise.[59] For Benjamin, this is a 'dialectical image' (or, as he says elsewhere, 'dialectics at a standstill', 'a constellation saturated with tensions'): a spatialized encounter between different times.[60] Applied to Huston's novel, the mark of the angel is a superimposition of different traumatic moments, a 'nœud de mémoire' / 'knot of memory',[61] with no resolution or redemptive outcome (in the novel, Saffie's son Emil dies, Saffie herself disappears, and Andràs grows old without ever seeing her again), yet whose paradoxical intersections must be read critically as the work of history in the present.

Contradictory intersections between different histories of extreme violence are certainly at the heart of Boualem Sansal's *Le Village de l'Allemand, ou le journal des frères Schiller*. The German father of the two boys Rachel and Malrich, who was, as an SS officer during the war, an active participant in the Final Solution of the Jews, becomes the victim himself of extreme violence when he and his wife are murdered by the GIA (Armed Islamic Group) in their Berber village in Algeria in 1994 during the bloody civil war. These contradictory positions are passed on to Rachel, who, in trying to come to terms with his father's involvement in different moments of extreme violence, identifies alternately as both perpetrator and victim, until the burden of this conflictual heritage proves too heavy to bear and he commits suicide. Malrich's perspective on the past, which is mediated through his reading of his brother's diary, is different to that of Rachel. If Rachel undergoes a tortuous entanglement with the past through conflicting identifications, Malrich simply equates Nazism and Islamic fundamentalism, in the same way, perhaps, that Andràs sees different histories of violence as repetition of the same in *L'Empreinte de l'ange*.

Sansal's narrative technique, however, casts doubt on a binary opposition between the approaches of the two brothers. Malrich's dedication at the beginning is to the teacher who has corrected his poor French; Malrich's diary often contains long inserts of text by Rachel; Rachel's apparently distinct diary entries are themselves housed within Malrich's broader editing (and his teacher's re-editing) of the text as a whole. In other words, the discrete nature of each voice is always undermined by the intervention of another voice, or other voices, speaking through it. On a broader scale, Sansal's technique highlights the ways in which history and memory are themselves always mediated: Rachel's understanding of and sensibility towards the Holocaust are largely shaped by the legacy of the father (and texts like Primo Levi's poem 'If this is a Man' / 'Si c'est un homme'); Malrich is further removed as his knowledge is shaped by the inheritance of Rachel's diary. Their subject positions as part of the 'post-memory' generation are never stable and discrete, but rather a constellation of different voices and texts. Mireille Rosello describes Sansal's technique as 'un mélange mémoriel spatio-temporel hybride' / 'a mixed spatio-temporal hybrid memory'.[62] In a similar vein, Debarati Sanyal points out,

> [a]lthough we are not invited to identify fully with either Rachel's melancholy sacralization of the Shoah or Malrich's crude instrumentalization, what is powerful in Sansal's experimentation with these approaches is the narrative's map of its alternating voices, temporalities, and histories. It is a map that traces convergences and even intersections – however dangerous – between distinct legacies and regimes of terror without yielding an unproblematic identity between them.[63]

In an age of identity politics, new cultural nationalisms and the 'guerre des mémoires',[64] Sansal's 'dangerous intersections' are controversial. For those, especially, who have a vested political, cultural or national interest in maintaining reductive (and often mythical) ethnocultural memories of the past, arguments that propose the interconnected nature of histories of violence are not always welcome. Sansal's novel is, thus, a risky endeavour that, nevertheless, raises important questions about history, memory, culture and politics.

Le Village de l'Allemand also highlights a central feature of all works of fiction that deal with extreme violence, namely, the cultural mediation of traumatic events and what that means for the concept of witnessing. If one thing emerges from all the works discussed in this chapter, it is perhaps the fact that we are all implicated in histories of violence, and often in highly ambiguous ways.[65] What fiction (even art in general) can bring to the question of our involvement in traumatic events, in ways that are beyond the remit of history and the law, is to disturb and refigure our responses. At its most powerful, it can tell a new story while simultaneously highlighting the dangers, in Delbo's words, of itself 'turning into a story'.

CHAPTER 10

Wretched of the Sea
Boat Narratives and Stories of Displacement
Subha Xavier

Stories about migration in contemporary French literature have prolifer-
ated since the 1970s, due to an acceleration in mass migratory flows which
were sometimes accompanied by a humanitarian crisis, not unlike the
situation Western Europe is responding to today. As migrants seek urgent
asylum from war-ridden countries such as Sudan, Afghanistan or Syria,
their ability to integrate linguistically or culturally into a new host country
factors low in a decision-making process premised foremost on physical
safety and bodily refuge. And so the emergence of a literature detailing
those horrific experiences of migration across an uninviting sea usually
takes another twenty years or more to emerge, once future writers have
settled into their host countries and mastered the required linguistic skills
to then produce the first waves of a new literary corpus. While we thus
await the works that will invariably rise out of today's migratory flows, it is
revealing to reconsider the novels of two of the world's most significant
immigration crises, which culminated in the boat narratives out of Haiti
and Vietnam, beginning in the 1990s. Two and three decades after the
Duvalier dictatorship and the end of the Vietnam/American War[1] propelled or exiled thousands of refugees on to the Caribbean seas and the
Pacific Ocean, French language writers such as Émile Ollivier (*Passages*,
1991), Néhémey Pierre-Dahomey (*Rapatriés*, 2017), Linda Lê (*Les
Évangiles du Crime*, 2007) and Kim Thúy (*Ru*, 2011) have narrativized
the experience of migration across perilous waters in ill-equipped vessels,
recalling for us a harrowing journey in search of more hospitable lands.[2]

Narratives of displacement by land, air or sea are not new to contemporary French literature, but scholarly efforts to categorize them as travelogues, migrant texts or refugee stories take us deep into the heart of the
critical distinctions that mar this type of writing. While the genre of the
travel narrative in French has had a marked history of colonial usage,
scholars such as Romuald Fonkua, Charles Fordick and Aedín Ní
Loingsigh have argued to reclaim it for the postcolonial text.[3] Forsdick

even suggests, more recently, that the term is elastic enough, when considered in its wider cross-cultural and multilingual usage, to describe the journeys of clandestine immigration and crossings by boat between Africa and Europe.[4] Migrant texts, as I have argued elsewhere, detail the experience of migration amidst the push and pull of national frameworks and nationalistic demands on writers, who are constantly negotiating for their work a place inside and outside the political boundaries within which their books are generated.[5] The refugee narrative, April Shemak reminds us, drawing on the UN High Commission for Refugees' legal designation, belongs to the narratives of 'escape and flight', which are also included in 'some of the most urgent and politicized' writings.[6] Of course, literature rarely falls neatly into just one genre, and if all narratives of displacement cross over into some form of at least two of these categories, the last of the three types grants this literature a pressing political character.[7]

Among refugee stories, those of people crowding onto ships and boats in complete desperation, choosing to risk their lives in near impossible crossings – despite the likelihood of being preyed on by smugglers, pirates and ultimately facing deportation – have become a veritable subgenre in and of themselves. Boat narratives are of course not unique to the Haitian and Vietnamese diaspora. There is a growing corpus of texts about African migration across the Mediterranean by Senegalese writers, for example, Abasse Ndione's *Mbëkë mi. À l'assaut des vagues de l'Atlantique* (2008) and Omar Ba's *Soif d'Europe : Témoignage d'un clandestin* (2008). Refugee narratives are a well-rehearsed reality in the North-African context as well, with numerous French language novels about emigration from Morocco, Algeria and Tunisia attesting to this fact.[8]

The designation 'boat people' dates back to a boat full of Haitian political refugees fleeing the Duvalier regime, which washed ashore on the beaches of South Florida in 1963.[9] Nearly a decade later, the term resurfaced to refer to the Vietnamese exodus beginning in May 1975, when, in the aftermath of the Vietnam/American War, the new Vietnamese government established re-education camps, new economic zones and nationalized private enterprise as part of its reconstruction strategies. Rising tensions between China and Vietnam, combined with natural disasters – a severe drought followed by the worst flooding in three decades – resulted in food scarcity, caused an already distraught, forcefully displaced, politically repressed and in some cases imprisoned population of ethnic Hoa Chinese and Vietnamese to take to the sea. The Chinese population of Vietnam was among the first to leave, incited by the government to do so – after other attempts at ethnic cleansing forced some 30,000 of them into re-education camps in 'New Economic Zones' – through the abetting of boat smugglers.[10] Early media coverage of the first boats leaving Vietnam portrayed the refugees as rich ethnic Chinese South Vietnamese carrying gold, and it is mainly to avoid recognizing these evacuees as refugees that the term 'boat people' first came into use in Vietnam and among the nations that would ultimately play host to this fleeing population.[11] The expression was simultaneously invoked to refer to the large numbers of Haitians reaching the shores of Miami by boat in a similar politicized refusal to acknowledge their status as refugees. In this case, the relative wealth of many of the earlier waves of migrants was used to delegitimize their requests for asylum and subsequent requests from more Haitian refugees, arguing that they were economic immigrants looking to improve their living conditions rather than genuine political refugees.[12]

Memorializing the Wreckage

The narratives of displacement detailing these terrifying journeys by Vietnamese and Haitian refugees have perhaps taken that much longer to emerge because of the unspeakable suffering and subsequent stigma attached to their plight as 'boat people'. In the case of Haiti, although a few authors made mention of the phenomenon before the 1990s,[13] most waited at least a decade after the last boats fleeing the Papa Doc dictatorship left Haiti to narrativize the experience. Even Émile Ollivier, a fluent speaker and writer of French at the time of migration, launched his writing career first – detailing and denouncing the political situation in Haiti – before venturing, only some fifteen years later, into the murky waters of the boat narrative. The difficulty inherent to this particular form of literary creation is poignantly summarized by Gaëlle Cooreman's notion of the 'triple disconnect' in this literature:

> [U]ne triple déconnexion, terme qui renvoie en premier lieu à leur dérive géographique, c'est-à-dire la nécessité de quitter l'île natale pour un Eldorado inconnu, qui se révélera toutefois peu hospitalier et même hostile. Deuxième déconnexion, l'écrivain postcolonial s'imposant de donner une voix à ses subalternes, un visage à ces fantômes/enfants dormant sur le fond de l'océan, est inévitablement confronté à l'écart entre lui, l'intellectuel, exilé 'réussi', et ses compatriotes pour qui il s'engage à parler. Finalement, cet auteur doit également affronter la déconnexion entre le vécu terrible des *boat people* et le monde de son lectorat, ignorant, voire indifférent par rapport à celui-ci.[14]

A triple disconnect, a term that refers first to their geographic drift, that is, the necessity to leave their native island for an unknown Eldorado, which reveals itself to be less than hospitable, even hostile. A second disconnect in that the postcolonial writer, attempting to give voice to the subaltern, a face to the ghosts/children sleeping at the bottom of the sea, is inevitably confronted with the gap that stretches out between him/her and his/her compatriots for whom s/he speaks. Finally, this writer must also confront the disconnect between the terrible lived experience of *boat people* and the world of his/her readers, uninformed, indeed indifferent to what they read.

The ethical onus to account for the suffering of those who survive the treacherous journey, as well as the many hundreds, even thousands, who perish in the crossing, is too heavy a burden for any writer to bear, and can only be paralleled with the challenges faced by writers of genocide literature.

Not surprisingly, references to the Middle Passage appear in Ollivier's novel, as they also will in Néhémy Pierre-Dahomey's *Rapatriés* over two decades later, as an eternal and unfinished cycle of crossing, drowning and exile.[15] The title of Ollivier's novel summons this history from the get-go, encapsulated in the book as memorial to a past that is here repeating itself. The boat that the sixty-seven refugees board for Miami in *Passages*, for example, is aptly named 'La Caminante', thereby linking this journey, and the vessel carrying its human cargo, with all those that preceded it. Martin Munro interprets this name, translated as 'traveller', as an ironic 'continuation of historical movement, of unrooted wandering.'[16] From the Spanish verb for walking, 'Caminante' also suggests the slowness and deliberateness of travel by foot. The days on the boat, it seems, linger on and on even as Brigitte Kadmon, the narrator and heroine of the voyage, tries to keep count of every single one. Time itself stands still on the seas, a meaningless string of rising and setting suns that breach their linear logic to reach into the abyss of history and spatially connect those who are separated by it. Time on the seas is adrift, but the boat reunites those who have been lost to the past with those currently on board, all those who have walked – journeyed onwards – along the same path. When the calmness of the water signals ominous weather ahead, the frightened passengers take part in a Vodoun ceremony of song and dance, invoking the assistance of their black African ancestry:

> Nègres de toutes les Nations : Nègre Rada, Nègre Petro, Nègre Ibo, Nègre Nago ! Nègres de toutes les nations : Nègre Mandingue, Nègre du Sénégal, Nègre du Congo, Nègre du Dahomey ! Nous nous inclinons de corps et

d'esprit. Nos os *marchent, marchent, et marchent.* Nous appelons tous les
esprits de l'Afrique. Maîtres de nos démolitions . . .[17]

Negroes of every nation: Rada Negroes, Petro Negroes, Ibo Negroes, Nago
Negroes! Negroes of every nation: Mandingue Negroes, Senegal Negroes,
Negroes from the Congo, Negroes from Dahomey! We bow down in body
and in spirit. Our bones are marching on and on and on. We call on all the
spirits of Africa. Those masters of our wreckage . . .[18]

The walking bones of the dead – 'masters of our wreckage' – and the living
are fused in songs made of 'mots qui avaient voyagé, ces mots de la grande
transhumance, échoués sur les rives de notre malheureux pays' / 'words
that had travelled, those words of the great transhumance, cast up on the
shores of our unfortunate country'.[19] Words, like the bones of their dead
ancestors, make their way through the Middle Passage, braving death to
join the 'boat people' many centuries later. Ollivier's novel takes on the
larger task of memorializing not one, but two great tragedies of history,
reminding his readers of how one forced crossing by black bodies is deeply
enmeshed in the other.

   In a world desensitized to the suffering of silent masses where death is
reduced to numbers, Ollivier interlaces his narrative with references to the
forgotten reality of Haiti's 'boat people'. Two-thirds of *La Caminante*'s
passengers perish on their terrifying sea voyage to Miami, but Ollivier's
twenty-two fictional survivors of the wreckage are brought ashore at West
Palm Beach the morning after another group of surviving refugees, we are
told, washed ashore at Golden Beach. Ollivier weaves the narrative of his
fictional boat people around that of the very real survivors of the boat full
of Haitian refugees that capsized off the southwest coast of Florida on
27 October 1981, when thirty-three people drowned, while the remaining
thirty-four swam ashore to Hillsboro beach.[20] Brigitte Kadmon and all her
surviving compatriots are taken to Florida's notorious Krome Detention
Center, where reports have tallied many decades of abuse, harassment and
intimidation of Haitian refugees.[21] In the voice of Régis, whose identity is
hidden until the very end of the novel, the narrator-collector of migrant
testimonials writes:

   De l'enfermement de l'île à la prison de Krome, de l'inventaire des ratés au
   catalogue des renoncements, le même délicat problème de la migrance, un
   long détour sur le chemin de la souffrance. Passagers clandestins dans le
   ventre d'un navire, nous visitons non des lieux mais le temps.[22]

   From the confinement on the island to the prison at Krome, from the
   inventory of failed attempts to the list of those who refused to depart, it was

all the same problem of migration, a long detour on the paths of suffering. Clandestine passengers in the belly of a ship, we don't visit places, only periods of time.[23]

Régis brings together the lives of migrants and refugees alike in the literal and metaphorical deployment of 'boat people' as a narrative trope for displacement, that is, the endless and painful crossing of time. Steeped in the 'boat people' experience, Ollivier contends, lie the various phases of migration that are nowhere felt as acutely or as horrifyingly as aboard the floating debris of human wreckage, or refugees lost at sea.

Boat Narratives as Anthropophagy

In his reading of *Passages*' timeless drifting at sea, Martin Munro links the passing of time on the boat to Maurice Blanchot's 'le pas au-delà'[24] / 'the step beyond', which comprises 'the ideal temporal state for the act of writing'.[25] Indeed, Ollivier's imaginary inhabits this alternate temporality which takes us from the sea to the page and back again, hence attempting to bypass the 'triple disconnect' through a new continuity of time, consciousness and identities in which the author can also partake. Franco-Vietnamese writer Linda Lê, however, suggests that any retelling of the 'boat people' experience in literary form results in a type of anthropophagy, feeding on human life for its existence. Lê's short story 'Vinh L.' in *Les Évangiles du Crime*, like Ollivier's *Passages*, weaves a *mise en abyme* of testimonial fiction, first through the writing of a plagiarist author who is denounced in a letter by a reader named Vinh L. An epistolary relationship ensues between the reader and the writer, who proceeds to cannibalize Vinh L.'s letters – or so we are told – to create a work of biographical fiction based on them. The narrator, now Vinh L. (or some form of him), recounts his shocking journey aboard a boat of refugees that is lost at sea for over a fortnight. The narrator and his accomplices murder and serve up the flesh of one of the dying men among them. Lê not only reminds us that survival is laden with guilt, tainted by the death of all those who perished along the way, but that the writerly and readerly function of this narrative genre is equally complicit in the deaths that line its literary success.

The parallels Lê draws between anthropophagy and refugee literature – even literature more generally – are realized through the trope of plagiarism, where the proscribed digestion and regurgitation of the words of others are realized in almost imperceptible ways. The more effective the plagiarist, the less likely we are to uncover traces of the assimilated text, let alone even suspect their existence. The boat lost at sea thus reproduces the writer's 'step beyond' time, in which, Lê tells us, egregious, gruesome and inhuman acts are not only possible, they are permissible and justifiable: 'En mangeant la chair de cet homme, j'ai dévoré le cordon ombilical qui me reliait à l'humanité. Pourtant, personne ne me rejette, car personne ne peut affirmer : « Moi, je n'aurais pas mangé ! »'[26] / 'By eating the flesh of that man, I devoured the umbilical cord that connected me to humanity. Yet, no one rejects me, since no person can say: "Me, I would not have eaten!"' Likewise, the letters proceed to cite writers whom the narrator only acknowledges by nationality, not by name, incorporating their words into his text with quotation marks that obliquely recognize the original authors, although not their source texts.[27] These unsanctioned borrowings are all the more well hidden because they appear in translation rather than in their original language of creation. Lê's intertextual references showcase the efficacy of the plagiarized text, just as the language of her short story (French, not Creole, Vietnamese, Lao or Khmer) betrays its potential for manipulation in the service of the literary genre. The proximity between literary plagiarism and erudition and culture is further invoked by the narrator as a pointless way to lessen, even nullify, the barbarism of his murderous act:

> J'encombre mon crâne, je le transforme en bibliothèque, en musée vivant, pour oublier que mon ventre est une morgue. Mais que peut-on attendre d'un homme qui a atteint le dernier degré de la barbarie et qui maintenant grimpe comme un forcené l'échelle de la culture ?[28]

> I cram my skull, I transform it into a library, into a living museum, to forget that my stomach is a morgue. But what can we expect from a man who has reached the last degree of barbarism and who now climbs the ladder of culture like a madman?

Culture and literature are nothing short of stuffing that gorges the guilty and complicit conscience into numbing acquiescence. Vinh L., the survivor/reader, sees into the mind of the plagiarist author as through a mirror, peering back at himself. The crime, in the survivor's mind, has less to do with the act of cannibalism itself than the pleasure derived both in eating and retelling the story. Writing provides a respite away from the turmoil of dehumanizing morals over to the higher plains of intellectual clarity and verbal lucidity, of which the survivor/reader will ultimately partake too: 'Cette boule dure qui pèse sur mon ventre, je vais l'introduire dans le broyeur de la littérature et il n'en sortira qu'une coulée de mots.'[29] / 'This hard lump that weighs on my stomach, I will introduce it into the grinder of literature and out will come only a flow of words.' Writers of boat narratives are expert evaders of life and responsibility, the text reminds us, they sniff the scent of human tragedy without ever breathing it in.[30]

The exploitative nature of boat literature that feeds on the misfortune of victims is repeatedly explored in relationship to the cannibalism of the writer/narrator/survivor, who acted 'pour la bonne cause' / 'for a good cause' and 'pour sauver sa peau et celle de quelques enfants'[31] / 'to save his life and that of a few children'. The use of children to at once heighten and temper the crime is a literary leitmotif that does not escape any of the boat narratives discussed in this chapter. In Vinh L.'s letters, there appear two young girls, one who seeks out the narrator/murderer many years later in search of answers to her amnesiac recollection of the fateful event on the boat. She cannot remember either eating, nor refusing to eat, the body. Another little girl, who watches as her mother's dead body is cast into the sea, later befriends the narrator in a bid to find the exact location of her mother's resting place. Lê paints these poignant couplings of fellow travellers with shared trauma in heartening and disturbing ways. Vinh L., though older and expectedly wiser, speaks kindly but refuses to offer solace to both female characters. Indeed, such negation is a function of the digestive trouble that will henceforth accompany his/their crime. Vinh L. and the unnamed young woman who seeks him out in France also admit to sexual impotency and frigidity ever since their experience aboard the boat. Although they staved off starvation and death, they are forever pursued by malnourishment and sexual incapacity, no longer able to participate in the pleasures of the body. The boat aborts the possibility of any real futures, as the characters are left with only imagined endings to their tale of terror, which they are now condemned to relive in literature and films about endlessly drifting people. The little girl promises to empty out the sea one day to find her mother's resting place,[32] while the young woman exits the text with 'les images d'un film dont elle allait peu à peu s'approprier le rôle principal' / 'the images of a film in which she will slowly assume the title role',[33] much as the narrator does in Lê's short story.

Wretched of the Sea

Néhémy Pierre-Dahomey's first novel *Rapatriés* is the most recent literary installment of the Haitian boat narrative, capturing a reality that continues across the Caribbean Sea to this day.[34] Like Ollivier, Pierre-Dahomey fled to France from Haiti by air, but he fictionalizes the horror of the 'boat people' experience through its deep connections to colonialism, Vodoun spirituality and global migration. Here again, the writer attends to what Cooreman identified as the 'triple disconnect' inherent to boat narratives by creating a story world that explores the refugee experience on the seas in its haunting real-world aftermath. The novel begins with a failed migration by boat whose survivors are deported back to Haiti and transferred to a temporary slum created specifically for them. The shanty town relegated to the outskirts of the city is christened by their shame as 'Rapatriés' / 'Repatriated people'. Pierre-Dahomey's heroine Belliqueuse Louissaint (Belli) attempts a crossing aboard the *Agwéton*, a sailboat preparing to make its last illicit voyage across the Caribbean Sea. The boat, named after Agwé, the loa and great Vodoun admiral of the seas, is piloted by Frère Fanon, recalling the celebrated theorist of decolonization, Frantz Fanon. If these two names alone do not foreshadow the boat's return to the sea and the human struggle to survive, the winds seal their fate. After a stormy night on the ocean, passengers fall overboard and a little girl named Fréda – after the loa of love Fréda Erzulie, also known as La Sirène, the mermaid wife of Agwé – disappears. In an act of hopeless desperation, Belli casts her infant child into the sea while awaiting her own death that will not come soon enough. Deported to Rapatriés after she and others are discovered adrift on the wreckage of the *Agwéton*, Belli starts her life again, but can no longer distinguish – much like Ollivier's and Lê's characters before her – between 'les parts de rêve, de souvenir et de démence'[35] / 'dreams, memories and dementia'. Although she will not return to the water again, Belli spends the rest of the novel trying to stave off drowning. Pierre-Dahomey returns to the trope of death by drowning to describe Belli's struggle to survive in Rapatriés and beyond, as though that 'interminable'[36] / 'endless' night thereafter extends into all time and space, as it did in *Passages*, in 'Vinh L.' and does also in Kim Thúy's *Ru*. Belli now lives in agony of drowning from within:

> Au compte-goutte, une dense solitude tentait de la noyer.[37]
> [. . .]
> Elle sentait dans son gosier s'accumuler des millilitres d'eau salée, comme une petite mer, mais quand elle ouvrait la bouche pour cracher les vagues, rien ne sortait. [. . .] C'était comme si elle se noyait de l'intérieur en même temps que ses glandes labiales subissaient une implacable sécheresse. Noyade et sécheresse, c'était la force terrible de cette angoisse inouïe.[38]

> As through a dropper, a dense solitude was trying to drown her.
> [. . .]
> She felt millilitres of salt water in her throat, like a small sea, but when she opened her mouth to spit out the waves, nothing came out. [. . .] It was

as though she was drowning from the inside at the same time as her labial glands were experiencing an implacable drought. Drowning and drought, it was the terrible force of this unimaginable anguish.

This opposition between the extreme aridity of land and the inescapable danger of the sea leaves Belli, as it did the passengers of *La Caminante*, in a no-man's land. As she slowly descends into madness, trying to reclaim 'des êtres à qui la mer et les circonstances interdisaient l'accès'[39] / 'beings to whom the sea and circumstances forbade access', she is haunted by the primal scene of the boat narrative, the night aboard the *Agwéton,* when she threw her child into the sea. On her deathbed, she summons, '*Agwéton, Agwéton* . . . faites venir Frère Fanon, que je sache enfin ce qui s'est passé cette nuit-là.'[40] / '*Agwéton, Agwéton* . . . have Brother Fanon come, so that I may finally know what happened that night.' Agwé and Fanon close the narrative just as they opened it, in a gesture that ties the boat through Agwé (and Fréda) to the Middle Passage and Africa; and through Frantz Fanon to the psychopathology of the colonized and the 'boat people' of today. The wretched of the earth have become the wretched of the sea.

Pierre-Dahomey creates a powerful portrait of the 'boat people' psyche in detailing the multiple ways in which migrants are *lost* to the sea. The loss of Belli's first child will be followed by others; a daughter succumbs to tuberculosis, another is adopted and taken to France, while a third one is adopted by Canadians. Her eldest and only son disappears, turning into a feared presidential hitman. 'La perte d'un enfant est toujours l'amputation d'une maman'[41] / '[T]he loss of a child is always the amputation of a mother', moans her daughter Bélial's adopted French mother in words that ring far more true to Belli. Each of her living children are separated by seas, carrying with them an emptiness that they cannot fill, much less comprehend. Belli's resilience and resolve are completely worn down when her visa for France is refused. It then becomes clear to her that she will never again be reunited with her children, that she will never be able to make that long desired crossing by sea or by air. Madness in Belli, as in Vinh L. expresses itself as a form of verbal lucidity, the stories flow out of her in captivating ways. Belli's rantings gain her a faithful audience in the capital city among school children and university students, who are amused and enthralled by her. Even as her health declines and her body collapses, her mind enjoys the type of clarity that Vinh L. also relished in the depths of despair: 'Il y a, dans l'extrême malheur, de la jouissance à voir clair.'[42] / 'There is, in extreme misfortune, a pleasure in seeing clearly.' Belli is 'born again into madness'[43] and is rebaptized as Manzè Filo (or Miss Philosophy in Creole) by the populace. When her former lovers go in search of her on the streets of Port-au-Prince, they uncover her new reputation as a speaker of all languages and knower of all things. Manzè Filo is a 'parolière de la rue, celle qui avait eu la conscience brute de sa situation de manque'[44] / 'street lyricist, who has attained a state of raw consciousness around her situation of lack'. From migrant to pariah, motherhood to childlessness, Belli awakens to the consciousness of the wretched of the sea who have looked into the eye of their destiny. For Frantz Fanon's colonized people, for whom the 'la valeur la plus essentielle, parce que la plus concrète, c'est d'abord la terre : la terre qui doit assurer le pain et, bien sûr, la dignité' / 'most essential value, because the most concrete, is first and foremost the land: the land which will bring them bread and, above all, dignity',[45] Pierre-Dahomey's novel, we might argue, posits the open border as that which brings freedom, safe passage and human community to the boat migrant. Upon her final exile back to Rapatriés, a dying Belli loses all ability to speak, she is confined to the silence in which she eternally relives her time on the seas, returning once more to the endless cycle of night that strips her of all lucidity. Left to drown in Agwé's waters, which Frère Fanon can no longer navigate for her, she is a boat migrant abandoned at sea, who gives her child over to the sea so he cannot be taken away from her.

Human Remains

Kim Thúy's novella *Ru* and most recent novel *Vi* return to the Vietnamese boat narrative and the mass exodus of refugees, who made their way from Vietnam to refugee camps in Malaysia and Indonesia while awaiting paperwork for entry by air to countries like the United States, Canada and France.[46] *Ru* takes us along the sinuous pathway of memories belonging to a young refugee girl from Saigon in Montreal. Nguyên An Tịnh boards a crowded boat from Vietnam to a peninsular Malaysian refugee camp and the novel rocks back and forth – like a lullaby – between her stories on land and those at sea, between her departure and flight to safety and her arrival and settlement in Canada. Her boat narrative, unlike the others discussed in this chapter, includes the heart-wrenching account of her family's stay in a camp designed for 200, but occupied by 2,000 refugees. As was the case for many other camps intended for those fleeing Vietnam, and most notoriously the camp in Pulau Bidong that was set up to welcome 4,500 refugees and once sheltered nearly 40,000, the temporary living conditions were shockingly inadequate. Thúy's protagonist is relieved to be among those who are not abandoned, or worse, towed back to sea. Nonetheless, for her it is not simply a question of life over death, but rather a trade-off which she couches in terms of the anonymity of mass drownings:

> Les autres qui avaient coulé pendant la traversée, n'avaient pas de noms. Ils sont morts anonymes. Nous avons fait partie de ceux qui ont eu la chance de se laisser choir sur la terre ferme. Alors nous nous sentions bénis d'être parmi les deux mille réfugiés de ce camp qui ne devait qu'accueillir que deux cents.[47]

> The others, those who had gone down during the crossing, had no names. They died anonymously. We were among those who had been lucky enough to wash up on dry land. We felt blessed to be among the two thousand refugees in a camp that was intended to hold two hundred.[48]

Even at the risk of malnourishment, illness and death at a refugee camp, it is the retention of one's identity that the young narrator privileges in life or in death.[49] Alexandra Kurmann and Tess Do's analyses of *Ru* and other Vietnamese boat stories point to the importance of burial rite practices and rituals of remembrance in Vietnam – without which the dead 'may become "wondering" or "hungry ghosts", specters that do not have family to facilitate, through ritual acts of remembrance, their transformation from the common dead into family ancestors or spirits'.[50] In *Ru*, it is precisely the fear of the common dead or what Valérie Loichot calls the 'unritual' – or 'the obstruction of the sacred'[51] – that drives the will to life of the refugees, as though clinging to what makes them most human. 'The stripping of rituals is a fundamental attempt to uncouple humans from their humanity', argues Loichot.[52] This search to retain one's humanity in the face of the inhuman is what brings the starved and forlorn refugees to lands that are not always as hospitable as one would hope. Thúy's descriptions of the boats, just as those of the refugee camp in Malaysia, point to the extreme insufficiency of the means available to salvage one's threatened humanity when basic human needs are scarcely, if at all, met. Thúy's descriptions of the camp through the narrative voice of Tịnh are an endless quest to find the human in a place that is supposed to restore humanity to those who have scaled the brink of the inhuman, escaping only narrowly. The narrative vignettes return time and again to those 'trous béants remplis d'excréments accumulés par les deux mille personnes du camp' / 'gaping holes filled with the excrement of two thousand people',[53] the nauseating smells, insects and vermin that thrive on human waste. The shelter the refugees build for themselves – secretly cutting down trees in the forest for piles they covered with cheap blue canvas – hardly keeps out the rain as the ground beneath them sinks deeper and deeper into the clay earth. Food is served as rations of rotten fish flung to the ground once each day. Although the passages devoted to the Malaysian refugee camp are few, they are nonetheless some of the most poignant ones of the novel, as the beauty of Thúy's prose accentuates the dissonance between her language and what is described:

> Si un musicien s'était trouvé là, il aurait entendu l'orchestration de toute cette eau frappant la paroi des boîtes de conserve. Si un cinéaste avait été présent, il aurait capté la beauté de cette complicité silencieuse et spontanée entre gens misérables.[54]

> If a musician had been there, he would have heard the orchestration of all that water striking the sides of the tins. If a filmmaker had been there, he would have captured the beauty of silent and spontaneous complicity between wretched people.[55]

So Tịnh imagines another narrator, a musician or a film maker, who might render the abject more pleasing to the senses, in lieu of her failing words. A scene reimagined in hypotheticals exposes language's ability to heighten the contrast between signifier and signified, and therein dampen the reader's ability to recognize refuge when it does not sound like or look like what it is supposed to be.

Scholars and critics of *Ru* have celebrated the novella as an example of 'refugee gratitude'[56] and a model of immigrant integration into Canadian society, all the more so because of the easy parallels between the life of the narrator and that of the author.[57] Yet, as Alexandra Kurmann's reading of *Ru* through Edouard Glissant's concept of 'le Détour' demonstrates, Thúy's writing resists a simple logic of gratitude and praise for her host countries by producing contradictory digressions in descriptions of welcome practices in the text.[58] Ching Selao also points to this important twist in Thúy's debut work by returning to the French meanings of 'ru' in particular, where pain figures prominently in the word's figurative sense:[59] 'In French, *ru* means a small stream, and figuratively, a discharge – of tears, of blood, of money.'[60] Tears, blood and money accordingly line this boat narrative and migrant text, which reads as redemptive only because it falls prey to the nationalistic longings of its host country. Hidden within its language of gratitude lies an experience of suffering that the narrator carries with her throughout. The achievement of the 'American dream' by Tịnh's aunt and step-uncle – who live in a beautiful stone house with rose gardens and travel first class – is therefore interlaced with memories of the Malaysian refugee camp. The same uncle, we are told, crawled more slowly than his eight-month-old daughter because he was suffering from malnutrition, and the same aunt used the one needle she had to sew clothes so she could buy milk for her daughter.[61] Likewise, Tịnh's first encounter with the Canadian delegation at the Malaysian camp is a dehumanizing one. Although she has been learning English for months, the medical examiner does not speak to her. Instead, he tugs on the elastic of her pants to note down her sex. She proceeds to excuse the debasing gesture by invoking the similarity between scrawny refugee boys and girls, adding a few more sentences to further justify her brutal treatment:

> Et puis, le temps pressait : nous étions tellement nombreux de l'autre côté de la porte. Il faisait si chaud dans cette petite salle d'examen aux fenêtres ouvertes sur une allée bruyante, où des centaines de personnes bousculaient leur sceau d'eau à la pompe. Nous étions recouverts de plaques de gale et de poux, et nous avions tous le visage de gens perdus, dépassés.[62]

> And time was short: there were so many of us on the other side of the door. It was terribly hot in the small examining room with its windows open onto a noisy alley where hundreds of water buckets collided at the pump. We were covered with scabies and lice and we all looked lost, beyond our depth.[63]

And yet those few lines condemn everything they appear to explain away. While some people struggle to get water from the camp's sole pump, others, dejected and pest-ridden, wait passively as their bodies are inspected like animals. In juxtaposing the life that awaits them outside the examination room – noisy shoving of people desperate for water and survival at the camp – with that inside the examination room – silently dehumanizing medical exam by outside country – it is at once clear why the narrator and her compatriots allow themselves to be subjected to such violence. Although it is on land, the refugee camp still reads as an extension of the boat narrative, as its inhabitants flee its oppressive and menacing confines for all that remains of the human.

Boats and Books Still Adrift

We can only read boat narratives from the Haitian and Vietnamese diaspora as a harbinger of many more literary voices still adrift at sea or making their way on land to their writerly end. As readers, critics and scholars, these texts confront us with our own anthropophagic nature, our perverse fascination with the wretched of the sea and our calculated desire to count rather than ritualize the dead. Boat narratives and stories of displacement by sea search for what remains of the human in the memorialized wreckage of human remains. In years to come, more stories will undoubtedly emerge in French from the refugees of Calais and Dunkirk, the migrant Roma camps in France and Europe, the multitude of asylum seekers at Canadian borders, and the many survivors of lethal boat journeys across the Mediterranean each day. Vietnamese and Haitian boat literature challenges our imaginary around forced migration in the age of the Anthropocene and prepares the literary shorelines for what is yet adrift.

CHAPTER 11

Urban Dystopias

Gillian Jein

Again it may be asked: can we talk about violence when nobody is
committing direct violence, is acting?
Johan Galtung, 'Violence, peace, and peace research' (1969)[1]

In France, the democratization of culture through education and technology has been accompanied by new forms of social, economic and spatial
inequality most readily tangible on the peripheries of major cities, and in
particular on the eastern edges of its global capital. Henri Lefebvre pre-
saged these inequalities in *Le Droit à la ville / The Right to the City* (1968),
wherein he apprehended the accelerated growth of the *banlieues* (or suburbs)[2] as decisive in the shift from the circumscribed city to generalized
urbanization.[3] As Lefebvre commented later in 1985, 'les banlieues étaient
le spectre de la ville' / 'the banlieues were the spectre of the city',
representing the failure of the state's urban governance to provide a
qualitative urban space that served the working classes.[4] While in the
1950s and 1960s, the term 'banlieues' retained positive connotations of
larger living spaces, fresh air, light and modernized living conditions,[5] by
the early 1980s, a discursive imaginary of deprivation and delinquency had
emerged in the press around the *cités*, or suburban high-rise housing
estates.[6] Both an affirmation of existence and a cry of revolt, the advent
of 'beur', and later, '*banlieue* literature', made visible the complex realities
and everyday lives which such discourses reduced to stereotypes. In syn-
ergy with the 1981 riots of Minguettes[7] and the 'Marche des Beurs' / 'the
Beur March', foundational works, such as Mehdi Charef's *Le thé au Harem
d'Archi Ahmed* (1983) / *Tea in the Harem* (1989), led the way for a
generation of authors whose writing raised questions of ethnicity and
difference, attesting to the experience of the marginal, the postcolonial
and suburban, and contesting the limits and idealism of French republicanism.[8] Within literary theory, postcolonialism endorsed the heterogeneity of notions of 'rootedness', taking up postmodernism's attendance to

fractured subjectivities, but with a keen concern to ground such fractures in external social and historical structures. In these evolutions, the space of the city has been formative. Defined by the heterogeneity of their cultural, historical and spatial intersections, urban and suburban spaces become primary sites for testing the practical limits of national identity and the disjunctures at the heart of the Republic's supposed indivisibility. Importantly, these disjunctures are often mapped spatially as fractures between 'centre' and 'periphery', with the centre standing for *intra muros* Paris, or the high cultural spaces of urban elites more generally, and the periphery representing those who are geographically, culturally, ethnically and economically on the margins.

Departing from understandings that position the periphery as a tension within 'the national', or a site from which to explore questions of ethnicity or the limits of Republicanism, the authors examined here – Lydie Salvayre, Joy Sorman and Didier Daeninckx – suggest *the global city* as a ground for the affective exploration of the new inequalities emergent in the context of 'grand urbanism' and the neoliberal planning and political priorities of twenty-first-century France.[9] In the era of Grand Paris and in the aftermath of the Charlie Hebdo attacks, media and state discourses[10] present a seemingly schizophrenic image of the urban peripheries. On the one hand, in response to terrorism, they construct the banlieues in terms akin to Julia Kristeva's notion of the 'abject', 'outsider spaces'.[11] On the other, the Grand Paris project intensifies production of the banlieues as speculative, flexible and collaborative spaces, whereby Paris extends into its suburbs, and in doing so reimagines itself as global powerhouse. Both discourses, however, work together to justify the extensive imposition of state infrastructures that are geared towards 'governing and controlling urban change',[12] and both are part of the same imaginary that posits the suburbs as outlier zones in need of regeneration, integration and architectural as well as cultural rehabilitation. Such discursive meshes combine to create what Jacques Rancière articulates as 'un espace commun' / 'a common space' that makes forms of domination *appear* as if they are founded on a sensible and obvious system.'[13] In effect, Rancière implies the *invisibility* of these forms of domination, and their disappearance behind veils of normativity. The exposure of such 'sensible and obvious' systems[14] is an important preoccupation of twenty-first-century literature on the city, and the novels selected for inclusion here attest to a continued mobilization of 'the peripheral', albeit in order to render visible contemporary social tensions around the right to speak, to dwell and to justice under conditions of urban neoliberalism. To clarify, this chapter understands 'neoliberalism' as a regime of capital accumulation whose primary means of production is no longer manufacturing; rather, production is now concerned with the information, service, tourist, cultural and FIRE (finance, insurance, real estate) industries.[15] A system in which all aspects of life are permeated by market logic and the optimization of market agendas, by extension neoliberalism constitutes a project to buttress elite power by reorganizing wealth in the hands of a 'transnational capitalist class'.[16] Literature is a mode of storying through which the affects and spatial manifestations of neoliberalism are brought into view, and the writers examined here all emphasize peripheral spaces as sites where the sociocultural damage arising from such global macro-systems might be exposed on the local, micro and affective levels. Thus, while this micro-level exploration has a longstanding tradition in French urban fiction, contemporary literature's attention to the grain of ordinary spaces in the global city suggests a move towards a post-national problematization of urban inequalities and dispossession.[17]

To unpack these themes, the chapter examines how these authors' different generic strategies disclose the structural and symbolic violence that underpins the separations of centre and periphery – separations not necessarily geographical but that, within tight proximities, work to maintain distance between social classes. To prepare the terrain, we expand the notion of 'violence', drawing on the peace theorist Johan Galtung's (b. 1930) concept of 'structural violence', and later on, Pierre Bourdieu's related notion of 'symbolic violence'. The chapter proceeds chronologically to analyse the manifestations of structural and symbolic violence in the novels, *Les Belles Âmes* (2000) by Lydie Salvayre, *Gros Œuvre* (2009) by Joy Sorman and *Artana ! Artana !* (2018) by Didier Daeninckx.[18] A central line of enquiry hinges on how these writers' recent treatments of urban peripheries (both spatial and subjective) demonstrate literature's capacity to make visible that which is usually beyond view: those normative structures that underscore late capitalist society's defining logic of separation. Analysed here in terms of a tension between discourse and signification on the one hand, and literature's attention to misrecognition, bodies and silence on the other, the chapter traces how these writers' depictions of the global city construct a site wherein invisible violence is made manifest.

Invisible Violence

In his treatise on violence, Slavoj Žižek, discusses the French and world media's sensational coverage of the riots that spread outwards from Clichy-sous-Bois in November of 2005. Žižek diagnoses the fetish for somatic (physical/subjective) violence as symptomatic of a denial of the structural violence pervading neoliberal systems, asking whether there is

> not something suspicious, indeed symptomatic, about this focus on sub-jective violence [...]? Doesn't it desperately try to distract our attention from the true locus of trouble, by obliterating from view other forms of violence and thus actively participating in them?[19]

Žižek implies a political necessity behind the fixation on this physical drama, as something enabling of more insidious, systemic forms of vio-lence, forms that Johan Galtung in 1969 theorized about under the umbrella term, 'structural violence'.[20] In his seminal essay, 'Violence, peace, and peace research', Galtung prioritizes the role of *non-visible* forms of violence in creating systemic inequalities within societies. Reconceptualizing the physical bias attendant to definitions of 'violence', Galtung states that violence is *'present when human beings are being influenced so that their actual somatic and mental realizations are below their potential realizations'*; violence constitutes the *'difference between the poten-tial and the actual*, between what could have been and what is'.[21] If suffering is caused when it would have been avoidable, then violence is at work and this suffering is not necessarily attributable to a specific agent. Thus, Galtung makes a distinction between 'personal' (physical or somatic) violence and 'structural violence'. 'Personal' violence is that highly visible, dramatic and interpersonal form of suffering of which Žižek speaks. This is physical harm perpetrated by subjects, and it captures action across multiple scales: international wars, minor civil conflicts, urban riots, collective physical violence, domestic violence, homicide and suicide. Such violence can be readily apprehended by language; it is 'grammatical', being 'easily captured and expressed verbally since it has the same structure as elementary sentences in (at least Indo-European) languages: subject-verb-object'.[22] However, as the novels examined here demonstrate, this subject-object violence often dissimulates deeper sys-temic violent forms, which Galtung names as 'structural, built into the structure'.[23]

Structural violence consists in conditions that create and perpetuate social injustice and inequality: the avoidable limitations that prohibit access to a quality of life which would otherwise be possible. Present when power is unevenly distributed, such inequalities may be legal, political, religious, economic or cultural in type, and, Akhil Gupta suggests, their mechanisms are often embedded in institutions and operational through their hierarchies.[24] Cities – as territories defined by a concentration of institutional powers – and, in particular, global cities as territories of concentrated corporate power are therefore important spaces for the study of structural violence.[25] Where this violence is habitually 'invisible' because its results are usually taken as norms, when we consider the 'real estate' of the city, competition for public space, delimitation of access to places, and the demarcation of property, then connections between space, economy, aesthetics and power come more easily into view. It is possible in the city to trace the manifestation of unequal spatial and social conditions. Moreover, urban literature, as a heterogeneous mode of storying the city, of revealing the historicity of urban structures (architectural, institutional and social), and of attendance to the micro-level affective experience of urban protagonists is precisely a means by which structural violence is rendered visible as a process that is sustained 'invisibly' over often long periods of time.

Harmful Othering: Highlighting Dark Tourism

It is through the perturbation of hierarchical logics, and of 'accepted' distinctions between centre and periphery in particular that Salvayre's 'banlieue' novels – *Les Belles Âmes* (2000) and *Passage à l'ennemie* (2003), as well as her non-fictional contribution, 'En français parfumé', to the collection *Des Nouvelles de la banlieue* (2008) – call into question the ingrained 'core-periphery' urban imaginary of Paris.[26] This disturbance of socio-spatial categories comes about through Salvayre's polyphonic style, which tests the limits of the 'hegemonic' voice and exposes its inadequacy to 'solve' or, even, to confront the realities of everyday life in the banlieues. In the diarized account *Passage à l'ennemie*, undercover cop Inspector Arjona's authoritarian language *evolves* upon contact with 'the enemy', his voice developing away from enumerative rules and descriptive lists towards linguistic and epistemological harmony with his suburban environment (the enemy). Thus, the grain of the voice becomes empathic and loving, altering upon everyday contact with the 'other' and opening a critical ground for reflection on the violence of discursive tropes. In 'En français parfumé', which consists of interviews conducted by Salvayre with inhabitants of Clichy-sous-Bois around the regeneration-demolition of the Grand Paris project, discourse is problematized through vocal multiplication. Constructed from nine separate, disconnected 'voices', the piece avoids an overarching narrative voice, includes untranslated responses in Spanish and Arabic, and any authorial intervention must be discerned from the responses of these voices to the author's (absent) questions. Moreover, 'Voice 6' creates a critically reflexive space, recuperating and reclaiming speech for the inhabitant, and seeming to take back power by withholding evidence from the 'author' – that figure sanctioned to speak on behalf, but also instead, of others: 'De quoi ? Non, j'ai rien à dire à des personnes qui nous prennent notre argent pour écrire des conneries qui servent à rien. C'est tout.' / 'About what? No, I have nothing to say to people who take our money to write stupid stuff which serves no purpose. That's all.'[27] Thus, Salvayre shatters the authorial voice, splinters subjectivities and multiplies voices, and seems to construct an alternative space to reveal and question how hegemonic discourse constitutes a reduction of 'the banlieue' at the same time as it makes alternative voices heard.

Les Belles Âmes, written prior to the urban crisis of 2005, is a relatively early articulation of the symbolic violence sustaining these centre-periphery imaginaries.[28] In this work, Salvayre's 'polyphonic and clashing comedy' performs to reveal the specific violence of language in the dominant class's appropriation of the banlieues,[29] and, given this linguistic emphasis, it is useful to read the novel through the lens of 'symbolic violence'. Pierre Bourdieu's extension of 'structural violence', 'symbolic violence' emphasizes the aesthetic, cultural dimensions of power distributions that foster structural inequalities within societies.[30] According to Bourdieu, contemporary social hierarchies as well as the resultant suffering inflicted are produced and maintained less by physical force than by forms of symbolic domination. Furthermore, these forms are so pervasive throughout the field of cultural production that their attendant value-laden and hierarchical systems are unconsciously assimilated and performed as norms. Salvayre's novel, through its exploration of the 'strategic seizure of the process of signification' by the dominant bourgeoisie, identifies discourse as a means of guaranteeing the hegemony of the centre over the periphery.[31] Salvayre's writing goes further than identification, however; the novel is also powerfully subversive of this symbolic hegemonic regime, effectively turning her bourgeois protagonists' discursive, linear communication on its head through the persistent use of satire, polyphony and authorial reflexivity, in order to destabilize what Laurent Dubreuil identifies as the 'structuring category' of 'the *banlieue*'.[32]

Dark Tourism's Symbolic Violence

From the outset, Les Belles Âmes hints at literature's agonistic position – being at once a form of cultural capital that potentially excludes those without access to its canonical fields, while also having the potential to create a space where normative discourse and middle-class morality might be ridiculed. The plot coheres around a tour bus transporting a group of thirteen upper middle-class Parisian tourists on a round-trip of 'l'Europe des démunis' / 'Destitute Europe', visiting one impoverished high-rise in each of Paris, Brussels, Berlin and Milan. Salvayre's characters comprise a microcosm of French society, the tourists being guided around the suburbs by the urban working class employed by the tour operator, Real Voyages. The latter characters include Jason, 'l'agent d'ambiance' / 'the atmosphere agent' and a violent (but often insightful) bully, Jason's girlfriend, Olympe, 'qui se tue à repasser les fringues des autres' / 'who kills herself ironing other people's clothes', and the bus driver, Vulpius, who 'connaît par cœur'[33] / 'knows by heart' the Parisian estate 'puisqu'il y habite' / 'because he lives there'. Embarked on a kind of poverty safari, the novel reveals this dark tourism as a vicious form of 'Othering', a way of looking and moving that strategically places the banlieues outside the bourgeois tourists' systems of normality and convention, and that justifies their neocolonial desire to reappropriate these spaces.[34] Dark tourism feeds off the split urban imaginary that informs Paris's relationship to its suburbs; where Paris is seen as the vital centre of modern, civilized life, while the banlieues are constructed as 'empty and dangerous hinterlands and stigmatized as places of savagery, disorder, lawlessness, and poverty'.[35] In its commodification of urban inequality, dark tourism designates the necessity of spaces of suffering, and the tourists equate this destitution with a kind of 'authenticity' or proximity to the 'Real'.[36] Each of Salvayre's bourgeois tourists, 'ces excités de la misère'[37] / 'those poverty perverts', corroborates the symbolic borders that must be maintained: for Faucher, the writer, suffering is prosaic material for his next novel; for the socialite, Miss Faulkircher, her brief encounter with poverty confirms her cultural capital and her 'edge'; for Mme Pite, travelling in the suburbs enables her to demonstrate her humanitarian nature; and finally, for Odile Boichard, it serves her self-narrative of political outrage and sense of superiority. In each instance, the person draws on the 'Other' to confirm the codes of the 'Same', the touristic experience being designed to guarantee the discrete borders of the suffering other, while packaged knowledge and mobilities maintain the tourists' worldview and confirm the social, political and historical status quo.

The micro-level affective damage of this othering is revealed through the character of Olympe. Representing oppressed peripheral femininity – she is of mixed race, young, poor, acquiescent of physical abuse – Olympe's arc perhaps testifies to Salvayre's modest hope that the subaltern might eventually speak. She distinguishes herself among her friends by wearing clothes from *Supermod*, 'Olympe est *Supermod*. *Supermod* constitue son appellation contrôlée. Ou son blason, comme on voudra.'[38] / 'Olympe is *Supermod*. *Supermod* is her brand name. Or, if you prefer, her family crest.' It is by consistently collapsing the registers – high to low and vice versa – that Salvayre renders visible the signifier as a singular, arbitrary component in the system of socio-symbolic hierarchies: 'Être *Supermod* ou ne pas être, *that is the question*.'[39] / 'To be or not to be *Supermod, telle est la question*.' However, when Olympe comes into contact with another layer of the code – the expensive, 'designer' outfits worn by Faulkircher – the value attached to *Supermod* is downgraded in the signification hierarchy and she feels insignificant, the collapse of her code effectively rendering her immaterial and leaving her feeling that she might disappear. In effect, Olympe misrecognizes as natural an arbitrary system of classification,[40] taking the veil of signification as a given. Salvayre accumulates examples of such symbolic misrecognition and the identitarian harm produced, harm which is largely experienced in terms of a separation – 'un infranchissable abîme'[41] / 'an impassable chasm' – and silence – 'Olympe redevient muette'[42] / 'Olympe resumes her silence'.

This same destabilization is produced as regards the working-class protagonists' connection to their suburban neighbourhoods. The othering gaze of the tourists is internalized by Olympe and Vulpius; they see themselves from without, and this shift in their field of vision affectively alters their relationship to the *cité*, destabilizing their cultural and spatial identities and filling them with a sense of deficiency. So, Vulpius is traumatized when he misrecognizes the tourist gaze as authoritative, and is led to undermine his own happiness (for he has been satisfied with life until now): 'il lui a suffi de deux heures à peine pour que la cité, son apart et sa femme lui soient devenus insupportables'[43] / 'it barely takes two hours for his estate, his flat and his wife to become unbearable'. However, while Olympe and Vulpius are interested participants, invested in propagating the myths of the very system that harms them, the ending of Salvayre's novel asks how we might conceive a 'beyond' that defies this symbolic regime. If the tour bus spatializes social hierarchies and their affective violence, the question for Salvayre then becomes whether and how we can ever get off the bus.

Getting off the Bus

If Salvayre's reflexive interruptions and scathing tone work to undermine the authority of the tourists' discourse, in the final chapters she suggests it will take nothing less than a confrontation with horror to collapse this discourse. In the suburbs of Milan, the tourists enter a cavernous warehouse that provides shelter to a population of zombiesque drug addicts:

> Une usine éventrée. Noire de suie. Ouverte au vent. Glaciale. Nauséabonde. D'une saleté indescriptible. Dont la proximité avec Milan, ville riche s'il en est, ne fait qu'accuser la misère. À l'intérieur, des jeunes gens somnambuliques errent, pieds nus, en loques, avec des airs d'un autre monde et trébuchent en aveugle sur des décombres entassés où l'on distingue des seringues.
> Ils vivent là, dans l'attente de mourir.[44]

> An eviscerated factory. Black with soot. Exposed to the wind. Freezing. Stinking. Unspeakably filthy. The place's proximity to Milan, a rich city if ever there was one, only making its existence all the more shameful. Inside, young people wander around in a daze, barefoot, spaced out, blindly tripping over heaped piles of rubbish, including syringes.
> There they live, waiting for death.

This scene constitutes the novel's crisis point. Elsewhere, different voices vie for dominance, and discourse is quickly satirized or undermined; here, it is a confrontation with a Lacanian 'Real' that marks the limits of the symbolic regime.[45] Here, all the passengers are silenced, the horror witnessed exceeds any language through which it might be comprehended, and by implication, contained. Forced to acknowledge and confront the materiality of death, the real erupts and constitutes the rock against which the protagonists' fantasies and discursive solutions to poverty – humanitarianism, writing, property investment, gentrification – crash. When the tour guide attempts to recover the situation, he does so by fetishizing language, defining the semantic difference between 'esseulement' and 'solitude'. This recourse to language is an attempt, according to Kristeva's theory of abjection, to cover over the factitiousness of their relation to this abject reality,[46] and reveals the insufficiency of the tourists' humanitarian discourse when faced with real suffering.

However, while Salvayre's novel demonstrates the pervasive and insidious way in which symbolic violence operates, her ending suggests an ambiguous hope for its precise refusal of trope or, as Kristeva might have it, a language that refutes the social contract of communication. The four companions, the tour guide, the driver, Olympe and Jason, leave the tour bus to get drunk at the side of the road, while the tourists are stranded helpless and, it seems, descending into madness. Finally, it is Olympe who finds a voice and leads the quartet in a toast: 'À nous la belle vie !' / 'To the good life.' Thus, if this journey to the banlieues has a pedagogical function on the one hand, serving to render visible the violence of middle-class Othering, on the other hand it provides a means to 'crash' the symbolic and to test the edges of the cultural system by drawing it into contact with the urban 'Real'. The closing scene sunders the tourists' worldview, and at the same time perhaps suggests that hope for resistance and recognition might lie in the banlieue inhabitants' convening of an alternative, if fragile, space of community.

Sorman's Structural Works

Problematizing the integrity or security of the 'centre', Joy Sorman's city is erected through a close attention to space, to what is out there to be faced and found, which, in contrast to Salvayre, lends her work an externality and a sense of the collective, shared experience that at once prohibits an entirely subjective appearance of any kind of interior. Sorman belongs to a generation of French female writers who are reconsidering the domestic and the relations of bodies in space. Her *L'Inhabitable* (2016) and *Gare du Nord* (2011) also make her part of a tradition of 'everyday' writing in French that evidences a concern to impart the materiality of the external world, and to explore the tangibility of spatial discourse – that of planning and renovation for example – as they intersect and alter human relationships in the urban environment.[47] And, indeed, it is something of a paradox that this writing's attention to the habitual and banal tends to reveal precisely the precarity of the habitual and the rarity of the banal. This paradox is explicitly framed in Sorman's treatment of 'habitat' in *Gros Œuvre*, which casts doubt on the possibility of 'dwelling' in the global neoliberal city. In *Gros Œuvre*, we explore the collapse in distinction between 'centre' and 'periphery' through this work's effective insinuation of precarity and the marginal into the discursive site of 'home'. This collection of thirteen short stories deploys a variety of genres – from science-fiction to fantasy to autobiography – to build a thematic assemblage around the concept of 'home', and what this might mean for urban inhabitants increasingly exposed to a precarity that is economic but also spatial, and that attends to the links between the architectural and subjective decomposition of notions of rootedness.

A Question of Habitat

This issue of habitat and inhabitation can be expanded usefully etymologically where it invokes 'to live, dwell, stay, remain', which is also a frequentative of *habere* 'to have, to hold, possess'.[48] For Sorman, these issues of possession, staying and dwelling are all called into question once one adopts a mode of attention that prioritizes marginality. Through evocation of 'homes' that resist normative definition, this book experiments with what it means to dwell in France in the twenty-first century.

The first essay, 'Un Castor' / 'A Beaver', sets out the thematic terrain developed throughout. Sam, the protagonist, is the human allegory of a beaver; he builds his house brick by brick over a period of twenty-five years. Prioritizing the corporeality of both Sam and house, this story weaves 'building' and 'being' into a symbiotic necessity: the structure and Sam require each other for their existence. This evokes a Heideggerean model of dwelling and being, whereby the manner in which we dwell *is* the manner in which we are – exist – and, furthermore, this dwelling constitutes how we *know* and access the world.[49] This is expressed through Sam's refusal to live a prefabricated, made-to-measure existence. Sam, 'ne veut pas de maison standard médiocre [. . .] pas confiance dans les mains des autres'[50] / 'does not want some standard, mediocre house [. . .] doesn't trust the hands of others'. The emphasis on home as an extension of man evokes an animalistic necessity that speaks to Richard Sennett's conception of 'craftsmanship' and its gradual erosion under neoliberalism.[51] Indeed, this conceptual nexus – building, dwelling, thinking – constitutes the foundation of humanist geography's emphasis on 'dwelling' as a stable and spiritual condition, but Sorman's work suggests the collapse of this possibility.[52] Beavers may be prolific builders – no other extant animal, apart from the human, does more to shape its landscape – but Sam is a lone beaver, and it seems more apt to interpret this analogy as an endangered animal working to stem an inexorable tide.[53] Stressing his singularity, Sorman suggests that Sam's is an isolated lodge, an eccentric, fragile bastion against the flow of commercial real estate and the standardized, machine-built housing of capitalist production lines. Sam's heterotopian habitat is, therefore, the opening and the exception in this work, the manifestation of Heidegger's idealized fusion of building, dwelling and thinking. Sam acts as a counter-position from which Sorman's exploration of the pathologies of home can better be laid bare.

In some cases, this opposition produces an entirely dystopian extension of Sam's organic connection to home, as with the character Akira in 'Célibataire II'. 'Akira habite dans une capsule et c'est l'avenir' / 'Akira lives in a capsule and that's the future', a capsule that sits alongside 139 other such capsules on the side of a tower that stretches 430 metres into the sky, a capsule Sorman reminds us that 'pourrait tout autant être

avec moi sur le terrain vague de la Goutte-d'Or'⁵⁴ / 'could just as easily be
here beside me on a vacant lot in northern Paris'. This vertical superstruc-
ture pushes the building-dwelling logic to the extreme, for here 'la structure hélicoïdale de l'ADN d'Akira a été reproduite pour construire cette
tour capsulaire'⁵⁵ / 'this capsular tower has been modelled from Akira's
DNA spiral'. In this case, the modular capsules resonate with a monadic
interchangeability, a collective isolation, catering for every human need
except interaction. While Sam's home is an extension of himself, Akira's
genetic architectural extension subsumes him, he 'se croit immergé dans
un sous-marin qui vole, voudrait ouvrir la fenêtre ronde [. . .] il n'y a pas de
poignée à ce hublot [. . .] embrasse la vitre et la ville, pleure puis étale les
larmes qui en séchant laissent une trace de sel'⁵⁶ / 'believes he is immersed
in a flying submarine, would like to open the round window [. . .] the
porthole has no handle [. . .] kisses the window and the city, cries then
smears his tears across the glass, which leave a trail of salt as they dry'. The
fantasy of synergetic fusion between human and building is repeated a
number of times throughout the book, but in each case the biotopic
architecture is pathologized by the human body's response: Akira is drawn
with his head pressed against the window, suspended, encased, a sweaty
residue from his forehead leaving a streaky trace on the utopian
glass bubble.

It is here that the figure of the home, or home understood in terms of
what Jean-François Lyotard terms the 'figural', comes into view.⁵⁷ *Gros
Œuvre* adopts home as a mode of enunciation, a stance from which the
author can assemble these misfit dwellings (the micro-scale of human
attachment to space) into a structural schema; the book's structural works
consist, therefore, in its assemblage of these myriad singular existences.
Literature operates as a collagistic machinery, whereby 'home' – the
material equivalent of signification's stability in one sense – is destabilized.
And this by an orchestration of external forces (the police's violent dis-
mantling of migrant camps, for example) and the internal, corporeal
experience of 'home' as container, as precarity, as madness. In this way,
'home' as a discursive, normative signification is deterritorialized in favour
of home as 'sense'. As Lyotard delineates, '*sens*' / 'sense' is an experience of
meaning, it constitutes an attachment to the mute exteriority, otherness
and materiality of things, but it cannot be separated out entirely from the
code, from 'signification'.⁵⁸ In *Gros Œuvre*, this deterritorialization of
home derives an understanding which suggests a view of precarity as
dwelling, of instability and unmooring as the new 'home'. Put another
way, if formerly precarity constituted a condition of the periphery, then

Sorman suggests the proliferation of precarity and, thereby, the periphery's infiltration of the centre.

Daeninckx: Real Fictions

Finally, in turning to a particularly 'urban genre', the *néo-polar* or detective novel, we encounter a particularly effective method of uncovering the structural injustices at work in the city. In much of Daeninckx's fiction, historical recovery is a strategic method for revealing structural violence,[59] and his recurrent protagonist, Inspector Cadin, has been instrumental in bringing to prominence the 'roman-historico-policier' / 'historico-detective novel'.[60] In the 2018 novel, *Artana ! Artana !*, however, Daeninckx replaces the professional detective with a veterinarian, Erik Ketezer, and while, in typical *polar* fashion, the novel overinvests signs with historical resonance to remind us of the persistence in the present of the Algerian War, the Holocaust or the 1961 Seine Massacre, these historical moments are relatively ancillary.[61] Rather than the past, the violent core that propels this *roman à clé* is contemporary political corruption in the context of the Grand Paris project and the extensive redevelopment of the banlieues.

Artana ! Artana ! is in keeping with the plot-driven impetus of *noir* fiction, and the process of uncovering – the identity of a murderer, but also the political agendas behind urban transformation – becomes a key mechanism enabling the narrative to weave lines of logical interconnection between people and places that seemingly exist in separate social, political and geographical spheres. The book tells the story of Ketezer's quest to find the murderer of Rayan, the brother of Sylvia, Ketezer's former lover. Sylvia, effectively the love of Ketezer's life, lies catatonic in a mental institution for the entirety of the book. The murder provides the catalyst for Ketezer's return to Courvilliers, Sylvia's hometown in Seine-Saint-Denis and where the couple lived together until she had the breakdown seven years previously. It is during his quest for the murderer that the veterinarian turned detective uncovers major political corruption that implicates the town's mayor, Patrick Muletier, and his mistress, Stéphanie Maumelet (responsible for town management and planning) in gerrymandering, embezzlement, cronyism and the rapid degradation and dissolution of urban community.

Daeninckx's novel is easily legible in tandem with contemporary political scandals that have beset Seine-Saint-Denis. Courvilliers, a fictional town in name, seems to be a synthesis of Saint-Denis, Bagnolet and, in particular, Aubervilliers, Daeninckx's long-term home. Patrick Muletier

'dont la plus grande des qualités a été d'épouser la fille du commandeur' /
'whose best quality was to have married the Commander's daughter' bears
a distinct resemblance to Aubervilliers' former PCF mayor, Pascal
Beaudot.[62] The corruption at the heart of the novel hinges on the
inordinate power wielded by a public officer, Pascal Ochualla, who, it
turns out, is also a gangster.[63] This character is likely drawn from the
Gharib K. affair: as in the case of Ochualla and his men, a municipal
officer, Gharib K., who had criminal convictions for drug trafficking and
aggravated theft, was promoted without sufficient qualifications or vetting.

The *roman à clé* involves threading reality through fiction, in order to
render visible and to critique that which is hidden from view. Indeed,
Daeninckx cites 'un silence, un manque, le fait de ne plus me retrouver
[...] dans ce que je lisais' / 'a silence, a lack, not finding myself [...]
represented in what I read' as the motivation for his work.[64] *Artana !
Artana !* is preoccupied with silence and, more importantly, with shattering
this silence to better distribute justice – the word 'artana' meaning 'blame'
or 'a mortal combat' in Sanskrit.[65] Silence performs as the enabling force
for both structural and physical violence; it is silence that guarantees the
persistence of violence, and by the same token, violence that ensures
silence is upheld. This is first of all evident in the way in which the novel
treats Rayan's murder. An extreme form of physical violence, murder
would seem to constitute the drama of Galtung's grammatical definition –
the subject-verb-object relation that has one body inflict mortal harm on
another. However, the connective tissue of the drama is disrupted at every
stage: the 'object' (Rayan's body) is not immediately present, and the
corpse must be identified and retrieved from a police station in
Thailand; the 'verb' relation is never revealed to us, we are never given a
description of the time, place or precise circumstances of Rayan's murder;
finally, the subject or murderer is a second-hand figure, our detective never
confronts him, we are never in his physical presence and Ketezer finally
learns of his untimely, violent death over the radio. Each link of the
grammatical chain that constitutes somatic violence is disarticulated.
Moreover, this strangely digressive murder catalyses the complex series of
detours and interconnections of seemingly dispersed geographical and
historical objects and events, so that the force of the novel lies in its
bringing into correspondence the trauma of silent bodies and the silent
trauma of the city. The detective, meanwhile, acts as a prosthetic voice,
whose questing is ultimately a quest after narrative, and this reminds us of
the detective's proximity to the urban theorist[66] and of the necessity of
narrative: it is narrative that resuscitates the meanings of those people,

buildings and spaces that cannot speak for themselves. Together, these interweavings combine to reveal the structural logic of violence that infiltrates both the affective, corporeal and urban, architectural scales.

This correspondence of flesh and stone is confirmed through the centrality of the cemetery as a spatial figure that establishes the novel's plot lines. In Courvilliers cemetery, Ketezer watches as Rayan's corpse is lowered into the ground, and this sight produces a reminiscence: the cemetery is where Sylvia's mental breakdown and her slippage into catatonia began. Her silence coincides with her arrest for urinating on the grave of Fabrice Ochualla, a city official and father of Pascal Ochualla, the key villain of the novel. Indeed, Sylvia's trauma and her relationship to Ochualla are revealed to parallel the trauma of the city itself. Never speaking, except through Ketezer's reminiscence, and never physically present until the closing pages, Sylvia is the void around which the plot orbits.

The graveyard also reminds us of the necessity of narrative to resuscitate the meanings of those who cannot speak for themselves. Narrative's capacity to bring into alignment past and present is reflected spatially in Daeninckx's historicization of the names engraved on the tombstones. These stories constitute a geology of urban mobilities, attesting the connection of individuals to global histories, containing evidence of mass migrations – from the Italians and Spanish to Kabyle and Chinese populations. The cemetery acts as a kind of heterotopic census of urban life and death, holding the memory of the city, not in monuments, but in stone silent proper names that require an interpreter to unlock their secrets. What emerges is an acknowledgement of the multidirectional, 'knotty' memoryscape of the city and the interconnection of personal and global histories; the permutations in urban space-time that have consequences for the individual as well as the collective experience of the city.[67] The cemetery performs, then, as the site where the writer confronts silence and activates the past, pulling meaning from the stones. It provides the spatial material through which the writer alerts the reader to the violence of forms of national forgetting, but also to the possibility of narrative resuscitation.

Exposing Grand Paris

The activation of silence through narrative is the driving force of Daeninckx's fiction,[68] and is especially important in the case of the urban periphery, often sidelined in French heritage discourse.[69] Daeninckx's work intercepts these discourses to refocus attention on their macro-scale political motivations and micro-scale affective dispossessions. Courvilliers's decline is conceived not only in terms of the built environment, but as a deterioration of communal values and, more specifically, of governance. This decline is mapped spatially by the consistent interruptions to Ketezer's movement around the town, which are observed as a series of separations – the town council building is cut off from the marketplace, 'et il faut traverser les rues au péril de sa vie'[70] / 'and you take your life in your hands crossing the street' to get there. The renovation and building works of the Grand Paris projects have disrupted the collective rhythms of the city. The noise of jackhammers causes the café terraces to vibrate, and danger and indifference define the urban space as the pedestrian zones are cut off.[71] The accumulation of architectural change, demolition or vacancy signal the decline in powers dedicated to the community: social space has been reduced drastically, the Trade Union Centre and the Communist Party Headquarters have been torn down and 'remplacés par ces ensembles immobiliers résidentialisés qui envahissent toutes les banlieues'[72] / 'replaced by those residential property blocks that are invading every suburb'. The streets are lined with estate agents, expensive greengrocers, money transfer agencies and makeshift international call centres, which, while they signal the mobilities inherent to Seine-Saint-Denis, also indicate the increasing separation between classes, and the emergence of gentrification and its attendant spatial and social standardization.

For Daeninckx, the institutional processes of planning and the control of public space are bound to the deliberate erasure of memory and to the trauma of bodies. As evidenced by the town's gravestones, this is a place whose history is the history of world migrations, and whose transnational spaces testify to France's interconnection with global conflict. However, the vast infrastructural works of the Grand Paris project are geared towards homogenous planning schemas, to streamlining the image of the city for global consumption, and in the process ripping out and erasing the traces of successive cultures from the cityscape. The Grand Paris renovations and the Olympic Games 2024, therefore, place Courvilliers at the centre of a vast accumulation of property speculation and encourage divestment in the town's diversity and its communal fabric, which are bulldozed in the interests of global markets and cosmopolitan wealth:

> Algériens, Portugais, puis Maliens avant que Turcs et Pakistanais n'ajoutent les récits de leurs déchirements à la longue histoire des convulsions du monde. Les bulldozers s'acharnent aujourd'hui à effacer les décors branlants de leurs derniers refuges. Place aux Jeux.[73]

Algerians, Portuguese, then Malians before the Turks and Pakistanis added the stories of their uprooting to the world's long history of uprooting. Today, the bulldozers are dedicated to erasing the last remaining signs of their rickety shelters. Make way for the Games.

Such social separation and property redistribution are defining of neo-liberalism's speculative manipulation of urban public space, or what David Harvey terms, 'accumulation by dispossession'.[74] The commodification and privatization effectively constitute the conversion of 'various forms of property rights' (common and collective as well as state) into exclusive private property rights. 'The state', as Harvey goes on to say, 'with its monopoly of violence and definitions of legality plays a crucial role in both backing and promoting these processes.'[75] Daeninckx's book effectively traces a battle for public space, as the effects of the mayor's corruption have infected the entire spectrum of urban connections. The community is dying because the corrupt structure deprives people of the chance to bring their power to bear on the municipal authorities, and effectively aims at the atomization of dissent and the disintegration of alternatives. Siphoning money away from public services, while ensuring that the gangsters have free rein to continue to operate their slumlord businesses and drug traf-ficking in peace, it is the veterinarian (a doctor dedicated, moreover, to interpreting the illnesses of creatures who cannot speak for themselves), who connects the dots. Ketezer's walks through the cityscape – where he interacts with locals, stopping to help those in need (women, the disabled, the elderly) – work to produce an interconnecting mesh that highlights the everyday extensions of these insidiously violent structures. Daeninckx's chain of connections positions this distortion of power as the infringement of citizens' right to the city, where, in the scenario of corrupt power, the ghetto becomes desirable.[76] As one character, Omar Belaïd, suggests, this corruption has sabotaged the citizens' access to both public and private space: 'À Courvilliers, ils ont créé le ghetto, de manière délibéré ... Du logement social à tire-larigot pour maîtriser la sociologie électorale, un abandon du parc privé qui s'est transformé pour partie en terrain de jeux des marchands de sommeil.'[77] / 'In Courvilliers, they've deliberately created a ghetto ... building copious amounts of social housing to control electoral demographics, neglecting their responsibilities towards private property, which is becoming a playground for slumlords.'

It is Daeninckx's attendance to the effects of such processes on the corporeal and affective levels which brings into view the trauma wrought. As Rosalyn Deutsche points out in her discussion of Roman Polanski's *Chinatown* (1974), the detective's action mirrors that of the urban theorist for the way in which he collates minor evidences to forge a systemic idea of the city.[78] Moreover, for Deutsche, it is the genre's acknowledgement of that theorist's affective immersion in the world that matters, for here it becomes possible to eschew homogenous models of dominant power structures, and instead connect theory to the practice of bodies in urban space. As with Jake's affective loss in *Chinatown*, so too in *Artana ! Artana !* the body is the primary site for the translation of institutional corruption into tangible terms, where the correlation between state corruption and the silent, broken human body is performed as a sequential logic – the one leading to the other. In this scenario, structural violence is not an abstraction that can necessarily be remedied through discourse, whether legal or economic, and justice is never complete or sufficient. Rather, the perversion of power structures results in a corporeal and psychological trauma that resists even the hero-detective. Thus, the bodies encountered on the street correspond to the dilapidation of the urban environment:

> Je mets plusieurs minutes à prendre conscience de ce qui a changé plus profondément encore que le décor : le délabrement des corps. Sans même m'en rendre compte, je détourne la tête à plusieurs reprises en croisant des hommes, des femmes, qui portent les stigmates de l'exclusion, dents abîmés, cheveux sales, vêtements élimés.[79]

> It takes me a couple of minutes to realize that, more than the architecture, it is human bodies that have deteriorated the most. Without even realizing, more than once my head is turned by the sight of men and women bearing the signs of exclusion – rotten teeth, dirty hair, ragged clothes.

The litany of broken bodies is presided over by an indifferent police force, so that legitimate and illegitimate forms of violence combine to strangle any sense of communal belonging. As it turns out, the corruption has enabled a paedophile, Pascal Ochualla, to take the local school children abroad on exchanges to Thailand. And it is here that Ochualla has repeatedly sexually abused Sylvia, and here that Rayan will later be murdered for his discovery of this fact.

In the end, while it is clear that the book suggests alternative models of urban management and life (mainly through Ketezer's kind-hearted encounters and ability to listen to others), it is less certain whether these can ever be separated from the trauma already endured. When Ketezer finally discovers Rayan's letter to Sylvia, which discloses knowledge of his sister's abuse, it becomes clear that Ochualla has murdered Rayan to silence him. Ochualla is therefore the source of both silences – the dead body of Rayan and the catatonic Sylvia. This revelation provides knowledge, but it does not lead to any change in state – Sylvia does not open her mouth or acknowledge Ketezer's new-found realization. She has known this all along, has suffered it. However, we might argue that this irresolution, typical of *noir* fiction, is suggestive too of a certain counter-discourse that refuses state and planning discourses on urban space. Where the latter see solutions in refined models and overarching reconstruction (that involves demolition), the novelist registers the interpersonal, affective trauma and refuses the model, and in doing so underscores the necessity of affective responses to uncover structural violence. Through its plot-driven structures, the novel weaves logical lines between the global contexts of governance, World Games, land values and the corruption, and the impact of such abstractions on the tangible, material city and its inhabitants.

Conclusion

This chapter has examined the mobilization of the 'periphery' as a space from which to articulate and map the affective impact of structural violence in the era of neoliberal urbanism. Through engagement with three novelists of the urban margins, we explored a variety of generic strategies for rendering visible that violence performed by social, institutional and linguistic structures, and which in the twenty-first century suggest the spread of precarity, economic and cultural inequalities and the collapse of bourgeois bastions for making sense of the city. In *Les Belles Âmes*, satire and polyphony disrupt the discrete symbolic borders separating centre and periphery, while in *Gros Œuvre*, Sorman prioritizes the interaction of the sensory and corporeal with the (in)tangibilities of places in which to dwell. In *Artana ! Artana !* the body and the city are aligned, one registering the trauma of the other as mutual victims of the hidden forces of corrupt power. In their various ways, these writers refute the integrity of liberal ideologies by exposing neoliberalism's attachment to discourses of regeneration and integration as a means to perpetuate urban inequalities. Rendering visible the affects of such inequalities, these narratives make structural violence appear by bringing into language its impact on the psychology and corporeality of urban existence.[80] Where discourses on the banlieues may work to maintain the discrete separation of centre and periphery, literature's attendance to the grain of the global city's inequalities works at collapsing such distinctions, at implicating each in the existence of the other. Read in this way, this micro-level, high-resolution mode of attention suggests that it is by zooming in, by moving closer that a 'broader horizon' of systemic socio-spatial violence of neoliberalism might come into view, and, we might suggest, this becoming visible might constitute a step towards sustained critique of the neoliberal city and create a space where we might begin to imagine alternatives.

CHAPTER 12

Imagining Civil War in the Contemporary French Novel

Martin Crowley

One of the striking features of the debate between Emmanuel Macron and Marine Le Pen, televised on 3 May 2017 in the run-up to the second round of the French presidential elections, was Macron's recourse to the language of civil war. Leaning on a reference to comments by political scientist Gilles Kepel, Macron claimed that the social division exacerbated and exploited by Le Pen's Front National played perfectly into the hands of France's 'terrorist' enemies, and he used the notion of civil war to capture this division: 'Ce qu'ils attendent, le piège qu'ils nous tendent, c'est celui que vous portez, c'est la guerre civile.'[1] / 'What they want, the trap they are setting us, is the very one you are helping to make, that is civil war.' Warming to his theme, he repeated the charge of laying the groundwork for civil war twice within the following forty seconds. Nor was this his only public use of this language: addressing the European Parliament on 17 April 2018, he described the opposition between newly successful authoritarian nationalists and upholders of the ideal of transnational European democracy in terms of the return of civil war to Europe.[2]

Macron is not alone in his fondness for the language of civil war. For the acute questions of division, exclusion or secession pressing urgently on French social and political life have seen this language revived throughout recent French political discourse. While Macron's uses pit socially liberal free-marketeers against identitarian populists, elsewhere in French debates the term is generally used to evoke the scale of the alienation of the impoverished outer housing estates or *cités*, especially as this is held to be expressed through identification with Islamist insurgency. Thus, essays by Ivan Rioufol and David Djaïz, from right and left, respectively, entitled *La Guerre civile qui vient* / The Coming Civil War (2016) and *La Guerre civile n'aura pas lieu* / Civil War Will Not Happen (2017), may offer different reasons for using the term (respectively, the supposed actual secession of the *banlieues*, and terrorist attacks on French citizens by French citizens); however, despite their mirror-image titles, they fundamentally agree that the *cités* are in thrall to a secessionist Islamism which threatens the unity and authority of the nation-state.[3] In these cases, the figure of 'civil war' articulates what Émile Chabal calls a 'neo-Republican' doubling-down on themes of integration in response to renewed fears of social division: its threat of fracture acts as a counterpart to 'l'unité nationale' / 'national unity'.[4]

The figure of civil war has a distinguished record in French social history, of course, usually in the guise of 'la guerre franco-française' / 'French-against-French war'. In 1985, Jean-Pierre Azéma, Jean-Pierre Roux and Henry Rousso wrote that 'Depuis près de deux cents ans, des crises majeures fracturent périodiquement l'unité nationale, plongeant la France dans une guerre civile plus ou moins violente, plus ou moins ouverte.' / 'For more than two hundred years major crises have periodically broken national unity, plunging France into more or less violent, more or less open civil war.'[5] They are referring particularly to 1789 (especially the conflict in the Vendée), the Commune (famously discussed by Marx as 'the civil war in France'), the Dreyfus affair, Vichy and the Algerian War, as well as a longer reach backwards to the Wars of Religion. Since I am neither a social historian nor a prophet, however, I am not proposing here either to examine this lineage or to assess the likelihood of civil war in France, whether parsed in ethno-confessional or other terms. If I do want to look at the figure of civil war, though, this is because it plainly focuses with particular intensity on questions of social division, its secessionist aspect suggesting with singular urgency the 'social segregation' starkly mapped in France's urban geography.[6] What interests me about the term is less its diagnostic accuracy, then, than its presentation of the dynamics of division, exclusion and secession – and the ways in which these function as a topic and a test for contemporary cultural forms, in particular the contemporary novel.

Civil war features in a number of recent French novels. It offers a significant plot line in Michel Houellebecq's *Soumission* (2015) / *Submission* (2016), before vanishing with Houellebecq's habitual disdain for the well-made plot. It hovers around Sabri Louatah's *Les Sauvages* (2012–2014) / *The Savages* (2018), in the alienation of the *banlieues* and the possibility of elective communities opaque to the state.[7] It is the central focus of three: *Guerilla* (2016) by Laurent Obertone, *Les Événements* (2014) by Jean Rolin and *Fabrication de la guerre civile* (2016) by Charles Robinson.[8] Given the nature of civil war, the crucial feature of these novels is their configuration of social division. Rolin's has France divided between anarchists, Islamists, nativists and mercenary criminal gangs; Obertone's sees the rabble from the *cités* run amok, while more or less fatuous Islamists and a lone-wolf, anti-PC avenger make murderous hay; Robinson's is set in the *cités* and interrogates their exclusion or possible secession from the Republic. Across all three, as often occurs in relation to civil war, the invocation of its conflictual dynamic produces an indivisible remainder, some part or other that will not fit the pattern as a whole. It is this structure, and its relation to the novel form, that I want to examine here through a close reading of Robinson's *Fabrication de la guerre civile*. The horizon of my reflexions will be the question of the novel's relation to the space of the nation; the detail of these reflexions will address the configuration of this relation in the novel's linguistic texture. The alignment between the novel as form and the nation as imaginary and real political entity has long been attested, and indeed constitutes a major factor in the novel's 200-year ascendancy as the Western cultural form of reference.[9] Against this background (and after the waning of this ascendancy), how might a contemporary novel negotiate its relation to ideas of nationhood? Specifically, in the French context: how might such a novel address in its formal strategies the sterile and factitious strife between universalism and particularism programmed by the organization of French political discourse around the categories of Republicanism? As we have already seen in the examples above, the centrality of this strife in this context is the major driver of the revived language of 'civil war'; this topic accordingly emerges as a key site at which the novel's relation to its contemporary context might be explored. How might a contemporary novel want to position itself in relation to the nation? What techniques might it use to do this? And how might these techniques facilitate – or perhaps compromise – this ambition?

'Tout dire'

First, though, we need some consideration of the relation between literature and politics in the discursive regime of Western modernity; to which end, I propose to recruit Jacques Derrida, Jacques Rancière and Chantal Mouffe.

From Derrida and Rancière, first, I take the suggestion that 'literature' (in the current meaning of the term) must be distinguished from other, related terms such as 'belles-lettres' or 'poetry', and defined as inherently modern. Derrida's definition links the emergence of 'literature' (in the current sense of the term) to 'l'espace de la liberté démocratique (liberté de la presse, liberté d'opinion, etc.)' / 'the space of democratic freedom

(freedom of the press, of opinion, etc.)' and identifies it with an exorbitant 'droit de tout dire', the right to say everything and anything.[10] Literature and democracy are inseparable, claims Derrida: this may not always be respected in fact, and one may well be present without the other in all kinds of regimes – but they share as their core principle an expansive, irredentist commitment to discursive freedom. Rancière gives this a further historical inflection: defining what he calls the 'democracy of literature', first theorized and practised by the Romantics, as 'le régime de la lettre en liberté que chacun peut reprendre à son compte' / 'the regime of the free letter, which everyone can lay their hands on'.[11] He identifies this regime with 'la grande loi de l'égalité de tous les sujets et de la disponibilité de toutes les expressions' / 'the great law of the equality of all subjects and the availability of all expressions', as enacted in the progressive entry into political life of the voices of the bourgeoisie and, later, the proletariat.[12] *Anyone* can say anything and everything, and *in any way*.

For Rancière, of course, such a *prise de parole* is the very definition of politics; that is, as an entry into the litigious conflict that determines which beings count, and which do not – those who speak, and those (the uncounted, the 'sans-part') who merely make noise.[13] As this suggests (and as Derrida emphasizes), literature's unfettered 'droit de tout dire' / 'right to say everything and anything' is mostly a matter of principle. Like other 'rights' and 'capacities' declared as part of the West's self-designation as 'modern' (which proved strangely compatible with their practical, primarily colonial refusal), this has of course been honoured as much in the breach as in the observance: namely, in the struggles over the right of anyone to say anything and everything, in any way, that form the history of 'literature' as a modern quasi-institution, and of the discursive regime through which this 'modernity' self-defines, namely, liberal representative democracy. Which brings us to Chantal Mouffe.

In Mouffe's account, to work as it should, this regime needs to be structured by what she calls 'agonistic pluralism'. Although its space is defined by conflict, this conflict is founded on a deep agreement: for the parties in question accept that they share a common ground, namely, the protocols regulating the discursive space itself. Any conflict that remains concerns only the interpretation of the values framing this space, not the values themselves. This 'conflictual consensus', as Mouffe terms it, ensures that these actors encounter each other as *legitimate adversaries* within the shared space of what she calls *agonism*.[14] This process is always incomplete, however; for Mouffe, *antagonism* is ineradicable. The formation of any temporarily hegemonic social order, she writes, 'implies the establishment of frontiers, the determination of a space of inclusion/exclusion'.[15] Actors who refuse the protocols – or whom the protocols exclude – remain on the outside, not just as Rancière's 'sans-part', but as Schmittian *enemies*, parties who, as Mouffe puts it, 'do not belong to the same space of representation'[16] or 'who have no common symbolic space'.[17]

Thus framed, then, my object here is the contemporary French novel as a site for the representation of social conflict, and the question of this site as a form of common ground. It will accordingly be important for my exploration that the novel on which I am going to focus bears all the hallmarks of prestige, high literary culture. For one sign of the persisting modern alignment between 'literature' and representative democracy is the still widespread notion that inclusion within the novel, especially, constitutes a form of social recognition of otherwise under-represented voices (whether of characters or of authors), a happily democratic redistribution of the cultural capital which just about remains attached to the 'literary', in which its forms (again, especially the novel) are understood as constitutively open, inclusive and mixed. Indeed, a well-established view of the novel as expansively pluralist, for example – negatively crystallized in Henry James's criticism of mid-Victorian novels as 'large, loose, baggy monsters' – can easily be aligned with the ideal self-image of liberal government as proceeding by 'deliberative democracy'.[18] So my guiding questions will be: how does a literary novel emanating from the centre of cultural power engage these dynamics of antagonism, especially when it is typified by the classically literary desire to 'tout dire', bringing individuals, groups and languages together on the common ground of its discursive pluralism? How does its form map the fault line between agonism and antagonism (singularly sharp in the case of civil war, of course, whose logic is exactly the refusal of common ground)? And how does its negotiation of these questions in the details of its form organize its treatment of social division in contemporary France?

'Keski space'

Charles Robinson published *Fabrication de la guerre civile* in 2016 with Le Seuil, who in 2011 had also published its predecessor, *Dans les cités*. The novel's plot concerns a local authority's decision to demolish a section of social housing and 'relocate' (i.e. evict) the current residents, and the route from this decision to a large-scale, violent insurrection by a significant section of this population. For our purposes, it is noteworthy that Robinson's twin novels, both concerned with spaces of exclusion, emanate from a centre of literary cultural capital, appearing in the eminent 'Fiction et Cie' series, whose signature cover style presents them as high Modernist prestige objects.[19] Prima facie, then, they are at a very different angle to the territory they engage than, for example, other more or less prestigious *banlieue* literature understood as emerging from that territory.[20] As we will see, Robinson's novel is keenly aware of the effects of this angle on its attempt to engage with this space. And its author is no less aware of the cultural capital and classic literary pluralism his work mobilizes. He situates himself in the lineage of '[la] grande littérature, [la] littérature classique' / 'great literature, classic literature', especially 'les Russes du dix-neuvième' / 'the nineteenth-century Russians'; and his aim might well be interpreted as 'tout dire'. As he puts it, the 'enjeu stylistique' / 'stylistic effort' of *Fabrication de la guerre civile* is 'comment je peux embarquer tout ça' / 'how I can load it all on'; that is, his chosen ingredients of classic literature, contemporary experimental literature (which he already defines as mixing heterogeneous elements) and 'la culture populaire, la culture urbaine, la culture des cités' / 'popular culture, street culture, the culture of the projects': '*Fabrication de la guerre civile*, le point de départ, c'est essayer d'inventer un style qui soit capable d'attraper tout ça'[21] / 'the starting point for *Fabrication de la guerre civile* was how to invent a style that could catch all of that'.

Alongside commentators such as Rioufol and Djaïz, Robinson frames the question of civil war in terms of the possible secession of the *cités*. And he does suggest that this conflict can include an ethnic dimension. Late in the novel, the character Saï declares: 'Avec les Français, on peut pas s'entendre.' / 'We just can't get along with the French.' Once his inter-locutor has confirmed that by 'Français' / 'French', he means 'Blancs' / 'Whites', he continues: 'Et les Blancs, ils sont pas racistes, ils veulent bien épicer les droits de l'homme avec des musulmans. Mais il faut que ça change rien à la douce France. Pas toucher la photo. Vous êtes chez vous : là, dans l'ombre. Chut.'[22] / 'And the Whites, they're not racist, they're quite happy to spice up the rights of men with some Muslims, so long as that doesn't change anything in sweet France. No switching the image. Here you stay in your place, right there, in the shadows. Shut up.' Mostly, however, Robinson's novel maps the fracture defining its social field not ethno-religiously, but in broadly Republican, even 'neo-Republican' terms: as social segregation via territorial separation. At its heart, consequently, is the relation between exclusion and secession – with a good dose of self-conscious musing on the novel's place in the face of these dynamics.

As Saï exposes the exclusion operated by pseudo-integration ('Vous êtes chez vous'), he specifies that this is also a silencing: 'Chut.' Deploying the mongrel tendencies of his genre, Robinson composes *Fabrication de la guerre civile* as a space of classically novelistic discursive pluralism, in which the 'noise' of the uncounted ('sans part') is included as speech. Not through mere transcription, though. With due creative diligence, he insists that 'on n'est pas dans un copié-collé d'une langue, c'est pas du tout du verbatim : la langue que parlent les personnages est un état de la langue inventé, qui n'est pas exactement celle qu'on entend à la rue'[23] / 'this is not a cut-and-paste job of a particular way of speaking, it's not trying to be verbatim: the way these characters speak is an invented state of the language, which is not exactly what you hear in the street'. Through this process of invention, Robinson nevertheless wants to inscribe something like the language of the excluded as a medium of powerful self-assertion. For the creativity he celebrates in this language as 'un usage de la langue extrêmement vif, dans les accents, dans l'invention de vocabulaire'[24] / 'an extremely sharp use of language, in the accents, in the invention of new vocabulary' also forms it as a site and a strategy of confrontation. Citing Sun Tzu's *Art of War*, he says: 'la langue dans les cités, c'est un champ de bataille. C'est le lieu où on peut apparaître, et c'est le lieu où on peut remporter les combats.'[25] / 'language in the projects is a battlefield. It's the place where you can win out.' For those without economic or cultural capital, this reworked language is a key asset: as the novel's narrative voice puts it, 'Ont-ils les armes pour lutter d'égal à égal, chers amis de la raison administrative française ? Non. Et bien ils déplacent le conflit, et ce n'est pas couillon.'[26] / 'Do they have the arms to fight on equal terms, dear friends of French administrative reason? No. So they shift the conflict elsewhere, that's not stupid.' This displacement is also a *détournement* of dominant codes, which the novel presents as a kind of Voodoo:

> À la possession de richesses s'oppose la possession magique. Esquiver l'esclavage, prendre sa revanche sur le citoyen d'État. Ce sur quoi tu ne peux agir, tu peux t'en saisir dans ce champ de bataille institué qu'est la langue devenue envoûtement.[27]

> There's a kind of magic possession that stands against possession of riches. Dodging slavery, getting your own back on the citizen of the State. All that you can't change, you can get hold of it in the battlefield of language that's got high.

In this reconfigured sign system, 'tous les rejets et détritus sont désormais investis de puissance magique' / 'all the rejects and waste now have a sort of magic power', which power lies in 'une résistance et une pratique qui sait fausser les rapports imposés'[28] / 'a form of resistance and practice that knows how to bend imposed relations'.

The language of Robinson's fictional *cité* and its inhabitants, then, asks to be understood as an inventive practice of evasion and resistance. When its usages display alternative contextual protocols, this is signalled by typographical variations mimicking the visual form of the language in question (as in various examples of graffiti and textspeak[29]). Most frequently, Robinson uses alternative orthography to indicate both what the usual euphemism would call 'non-standard' pronunciation and the currency of this as the local medium: thus, 'keski space ?' (qu'est-ce qui se passe ?) / 'what's going down?'; 'ki peton vrémen konsidéré kom 1 ami ?' (qui peut-on vraiment considérer comme un ami ?) / 'who can you really consider a friend?', or

> Si tu reçois un chargeur,
> dans les Cités
> ékout mon konsey : garde la
> dernière balle pour twa.[30]

> If you get a piece
> in the projects
> listen to my advice: keep the
> last bullet for yourself.'

Occasionally, the narrative voice glosses its own role as translator:

M évolue à sa guise sur le territoire géré par Budda.
Budda ne pense pas « à sa guise ». Budda pense : Cet enkulé fait ce qu'il veut.[31]

M strikes his own course in Budda's territory.
Budda doesn't think 'his own course'. Budda thinks: 'that fucker is doing what he wants'.

Indicating its double procedure of presenting the locals' language as it might sound and translating this into 'standard' French without effacing it, the novel foregrounds its intention that the voice of the rabble should be heard, their 'noise' included as speech via the classic pluralism of the novel.

Beyond the idealist sentimentality of such an interpretation, however, the novel suggests that its terrain is more complex than this simple opposition between 'local' and 'standard' would allow. Typographical variation is also used, for example, in the replication of the visual appearance of graffiti tags, or in the typewriter-style font used to mark the entries from his mother's *Petit Larousse* used by Budda to generate passwords for his drug runners – whose thoughts on this *niveau de langue* / *register* offer further commentary on the meaning of *its* inclusion:

> Putain, songe DoBoï en frappant à la porte. C'est quoi, ces mots tout bizarres de la langue ? À quoi ça peut servir ?
>   Ils les ont inventés juste pour t'humilier ou kwa ?[32]

> Fuck, thinks DoBoï as he knocks on the door. What the fuck are all these weirdo words? What's that about?
>   Did they make them up just to humiliate you or what?

The terrain is plural, and contested: not least inasmuch as it already features the language of the state and its apparatuses. So this is not a simple relation of internal isolation, but rather an intrication, whose various languages are vectors of social power. In addition to the impeccably standard French of the former mayor,[33] we have (as in these examples): the prefabricated sensationalism of media cliché ('*Les Cités de non-droit. Tombées sous la coupe des bandes. La République a abandonné le terrain depuis des années. Un membre d'une bande a accepté de nous parler, de témoigner. Sous couvert de l'anonymat.*'[34] / '*No-go zones. Controlled by gangs. The Republic pulled out years ago. A gang-member agreed to speak to us. Under the cover of anonymity.*'); the solidarity of media and state ('Un correspondant AFP réévalue à la hausse le nombre des émeutiers. Notre détermination. La République ne cédera.'[35] / 'A correspondent from AFP reports a rise in the number of rioters. Our determination. The Republic will not give way.' Or '*Toutes les personnes évacuées ont été prises en charge pour relogement*, avait tweeté la préfecture de police après les expulsions.'[36] / '*All tenants evacuated have been offered alternative lodgings*, tweeted the police officials after the evictions.'); and the easy compatibility between an official discourse of civil rights and the reality of securitization ('Respect – Transparence – Égalité de traitement | Nos engagements pour une vidéosurveillance de qualité'[37] / Respect – Transparency – Equality of treatment | Our commitment to quality telesurveillance'). Significantly, however, none of these examples of dominant discourse is typographically marked; this may signal something of the text's own discursive position, as we will discuss below.

The text, and by implication its territory, become a space of conflictual linguistic plurality. Robinson's 'langue des cités' is the clash and the interpenetration of all manner of languages, differently powerful. Not least because the *cité* itself is home to all manner of people. Instead of anonymity ('la foule' / 'the crowd'; 'la racaille' / 'the plebs', and so on), we have a highly internally differentiated population, which alongside those with no stake in the Republic also features the so-called 'deserving poor', others who think of themselves as impeccably respectable in comparison to their feckless, sponging neighbours, and still others who strive for social mobility through education and some more or less precarious profession: 'La fraction qui a pris l'ascenseur républicain. Objectif : promotion sociale.'[38] / 'The fraction that took the Republican elevator. Destination: upward mobility.' Alongside a critique of the bankruptcy of the (neo)liberal ideology of self-improvement and self-management, Robinson thus makes the standard liberal move of underlining that this demographic is less homogeneous than the media clichés suggest, as he writes: 'Dans les Cités aussi on forme des chirurgiens-dentistes, des designers d'objet, des écoconcepteurs, des ingénieurs gouvernance des risques, des auxiliaires de la vie politique.'[39] / 'You also find dental surgeons who grow up in the projects, designers, ecoconceptors, risk management specialists, staffers in political life.' But his emphasis on the conflictual configuration of this space takes him somewhere more interesting than this standard move.

The conflictual complexity of Robinson's territory (both the territory his novel represents and the linguistic territory it forms) blocks any homogenization of its population (including in relation to conflict – we have class war, gang war, individual vengeance, insurrection for its own sake). So his novel refuses the liberal-rationalist-pluralist fantasy of inclusion as discursive participation in a transparent self-representation of the social field. Instead, it forms a version of Mouffe's 'conflictual consensus', in which the range of parties is included without any abstract neutralization of the conflict between them – whence the significant presence of the languages of social domination.

But it would be too easy to leave the novel enjoying this air of consensus (however supposedly 'conflictual'). For it knows what Mouffe emphasizes; namely, that the agreement on common ground that sublimates antagonism into agonism is always incomplete, and always leaves a remainder of antagonism, an 'illegitimate' enemy. And the question it invites is whether, as a high literary novel, it is capable of indicating this antagonistic outside *as outside*.

Cross-cut by lines of force, Robinson's novel is a space not of co-existence, but of confrontation. It is indeed a battleground. Of the educating crusade of the Third Republic ('aux temps glorieux de la conquête alphabétique sur les campagnes environnantes'[40] / 'the glorious days in which literacy was rolled out to the surrounding regions'), little remains but the notion of the territory as ground to be won. When the local mayor says they have lost ground, he means this literally; thanks to the narrative's satirical edge, his staff even includes a deputy in charge of gaining ground back ('adjoint chargé de la Reconquête du territoire'). Municipal strategies to inculcate 'civilité' ('des actions de sensibilisation' / 'awareness raising actions') blend smoothly into social control, ('nos Cités chaque jour plus sûres | bientôt ici, la vidéosurveillance' / 'our projects are getting safer everyday | telesurveillance coming soon'),[41] and according to the novel's narrative voice, the Republic seeking to regain control of the territory has itself produced and segregated the unruly populations it wishes to subdue:

> Le droit ne peut rien pour eux. Ils ne possèdent rien, ils n'attendent rien. [. . .] Ce n'est pas important que l'on ferme les Cités par des murs, que l'on arrête les trains dans cette direction, que l'on déploie l'armée autour pour qu'ils ne sortent pas. Le fait important, c'est que pour la première fois depuis bien longtemps des gens auront échappé à l'État, et vivront à nouveau à sa marge. [. . .] Des groupes entiers de population, avec femmes et enfants, sur plusieurs générations, dans des territoires séparés.[42]

> The law can do nothing for them. They own nothing, they expect nothing. [. . .] It is not important that the projects are being walled in, that the trains have ceased to stop there, that the army is being used to keep people from getting out. The important thing is that for the first time in a long while, people have escaped the State and are living on its margins. [. . .] Whole groups of the population, with women and children, several generations together, in separate territories.

Setting the *cités* apart the better to control them (in the logic of the colonial *bagne* / 'jail' or Guantánamo Bay), the state deploys a method of segregation it takes for a strategy of remote control, and thereby produces the very separation which makes control appear necessary while programming its failure.

The novel's use of the civil war motif of secession/expulsion thus serves to articulate contemporary French debates about the extent and causes of territorial segregation within the Republic. And those of its *citéens* who confront what they call the 'ripoublik'[43] do indeed articulate their dynamic as one of secession from the state. Attempting to subtract themselves from state control, they are returning to the origins of the *cité* as the *polis*: 'Cité désigne à l'origine des villes administrées par leurs habitants, dotées de pouvoir de police et levant l'impôt, assurant seules leur fonctionnement. Assumons.'[44] / 'The term 'Cité' originally meant a town administered by its own citizens, with the powers to police and to levy taxes on a self-governing basis. Let's take up that mantle.' As Saï puts it: 'À quoi ça sert d'être une Cité si n'importe qui peut entrer ?'[45] / 'What use is it being a

Cité if anyone can come in?' This is conflict without consensus – and precisely the refusal of common ground. The state is the enemy, its various agents deserving violent retribution. Against 'les forces fascistes de coloni-sation'[46] / 'the fascist forces of colonization', those in revolt seek the resources for continued armed conflict while hijacking the now respectable insurrectionary iconography of the Republic (here, Delacroix's huge canvas 'Liberty Guiding the People') to underscore its latter-day hypocrisy:

> Marianne en flanelle, joli foulard turquoise masquant son nez, est-ce le ninja pastel ? Hissée sur la barricade [. . .], sa robe s'est fendue lorsqu'elle est grimpée et tout le monde peut admirer le galbe gracieux de son joli sein.[47]

> Marianne in flannel, with a nice turquoise scarf tied over her nose, is that ninja pastel? Her dress ripped when she climbed up on a barricade and everyone can admire the smooth curve of her pretty tit.

Nor does this have anything to do with reform or revolution. The rioters agree with Giorgio Agamben that, 'The novelty of the coming politics is that it will no longer be a struggle for the conquest or control of the State, but a struggle between the State and the non-State':[48]

> Ce n'est pas une révolution [. . .], le vaudou ne peut pas faire la révolution, ce n'est pas sa fonction. Ce n'est pas un soulèvement. Ce n'est ni une colère, ni une vengeance. C'est la libération, c'est presser très fort le bouton OFF.[49]

> This is not a revolution [. . .], voodoo can't make revolution, that's not its function. It's not an uprising. It's not anger, nor revenge. It's liberation. It's pressing the OFF button really hard.

If Robinson's novel here appears to channel the comments of an Alain Finkielkraut on the 2005 riots, the effect of this is not to lament (however lucidly) the rejection of the Republic: it is rather to suggest that for the characters in question, whether or not the 'cité' has its origins in the autonomy of the *polis*, the contemporary *cités* are not part of the *polis*, and nor do they want to be.[50] If we meet here the 'blank space' version of secession in the French context, this indicates nothing so much as its determination as the wholly unimaginable other side of the Republican public space of social visibility and control. Wholly unimaginable, that is, from that Republican space. These are not the noisy uncounted, insisting that the counted hear their speech; the obligatory Republican-philosophical template of ancient Athens is not their frame of reference. 'Notre Agora, c'est les emmerdes' / 'Our Agora, it's the shit going down', says the narrative voice:[51] in the *cité*, not the *polis*, 'we' are already speaking.

The 'nous' to which the narrative voice here lays claim is also contested, however. Far from *staging* these dramas of conflict and consensus, the novel is *caught up in* them. By folding literary allusions into his novel's fabric, for example, Robinson makes it plain that the cultural and commercial institution of literature is firmly on the side of the powers that be, however heterodox or combative it might once have been.[52] And crucially, to his delineation of the plural make-up of the *cité*'s population, and the various elevated positions attained by some of its inhabitants, Robinson adds that of *novelist*. For the text's narrator and most frequent focalizer turns out to be one 'Charles', a participant-observer who, having grown up in the area, is now engaged in writing a novel about it. This figure is unsurprisingly self-conscious: 'Difficile de savoir si je me sens anthropologue, archéologue face aux ruines d'une civilisation, ingénieur cherchant ce qui pourrait être réparé, simple voyeur'[53] / 'Difficult to know whether I feel like an anthropologist, an archaeologist staring at the ruins of a civilisation, an engineer wondering what can be mended, or a simple voyeur', he muses at one point. Other characters interrogate him as to the nature of his role, and alongside embedding the text within the wider œuvre of Charles Robinson via a 'revision notes'-style exercise on the novel's predecessor,[54] he also insists to the reader that he is of this territory: 'Je ne suis pas un touriste. J'ai passé là toute mon adolescence.' / 'I'm not a tourist. I grew up here.' This is questioned, however, by those who live there, not least his one-time best friend Saï, who comments, 'Je suis sûr que tu fumes de la merde dans ta capitale' / 'I'm sure you smoke shit in your capital', and subsumes him among the forces of the other side: 'Qui voudrait se battre de votre côté ? À part les flics.' / '[W]ho would want to fight on your side? Except the cops?'[55] If we accept the text's invitation and identify 'Charles' with Charles Robinson, this association with the forces of the centre is confirmed by the alignment at work in Robinson's interview comment that, 'L'idée du livre [. . .] c'est vraiment d'essayer de comprendre comment tout ce qui se passe, qui peut *nous* sembler très étrange, quand *on* en voit quelques images dans un journal télévisé, d'essayer, d'être placé au cœur de ça.'[56] / 'The idea of the book [. . .] is to try and understand what is happening, which might seem really strange to us, when you just see the news reports, to try and be at the heart of it.' Charles is indeed at the heart of it – but the effect of this is to delineate sharply the lines of force by which the territory is traversed, and in which he, like everyone, is caught. Indeed, according to Saï, his absorption into the mainstream is such that his novel is doomed to failure:

– Tu ne pourras pas déclencher une guerre.

– Déclencher ? Ben tu vois, il est pourri, ton livre. T'as rien compris aux Cités. La guerre, elle est déjà là et ce n'est pas nous qui l'avons commencée.[57]

– You will never set a war in motion.

– Set it in motion? You know, your book is a pile of crap. You don't understand shit about the projects. The war's already there and it wasn't us that set it in motion.

Robinson's self-conscious literariness is not just dutiful Modernist posturing, then. Charles's capture within the novel's lines of force, as representative of literary culture's alignment with procedures of domination, articulates the novel's major dilemma. From its side of the battle lines, that of a Republican policy of integration whose reality is attempted remote control by abandonment and segregation, its novelistic representation of the insurgent *citéens* can only betray them by sublimating their antagonism into the agonistic pluralism defining its form. Robinson's novel may well understand itself as a space of confrontation, but it also understands that it is bound to neutralize this. As Charles says when debating the future of the *cités* with Saï: 'La séparation est un fantasme.'[58] / 'Separation is fantasy.' And this is his novel's double bind. Yes, it can show the limits of its constitutive drive towards inclusion, or attend with self-conscious irony to its own translation of characters' 'noise' into 'speech', but as a literary novel, how can it resist instantiating itself as a kind of common ground? And what is worse, given its knowledge of its inevitable alignment with the current dominant order, as an object wielding major cultural capital, how can it avoid gathering up in its mainstream Republican embrace the self-designated enemies of the 'ripoublik'? Refashioning their unimaginable other space in its own image? Only a form immanent to its territory and refractory to the state can avoid this, and in so doing, reproduce the structure of secession. Which a novel emanating from the centre of social power simply cannot do.

But sublimation is always incomplete. This fault line is less within the space of Robinson's novel than between the novel itself – as a whole – and its most significant part. Which thereby ends up inside *and* outside, inscribed within as refusing such heteronomous inscription. This is a complex figure, to be sure (a part contained within a whole defined as unable to contain it), but such is the result of the encounter here between the generous minded inclusivity of the novel as genre, and this particular novel's attempt to honour a rebel rejection of any inclusion whatsoever.

The novel's exorbitant tendency to include even what it is not including is highlighted at one point by a reference to our narrator's presence within the action: after we read a scandalous comment from a municipal official, a colleague asks, 'Charles, vous ne prenez pas ça en note, merci.'[59] / 'Charles, don't go writing that down please.' Too late, of course: the novel can only mark the withdrawal of an element by *including* it *as withdrawn*. If, for Charles, the Republic seeks to control the *cités* remotely, holding them at a distance the better to keep them bound in, so inversely is Robinson left with the secessionist part of his population straining to form an outside, and so forming an internal remainder antagonistically rejecting the discursive politics of the literary novel in which they find themselves. The enemy within.

There's Always Something Left Behind

The agonistic pluralism which defines the literary novel thus retains antagonistic refusal as an inassimilable remainder *within and beyond* the common ground of adversarial relation. In Agamben's reflexions on the Ancient Greek theory of civil war as *stasis*, civil war itself emerges as just such a remainder, as 'the becoming-political of the unpolitical (the *oikos*) and the becoming-unpolitical of the political (the *polis*)'.[60] Within the Republic ('une et indivisible'), the figure of civil war produces a differently indivisible leftover, whether civil war itself or that part of the social body which comes to figure its impossible logic as a part both within and without the whole.

Impossible, and perhaps fractal. What if, to the remainders of civil war, we had to add what even this paradoxical internal exile has had to jettison? The question of confessional allegiance, for example: in good Republican fashion (and unlike Louaath, say, whose *Les Sauvages* is structured by the overlaying of social, ethnic and religious divisions), Robinson declines to parse his population in confessional terms – no doubt, in order to refuse the caricatural, single-issue focus on Islamism we find in authors such as Rioufol and Djaïz (and indeed Houellebecq). Or the question of gender. All but one of the key actors in Robinson's story are male; almost without exception, women feature as lovers (past or present) or mothers, consistently evoked secondarily, in relation to male characters for whose thoughts and feelings they serve as objective correlatives. Only one female character is granted anything by way of significant interiority: Angela, the municipal official charged with managing the 'relocation' of the *cité*'s residents on the ground. But Angela's role is primarily structural, on the one hand, and narrative, on the other. As the point of contact between the

residents and the mayor's office, she forms a privileged space in which the
tensions and interactions between the two sides may be registered. And
when Saï triggers the climactic uprising by occupying the *mairie*'s local
administrative office, taking Angela and a male colleague hostage, this
captivity culminates in her sexual assault. Indeed, as the start of the
uprising immediately follows her near-rape, the uprising functions in
narrative terms as the displaced climax to her abuse, the attack on her
body synecdochically continuous with the attack on the Republic she is
charged with embodying. The limits of Robinson's female characterization
would appear to be emphatically sexual, and his plot structure arguably
misogynist. Indeed, even when the Republican imagery of a bare-breasted
Liberty is being satirized, as we saw above, it is also being repeated: for all
that this scenario presents a newly urban Marianne, it is still her breast that
is exposed, and as a rule any agency possessed by Robinson's women is
defined relative to that of his male protagonists.[61]

Occluding religion and relegating gender to the habitual terms of a
patriarchal symbolic economy, granting agency primarily to the male citizen
as supposed 'abstract individual' (whose ethnic diversity is swept up in this
familiar pseudo-universalism), Robinson's blind spots ironically join the
defining inclusivity of his form in aligning him with the Republicanism
his novel analyses so sharply. But even this alliance of inclusion and
exclusion leaves a further remainder in its turn. As its flats are progressively
cleared in preparation for demolition, Robinson's *cité* accommodates new
residents, who pay over the odds to squat these abandoned spaces. Although
composed of 'un patchwork d'Africains de l'Est non francophones'[62] / 'a
patchwork of non-French-speaking East Africans', these more or less illegalized migrants are designated by the locals indifferently as 'les Somaliens',
and are despised in the most classic of racist clichés:

— Putains de Somaliens, dit quelqu'un.
— Personne ne les a vus venir, dit quelqu'un. Ils entrent là. Comme des
   rats. Personne ne peut les empêcher.[63]
— Fucking Somalis, said someone.
— Nobody saw them coming, said someone. In they come. Like rats.
   No-one can stop them.

The novel attends to their plight, and registers their language, to an
extent — to the extent that they figure in this territory at all, that is.
A source of shady income, installed and expelled at will, they fade in and
out of the narrative, inassimilable even for those remainders that inhabit
the conflictual space of impossible secession. A part of no whole, exscribed
by even the most contestatory gesture of inscription.

At which point, and despite Saï's hostility towards 'les Français', we might wonder whether there might not also be something all too domestic about the figure of civil war. Might even Robinson's secessionists, hijacking the iconography of the Republic and repeating its exclusions, not still be engaged in another 'very French war'? If we put *Fabrication de la guerre civile* alongside the films about illegalized migrants that Sylvain George groups under the heading, 'Des figures de guerre', for example, does it not look rather chauvinistic?[64] When compared to Europe's war on refugees, say, whose outsourcing of the interior recruits Turkish, Libyan and Sudanese security forces, and whose internal remainder is the legal limbo of detention centres.[65] Just as the term 'fracture sociale' / 'social fracture' has served to render 'new and disruptive post-colonial narratives of second-generation identity politics or post-colonial racism' digestible within 'an existing neo-republican framework', as Émile Chabal puts it,[66] so might the figure of civil war – and quite possibly even the baggy inclusivity of the novel, which here at least proves still hard to separate from the nation – exert similarly centripetal force, gathering the issue of conflict into questions of social exclusion and inclusion which maintain the unity of the Republic as the key reference point. Perhaps, ultimately, 'civil war' is just too civil.

Notes

Introduction

1 Arjun Appadurai's *Modernity at Large. Cultural Dimensions of Globalization* (Minneapolis, MN: University of Minnesota Press, 1996) is a foundational text for this approach.

2 William Marx, 'Entretien', in François Bégaudeau, Arno Bertina, Mathieu Larnaudie, Olivier Rohe and Joy Sorman (eds.), *Devenirs du roman* (Paris: Inculte/Naïve, 2007), pp. 52–53: 'la crise existentielle de la littérature est une conséquence nécessaire de l'autonomisation, alors c'est aussi en France que la dévalorisation doit être le plus visible. [. . .] Par comparaison, la situation littéraire dans les pays anglophone est beaucoup moins tranchée : jamais les écrivains n'y ont été portés au pinacle comme ici, jamais ils ne se sont coupés complètement du réel, jamais ils n'ont mis leur art en accusation avec autant de violence qu'en France.' / 'the existential crisis of literature is a necessary consequence of its autonomy, so it had to be in France that its devalorization would be most visible. [. . .] In comparison, the situation with literature in Anglophone countries is much less marked: writers have never been so absolutely valued as they have here; they have never been so cut off from the real; and they have never shown such violence in accusation of their art as in France.'

3 Marx, 'Entretien', p. 53. Marx anticipates a small 'pincement de cœur' / 'twinge of the heart' at having to say goodbye to this 'hautaine beauté' / 'haughty beauty'.

4 Pierre Nora's considerable influence in the field of French literary and historical studies is also due to his multi-volume work *Les Lieux de Mémoire* (Paris: Gallimard, 1984–1992, 3 vols.); *Realms of Memory. Rethinking the French Past*, trans. Arthur Goldhammer (New York, NY: Columbia, 1996).

5 Annie Ernaux, *Les Années* (Paris: Gallimard, 2008), p. 136.

6 Ernaux, *The Years*, trans. Alison L. Strayer (New York, NY: Seven Stories Press, 2017), pp. 123–124.

7 The 'loi Lang' differentiated books from other cultural products by allowing only a 5% margin on the editor's listed price, in order to stop discounting processes driving marginal production out of the market.

8 On this tendency, see Simon Kemp, *French Fiction into the Twenty-First Century* (Cardiff: University of Wales Press, 2010).

9 Dominique Viart, 'Le Moment critique de la littérature. Comment penser la littérature contemporaine ?', in Bruno Blanckeman et Jean-Christophe Millois (dirs.), *Le Roman français aujourd'hui. Transformations, perceptions, mythologies* (Paris: Prétexte, 2004), pp. 13, 16.

10 Marc Fumaroli, *L'État culturel. Une religion moderne* (Paris: Fallois, 1990).

11 Alain Badiou, *Le Siècle* (Paris: Éditions du Seuil, 2005), p. 153. See also Gisèle Sapiro, Myrtille Picaud, Jérôme Pacouret and Hélène Seiler, 'L'amour de la littérature : le festival, nouvelle instance de production de la croyance', in *Actes de la recherche en sciences sociales*, n° 206–207 (2015), pp. 108–137.

12 François Cusset, *La décennie. Le grand cauchemar des années quatre-vingt* (Paris: La Découverte, 2006), p. 328.

13 See Lionel Ruffel, *Brouhaha* (Paris: Verdier, 2016).

14 Of particular note was Denis Hollier's *A New History of French Literature* (Cambridge, MA: Harvard University Press, 1989) and more recently Susan Rubin Suleiman's *French Global. A New Approach to Literary History* (New York, NY: Columbia University Press, 2010).

15 See www.francophonie.org/la-francophonie-en-bref-754.

16 Luc Pinhas, 'La Francophonie face à la globalisation éditoriale : politiques publiques et initiatives privées', in Gisèle Sapiro (ed.), *Les contradictions de la globalisation éditoriale* (Paris: Nouveau Monde éditions, 2009), pp. 117–129; Gisèle Sapiro, George Steinetz and Claire Ducournau, 'La Production des représentations coloniales et postcoloniales', *Actes de la recherche en sciences sociales*, n° 185 (2010), pp. 4–11; Claire Decournau, 'Qu'est-ce qu'un classique "africain"?', *Actes de la recherche en sciences sociales*, n° 206–207 (2015), pp. 34–49.

17 Pascale Casanova, *La République mondiale des Lettres* (Paris: Éditions du Seuil, 2008 [1999]); *The World Republic of Letters* (Cambridge, MA and London, UK: Harvard University Press, 2007). In her 2008 preface, Casanova acknowledges the specifically French 'literary-centrism' at work in her own ambition to write a totalizing survey of structural forces of the literary field, but suggests that this project could also only take form because of the already ongoing erosion of that pre-eminence. (*La République mondiale des Lettres*, pp. XI–XVI.)

18 Casanova, *La République mondiale*, p. 490; *The World Republic*, p. 399.

19 Casanova, *La République mondiale*, p. 73; *The World Republic*, p. 44.

20 Casanova, *La République mondiale*, p. XIII.

21 Ibid.

22 Fredric Jameson's *The Geopolitical Aesthetic: Cinema and Space in the World Space* (London, UK and Bloomington, IN: BFI/Indiana University Press, 1995) is a foundational text for this approach.

23 Casanova, *La République mondiale*, p. 484, quoting Roland Barthes, *Sur Racine* (Paris: Éditions du Seuil, 1963), p. 145; Casanova, *The World Republic*, p. 394.

24 Barthes, *Sur Racine*, p. 145; Barthes, *On Racine*, trans. Richard Howard (Berkeley, CA: University of California Press, 1992), p. 153.

25 Ivan Jablonka, *L'Histoire est une littérature contemporaine. Manifeste pour les sciences sociales* (Paris: Éditions du Seuil, coll. La Librairie du XXIe siècle, 2018 [2014]). Jablonka has a range of editorial roles, including editor of the Collège-de-France-based online review publication *La Vie des idées/Books and Ideas*.

26 Jablonka, *L'Histoire est une littérature contemporaine*, p. 8: 'Contribuer, par l'écriture, à l'attrait des sciences sociales peut être une manière de conjurer le désamour qui les frappe à l'université comme dans les librairies.' / 'Writing can contribute to dispelling the disaffection that has befallen the social sciences among university students and the book-buying public.'

27 Jablonka, *L'Histoire est une littérature contemporaine*, pp. II–III.

28 Jablonka, *Histoire des grand-parents que je n'ai pas eus* (Paris: Éditions du Seuil, coll. La Librairie du XXIe siècle, 2012); *A History of the Grandparents I Never Had*, trans. Jane Kuntz (Stanford, CA: Stanford University Press, 2017); *Laëtitia, ou la fin des hommes* (Paris: Éditions du Seuil, coll. La librairie du XXIe siècle, 2016).

29 Jablonka, *L'Histoire est une littérature contemporaine*, p. 19.

30 Alexandre Gefen, *Réparer le monde. La Littérature face au XIXe siècle* (Paris: Corti, 2017). Dominique Rabaté also defined the 1980s as the moment when ' "écrire" redevient un verbe transitif' / 'when "writing" becomes a transitive verb again' (Dominique Rabaté, 'À l'ombre du roman. Propositions pour introduire à la notion du récit', in Bruno Blanckeman and Jean-Christophe Millois (dirs.), *Le Roman français aujourd'hui*), p. 47.

31 Jablonka, *L'Histoire est une littérature contemporaine*, p. VII.

32 Ibid., p. VIII.

33 Barthes, 'Ce que je dois à Khatibi', in *L'Œuvre de … Abdelkébir Khatibi* (Rabat: Marsam, 1997), pp. 121–123; Casanova, *La République mondiale des lettres*, p. 490.

34 Barthes, 'Ce que je dois à Khatibi', p. 123.

35 See in particular the works by Alec Hargreaves, *Voices from the North African Immigrant Community in France: Immigration and Identity in Beur Fiction* (Oxford, UK and New York, NY: Berg, 1991) and *Post-colonial Cultures in France* (London, UK and New York, NY: Routledge, 1997).

36 Tiphaine Samoyault, 'L'amitié', in *Le Goût du roman*, dir. Matteo Majorano (Bari: Edizoni B.A. Graphis, 2002), p. 79. See also Samoyault's longer study *L'excès du roman* (Paris: Maurice Nadeau, 1999), in which she grapples with what the task of the novel can be after the experiment of 'radical intransitivity'.

37 Samoyault, 'Un réalisme lyrique est-il possible ?', in Bruno Blanckeman et Jean-Christophe Milois (dirs.), *Le Roman français aujourd'hui. Transformations, perceptions, mythologies* (Paris: Prétexte, 2004), p. 83, referring to Philippe Forest's *Le Roman, le réel* (Nantes: Pleins feux, 1999). Forest, like Rabaté in *La Passion de l'impossible. Histoire du récit au XXe siècle* (Paris: Corti, 2018), anchors the 'novel' in its 'impossibility' throughout this essay.

38 See Oana Panaïté, 'La Querelle des bibliothèques ou la gêne de la critique française face à la littérature en français', *Nouvelles Études Francophones*, 28.1 (2013), pp. 145–161.

39 See Gisèle Sapiro and Cécile Rabot (eds.), *Profession, écrivain ?* (Paris: CNRS Éditions, 2017).

40 See the collective publication *Devenirs du roman* by the group that founded the review *Inculte*.

41 Roland Barthes's last lectures at the Collège de France were entitled 'Préparation du roman' and lasted through the years 1978–1980. They were published as *Préparation du roman. Cours au Collège de France*, ed. Nathalie Léger (Paris: Éditions du Seuil, 2003); *The Preparation of the Novel: Lecture Courses and Seminars at the Collège de France*, trans. Kate Briggs (New York, NY: Columbia University Press, 2010).

42 See Lionel Ruffel, *Brouhaha*.

43 See Véronique Montémont, '*Quelque chose noir* : le point de fracture ?', in *Textuel*, n° 55 (Paris: Université Paris Diderot, 2008).

Chapter 1

1 See, among others, Charles Forsdick and David Murphy (eds.) *Francophone Postcolonial Studies: A Critical Introduction* (London: Arnold, 2003); Farid Laroussi and Christopher L. Miller, 'French and Francophone: the challenge of expanding horizons', *Yale French Studies* 103 (2003); Alec G. Hargreaves, Charles Forsdick and David Murphy, *Transnational French Studies: Postcolonialism and Littérature-Monde* (Liverpool: Liverpool University Press, 2012).

2 Françoise Lionnet, 'Introduction. Francophone studies: new landscapes', in Françoise Lionnet and Dominic Thomas (eds.), *Modern Language Notes*, 118.4 (2003), pp. 783–786 (p. 784).

3 Charles Forsdick and David Murphy (eds.), *Francophone Postcolonial Studies: A Critical Introduction*, p. 12. Forsdick and Murphy further argue that 'much scholarship on the Caribbean archipelago [...] has tended to be produced according to the dominant languages spoken within the region, with the result that a polyglossic, pan-Caribbean space is fragmented into smaller spaces still defined along transatlantic axes in relation to their former colonial occupiers' (p. 12). The same holds true in relation to the Mediterranean.

4 Iain Chambers, 'Maritime criticism and theoretical shipwreck', *Publications of the Modern Language Association*, 125.3 (2010), pp. 678–684 (p. 680).

5 Susan Rubin Suleiman, *Risking Who One Is: Encounters with Contemporary Art* (Cambridge, MA: Harvard University Press, 1994), p. 3.

6 Ibid., p. 10.

7 Giorgio Agamben, *What Is an Apparatus? and Other Essays*, trans. David Kishik and Stefan Pedatella (Stanford, CA: Stanford University Press, 2009), p. 40.

8 Ibid., pp. 44–46.
9 Ibid., p. 47.
10 Hannah Arendt, *Between Past and Future: Eight Exercises in Political Thought* (New York: Penguin, 1993), p. 9.
11 Marianne Hirsch, *The Generation of Postmemory: Writing and Visual Culture After the Holocaust* (New York, NY: Columbia University Press, 2012), p. 5.
12 Jacques Derrida, *Acts of Literature*, ed. Derek Attridge (New York, NY: Routledge, 1992), p. 48.
13 Abdelkebir Khatibi, 'Pensée-Autre', in *Œuvres de Abdelkébir Khatibi III, Essais* (Paris: Éditions de la Différence, 2008), pp. 9–27 (p. 21). All translations into English are the author's, unless specified otherwise.
14 Ibid., p. 10.
15 Ibid., p. 13.
16 Ibid., p. 26.
17 Ibid., p. 26.
18 Khatibi, *Maghreb pluriel* (Paris: Denoël, 1983), p. 186. A collection of Khatibi's writing is published under the title *Plural Maghreb. Writings on Postcolonialism*, trans. P. Burcu Yalim (London: Bloomsbury Academic, 2019).
19 Khatibi, *Amour bilingue*, in *Œuvres de Abdelkébir Khatibi I, Romans et récits* (Paris: Éditions de la Différence, 2008), pp 205–284 (p. 238).
20 Khatibi, *Love in Two Languages*, trans. Richard Howard (Minneapolis, MN: University of Minnesota Press, 1990), p. 49.
21 Khatibi, 'Diglossia', in Anne-Emmanuelle Berger (ed.) *Algeria in Other's Languages* (Ithaca, NY: Cornell University Press, 2002), pp. 157–160 (p. 158).
22 Khatibi, *Figures de l'étranger dans la littérature française* (Paris: Denoël, 1987), p. 203.
23 Ibid., p. 205.
24 Khatibi, 'Diglossia', p. 158.
25 Khatibi, 'Paradigmes de civilisation', in *L'Œuvre de ... Abdelkébir Khatibi* (Rabat: Marsam, 1997), pp. 69–87 (pp. 86–87).
26 Roland Barthes, 'Ce que je dois à Khatibi', in *L'Œuvre de ... Abdelkébir Khatibi*, pp. 121–123 (p. 123).
27 Assia Djebar, *Ces Voix qui m'assiègent* (Paris: Albin Michel, 1999), p. 26.
28 Ibid., p. 27.
29 Ibid., p. 25.
30 Ibid., p. 27.
31 Ibid., p. 29.
32 Ibid., p. 30.
33 Ibid., p. 34.
34 Ibid., p. 44.
35 The phrase comes from Assia Djebar, *Algerian White*, trans. David Kelley and Marjolijn De Jager (New York, NY: Seven Stories Press, 2000), p. 230.
36 Djebar, *Ces Voix qui m'assiègent* (Paris: Albin Michel, 1999), p. 139.

37 Ibid., p. 140.
38 Ibid., p. 144.
39 See Patrick Crowley, 'Introduction. Travel, colonialism and encounters with the Maghreb: Algeria', *Studies in Travel Writing*, 21.3 (2017), pp. 231–242.
40 Assia Djebar, *Vaste est la prison* (Paris: Albin Michel, 1995), p. 143.
41 Djebar, *So Vast the Prison*, trans. Betsy Wing (New York, NY: Seven Stories Press, 1999), p. 145.
42 Djebar, *Vaste est la prison*, p. 121.
43 Djebar, *So Vast the Prison*, p. 123.
44 Djebar, *Ces Voix qui m'assiègent*, p. 203.
45 *Moriscos* are Spanish Muslims who, under relentless pressure from the Catholic Church, converted to Christianity. Many continued to practise Islam secretly.
46 Djebar, *Vaste est la prison*, p. 170.
47 Djebar, *So Vast the Prison*, pp. 174–175.
48 Djebar, *Vaste est la prison*, p. 168; *So Vast the Prison*, p. 172.
49 Djebar, *Vaste est la prison*, p. 168.
50 Djebar, *So Vast the Prison*, p. 173.
51 Djebar, *Vaste est la prison*, p. 170.
52 Djebar, *So Vast the Prison*, p. 174.
53 These included the *limpieza de sangre* or 'purity of blood' laws, which demarcated Christian lineages from mixed Andalusian genealogies.
54 Derrida, *Of Hospitality. Anne Dufourmantelle Invites Jacques Derrida to respond* (Stanford, CA: Stanford University Press, 2000), p. 144. Originally published as *De l'hospitalité. Anne Dufourmantelle invite Jacques Derrida à répondre* (Paris: Calmann-Lévy, 1997).
55 For a full analysis of Colette Fellous's novel in a Mediterranean context, see Edwige Tamalet Talbayev, *The Transcontinental Maghreb: Francophone Literature across the Mediterranean* (New York, NY: Fordham University Press, 2017), chapter 2.
56 Colette Fellous, *Avenue de France* (Paris: Gallimard, 2001), p. 31.
57 Ibid., pp. 32–33.
58 Ibid., p. 31.
59 Samia Kassab-Charfi, 'Entretien avec Colette Fellous', *Expressions maghrébines*, 11.2 (2012), pp. 145–157 (p. 149).
60 See Gilles Deleuze, *Difference and Repetition*, trans. Paul Patton (New York, NY: Columbia University Press, 1994), p. 208.
61 See Hélé Béji, *Désenchantement national. Essai sur la décolonisation* (Tunis: Elyzad, 2014).
62 Fellous, *Avenue de France*, p. 91.
63 Ibid., p. 84.
64 Réda Bensmaïa, *Experimental Nations* (Princeton, NJ: Princeton University Press, 2003), p. 8.
65 Fellous, *Avenue de France*, p. 23.
66 Fellous, *Plein Été* (Paris: Gallimard, 2007), pp. 65–66.

67 Fellous, *Avenue de France*, pp. 27–28.
68 Tahar Ben Jelloun, *Partir* (Paris: Gallimard, 2006), p. 12; *Leaving Tangier*, trans. Linda Coverdale (New York, NY: Penguin Books, 2009), p. 4.
69 Ben Jelloun, *Partir*, p. 256; *Leaving Tangier*, p. 253.
70 Ben Jelloun, *Partir*, p. 256; *Leaving Tangier*, p. 252.
71 Ben Jelloun, *Partir*, p. 263; *Leaving Tangier*, p. 260.
72 Ben Jelloun, *Partir*, p. 261; *Leaving Tangier*, p. 258.
73 Derrida, *Of Hospitality. Anne Dufourmantelle Invites Jacques Derrida to respond*, p. 2.
74 Sharon Kinoshita, 'Medieval Mediterranean literature', *Publications of the Modern Language* Association, 124.2 (2009), pp. 600–608 (p. 602).
75 Ranjanna Khanna, *Algeria Cuts: Women and Representation, 1830 to the Present* (Stanford, CA: Stanford University Press, 2008), p. 55.

Chapter 2

1 Frédéric Beigbeder, *Windows on the World* (Paris: Gallimard, collection Folio, 2004; first published by Grasset, 2003), p. 271.
2 Beigbeder, *Windows on the World*, trans. F. Wynne (London: Harper Perennial, 2005), p. 226.
3 Michel Houellebecq, 'Lettre à Lakis Proguidis', in Houellebecq, *Interventions 2* (Paris: Flammarion, 2009), pp. 151–156 (p. 153).
4 All translations are the author's, unless specified otherwise.
5 Michel Houellebecq and Jérôme Garcin, '"Je suis un prophète amateur": un entretien avec Michel Houellebecq', *Le Nouvel Observateur*, 25–31 August 2005, pp. 8–10 (pp. 9–10).
6 Johan Huizinga, *Homo Ludens: A Study of the Play Element in Culture* (London: Routledge, 1998), p. 13.
7 Ibid., p. 3.
8 Ibid., pp. 197–198.
9 Jean Baudrillard, 'Game with Vestiges: Interview with Salvatore Mele and Mark Titmarsh', trans. Ross Gibson and Paul Patton. First published in *On the Beach*, 5 (winter 1984). Reprinted in Mike Gain (ed.) *Baudrillard Live: Selected Interviews* (London: Routledge, 1993), pp. 81–95 (p. 95).
10 Fredric Jameson, *Postmodernism, or, The Cultural Logic of Late Capitalism* (London: Verso, 1991), pp. 10–11.
11 Jean-Philippe Toussaint, *M. M. M. M.* (Paris: Minuit, 2017), pp. 495–496. The extract is from the third novel in the quartet, *La Vérité sur Marie*.
12 Toussaint, *The Truth about Marie*, trans. Matthew B. Smith (Champaign, IL: Dalkey Archive Press, 2011), pp. 130–131.
13 Toussaint, *M. M. M. M.*, p. 542. The episode occurs in the fourth novel in the quartet, *Nue*.
14 Éric Chevillard, *Le Vaillant Petit Tailleur* (Paris: Minuit, 2003), p. 8.
15 Ibid., pp. 64–65.

16 Ibid., p. 48. Translations are the author's.

17 Christine Montalbetti, *Western* (Paris: P. O. L., 2005), p. 212.

18 Montalbetti, *Western*, trans. Betsy Wing (Champaign, IL: Dalkey Archive Press, 2009), p. 192.

19 Minimalism, the use of various kinds of formal economy in storytelling is seen by Warren Motte as one of the hallmarks of contemporary French literature, and a central element in the work of writers as diverse as Annie Ernaux, Jean Echenoz and Hervé Guibert. See Warren Motte, *Small Worlds: Minimalism in Contemporary French Literature* (Lincoln, NE: University of Nebraska Press, 1999).

20 Jean Echenoz, *Envoyée spéciale* (Paris: Minuit, 2016), p. 280; *Special Envoy: A Spy Novel*, trans. Sam Taylor (New York, NY: New Press, 2017), p. 225.

21 Echenoz, *Envoyée spéciale*, p. 270; *Special Envoy: A Spy Novel*, p. 218.

22 Echenoz, *Envoyée spéciale*, p. 206; *Special Envoy: A Spy Novel*, p. 164.

23 Echenoz, *Envoyée spéciale*, p. 154; *Special Envoy: A Spy Novel*, p. 125.

24 Echenoz, *Envoyée spéciale*, p. 188; *Special Envoy: A Spy Novel*, p. 154.

25 Éric Chevillard, *Le Vaillant Petit Tailleur*, p. 89.

26 Anne F. Garréta, *La Décomposition* (Paris: Grasset, 1999), pp. 211, 223.

27 François Bon, *Daewoo* (Paris: Fayard, 2004), p. 247; *Daewoo*, trans. Youna Kwak (New Orleans, LA: Diálogos Books, 2020).

28 Bon, *Daewoo* (Paris: Fayard, 2004), p. 78.

29 Olivier Rolin, *L'Invention du monde* (Paris: Éditions du Seuil, 1993), p. 21.

30 Dominique Viart, 'Les "fictions critiques" de Pascal Quignard', *Études françaises*, 40.2 (2004), pp. 25–37 (p. 26).

31 Michel Houellebecq, *Les Particules élémentaires* (Paris: Flammarion, 1998), p. 228.

32 Houellebecq, *Atomised*, trans. F. Wynne (London: Vintage, 2001), p. 272.

33 Emmanuelle Pireyre, *Féerie Générale* (Paris: L'Olivier, 2012), p. 160.

Chapter 3

1 'The End of History' was perhaps most famously declared by Francis Fukuyama in 1989 in the journal *The National Interest*, although his declaration was far from the first, nor the only one at this particular juncture. For a renewed projection of revolution see Comité invisible, *L'Insurrection qui vient* (Paris: La Fabrique, 2007).

2 Annie Ernaux, *La Place* (Paris: Gallimard, 1983), p. 11; *Positions*, trans. Tanya Leslie (London: Quartet Books, 1991), p. 2.

3 Ernaux, *La Place*, p. 113; *Positions*, pp. 98–99.

4 The tangential orientation of this framing relative to the central 'topic' of her father's life is reflected in the fact that it tends to be overlooked; see Michael Sheringham, 'Visible presences: fiction, autobiography and women's lives – Virginia Woolf to Annie Ernaux', *Sites*, 2.1 (1998), p. 17.

5 In *L'Écriture comme un couteau* (Paris: Stock, 2003, p. 87), she notes that above all else it was Pierre Bourdieu and Jean-Claude Passeron's book on the

forms of reproduction engendered by the education system, *Les Héritiers* (Paris: Les Éditions de Minuit, 1964), which pushed her to pursue the project that would become *Les armoires vides* (Paris: Gallimard, 1974).

6 See Karim Amellal, *Discriminez-moi ! Enquête sur nos inégalités* (Paris: Flammarion, 2005), pp. 171–175; Valérie Caillet, 'Le sentiment d'injustice chez les jeunes de banlieue. Le cas de l'école' in *Situations de banlieues. Enseignement, langues, cultures*, dir. Marie-Madeleine Bertucci and Violaine Houdart-Merot (Paris: Institut national de recherche pédagogique, 2005), p. 80.

7 Younès Amrani and Stéphane Beaud, *"Pays de Malheur !" Un jeune de cité écrit à un sociologue* (Paris: La Découverte, 2004), pp. 13, 15.

8 Ibid., p. 16.

9 Ernaux, *La Place*, p. 24; *Positions*, p. 13 (translation modified).

10 Ernaux, *L'Atelier noir* (Paris: Éditions des Busclats, 2011), p. 8.

11 Ibid.

12 Ibid., p. 10.

13 Ibid., p. 12.

14 Ernaux's work has been the object of considerable critical attention in both French and English and has also gradually been substantially translated. Critics have been particularly sensitive to the interplay between the work's claims to 'flatness' or objectivity and the evidence of composition; to its strategies for 'transpersonal' narration and the use of impersonal or collective pronouns (Michael Sheringham, *Everyday Life*, Oxford: Oxford University Press, 2006). The discussions are often organized around particular thematic constants: the question of familial heritage, the work of shame and desire, the narrative of her affair with a married man, the importance of photography (Loraine Day, *Writing Shame and Desire: The Work of Annie Ernaux*, Oxford: Peter Lang, 2007). The focus in this chapter on long insurmountable hesitations is intended to question the frequent critical emphasis on 'transgression' and on the idea of breaching a 'cultural divide' (Michael Sheringham, 'Visible presences: fiction, autobiography and women's lives – Virginia Woolf to Annie Ernaux', p. 19), or of enacting a fundamental 'rupture' (Carole Allamand, 'Annie Ernaux : à la serpe, à l'aiguille et au couteau', *The Romanic Review*, 97.2 (2006), p. 202).

15 Ernaux, *L'Écriture comme un couteau*, p. 35.

16 Ernaux, *La Place*, p. 47; *Positions*, p. 35 (translation modified).

17 Ernaux, *L'Atelier noir*, p. 12.

18 Michael Sheringham distinguishes between the possibility of 'playing up' the subjective component in a process of transcription of observed events, and 'playing back' their objective unfolding. Ernaux's method, he claims, corresponds to the latter (*Everyday Life*, p. 321).

19 Faïza Guène, *Kiffe, kiffe demain* (Paris: Hachette, 2004); *Just Like Tomorrow*, trans. Sarah Adams (London: Definitions, 2006).

20 Guène, *Kiffe, kiffe demain*, p. 110; *Just Like Tomorrow*, pp. 97–98.

21 Guène, *Kiffe, kiffe demain*, pp. 192–193; *Just Like Tomorrow*, p. 178.

22 Guène, *Kiffe, kiffe demain*, p. 193; *Just Like Tomorrow*, p. 179 (translation modified; Adams has 'I'm getting way too political').

23 Ernaux, *L'Écriture comme un couteau*, p. 39.

24 The recurrent reference for the 'roman total' is Marcel Proust, as we will discuss further, and she also refers to it as the 'grand roman-destin' (*L'Atelier noir*, p. 36).

25 Annie Ernaux with Philippe Lejeune in Fabrice Thumerel (ed.), *Annie Ernaux, une œuvre entre-deux* (Arras: Artois Presses Université, 2004), p. 257.

26 Michael Sheringham, *Everyday Life*, p. 323.

27 Ernaux, *La Place* (Paris: Gallimard, 1983), pp. 61–62; *Positions*, pp. 49–50.

28 Ernaux, *L'Écriture comme un couteau*, p. 89.

29 Ibid., p. 35.

30 Ernaux, *Journal du dehors* (Paris: Gallimard, 1993), p. 499; see also *L'Écriture comme un couteau*, p. 35: 'la sensation est critère d'écriture, critère de vérité' / 'sensation is the criteria of writing, the criteria of truth'.

31 Ernaux, *Journal du dehors*, p. 509.

32 Ernaux, *Exteriors*, trans. Tanya Leslie (New York, NY: Seven Stories Press, 1996), p. 509.

33 Ernaux, *La Honte* (Paris: Gallimard, 1997), p. 140. In *Se perdre*, she writes: 'je suis dans le creux où fusionnent mort, écriture, sexe' / 'I am in the pit where death, writing, sex enter into fusion' (Paris: Gallimard, 2001), p. 211; in *Le vrai lieu*, she invokes the image of dragging stones from the bottom of a river, before suggesting that it is also like 'la porte d'une cave qui s'ouvre' / 'the door of a cellar that opens' (Paris: Gallimard, 2014), p. 377.

34 François Bégaudeau, *Entre les murs* (Paris: Gallimard, 2006), pp. 208–209.

35 Bégaudeau, *The Class*, trans. Linda Asher (New York, NY: Seven Stories Press, 2009), pp. 202–203 (translation slightly modified).

36 Bégaudeau, *Entre les murs*, p. 24; *The Class*, p. 21.

37 Bégaudeau, *Entre les murs*, p. 255; *The Class*, p. 249.

38 Bégaudeau, *Devenirs du roman* (Paris: Naïve Records, 2007), p. 117.

39 Bégaudeau, *Entre les murs*, p. 274; *The Class*, p. 250.

40 See Edouard Louis, *Pierre Bourdieu. L'Insoumission en héritage* (Paris: Presses universitaires de France, 2013), including an essay by Ernaux.

41 Louis, *Histoire de la violence* (Paris: Éditions du Seuil, 2016), p. 95; *The History of Violence*, trans. Lorin Stein (London: Harvill Secker, 2019), p. 78. The translator has opted for a more childish expression here than the French 'faire le con'.

42 Louis, *Histoire de la violence*, p. 96; *The History of Violence*, p. 79.

43 Louis, *Histoire de la violence*, p. 97.

44 Louis, *The History of Violence*, pp. 80–81.

45 Louis, *Histoire de la violence*, p. 98; *The History of Violence*, p. 82.

46 Louis, *Histoire de la violence*, p. 97; *The History of Violence*, p. 81. The translation has abandoned the idiomaticity of speech here.

47 Louis, *Histoire de la violence*, p. 98; *The History of Violence*, p. 81.

48 Louis, *Histoire de la violence*, p. 80; *The History of Violence*, p. 64.

49 See Louis, *En Finir avec Eddy Bellegueule* (Paris: Éditions du Seuil, 2014); *The End of Eddy*, trans. Michael Lucey (London: Harvill Secker, 2017).

50 See Marion Dalibert 'En Finir *avec Eddy Bellegueule* dans les médias. Entre homonationalisme et ethnicisation des classes populaires', *Questions de communication*, 33 (2018), pp. 89–109.

51 Leslie Kaplan's first book *L'excès – L'usine* (Paris: P.O.L., 1982) / *Excess – The Factory*, trans. Julie Carr and Jennifer Pap (Oakland, CA: Commune Editions, 2018) draws on her experience as an 'établi', 'established' as a manual labourer, having like other Maoist militants chosen the direct experience of class warfare to the vanguardist position of the intellectual class to which she belonged.

52 Ernaux, *L'Événement* (Paris: Gallimard, 2000), p. 319; *L'Écriture comme un couteau*, p. 44.

53 Ernaux, *Les Années* (Paris: Gallimard, 2008), p. 252; *The Years*, trans. Alison L. Strayer (New York, NY: Seven Stories Press, 2017), pp. 229–230.

54 Ernaux, *Les Années*, p. 251; *The Years*, p. 228. Italics in the original. See note 18 for the importance of Proust in the elaboration of Ernaux's thinking.

55 Ernaux, *Les Années*, p. 250; *The Years*, pp. 227–228.

56 Ernaux, *Les Années*, p. 248; *The Years*, p. 225. See Leslie Kaplan, *Mon Amérique commence en Pologne* (Paris: P.O.L., 2009).

57 Kaplan, *Mathias et la Révolution* (Paris: P.O.L., 2016), pp. 114–117, 126–127, 188–190.

58 See her interview with Dominique Viart in Dominique Viart and Dominique Rabaté (eds.), *Écritures blanches* (Saint-Étienne: Publication de l'Université de Saint-Étienne, 2009), pp. 171–172.

59 Ernaux, *Les Années*, p. 251; *The Years*, pp. 227–228.

60 Kaplan, *Mathias et la Révolution*, p. 52: 'Mais où ? C'est vaste, la *banlieue*. – Je ne sais pas. À Gonesse, ou peut-être aux Lilas.' It is one hundred pages later that the possibility of Livry-Gargan is raised, p. 150. The *banlieue* is also discussed on p. 80.

Chapter 4

1 Michel Le Bris et al., *Pour une littérature voyageuse* (Brussels: Complexe, 1992). The notion of 'littérature voyageuse' might be translated as 'travelling literature'.

2 In many ways, a French-language version of *Granta*, this periodical would appear sporadically over the next decade. See Charles Forsdick and Katy Hindson, 'France, Europe, the World: *Gulliver*, or the journal as vehicle of literary transformation', in Charles Forsdick and Andrew Stafford (eds.), *La Revue: The Periodical in Modern French-Speaking Cultures* (Oxford: Peter Lang, 2013), pp. 115–135.

3 Simon Kemp, *French Fiction into the Twenty-First Century: The Return to the Story* (Cardiff: University of Wales Press, 2010). See also the Introduction in this volume.

4 See Michel Le Bris's editorial on the Festival's website.

5 Jean-Didier Urbain, *Ethnologue, mais pas trop* (Paris: Payot, 2003).

6 Anaïk Franz and François Maspero, *Les Passagers du Roissy-Express* (Paris: Éditions du Seuil, 1990); *Roissy Express. A Journey through the Paris Suburbs*, trans. Paul Jones (London: Verso, 1994).

7 'Toward a "world literature" in French', trans. Daniel Simon, *Contemporary French and Francophone Studies*, 14.1 (2010), pp. 113–117. Originally published in *Le Monde des Livres* on 15 March 2007.

8 Ibid., p. 113.

9 Ibid.

10 Ibid., p. 116.

11 Ibid.

12 Ibid.

13 Emily Apter, *Against World Literature: On the Politics of Untranslatability* (London: Verso, 2013), p. 178.

14 Ibid., p. 190.

15 Jonathan Arac, 'Edward W. Said: the worldliness of world literature', in Theo D'haen, David Damrosch and Djelal Kadir (eds.), *The Routledge Companion to World Literature* (Abingdon: Routledge, 2012), pp. 117–125 (p. 119).

16 Tzvetan Todorov, *La Littérature en péril* (Paris: Flammarion, 2007).

17 'Toward a "world literature" in French', p. 116.

18 Graham Huggan, *The Postcolonial Exotic: Marketing the Margins* (London: Routledge, 2001).

19 José Saldívar, *Trans-Americanity: Subaltern Modernities, Global Coloniality and the Cultures of Greater Mexico* (Durham, NC: Duke University Press, 2012), p. xvii.

20 Arthur Goldhammer, 'A few thoughts on the future of French studies', *French Politics, Culture & Society*, 32.2 (2014), pp. 15–20 (p. 20).

21 Ten writers responded to the survey, including Henri Troyat himself, as well as Irène Némirovsky, Jean Malaquais, Joseph Kessel and Julien Green. See Charles Forsdick, 'French literature as world literature: reading the translingual text', in John Lyons (ed.), *Cambridge Companion to French Literature* (Cambridge: Cambridge University Press, 2015), pp. 204–221 (pp. 207–208).

22 See Sara Kippur, *Writing It Twice: Self-Translation and the Making of a World Literature in French* (Evanston, IL: Northwestern University Press, 2015).

23 Andreï Makine, *Cette France qu'on oublie d'aimer* (Paris: Flammarion, 2006), p. 23.

24 Vassilis Alexakis, *Les Mots étrangers* (Paris: Gallimard (Folio), 2004 [Paris: Éditions Stock, 2002]), p. 75. Author's own translation.

25 Cited by Marie-José N'Zengou-Tayo, 'Literature and diglossia: the poetics of French and Creole "interlect" in Patrick Chamoiseau's *Texaco*', *Caribbean Quarterly*, 43.4 (1997), pp. 81–101 (p. 81).

26 Stanka Rodovic, 'Creole language and space: entertaining Patrick Chamoiseau's *Texaco*', *Nottingham French Studies*, 56.2 (2017), pp. 139–150 (p. 140).

27 For a detailed discussion, see N'Zengou-Tayo, 'Literature and diglossia'.
28 Kavita Ashana Singh, 'Translative and opaque: multilingual Caribbean writing in Derek Walcott and Monchoachi', *Small Axe*, 18.3 (2014), pp. 90–106 (p. 91).
29 Patrick Chamoiseau, 'Autour des grands mystères: récitation pour M. Monchoachi', in Béatrice Bonhomme, Idoli Castro and Evelyne Lloze (eds.), *Dire le réel aujourd'hui en poésie* (Paris: Hermann, 2016), pp. 37–41 (p. 40). Author's own translation.
30 Gemma King, *Decentring France: Multilingualism and Power in Contemporary French Cinema* (Manchester: Manchester University Press, 2017).
31 Karim Miské, *Arab Jazz* (Paris: Hamy, 2012).
32 Katalin Molnár, *Konférans pour lé zilétré* (Romainville: Al Dante, 1999), p. 8.
33 'Nous sommes plus grands que nous' launched at the Étonnants voyageurs festival 2017, and published in weekly broadsheet 1, 31 May 2017. Author's own translation.
34 Patrick Chamoiseau, *Frères migrants* (Paris: Éditions du Seuil, 2017), p. 136.
35 Abasse Ndione, *Mbëkë mi: à l'assaut des vagues de l'Atlantique* (Paris: Gallimard, 2008).
36 Ibid., p. 11.
37 Mahmoud Traoré, *'Dem ak xabaar', partir et raconter: récit d'un clandestin africain en route vers l'Europe* (Paris: Nouvelles Éditions Lignes, 2012).

Chapter 5

1 Fredric Jameson, *Postmodernism* (Durham, NC: Duke University Press, 1991), p. 5.
2 For a consideration of Boris Vian's involvement with the Série Noire, see Alistair Rolls and Deborah Walker, *French and American Noir* (London: Palgrave, 2009).
3 Jean-Patrick Manchette, *Chroniques* (Paris: Rivages, 1996), p. 12. All translations are the author's, unless specified otherwise.
4 Christophe Guilluy, *La France périphérique* (Paris: Flammarion, 2015).
5 Eric Libiot, 'Le Roman noir est militant', *L'Express.fr*, 3 March 2015, www .lexpress.fr/culture/livre/jean-bernard-pouy-le-roman-noir-est-militant_ 1657515.html, last accessed 9 April 2019.
6 Simon Kemp, *Defective Inspectors* (Oxford: Legenda, 2006). See also Chapter 2 of this volume.
7 Ari J. Blatt, 'Tanguy Viel's manic fictions', *Contemporary French and Francophone Studies*, 14.4 (September 2010), pp. 373–380 (p. 373).
8 Tanguy Viel, *La Disparition de Jim Sullivan* (Paris: Minuit, 2013), p. 9. The forthcoming English translation by Clayton McKee is to be published by Dalkey Archive Press, Dublin (2020).
9 Ibid., p. 12.
10 Ibid., p. 60.
11 Ibid., p. 34.

12 Ibid., p. 23.

13 Ibid., p. 25.

14 Viel, 'Quelques remarques sur la littérature américaine', *Vacarme*, 62.1 (2013), pp. 50–64 (p. 51).

15 Ibid., p. 52.

16 Sylvie Cadinot-Romerio, '*La Disparition de Jim Sullivan* ou le désir d'en finir', *Littérature*, 179.3 (2015), pp. 84–97 (p. 90).

17 Viel, *La Disparition de Jim Sullivan*, p. 32.

18 Ibid., p. 120.

19 Alice Richir, 'Hétérogénéisation de l'énonciation dans l'œuvre de Tanguy Viel', *Tangence*, 105 (2014), p. 55–68 (p. 59).

20 Viel, *La Disparition de Jim Sullivan*, p. 58.

21 James Quandt, 'Flesh and blood: sex and violence in recent French cinema' in Tanya Horeck and Tina Kendall (eds.), *The New Extremism in Cinema* (Edinburgh: Edinburgh University Press, 2011), pp. 18–25 (p. 18).

22 Alain-Philippe Durand and Naomi Mandel, 'Introduction' to Alain-Philippe Durand and Naomi Mandel (eds.), *Novels of the Contemporary Extreme* (London: Continuum, 2006), pp. 1–5 (p. 1).

23 Quandt, 'More moralism from that "wordy fuck" ' in Tanya Horeck and Tina Kendall (eds.), *The New Extremism in Cinema*, pp. 209–213 (p. 213).

24 Writing about the New French Extremity, film journalist Jonathan Romney suggests that these films have their heritage in French literature, citing the influence of Sade, Lautréamont and Georges Bataille on contemporary extreme output. Romney also notes that contemporary writing (he highlights Houellebecq, Despentes and Darrieussecq) also has extreme qualities that, we suggest, form something approaching an osmotic relationship with contemporary film. Romney, 'Le sex and violence', *Independent.co.uk*, 12 September 2004, www.independent.co.uk/arts-entertainment/films/features/le-sex-and-violence-546083.html, last accessed 9 April 2019.

25 Viel, 'Quelques remarques sur la littérature américaine', pp. 50–64 (p. 51).

26 Naomi Mandel, ' "Right here in nowheres": *American Psycho* and violence's critique', in Alain-Philippe Durand and Naomi Mandel (eds.), *Novels of the Contemporary Extreme*, pp. 9–19 (p. 9).

27 Victoria Best and Martin Crowley, *The New Pornographies* (Manchester: Manchester University Press, 2012), p. 13.

28 As explored in Anger's notorious *Hollywood Babylon* (1975).

29 Nelly Kaprièlian, 'Qu'est-ce qu'un roman rock ?', *LesInrocks.com*, 27 November 2011, www.lesinrocks.com/2011/11/27/livres/livres/quest-ce-quun-roman-rock, last accessed 9 April 2019.

30 It is worth noting that Houellebecq himself has underlined his own 'rock' credibility by collaborating with musicians Bertrand Burgalat, Jean-Claude Vannier and the aforementioned Iggy Pop at various points in his career.

31 Michel Houellebecq, *Sérotonine* (Paris: Flammarion, 2019), p. 227; Houellebecq, *Serotonin*, trans. Shaun Whiteside (London: William Heinemann, 2019), p. 198.

32 Seth Armus, 'The American menace in the Houellebecq affaire', *French Politics and Society*, 17.2 (spring 1999), pp. 34–42 (p. 36).

33 Ibid.

34 Houellebecq, *Les Particules élémentaires* (Paris: Flammarion, 1998), p. 262.

35 Houellebecq, *Atomised*, trans. Frank Wynne (London: Vintage, 2001), p. 252.

36 See Russell Williams, 'Michel Houellebecq and crime fiction: between *polar* and *poésie*', *Revue Critique de Fixxion Francaise Contemporaine*, 10, pp. 148–159.

37 Virginie Despentes, *King Kong Théorie* (Paris: Grasset, 2006), p. 9; *King Kong Theory*, trans. S. Benson (London: Serpent's Tail, 2010), p. 1.

38 Jacinthe Dupuis, 'De victime à hors-la-loi : l'émancipation par la transgression dans *Baise-moi* et *Thelma et Louise*', *Entrelacs*, 9 (2012), https://journals.openedition.org/entrelacs/351, last accessed 19 April 2019.

39 Despentes, *Baise-Moi* (Paris: Florent-Massot, 1994), p. 72; *Baise-Moi*, trans. Bruce Benderson (New York, NY: Grove Press, 2003), p. 66.

40 Despentes, *Baise-Moi*, p. 75; *Baise-Moi*, trans. Bruce Benderson, p. 68.

41 Despentes, *Baise-Moi*, p. 118; *Baise-Moi*, trans. Bruce Benderson, p. 117.

42 Despentes, *Baise-Moi*, p. 36.

43 Ibid., p. 87.

44 'Vernon Subutex, c'est un livre qui s'écoute', *Clique.tv*, www.clique.tv/vernon-subutex-cest-un-livre-qui-secoute-la-playlist-de-vernon-subutex-3, last accessed 9 April 2019.

45 Despentes, *Vernon Subutex*, Vol. 1 (Paris: Grasset, 2016), p. 205; *Vernon Subutex*, Vol. 1, trans. Frank Wynne (London: Maclehose Press, 2017), p. 168.

46 Bruno Pellegrino, Aude Seigne and Daniel Vuataz, *Stand-By, Saison 1* (Geneva: Zoé, 2018), p. 173.

47 James C. McKinley Jr. and Jan Ransom, 'Manhattan nanny is convicted in murders of two children', *NYTimes.com*, 18 April 2018, www.nytimes.com/2018/04/18/nyregion/nanny-trial-verdict.html, last accessed 19 April 2019.

48 Leïla Slimani, *Chanson Douce* (Paris: Gallimard, 2016), p. 64; *Lullaby*, trans. Sam Taylor (London: Faber & Faber, 2018), p. 52.

49 Slimani, *Chanson Douce*, p. 158; *Lullaby*, p. 140.

50 Slimani, *Chanson Douce*, p. 16; *Lullaby*, p. 4.

51 Slimani, *Chanson Douce*, p. 28; *Lullaby*, p. 16.

52 Joyce Carole Oates, *The New Yorker*, 19 February 2018, www.newyorker.com/magazine/2018/02/26/the-domestic-thriller-is-having-a-moment, last accessed 9 April 2019.

53 Novelist Alain Mabanckou reportedly rejected a similar proposal from the president; see Alain Mabanckou, 'Francophonie, langue française : lettre ouverte à Emmanuel Macron', *BiblioObs*, 15 January 2018, https://bibliobs.nouvelobs.com/actualites/20180115.OBS0631/francophonie-langue-francaise-lettre-ouverte-a-emmanuel-macron.html, last accessed 9 April 2019.

Chapter 6

1 Michel Houellebecq, *Les Particules élémentaires* (Paris: J'ai Lu, 2016 [1998]), pp. 36–37; *Atomised*, trans. Frank Wynne (London: Vintage, 2001), p. 39.

2 A full discussion of the social context of the *Charlie Hebdo* attacks is beyond the scope of this chapter. On that subject, see Alessandro Zagato (ed.), *The Event of 'Charlie Hebdo': Imaginaries of Freedom and Control* (Oxford and New York: Berghahn, 2015).

3 For an overview of the institutional consecration of the *bande dessinée*, see chapter 9 (pp. 229–248) of Laurence Grove, *Comics in French* (Oxford, UK and New York, NY: Berghahn, 2013 [2010]).

4 On this development and for an overview of BD trends from the end of the twentieth century to the second decade of the twenty-first, see Laurence Grove, *Comics in French*, in particular chapters 6 (pp. 117–154) on 'The Twentieth Century' and 7 (pp. 155–206) on 'Contemporary BD'.

5 See Zep, *Nadia se marie* (Grenoble: Glénat, 2004).

6 See Vladimir Propp, *Morphology of the Folktale*, ed. Louis Wagner, trans. Laurence Scott (Austin, TX: University of Texas Press, 1968 [1928]).

7 All are published by Éditions Albert-René of Paris.

8 For an introduction to the notion of literary classics adapted to comics, and a selection of analytical studies drawing largely on English-language traditions, see Stephen E. Tabachnick and Esther Bendit Saltzman (eds.), *Drawn From the Classics: Essays on Graphic Adaptations of Literary Works* (Jefferson, NC: McFarlane, 2015).

9 https://boutique-comedie-francaise.fr/bandes-dessinees/151-l-avare-moliere-bd-texte-integral.html

10 The field of adaptation studies is a domain in its own right and one outwith the scope of this current discussion. For an overview of the issues and questions raised, see, for example, Linda Hutcheon, *A Theory of Adaptation* (New York, NY: Routledge, 2006).

11 Louis-Ferdinand Céline, illustrated by Jacques Tardi, *Voyage au bout de la nuit* (Paris: Futuropolis, 1988). For a stylistic analysis of this work, see Armelle Blin-Rolland, 'Narrative techniques in Tardi's *Le Der des ders* and *Voyage au bout de la nuit*', *European Comic Art*, 3.1 (2010), pp. 23–36.

12 Enrique Corominas, *Dorian Gray d'après Oscar Wilde* (Paris: Daniel Maghen, 2011).

13 The volume is unpaginated.

14 Jacques Ferrandez and Albert Camus, *L'Étranger* (Paris: Gallimard, 2013).

15 Michel Houellebecq and Alain Dual, *Plateforme* (Paris: Les Contrebandiers, 2014).

16 See, for example, volume 4.1 (2004) of the online journal of popular culture, *Belphégor*, which is largely dedicated to BD and autobiography, https://dalspace.library.dal.ca/handle/10222/31206. See also Elisabeth El Refaie, *Autobiographical Comics: Life Writing in Pictures* (Jackson, MS: University Press of Mississippi, 2012).

17 See Laurence Grove, 'Autobiography in early *bande dessinée*', *Belphégor*, 4.1 (2004), https://dalspace.library.dal.ca/handle/10222/47694.
18 The series is published by Ego comme X of Angoulême.
19 Dominique Goblet, *Faire semblant c'est mentir* (Paris: L'Association, 2007). Available in English as *Pretending Is Lying*, trans. Sophie Yanow (New York, NY: New York Review Books, 2017).
20 In this case, all the more so, as Goblet chose the crash incident as a TV trauma of the time, although it did not actually correspond to the time of the shutting in the attic. See Thierry Groensteen's chapter on 'Pretending is lying' (pp. 111–125) in *The Expanding Art of Comics: Ten Modern Masterpieces*, trans. Ann Miller (Jackson, MS: University Press of Mississippi, 2017). Other French-language works in Groensteen's choice of ten are Moebius's *Garage hermétique* (1979) and David B.'s *L'Ascension du haut mal* (1996–2003). David B. likewise plays a leading role in the proliferation of autobiographical *bandes dessinées*.
21 Julie Doucet, *Ciboire de Criss* (Paris: L'Association, 2004).
22 The 'gutter' is the space between two frames in which imagined linking action occurs.
23 *Cœurs Vaillants*, 2 January 1955, p. 3.
24 On the role played by *Pilote* in the development of the *bande dessinée*, see Laurence Grove, *Comics in French*, in particular chapter 6 (pp. 117–154) on 'The twentieth century', and Wendy Michellat, *French Cartoon Art in the 1960s and 1970s:* Pilote hebdomadaire *and the Teenager* Bande Dessinée (Leuven: Leuven University Press, 2018).
25 See www.bdangouleme.com/933,le-festival-d-angouleme-aime-les-femmes-mais-ne-peut-pas-refaire-l-histoire-de-la-bande-dessinee.
26 The lack of secondary literature on *Ah ! Nana* is telling in itself. See, however, Catriona MacLeod, '*Ah ! Nana*: the forgotten French feminist comics magazine', *Comics Forum* (2011), https://comicsforum.org/2011/09/16/ah-nana-the-forgotten-french-feminist-comics-magazine-by-catriona-macleod. See also Trina Robbins, 'The two glorious years of *Ah ! Nana*', *Comics Forum* (2011), https://comicsforum.org/2011/09/26/the-two-glorious-years-of-ah-nana-by-trina-robbins.
27 There are three Julie Bristol albums: Chantal Montellier, *La Fosse aux serpents* (Tournai: Casterman, 1990); *Faux sanglant* (Paris: Dargaud, 1992); *L'Île aux démons* (Paris: Dargaud, 1994).
28 All are published by Allary of Paris. Available in English as *The Arab of the Future*, volumes 1 to 3, trans. Sam Taylor (London: Two Roads, 2016–2018).
29 The books were published by L'Association (Paris).
30 The film's English-language title is *The French Kissers*. On Sattouf's intermediality, see Guillaume Lecomte, 'Adapting the rhetoric of authentication of Riad Sattouf's *La Vie secrète des jeunes*', *European Comic Art*, 10.1 (2017), pp. 41–57.
31 The volumes were published by L'Association. The two-volume English translation (London: Jonathan Cape, 2003–2004) is by Blake Ferris and Mattias Ripa (vol. 1) and Anjali Singh (vol. 2). The film was a co-creation by Satrapi and Vincent Paronnaud.

32 (Paris: Les Arènes).

33 Marguerite Abouet and Clément Oubrerie, *Aya de Yopougon : Intégrale*, 2 vols. (Paris: Gallimard, 2016). The work originally appeared in six volumes from 2005 to 2010. The work is available in English as *Aya: Life in Yop City*, trans. Helge Dascher (Montreal: Drawn and Quarterly, 2013 [2012]).

34 For more on the notion of transnationalism and BD, see Laurence Grove, '*Bande Dessinée*: the Ninth Art of France that is not really French', from which this section on *Aya* is taken. The chapter is in Charles Forsdick and Claire Launchbury (eds.), *Transnational French Studies*, forthcoming from Liverpool University Press.

35 On Dz-Manga, see Alexandra Gueydan-Turek, 'The rise of Dz-manga in Algeria: globalization and the emergence of a new transnational voice', *Journal of Graphic Novels and Comics*, 4.1 (2013), pp. 161–178.

36 Early scholarship in this direction has included the special *bande dessinée* issue, no. 145 (2001), of *Notre Libraire : Revue des Littératures du Sud*, which pays particular attention to the styles, content and influences of BD in Africa, and no. 32 (2000) of *Africultures*, whose topic is 'BD d'Afrique'. On *québecoise* BD, see, for instance, Mira Falardeau, *La Bande dessinée au Québec* (Montreal: Boréal, 1994). More recently, issue 5.1 (2012) of *European Comic Art* was dedicated to Quebec. However, these are no more than a sample of publications dedicated to a subject area that is increasingly attracting attention.

37 See for example, Laurence Grove, '*Bande dessinée* studies: *état présent*', *French Studies*, 68.1 (2014), pp. 78–87; see also chapter 9 (pp. 229–248) of Laurence Grove, *Comics in French*. The *International Journal of Comic Art* also features regular sections on the development of comics studies.

38 Luc Boltanski, 'La Constitution du champ de la bande dessinée', *Actes de la Recherche en Sciences Sociales*, 1 (1975), pp. 7–59.

39 See https://journals.openedition.org/comicalites.

40 *Titeuf, le film*, directed by Zep, was released in 2011. Of the exhibitions, potentially the most high-profile was the 2007 *Zizi sexuel : L'Expo* at the Paris Villette science centre.

41 Jean-Christophe Menu, *Plates-bandes* (Paris: L'Association, 2005).

42 For an overview of the different collections and diversity of publications from the 1990s onwards, see L'Association's website, www.lassociation.fr/fr_FR/#!accueil.

43 See https://6pieds-sous-terre.com.

44 As of early 2020, the last update is June 2014.

45 Published by 6 Pieds Sous Terre.

46 See *Pause* (Paris: La Cafetière, 2017), n. p.

Chapter 7

1 Rolin's Russia-themed works include *En Russie*; *Bakou, derniers jours*; *Sibérie*; *Le Météorologue* and, co-authored with Jean-Luc Bertini, *Solovki, la bibliothèque perdue*.

2 Maureen Demidoff, 'Oliver Rolin : infatigable voyageur en Russie', *Russie Info*, 27 May 2018, www.russieinfo.com/olivier-rolin-infatigable-voyageur-en-russie, last accessed 15 October 2018.

3 Grégoire Leménager, 'Comment peut-on aimer la Russie ?', *Le Nouvel Observateur*, 28 November 2014, https://bibliobs.nouvelobs.com/romans/20141128.OBS6463/comment-peut-on-aimer-la-russie.html, last accessed 15 October 2018.

4 Emmanuel Carrère, *Un roman russe* (Paris: P.O.L. Folio, 2007); *My Life as a Russian Novel*, trans. Linda Coverdale (London: Vintage, 2018); Emmanuel Carrère, *Limonov* (Paris: P.O.L., 2011); *Limonov: The Outrageous Adventures of the Radical Soviet Poet Who Became a Bum in New York, a Sensation in France, and a Political Antihero in Russia*, trans. John Lambert (New York, NY: Farrar, Straus and Giroux, 2014).

5 *Retour à Kotelnich* was first released in 2003.

6 Carrère, *Un roman russe*, p. 213; *A Russian Novel*, p. 252.

7 Frédéric Beigbeder, *Au secours pardon* (Paris: Grasset, 2007); Patrick Deville, *Viva* (Paris: Éditions du Seuil, 2014).

8 Charlotte Krauss, *La Russie et les Russes dans la fiction française du XIX siècle (1812–1917)* (Amsterdam: Rodopi, 2007), p. 17.

9 The journey was organized by the French Ministry of Foreign Affairs and the Ministry of Culture and Communication.

10 Mathias Enard, *L'Alcool et la nostalgie* (Arles: Actes Sud, 2011); Sylvie Germain, *Le Monde sans vous* (Paris: Albin Michel, 2011); Dominique Fernandez, *Transsibérien* (Paris: Grasset, 2012); Maylis de Kerangal, *Tangente vers l'Est* (Paris: Gallimard, 2012); Danièle Sallenave, *Sibir* (Paris: Gallimard, 2012); Olivier Rolin, *Sibérie* (Paris: Verdier, 2016). It is believed that, although Cendrars lived in Russia for a time, he never actually travelled on the Trans-Siberian Express.

11 Alain Guillemoles, 'Dans le Transsibérien : des écrivains français à la rencontre du peuple russe', *La Croix*, 14 June 2010, www.la-croix.com/Culture/Actualite/Dans-le-Transsiberien-des-ecrivains-francais-a-la-rencontre-du-peuple-russe-_NG_-2010-06-14-552989, last accessed 20 February 2019.

12 Quoted by Krauss, *La Russie et les Russes*, p. 8. All translations into English are the author's, unless specified otherwise.

13 Léon Robel, *Histoire de la neige : La Russie dans la littérature française* (Paris: Hatier, 1994).

14 Janine Neboit-Mombet, *L'Image de la Russie dans le roman français, 1859–1900* (Clermont-Ferrand: Presses Universitaires Blaise-Pascal, 2005).

15 Ibid., p. 12.

16 Charlotte Krauss, *Inna Gorbatov, Catherine the Great and the French Philosophers of the Enlightenment: Montesquieu, Voltaire, Rousseau, Diderot and Grimm* (Washington, WA: Academica, 2006).

17 Of importance is also Eugène-Melchior de Voguë's *Le Roman russe* (1886), which introduces French readers to the works of Gogol, Turgenev, Tolstoy and Dostoyevsky. For a discussion of *Le Roman russe*, see Pauline Gacoin Lablanchy, 'Le Vicomte Eugène-Melchior de Voguë et l'image de la Russie dans la France de la IIIe République', *IRICE*, 1.39 (2014), pp. 65–78.

18 Krauss, *La Russie et les Russes*, p. 108.

19 Neboit-Mombet, *L'Image de la Russie*, p. 427.

20 Ibid., pp. 428–429.

21 Krauss, *La Russie et les Russes*, p. 274.

22 Ibid., p. 167.

23 Neboit-Mombet, *L'Image de la Russie*, pp. 433–434.

24 Krauss, *La Russie et les Russes*, p. 395.

25 Biographical notes give Penza, Krasnoyarsk, Divnogorsk or Novgorod as Makine's birthplace. The novel won the Prix Goncourt, the Prix Médicis and the Prix de Goncourt des Lycéens.

26 Makine's first doctoral thesis addressed the representation of childhood in French literature, while his second thesis was concerned with the prose of Ivan Bunin. For what seems like a verifiable biography of Makine, see Adrian Wanner, 'Andreï Makine: "Seeing Russia in French"', in *Out of Russia: Fictions of a New Translingual Diaspora* (Evanston, IL: Northwestern University Press, 2011), pp. 19–49.

27 These are *La Fille d'un héros de l'Union soviétique* (1990) (*A Hero's Daughter*, 2003) and *Confession d'un porte-drapeau déchu* (1992) (*Confessions of a Fallen Standard Bearer*, 2000).

28 Véronique Porra, 'Un Russe en Atlantide : Andreï Makine, du discours littéraire à la citoyenneté', in János Riesz and Véronique Porra (eds.), *Français et Francophones : Tendances centrifuges et centripètes dans les littératures françaises/francophones d'aujourd'hui* (Bayreuth: Schultz & Stellmacher, 1998), pp. 67–85.

29 Among the awards Makine has received are the Prix RTL for *La Musique d'une vie* (2001) (*A Life's Music*, 2002), the Prix de la Fondation Prince de Monaco (2005) for the entirety of his œuvre, and the Prix Wartburg de Littérature for *Le Pays du lieutenant Schreiber* (2014) (*Lieutenant Schreiber's Country: The Story of a Forgotten Hero*, 2018).

30 The Académie française is a venerated institution dedicated to safeguarding and regulating the French language through the publication of an official dictionary and the award of important literary prizes.

31 Makine's controversial address can be viewed here in full: www.youtube.com/ watch?v=qJur4JhQ6-A, last accessed 1 September 2018.

32 In 2011, after a French scholar had observed similarities between *20,000 femmes dans la vie d'un homme* and *Le Testament français,* Makine came clean about writing under a pen-name. For more details, see Astrid de Larminat, 'Osmonde sort de l'ombre', *Le Figaro*, 30 March 2011, www.lefigaro.fr/livres/ 2011/03/30/03005-20110330ARTFIG00656-osmonde-sort-de-l-ombre.php, last accessed 17 October 2018.

33 Andreï Makine, *Au temps du fleuve Amour* (Paris: Gallimard folio, 1996); *Once Upon the River Love*, trans. Geoffrey Strachan (London: Penguin, 1999).

34 Makine retraces the tsarina's life in *Une femme aimée* (Paris: Éditions du Seuil, 2013); *A Woman Loved*, trans. Geoffrey Strachan (London: Maclehose Press, 2015).

35 Makine, *Le Testament français* (Paris: Gallimard folio, 1995), p. 142; *Le Testament français,* trans. Geoffrey Strachan (London: Sceptre, 1997),

p. 109. See also *Au temps du fleuve Amour*, where Makine describes Russia's past thus: 'Dès le début du siècle, l'histoire, tel un redoutable balancier, s'est mis à balayer l'Empire par son va-et-vient titanesque. Les hommes partaient, les femmes s'habillaient de noir. Le balancier mesurait le temps : la guerre contre le Japon ; la guerre contre l'Allemagne ; la Révolution : la guerre civile …' (p. 22) / 'From the start of the century, history, like a titanic pendulum, had begun to sweep fearsomely to and fro across the empire. The men went away; the women dressed in black. The pendulum kept the measure of the passing time: the war against Japan; the war against Germany; the Revolution; the civil war …) (p. 10).

36 Alexander Solzhenitsyn, *The Gulag Archipelago 1918–56: An Experiment in Literary Investigation*, trans. Thomas P. Whitney and Harry Willets (London: Havrill, 2003), p. 211.

37 The purges Makine refers to here are known as the Great Terror (1936–1938).

38 While Moscow is the scene of Olya's moral downfall in *La Fille d'un héros de l'Union soviétique*, Leningrad/St. Petersburg is systematically portrayed as the hub of Western-imported moral decadence and political dissent, and, post-1991, of predatory capitalism, violence and corruption. This is particularly the case in *La Vie d'un homme inconnu* (Paris: Éditions du Seuil, 2009); *The Life of an Unknown Man*, trans. Geoffrey Strachan (London: Sceptre, 2010), and *La Femme qui attendait* (Paris: Éditions du Seuil, 2004); *The Woman Who Waited*, trans. Geoffrey Strachan (London: Sceptre, 2006).

39 Svetlana Boym, *Common Places: Mythologies of Everyday Life in Russia* (Cambridge, MA: Harvard University Press, 1994), p. 41.

40 Wallace L. Daniel, *The Orthodox Church and Civil Society in Russia* (College Station, TX: Texas A&M University Press: 2006), p. 74. The *mir* was disbanded in 1929 by Stalin.

41 *La Terre et le ciel de Jacques Dorme* (Paris: Mercure, 2003); *The Earth and Sky of Jacques Dorme*, trans. Geoffrey Strachan (New York, NY: Arcade 2005).

42 Andreï Makine, *L'Archipel d'une autre vie* (Paris: Éditions du Seuil, 2016), pp. 53–54.

43 Ibid., p. 76. Translations are the author's own. Geoffrey Strachan's translation (*The Archipelago of Another Life*) is due for publication in 2019.

44 For instance, the three central characters of *Au temps du fleuve Amour* break out of their culturally stilted universe when they travel to Vladivostok, Russia's largest port on the Pacific coast which is a gateway to Japan. The trip provides the youths with a taste of freedom and anticipates their later defection to the West.

45 *The Great Religions of the Modern World*, ed. Edward J. Jurij (Princeton, NJ: Princeton University Press, 2015), p. 304.

46 For a detailed analysis of this trope, see Helena Duffy, 'L'Écrivain ne se meurt pas ou la Résurrection dans l'œuvre d'Andreï Makine', in Murielle Lucie Clément (ed.), *Autour des écrivains franco-russes* (Paris: L'Harmattan, 2008), pp. 153–167.

47 For Makine's representation of Jews, see Helena Duffy, *World War II in Andreï Makine's Historiographic Metafiction: 'No One Is Forgotten, Nothing Is Forgotten'* (Amsterdam: Brill, 2018).

48 Makine, *L'Archipel*, p. 68.

49 Ibid., p. 207.

50 *Le Crime d'Olga Arbélina* (Paris: Mercure, 1998); *The Crime of Olga Arbyelina*, trans. Geoffrey Strachan (New York, NY: Arcade, 1999).

51 Together with rubber plants, geraniums and all other 'domestic trash', the gramophone was condemned by the communists who banned it from post-revolutionary living spaces. See Svetlana Boym, *Common Places*, p. 38.

52 Antoine Volodine, *Écrivains* (Paris: Éditions du Seuil, 2010); Lutz Bassman, *Les Aigles puent* (Paris: Verdier, 2010); and Manuela Draeger, *Onze rêves de suie* (Paris: L'Olivier, 2010).

53 Conversely, in *Le Post-exotisme en dix leçons, leçon onze*, the authorial narrator uses the first-person singular, but points out that '[l]a première personne du singulier sert à accompagner la voix des autres, elle ne signifie rien' / '[t]he first person singular serves to accompany the voice of others, it signifies nothing more'. Antoine Volodine, *Le Post-exotisme en dix leçons, leçon onze* (Paris: Gallimard, 1998), p. 19; *Post-Exoticism in Ten Lessons, Lesson Eleven*, trans. J. T. Mahany (Rochester, NY: Open Letter, 2015), p. 18.

54 Grégoire Leménager, 'Entretien avec Antoine Volodine, "Je ne suis pas un cas psychiatrique" ', *Le Nouvel Observateur*, 24 August 2010, https://bibliobs .nouvelobs.com/romans/20100824.BIB5527/antoine-volodine-je-ne-suis-pas-un-cas-psychiatrique.html, last accessed 11 October 2018.

55 Volodine, *Le Post-exotisme*, p. 19; *Post-Exoticism,* p. 18.

56 Geoff Shullenberger, 'From elsewhere to elsewhere', *Los Angeles Review of Books*, https://lareviewofbooks.org/article/from-elsewhere-to-elsewhere, last accessed 17 October 2018. For a study of Volodine's attitude towards language, see Frédérik Detue, 'Des langues chez Volodine : un drame de la survie', *Littérature*, 151 (2008), pp. 75–89.

57 Lionel Ruffel, *Volodine Post-exotique* (Nantes: Cécile Défaut, 2007), p. 125.

58 David Bellos, 'French as a foreign language: the literary enterprise of Antoine Volodine', *Studies in 20th & 21st Century Literature*, 36.1 (2012), pp. 100–116 (p. 104). In the interview conducted by Sara Bonomo, Volodine explains the internationalism of his characters' names thus: 'L'objectif est d'obtenir quelque chose de vraisemblable et agréablement bizarre.' / 'The objective is to obtain something plausible and pleasantly bizzare.' Quoted by Dominique Soulès, *Antoine Volodine : Affolement des langues* (Villeneuve d'Ascq: Presses Universitaires de Septentrion, 2017), p. 105.

59 As an example of these archaic or obscure words, one can quote the adverb 'saumâtrement' / 'brakishly', and as examples of neologisms 'suruquer', 'tromboneuse', 'volatilisation', 'crocodilement', 'romånce' or 'shaggå'. See Soulès, *Antoine Volodine*, pp. 163–165 and p. 209.

60 For example, in *Dondog* the eponymous character says 'Nous transpirions à ruisseaux', whereas the customary French expression would be 'Nous suions à grosses goûtes' (Soulès, *Antoine Volodine*, p. 146).

61 Jean-Didier Wagneur, 'Introduction', *SubStance*, 32.2 (2003), pp. 3–11 (p. 3).

62 Bellos, 'French as a foreign language', p. 101.

63 These include 'Elli Kronauer' and 'Maria Soudaïeva'.

64 Volodine's first novels were published by Denoël in the series 'Présence du futur', and in 1987 *Rituel du mépris* was awarded the Grand prix de la science-fiction français. According to Ruffel, even now Volodine's work is still seen by many as renewing the genre of science-fiction. Ruffel, *Volodine Post-exotique*, p. 30; Wagneur, 'Introduction', pp. 4–5.

65 The name seems to derive from the Russian noun '*boloto*', which, fittingly, means 'bog' or 'letch'.

66 Wagneur, 'Introduction', p. 3.

67 Volodine, *Le Post-exotisme*, p. 51; *Post-Exoticism*, p. 41.

68 Volodine, *Le Post-exotisme*, p. 59; *Post-Exoticism*, p. 52.

69 Sara Bonomo, 'Entretien avec Antoine Volodine', in Matteo Majrano (ed.), *Le Goût du roman* (Bari: B.A. Graphis, 2002), pp. 243–254 (p. 244). Quoted by Magdalena Silvia Mancas, 'Du post-exotique postmodernisme et du postmodernisme exotique : stratégies narratives chez Antoine Volodine', in Wolfgang Asholt and Marc Dambre (eds.), *Un retour des normes romanesques dans la littérature française contemporaine* (Paris: Presses Sorbonne Nouvelle, 2018), pp. 181–195, paragraph 1.

70 Mancas, 'Du post-exotique postmodernisme et du postmodernisme exotique', paragraph 12.

71 Dominique Viart, 'Situer Volodine ? Fiction du politique, esprit de l'histoire et anthropologie littéraire du *post-exotisme*', in Anne Roche (ed.), *Écritures contemporaines : Antoine Volodine, fictions du politique* (Paris: Minard, 2006), pp. 29–66 (p. 54).

72 Volodine, *Terminus radieux* (Paris: Éditions du Seuil, 2014), p. 502; *Radiant Terminus*, trans. Jeffrey Zuckerman (Rochester, NY: Open Letter, 2017), p. 376.

73 Volodine, *Terminus*, pp. 10, 63, 81, 531; *Radiant Terminus*, pp. 8, 47, 60, 401.

74 Interview with Antoine Volodine, www.youtube.com/watch?v= wystdZmsFac. While *Terminus* was awarded the prestigious Prix Médicis, Volodine has also won the Prix Wepler and the Prix du Livre Inter for *Des anges mineurs* (1999) (*Minor Angels*, 2004), and the Bourse de Jean Gattégno du Centre national du livre for *Macau* (2008).

75 Volodine, *Terminus*, p. 502; *Radiant Terminus*, p. 376.

76 It is noteworthy that while Kronauer is the surname of Volodine's alias, both Kronauer and Marachvili feature among the defeated revolutionaries in *Post-exotisme*.

77 Volodine, *Terminus*, p. 96; *Radiant Terminus*, p. 71.

78 'Ilya Muromets and Nightingale the Robber', *An Anthology of Russian Folk Epics*, trans. James Bailey and Tatyana Ivanova (London: M. E. Sharpe, 1998), pp. 25–36. Sung by Aldolay Schulhoff, this *bylina* is one of the novel's intertexts. Volodine, *Terminus*, p. 124; *Radiant Terminus*, p. 92.

79 Volodine, *Terminus*, p. 46.

80 Ibid., p. 35.

81 Writing under the pen-name 'Elli Kronauer', Volodine himself has published several volumes of epic narrative poems called *byliny*.

82 A. Ross Johnson and R. Eugene Parta, *Cold War Broadcasting: Impact on the Soviet Union and Eastern Europe* (Budapest: Central European University Press, 2010), pp. 239–240.

83 Volodine, *Terminus*, p. 190; *Radiant Terminus*, p. 142.

84 Volodine, *Terminus*, pp. 190–191; *Radiant Terminus*, p. 142. On shamanism, see Mihály Hoppál, 'Cosmic symbolism in Siberian shamanhood', in Art Leete and R. Paul Firnhaber (eds.), *Shamanism in the Interdisciplinary Context* (Boca Raton, FL: BrownWalker, 2004), pp. 178–190.

85 Sigmund Freud, 'Totem and taboo', trans. James Strachey et al. *The Standard Edition of the Complete Psychological Works of Sigmund Freud*, vol. 13 (London: Hogarth, 1912–1913), pp. 1–161.

86 Volodine, *Terminus*, p. 597; *Radiant Terminus*, p. 453.

87 Volodine, *Terminus*, p. 211; *Radiant Terminus*, p. 157.

88 Volodine, *Terminus*, p. 46; *Radiant Terminus*, p. 34.

89 Mervyn Matthews, *Privilege in the Soviet Union: A Study of Elite Life-Style under Communism* (New York, NY: Routledge, 1978), pp. 119–121.

90 Volodine, *Terminus*, p. 213.

91 Ibid., p. 159.

92 Linda Hutcheon, *A Poetics of Postmodernism: History, Theory, Fiction* (Oxford: Routledge, 1988).

93 Elisabeth Wesseling, *Writing History as a Prophet: Postmodernist Innovations in a Historical Novel* (Amsterdam: John Benjamin's Publishing Company, 1991), p. 110.

94 Hutcheon, *A Poetics of Postmodernism: History, Theory, Fiction*, p. 62.

95 Cecil C. Konijnendijk, *The Forest and the City: The Cultural Landscape of Urban Woodland* (New York, NY: Springer, 2018), p. 38; D. L. Ashliman, *Folk and Fairy Tales: A Handbook* (Westport, CT: Greenwood Folklore Handbooks, 2004), p. 6.

96 Volodine, *Terminus*, p. 14; *Radiant Terminus*, p. 11.

97 Volodine, *Terminus*, pp. 95–96; *Radiant Terminus*, p. 71.

98 Konijnendijk, *The Forest and the City*, p. 29.

99 Makine's novels feature many rape scenes, including the rape of the red-haired prostitute in *Au temps du fleuve Amour*, Charlotte's rape in *Le Testament français* or the rape of a Polish woman by Soviet soldiers in *Requiem pour l'Est*.

100 Volodine, *Terminus*, p. 153.

101 Volodine, *Terminus*, p. 479; *Radiant Terminus*, p. 372.

102 Volodine, *Terminus*, p. 551; *Radiant Terminus*, p. 418.
103 Kronauer's wife, Irina Echenguyen, is gang-raped during the fall of the Orbise (the fictionalized Soviet Union) in the hospital where she is recovering from a serious illness; Kronauer and Ilyushenko fear that the soldiers and prisoners travelling on the train may rape the dying Vassilissa; Umrug Batyushin's mother is repeatedly raped by a group of vagrants and so is Myriam Umarik.
104 Soulès, *Antoine Volodine*, p. 212.
105 The accusation that Solovyei and his daughters repeatedly level at Kronauer is that he is accompanied by dead or dying women. Volodine, *Terminus*, p. 171; *Radiant Terminus*, p. 155. Let us also note that before being murdered by the enemies of the Orbise, Kronauer's wife is raped. It is thus suggested that sexual intimacy inevitably leads to the woman's death.

Chapter 8

1 Jacques Roubaud, *Peut-être ou la nuit de dimanche* (Brouillon de prose) *Autobiographie Romanesque* (Paris: La librairie du XXIe siècle, 2018), p. 83. As yet untranslated. Translations are the author's.
2 Mary Cappello, 'Wending artifice: creative nonfiction', in Maria DiBattista and Emily O. Wittman (eds.), *The Cambridge Companion to Autobiography* (Cambridge: Cambridge University Press, 2014), pp. 237–251 (p. 241).
3 Philippe Lejeune, *Le Pacte autobiographique* (Paris: Éditions du Seuil, 1975).
4 Serge Doubrovsky, *Fils* (Paris: Galilée, 1977).
5 For debates on innovation in autofiction, see Serge Doubrovsky, Jacques Lecarme and Philippe Lejeune (eds.), *Autofictions et cie.*, Cahiers du RITM, 6 (Nanterre: Université Paris X-Nanterre, 1993).
6 See Sylvie Jouanny and Élisabeth le Corre, *Les Intermittences du sujet : écritures de soi et discontinu* (Rennes: Presses Universitaires de Rennes, 2016).
7 Suzette A. Henke, *Shattered Subjects: Trauma and Testimony in Women's Life-Writing* (New York, NY: St. Martin's Press, 1998).
8 Georges Perec, *W ou le souvenir d'enfance* (Paris: Éditions Denoël, 1975).
9 Philippe Forest, *L'Enfant éternel* (Paris: Gallimard, 1998). See also Forest's *Le Roman, le je* (Paris: Pleins Feux, 2001).
10 See Shirley Jordan, '*État Présent :* autofiction in the feminine', *French Studies*, 67 (2012), pp. 76–84.
11 On the 'pact of doubt' in Angot, see Gill Rye ' "Il faut que le lecteur soit dans le doute": Christine Angot's literature of uncertainty', in Gill Rye (ed.), *Hybrid Voices, Hybrid Texts: Women's Writing at the Turn of the Millennium*, special issue of *Dalhousie French Studies*, 68 (2004), pp. 117–126.
12 Mairéad Hanrahan, *Cixous's Semi-Fictions: Thinking at the Borders of Fiction* (Edinburgh: Edinburgh University Press, 2016).
13 Annie Ernaux, *Mémoire de fille* (Paris: Gallimard, 2016).
14 Karin Schwerdtner, *Le (beau) risque d'écrire. Entretiens littéraires* (Quebec: Éditions Nota bene, 2017); Anna Rocca and Kenneth Reeds (eds.), *Women*

Taking Risks in Contemporary Autobiographical Narratives (Newcastle upon Tyne: Cambridge Scholars Publishing, 2013).

15 For analysis of *autofiction* in Angot, including this episode, see Marion Sadoux, 'Christine Angot's *autofictions*: literature and/or reality?', in Gill Rye and Michael Worton (eds.), *Women's Writing in Contemporary France. New Writers, New Literatures in the 1990s* (Manchester: Manchester University Press, 2002), pp. 171–181.

16 Capello, 'Wending artifice', p. 243.

17 Névine El Nossery, *Témoignages fictionnels au féminin. Une réécriture des blancs de la guerre civile algérienne* (Amsterdam: Rodopi, 2012).

18 Paul John Eakin, *Living Autobiographically. How We Create Identity in Narrative* (Ithaca, NY and London, UK: Cornell University Press, 2008).

19 Alison James, 'Jacques Roubaud and the ethics of artifice', *French Studies*, 63.1 (January 2009), pp. 53–65 (p. 53).

20 Roubaud, *Peut-être*.

21 Ibid., p. 5.

22 Capello, 'Wending artifice', pp. 237–238.

23 James, 'Jacques Roubaud and the ethics of artifice', p. 11.

24 Roubaud, *Peut-être*, p. 33.

25 Ibid., p. 5.

26 Ibid.

27 Ibid.

28 Ibid., pp. 5–6.

29 Ibid., p. 7.

30 Ibid., p. 8.

31 Ibid., p. 11.

32 Marguerite Duras, *L'Amant* (Paris: Éditions de Minuit, 1984), pp. 18–19; *The Lover*, trans. Barbara Bray (London: Flamingo, 1986), p. 15.

33 Roubaud, *Peut-être*, p. 14.

34 Ibid., p. 12.

35 Ibid., p. 171.

36 Ibid., p. 170.

37 Ibid., p. 171.

38 Ibid., p. 61.

39 Ibid., p. 177.

40 Marie NDiaye, *La Cheffe,* roman *d'une cuisinière* (Paris: Gallimard, 2016). Translations are the author's. Jordan Stump's translation (*The Cheffe: A Cook's Novel*) is due for publication in 2019.

41 See Lorraine York, *Margaret Atwood and the Labour of Literary Celebrity* (Toronto: University of Toronto Press, 2013), p. 160.

42 Marie NDiaye, *Autoportrait en vert* (Paris: Mercure de France, 2005); *Self Portrait in Green*, trans. Jordan Stump (San Francisco, CA: Two Lines Press, 2014).

43 Noelle Giguere, 'Strange and terrible: understanding the risks of self-definition in Marie NDiaye's *Autoportrait en vert*', in Anna Rocca and

Kenneth Reeds (eds.), *Women Taking Risks in Contemporary Autobiographical Narratives* (Newcastle upon Tyne: Cambridge Scholars Publishing, 2013), pp. 59–70.

44 NDiaye, *La Cheffe*, p. 46.
45 Ibid., p. 9.
46 Ibid., p. 10.
47 Marie NDiaye, *Comédie Classique* (Paris: P.O.L., 1987).
48 NDiaye, *La Cheffe*, p. 93.
49 Ibid., p. 232.
50 Ibid., p. 11.
51 Ibid.
52 Ibid., pp. 220–221.
53 Ibid., p. 11.
54 Ibid., p. 233.
55 Ibid., p. 9.
56 Ibid., p. 15.
57 Ibid., p. 14.
58 Leah D. Hewitt, *Autobiographical Tightropes* (Lincoln, NE and London, UK: University of Nebraska Press, 1990), p. 1.
59 The contemporaneity of *Peut-être* is highlighted very precisely by the collection in which it is published: Seuil's 'La Librairie du XXIe Siècle'.

Chapter 9

1 For general overviews on these issues relating to literature and the Holocaust, see for example Marie Bornand, *Témoignage et fiction : les récits de rescapés dans la littérature de la langue française, 1945–2000* (Paris: Librairie Droz, 2004); Catherine Coquio, *La Littérature en suspens. Écritures de la Shoah : le témoignage et les œuvres* (Paris: L'Arachnéen, 2015); Karla Grierson, *Discours d'Auschwitz : littérarité, représentation, symbolisation* (Paris: Honoré Champion Editeur, 2003); Clara Lévy, *Écritures de l'identité. Les écrivains juifs après la Shoah* (Paris: Presses Universitaires de France, 1998); Miriam Ruszniewski-Dahan, *Romanciers de la Shoah. Si l'Écho de leurs voix faiblit* (Paris: L'Harmattan, 1999).
2 Annette Wieviorka, *L'Ère du témoin* (Paris: Plon, 1998); *The Era of the Witness*, trans. J. Stark (Ithaca, NY: Cornell University Press, 2006).
3 Robert Antelme, *L'Espèce humaine* (Paris: Gallimard, 1957 [1947]), p. 9.
4 Antelme, *The Human Race*, trans. J. Haight and A. Mahler (Marlboro, VT: Marlboro Press, 1992), p. 3 (translation modified). (Henceforth, all unreferenced translations are the author's.)
5 Cathy Caruth, *Unclaimed Experience: Trauma, Narrative, and History* (Baltimore, MD and London, UK: Johns Hopkins University Press, 1996), p. 5. Of the extensive literature on testimony and writing, see for example Maurice Blanchot, *L'Écriture du désastre* (Paris: Gallimard, 1980); Shoshana

Felman and Dori Laub, *Testimony: Crises of Witnessing in Literature, Psychoanalysis and History* (New York, NY and London, UK: Routledge, 1992); Jacques Rancière, 'S'il y a de l'irreprésentable ?', in *Le Destin des images* (Paris: La Fabrique, 2003), pp. 123–153; and Susan Rubin Suleiman, *Crises of Memory and the Second World War* (Cambridge, MA: Harvard University Press, 2006).

6 Delbo actually wrote parts of her work immediately after the war, but did not publish it until much later. The Spanish writer Jorge Semprun also waited sixteen years before publishing his first work, *Le Grand voyage*, based on his experience in Buchenwald during the war.

7 Charlotte Delbo, *Aucun de nous ne reviendra* (Paris: Éditions de Minuit, 1970); *None of Us Will Return*, trans. R. C. Lamont (New Haven, CT and London, UK: Yale University Press, 1995).

8 Delbo, *Aucun de nous*, p. 45; *None of Us Will Return*, p. 26 (translation modified).

9 Delbo, *Aucun de nous*, p. 45; *None of Us Will Return*, pp. 26–27.

10 Delbo, *Aucun de nous*, pp. 29–30 and pp. 177–178, respectively; *None of Us Will Return*, pp. 17–18 and pp. 110–111.

11 Delbo, *Aucun de nous*, pp. 9–12; *None of Us Will Return*, pp. 3–5.

12 Michael Rothberg, *Traumatic Realism: The Demands of Holocaust Representation* (Minneapolis, MN: University of Minnesota Press, 2000). See also Lawrence Langer, *Holocaust Testimonies: The Ruins of Memory* (New Haven, CT: Yale University Press, 1991).

13 Delbo, *Aucun de nous*, 'La jambe d'Alice', pp. 67–68, 'La soif', pp. 114–123, 'La tulipe', p. 97, and 'Le printemps', pp. 176–183, respectively; *None of Us Will Return*, 'Alice's Leg', p. 41, 'Thirst', pp. 70–75, 'The Tulip', pp. 60–61, and 'Springtime', pp. 109–113.

14 David Rousset, *L'Univers concentrationnnaire* (Paris: Éditions de Minuit, 1965 [1946]); *The Other Kingdom*, trans. R. Guthrie (New York, NY: Reynal and Hitchcock, 1947).

15 Jean Cayrol, '*Nuit et brouillard* (commentaire)', in *Nuit et brouillard* (Paris: Fayard, 1997), pp. 17–43 (p. 17). See also Griselda Pollock and Max Silverman (eds.), *Concentrationary Cinema: Aesthetics as Political Resistance in Alain Resnais's* Night and Fog (New York, NY and Oxford, UK: Berghahn, 2011).

16 Jean Cayrol, *Lazare parmi nous* (Paris: Éditions du Seuil, 1950), p. 18; 'Lazarus among us', trans. K. Tidmarsh, in Griselda Pollock and Max Silverman (eds.), *Concentrationary Art: Jean Cayrol, the Lazarean and the Everyday in Post-war Film, Literature, Music and the Visual Arts* (New York, NY and Oxford, UK: Berghahn, 2019).

17 Theodor Adorno and Max Horkheimer, *Dialectic of Enlightenment* (London: Verso, 1997 [1944]). See also Zygmunt Bauman, *Modernity and the Holocaust* (Cambridge: Polity Press, 1989).

18 Delbo, *Aucun de nous*, pp. 182–183; *None of Us Will Return*, pp. 113–114 (translation modified). For works that give an overview of Delbo's writing on

Auschwitz and after, see 'Dossier Charlotte Delbo', *Témoigner entre Histoire et Mémoire*, 105 (octobre–décembre 2009); Nicole Thatcher, *A Literary Analysis of Charlotte Delbo's Concentration Camp Re-presentation* (Lewiston, NY and Lampeter, Wales: Edwin Mellen Press, 2000).

19 Suleiman, *Crises of Memory*; Marianne Hirsch, *Family Frames: Photography, Narrative and Postmemory* (Cambridge, MA: Harvard University Press, 1997).

20 Georges Perec, *W ou le souvenir d'enfance* (Paris: Denoel, 1975), p. 89; *W or the Memory of Childhood*, trans. D. Bellos (London: Vintage Books, 2011), p. 6 (ellipsis is on p. 61 of the translation).

21 Perec, *W*, p. 17; *W or the Memory*, p. 6.

22 Perec, *W*, back cover.

23 Michael Sheringham, *French Autobiography: Devices and Desires* (Oxford: Oxford University Press, 1993), p. 323.

24 For a similar reading of Alain Resnais's film *Hiroshima mon amour* (1959), see Caruth, *Unclaimed Experience*, p. 27. We can apply the same reading to Modiano's *Dora Bruder*, Huston's *L'Empreinte de l'ange* and Sansal's *Le Village de l'Allemand*, all of which will be discussed later.

25 Perec, *W*, pp. 63–64; *W or the Memory*, p. 42.

26 'parachute, bras en écharpe, bandage herniaire : cela tient de la suspension, du soutien, presque de la prothèse' (Perec, *W*, p. 81) / 'parachute, sling, truss: it suggests suspension, support, almost artificial limbs' (*W or the Memory*, p. 55). In a typically Perec-ian move, 'les bretelles des pantalon de Charlot' (Perec, *W*, p. 45; *W or the Memory*, p. 26) transmute into the name 'Perec', via 'bretzel' and 'Peretz' (Perec, *W*, p. 50; *W or the Memory*, p. 35).

27 For a fascinating discussion of the 'homeopathic' effect of the child's game in Freud's theory, see Eric L. Santner, *Stranded Objects: Mourning, Memory and Film in Postwar Germany* (Ithaca, NY and London, UK: Cornell University Press, 1990).

28 Perec, *W*, p. 62; *W or the Memory*, p. 41.

29 See Claude Burgelin, *Georges Perec* (Paris: Éditions du Seuil, 1988), p. 146.

30 Perec, *W*, p. 59; *W or the Memory*, p. 41.

31 For general works on Perec, see Catherine Dana, *Fictions pour mémoire : Camus, Perec et l'écriture de la Shoah* (Paris: L'Harmattan, 1998); Philippe Lejeune, *La Mémoire et l'oblique : Georges Perec autobiographe* (Paris: P.O.L., 1991); Anne-Lise Schulte Nordholt, *Perec, Modiano, Raczymow : la génération d'après et la mémoire de la Shoah* (Amsterdam: Rodopi, 2008); 'Pereckonings: reading Georges Perec', *Yale French Studies* (special issue), 105 (2004).

32 Patrick Modiano, *Dora Bruder* (Paris: Gallimard, 1997), p. 73; *Dora Bruder*, trans. Joanna Kilmartin (Berkeley, CA and London, UK: University of California Press, 1999), p. 60.

33 Modiano, *Dora Bruder*, 1997, p. 144.

34 Ibid., pp. 28–29.

35 Modiano, *Dora Bruder*, 1999, p. 21.

36 See Andreas Huyssen, *Present Pasts: Urban Palimpsests and the Politics of Memory* (Stanford, CA: Stanford University Press, 2003).

37 Modiano, *Dora Bruder*, 1997, p. 65; *Dora Bruder*, 1999, p. 53.
38 For discussions of the 'spectral imaginary' in French literature (including analyses of Perec and Modiano), see Jutta Fortin and Jean-Bernard Vray (eds.), *L'Imaginaire spectral de la littérature narrative française contemporaine* (Saint-Étienne: Publications de l'Université de Saint-Étienne, 2013). For general works on Modiano, see Ora Avni, *D'un passé l'autre : aux portes de l'histoire avec Patrick Modiano* (Paris: L'Harmattan, 1997); Dervila Cooke, *Present Pasts: Patrick Modiano's (Auto)Biographical Fictions* (Amsterdam: Rodopi, 2005); John Flower (ed.), *Patrick Modiano* (Amsterdam, Netherlands and New York, NY: Rodopi, 2007); Martine Guyot-Bender and William VanderWolk (eds.), *Paradigms of Memory: The Occupation and Other Hi/Stories in the Novels of Patrick Modiano* (New York, NY: Peter Lang, 1998); Akane Kawakami, *A Self-Conscious Art: Patrick Modiano's Postmodern Fictions* (Liverpool: Liverpool University Press, 2015 [2000]); William VanderWolk, *Rewriting the Past: Memory, History and Narration in the Novels of Patrick Modiano* (Amsterdam: Rodopi, 1997).
39 See Charles Forsdick, '« Direction les oubliettes de l'histoire »: witnessing the past in the contemporary French *polar*', *French Cultural Studies*, 12.36 (2001), pp. 333–350.
40 The exact number of those killed is not known. For the most comprehensive account of this moment in French history, see Jim House and Neil Macmaster, *Paris 1961: Algerians, State Terror and Memory* (Oxford, UK and New York, NY: Oxford University Press, 2006).
41 '*Meurtres pour memoire* gives the lie to the idea of the archive as a mere repository of documents. It is demonstrated rather to be a highly orchestrated space of history, in which representations of the past are molded to suit present-day interests.' Claire Gorrara, 'Reflections on crime and punishment: memories of the Holocaust in recent French crime fiction', *Yale French Studies*, 8 (2005), pp. 131–145 (p. 138).
42 Daeninckx, *Meurtres pour mémoire* (Paris: Gallimard, 1984), pp. 210–211; *Murder in Memoriam*, trans. Liz Heron (London: Serpent's Tail, 1991), p. 171.
43 See Hannah Arendt, *Eichmann in Jerusalem: A Report on the Banality of Evil* (New York, NY: Viking Press, 1963). For an analysis of Delbo and Arendt, see Jennifer L. Geddes, 'Banal evil and useless knowledge: Hannah Arendt and Charlotte Delbo on evil after the Holocaust', *Hypatia*, 18.1 (winter 2003), pp. 104–115.
44 Of the many discussions of history and memory, see especially Pierre Nora, 'Entre mémoire et histoire: la problématique des lieux' in Pierre Nora (ed.), *Les Lieux de mémoire, tome 1 : La République* (Paris: Gallimard, 1984), pp. xvii–xlii; Paul Ricœur, *La Mémoire, l'histoire, l'oubli* (Paris: Éditions du Seuil, 2000); Saul Friedlander, 'Trauma, memory and transference', in Geoffrey H. Hartman (ed.), *Holocaust Remembrance: The Shapes of Memory* (Oxford: Blackwell, 1994), pp. 252–263; and Dominick LaCapra, *History and Memory After Auschwitz* (Ithaca, NY and London, UK: Cornell University Press, 1998).

45 In fact, as Roger Thiraud was born in Drancy, his work is a journey that combines personal memory and collective history. Claudine adopts a similar approach in her own doctoral work on the area known as 'the zone' by the old city walls of Paris.

46 Thierry Jonquet, *Les Orpailleurs* (Paris: Gallimard, 1993), pp. 371–374.

47 Daeninckx, *Meurtres pour mémoire*, p. 215; *Murder in Memoriam*, p. 174. Referring to the peeling away of the poster in the epilogue, Margaret Atack shows how this technique is typical of Daeninckx's work as a whole, as 'it effects a re-opening onto the interminable repetition of surprise encounters with a previously buried past', 'From *Meurtres pour mémoire* to *Missak*: literature and historiography in dialogue', *French Cultural Studies*, 25.3–4 (2014), pp. 271–280.

48 For reading crime fiction through the prism of the palimpsest, see Angela Kimyongur and Amy Wigelsworth (eds.), *Rewriting Wrongs: French Crime Fiction and the Palimpsest* (Newcastle upon Tyne: Cambridge Scholars Publishing, 2014).

49 Jean-Paul Sartre, *Situations V : Colonialisme et néo-colonialisme* (Paris: Gallimard, 1964), p. 163.

50 Aimé Césaire, *Discours sur le colonialisme* (Paris: Présence Africaine, 2004 [1955]), p. 14; *Discourse on Colonialism*, trans. J. Pinkham (New York, NY: Monthly Review Press, 2000 [1972]), p. 36.

51 See, for example, Catherine Coquio (ed.), *Parler des camps, penser les génocides* (Paris: Albin Michel, 1999); Tzvetan Todorov, *Les Abus de la mémoire* (Paris: Arléa, 2004); and Enzo Traverso, *Le Passé, modes d'emploi : Histoire, mémoire, politique* (Paris: La Fabrique, 2005).

52 See, for example, Henry Rousso, *Le Syndrôme de Vichy (1944–198...)* (Paris: Éditions du Seuil, 1987) and Richard J. Golsan, *Vichy's Afterlife: History and Counterhistory in Postwar France* (Lincoln, NE: University of Nabraska, 2000). In a reverse use of the parallel history for political purposes, Jacques Vergès, the chief lawyer acting for the accused at the trial of Klaus Barbie, the infamous 'butcher of Lyon' in Nazi-occupied France during the war, compared Barbie's crimes to those committed by the French in Algeria, in order 'to attenuate the charges against Barbie' (Forsdick, '« Direction les oubliettes de l'histoire »', p. 344). See Lynne Higgins, 'The Barbie Affair and the trials of memory', in Richard J. Golsan (ed.), *Fascism's Return: Scandal, Revision and Ideology since 1980* (Lincoln, NE and London, UK: University of Nebraska Press, 1998), pp. 200–217.

53 Hannah Arendt, *The Origins of Totalitarianism* (New York, NY: Schocken Books, 2004 [1951], preface to first edition, p. xxvii.

54 See, for example, Michael Rothberg, *Multidirectional Memory: Remembering the Holocaust in the Age of Decolonization* (Stanford, CA: Stanford University Press, 2009); Debarati Sanyal, *Memory and Complicity: Migrations of Holocaust Remembrance* (New York, NY: Fordham University Press, 2015); Max Silverman, *Palimpsestic Memory: The Holocaust and Colonialism in French and Francophone Fiction and Film* (New York, NY and Oxford, UK:

Berghahn, 2013); Lucy Bond, Stef Craps and Pieter Vermeulen (eds.), *Memory Unbound: Tracing the Dynamics of Memory Studies* (New York, NY and Oxford, UK: Berghahn, 2017).

55 Nancy Huston, *L'Empreinte de l'ange* (Arles: Actes Sud, 1998), pp. 185–186.
56 Huston, *The Mark of the Angel*, trans. N. Huston (New York, NY: Vintage International, 1999), pp. 186–187.
57 Huston, *L'Empreinte de l'ange*, p. 184; *The Mark of the Angel*, p. 185.
58 Huston, *L'Empreinte de l'ange*, p. 219; *The Mark of the Angel*, p. 221.
59 Walter Benjamin, 'Ninth thesis on the philosophy of history', in *Illuminations* (London: Collins-Fontana Books, 1973), p. 249.
60 Walter Benjamin, *The Arcades Project*, trans. H. Eiland and K. McLaughlin (Cambridge, MA and London, UK: The Belknap Press of Harvard University Press, 1999), p. 463.
61 The concept of 'nœuds de mémoire' is a transnational and transcultural challenge to the more monolinear definition of memory proposed by Pierre Nora in his three-volume work entitled *Les Lieux de mémoire* (Paris: Gallimard, 1984, 1986, 1992). See Michael Rothberg, Debarati Sanyal and Max Silverman (eds.), 'Nœuds de mémoire: multidirectional memory in post-war French and Francophone culture', *Yale French Studies*, 118/119 (2010).
62 Mireille Rosello, 'Guerre des mémoires ou "parallèles dangereux" dans *Le Village de l'Allemand* de Boualem Sansal', *Modern and Contemporary France*, 18.2 (2010), pp. 193–211. See also Caroline Beschea-Fache, 'Transnational heritage in Boualem Sansal's *The German Mujahid*', *Culture, Theory and Critique*, 53.2 (2012), pp. 163–179.
63 Sanyal, *Memory and Complicity*, p. 256.
64 See Benjamin Stora, *La Guerre des memoires : La France face à son passé colonial* (Entretiens avec Thierry Leclère) (Paris: Éditions de l'Aube, 2007) and Pascal Blanchard and Isabelle Veyrat-Masson (eds.), *Les Guerres de memoires. La France et son histoire : enjeux politiques, controverses historiques, stratégies médiatiques* (Paris: La Découverte, 2008).
65 See, for example, Astrid Erll and Ann Rigney (eds.), *Mediation, Remediation and the Dynamics of Cultural Memory* (Berlin: De Gruyter, 2009), and Alison Landsberg, *Prosthetic Memory: The Transformation of American Remembrance in the Age of Mass Culture* (New York, NY: Columbia University Press, 2004).

Chapter 10

1 In Vietnam, this war is called the American War, while the Americans call it the Vietnam War, hence my use of the oblique.
2 There has also been a proliferation of English language works about these two crossings. For Haitian-American writers, see Felix Morisseau-Leroy's poem 'Boat people', in *Haitiad & oddities* (Miami, FL: Pantaléon Guilbaud, 1991); Edwidge Danticat's novel, *Breath, Eyes, Memory* (New York, NY: Soho, 1994), her collection of essays, *Create Dangerously: The Immigrant Artist at*

Work (Princeton, NJ: Princeton University Press, 2010), and short stories, 'Children of the sea', in *Krik? Krak!* (New York, NY: Vintage, 1996), pp. 1–29, and 'Without inspection', *New Yorker*, 14 May 2018, www .newyorker.com/magazine/2018/05/14/without-inspection. For works by Vietnamese-Americans, see Mary Terrell Cargill and Jade Quang Huynh (eds.), *Voices of Vietnamese Boat People: Nineteen Narratives of Escape and Survival* (Jefferson, NC: McFarland, 2000); Carine Hoang (ed.), *Boat People: Personal Stories from the Vietnamese Exodus 1975–1996* (New York, NY: Beaufort Books, 2013); and Viet Thanh Nguyen's collection of short stories, *The Refugees* (New York, NY: Grove/Atlantic, Inc., 2017). See also Vietnamese-Australian writer Nam Le's collection of short stories, *The Boat* (New York, NY: Vintage, 2008), which was also adapted into an interactive webcomic by Matt Huyhn, *The Boat* (Australia: Special Broadcasting Service, 2015), www.sbs.com.au/theboat.

3 Romuald Fonkoua, *Les Discours de voyages : Afrique-Antilles* (Paris: Karthala, 2001); Charles Forsdick, *Travel in Twentieth-Century French and Francophone Cultures* (Oxford: Oxford University Press, 2005); Aedin Ní Loingsigh, *Postcolonial Eyes: Intercontinental Travel in Francophone African Literature* (Liverpool: Liverpool University Press, 2009).

4 Charles Forsdick, 'Francophone postcolonial travel writing', in Robert Clarke (ed.), *The Cambridge Companion to Postcolonial Travel Writing* (Cambridge: Cambridge University Press, 2017), pp. 93–108.

5 Subha Xavier, *The Migrant Text. Making and Marketing a Global French Literature* (Montreal: McGill-Queens University Press, 2016).

6 April Shemak, 'Refugee and asylum seeker narratives as postcolonial travel writing', in *The Cambridge Companion to Postcolonial Travel Writing*, p. 188.

7 Shemak further notes that refugee narratives are 'largely focused on obtaining justice, raising awareness, producing empathy for refugees and asylum seekers, or gaining asylum in a host nation' ('Refugee and asylum seeker narratives', p. 188).

8 Hakim Abderrazak coins the term *illiterature* to describe literature about clandestine boat crossings of the Mediterranean; his literary examples of choice are Tahar Ben Jelloun's *Partir* (2006), Youssouf Amine Elalamy's *Les Clandestins* (2000) and Mahi Binebine's *Cannibales : Traversées dans l'enfer de Gibraltar* (1999), although he mentions many other works of *illiterature* from Morocco, Algeria and Tunisia. See Hakim Abderrazak, *Ex-Centric Migrations* (Bloomington, IN: Indiana University Press, 2016). In Arabic, the term *harragas* (or 'burners') is commonly used for undocumented migrants attempting to cross over from North Africa to Europe in boats. See also Papa Samba Diop, *Archéologie du roman sénégalais* (Paris: L'Harmattan, 2010) and Mahriana Rofheart, *Shifting Perceptions of Migration in Senegalese Literature, Film and Social Media* (Lanham, MD: Lexington Books, 2013).

9 Gaëlle Cooreman, '« La Mer, la plage, l'épouvante » : l'imaginaire des *boat people* haïtiens dans la littérature caribéenne anglophone et francophone', *Esprit Créateur*, 51.2 (summer 2011), p. 34.

10 See Howard Adelman, 'Indochinese refugee resettlement: causes of the exodus. Part I of IV: 1975–1978 Refugees from Vietnam', 20 May 2015, https://howardadelman.com/2015/05/20/indochinese-refugee-resettlement-causes-of-the-exodus-part-i-of-iv-1975-1978-refugees-from-vietnam, last accessed 15 April 2019.

11 See B. Martin Tsamenyi, 'The "boat people": are they refugees?', *Human Rights Quarterly*, 5.3 (1983), pp. 348–372.

12 It is important to note that Cuban refugees who were also making the journey by raft or boat to the shores of Florida after the 1959 Cuban Revolution were treated very differently by the US government, regardless of their socioeconomic status, and were considered eligible for asylum as refugees. For the discrepancy in the treatment of these two populations of asylum seekers, see April Shemak, *Asylum Speakers: Caribbean Refugees and Testimonial Discourse* (New York, NY: Fordham University Press, 2010), pp. 49–54.

13 Gaëlle Cooreman provides a complete history of Haitian boat people literature, from its inception in Frankétienne's 1968 novel, *Mûr à crever* (2004), Anthony Phelp's 1983 poem 'Même le soleil est nu ...' (1992) and Jean-Claude Charles's first novel dedicated to the phenomenon, *De si jolies petites plages* (1982), to novels by Émile Ollivier (*Passages*, 1991), Louis-Philippe Dalembert (*L'autre face de la mer*, 1998), Marie-Célie Agnant (*Alexis d'Haïti*, 1999; *Alexis, fils de Raphaël*, 2000) and Maryse Condé (*Haïti chérie*, 1991; *Rêves amers*, 2001), as well as several other works in English and Spanish. See Cooreman, '« La Mer, la plage, l'épouvante »', pp. 34–46.

14 Cooreman, 'Cheminer seul et subaltern : *Passages* d'Émile Ollivier ou la triple déconnexion des *boat people* haïtiens', *Francofonia*, 52 (spring 2007), pp. 19–20. (All translations are the author's own, unless otherwise specified.)

15 The Middle Passage was the name given to the second leg of the triangular slave trade route.

16 Martin Munro, 'Unfinished journeys: exile, Africanity, and intertextuality in Émile Ollivier's *Passages*', *Journal of Modern Literature*, 29.2 (winter, 2006), p. 41.

17 Émile Ollivier, *Passages* (Paris: Serpent à Plumes, 1991), p. 129 (my emphasis added).

18 Ollivier, *Passages*, trans. Leonard W. Sudgen (Victoria, BC: Ekstasis Editions, 2003), p. 103.

19 Ollivier, *Passages*, 1991, p. 129; Ollivier, *Passages*, 2003, p. 103.

20 See Gregory Jaynes, 'Thirty-three Haitians drown as boat capsizes off coast of Florida', *New York Times*, 27 October 1981, www.nytimes.com/1981/10/27/us/33-haitians-drown-as-boat-capsizes-off-florida.html, last accessed 15 April 2019. There were many other such tragedies, but few that made the national news as this one did.

21 See Larry Rohter, 'U.S. accused of abuse of Haitians at a center', *New York Times*, 5 June 1992, www.nytimes.com/1992/06/05/us/us-accused-of-abuse-of-haitians-at-a-center.html, last accessed 15 April 2019. For more in-depth analysis of human neglect from a medical perspective, see Steven Nachman,

'Wasted lives: tuberculosis and other health risks of being Haitian in a U.S. detention camp', *Medical Anthropology Quarterly*, 7.3 (1993), pp. 227–259. For general mistreatment of detained asylum seekers, see Evelyn Cartright, 'The plight of Haitian refugees in south Florida', *The Journal of Haitian Studies*, 12.2 (2006), pp. 112–124.

22 Ollivier, *Passages*, 1991, pp. 159–160.

23 Ollivier, *Passages*, 2003, pp. 127–128.

24 Maurice Blanchot, *Le Pas au-delà* (Paris: Gallimard, 1973), p. 8.

25 Munro, 'Unfinished journeys', p. 42.

26 Linda Lê, 'Vinh L.', in *Les évangiles du crime* (Paris: Christian Bourgois, 2009), p. 226.

27 He references Cătălin Avramescu's *Intellectual History of Cannibalism* (2003) as 'un philosophe roumain' (Lê, 'Vinh L.', p. 212) and Jun'ichirō Tanizaki as 'un japonais amoureux cannibale, dévoreur de chair féminine' / 'a Japanese cannibal lover, devourer of feminine flesh)' (Lê, 'Vinh L.', p. 213). A quote from Fernando Pessoa's poem 'Ambiente' (1927), written under his heteronym Álvaro de Campos, is credited to 'cet auteur portugais' / 'that Portuguese author' (Lê, 'Vinh L.', p. 21). A quote from Pier Pasolini's film *Porcile* (1969) appears as an epigraph to the short story, but reappears in the text with only a reference to the epigraph itself: 'je ruminais une phrase placée en exergue du texte' / 'I was ruminating on a sentence placed as an epigraph to this text' (Lê, 'Vinh L.', p. 216). Fyodor Dostoyevsky is cited with a quote from *Notes from the Underground* (1864) as 'un auteur russe' / 'a Russian author' (Lê, 'Vinh L.', p. 220), and Bohumil Hrabal as 'cet écrivain tchèque' / 'that Czech writer' (Lê, 'Vinh L.', p. 223). Oskar Kokoschka's play *Murderer, the Hope of Women* (1909) is mentioned and the playwright is described as 'un peintre viennois' / 'a Viennese painter' (Lê, 'Vinh L.', p. 244). Cesare Pavese is also cited from *The Business of Living: Diaries 1935–50* (Lê, 'Vinh L.', p. 255).

28 Lê, 'Vinh L.', p. 211.

29 Ibid., p. 256.

30 Ibid.

31 Ibid., p. 240.

32 Ibid., p. 245.

33 Ibid., p. 224.

34 See, for example, Kyra Gurney, 'Coast guard searching for missing Haitian child after migrant boat capsized,' *Miami Herald*, 1 January 2019, www .miamiherald.com/news/local/article223810825.html, last accessed 15 April 2019.

35 Néhémy Pierre-Dahomey, *Rapatriés* (Paris: Éditions du Seuil, 2017), p. 15.

36 Ibid., p. 13.

37 Ibid., p. 135.

38 Ibid., p. 155.

39 Ibid., p. 136.

40 Ibid., p. 191.

41 Ibid., p. 125.

42 Lê, 'Vinh L.', p. 220.

43 Pierre-Dahomey, *Rapatriés*, p. 159.

44 Ibid., p. 176.

45 Frantz Fanon, *Les damnés de la* terre (Paris: Maspero, 1961), p. 35; *The Wretched of the Earth*, trans. Richard Philcox (New York, NY: Grove, 2004 [1963]), p. 9.

46 Kim Thúy, *Ru* (Montreal: Lianna Lévi, 2010); *Ru: A Novel*, trans. Sheila Fischman (Toronto: Vintage, 2012).

47 Thúy, *Ru*, p. 24.

48 Thúy, *Ru: A Novel*, p. 14.

49 In fact, a few years after publishing *Ru*, Kim Thúy went in search of her registration at the Malaysian Red Crescent Society, which, along with other government agencies, had documented the refugees at the time. 'With the cards written out, we were given a second chance at life . . .', she said. See Faihan Ghani, 'Kim Thúy: from refugee to award-winning author', *Star2.com*, 21 July 2015, www.star2.com/people/2015/07/21/kim-thuy-from-a-refugee-to-award-winning-author.

50 Kurmann and Do cite Ann-Marie Leshkowich's work on memory and conflict in socialist Vietnam; see Alexandra Kurmann and Tess Do, 'Children on the boat: the recuperative work of postmemory in short fiction of the Vietnamese diaspora', *Comparative Literature*, 70.2 (June 2018), pp. 218–234 (p. 225).

51 Valérie Loichot, *Water Graves* (Charlottesville, VA: University of Virginia Press, 2020), p. 9.

52 Loichot, *Water Graves*, p. 10.

53 Thúy, *Ru*, p. 27; *Ru: A Novel*, p. 17.

54 Thúy, *Ru*, p. 25.

55 Thúy, *Ru: A Novel*, pp. 14–15.

56 Vinh Nguyen, 'Refugee gratitude: narrating success and intersubjectivity in Kim Thúy's *Ru*', *Canadian Literature*, 219 (winter 2013), pp. 17–36.

57 See, for example, John Barber, 'Kim Thúy's river of life', *Globe and Mail*, 5 February 2012; Jim Bartley, 'From riches to rags to riches', *Globe and Mail*, 10 February 2012; Louis-Bernard Robitaille, 'Départ en fanfare pour *Mãn* en France', *La Presse*, 21 May 2013, www.lapresse.ca/arts/livres/201305/21/01-4652663-depart-en-fanfare-pour-man-en-france.php, last accessed 15 April 2019.

58 Alexandra Kurmann, '*Aller-retour-détour*: transdiasporic nomadism and the navigation of literary prescription in the work of Kim Thúy and Thanh-Van Tran-Nhut', *Australian Journal of French Studies*, 55.1 (2018), p. 72.

59 Ching Selao, 'Oiseaux migrateurs : l'expérience exilique chez Kim Thúy et Linda Lê', *Voix et Images*, 40.1 (2014), p. 157.

60 Thúy, *Ru: A Novel*, n. p.

61 Thúy, *Ru*, p. 83; *Ru: A Novel*, p. 74.

62 Thúy, *Ru*, p. 28

63 Thúy, *Ru: A Novel*, p. 18.

Chapter 11

1 Johan Galtung, 'Violence, peace, and peace research', *Journal of Peace Research*, 6.3 (1969), 167–191 (p. 170).

2 Literally translated as 'suburb', but the term is often used reductively to refer to poor or 'populaire' / 'popular' housing estates on the outskirts of major cities.

3 Henri Lefebvre, *Le Droit à la Ville* (Paris: Anthropos, 1968).

4 Lefebvre, 'Entretien avec Henri Lefebvre : de l'urbain à la ville', *Techniques et architecture*, 359, pp. 112–113.

5 See, for instance, Marc Bernard, *Sarcellopolis* (Paris: Flammarion, 1964).

6 See Mustafa Dikeç, *Badlands of the Republic: Space, Politics, and Urban Policy* (London: Blackwell Publishing, 2007).

7 For more on the urban upheavals of 'L'été chaud des Minguettes' / 'Minguettes' hot summer', see Fabien Jobard, 'An overview of French riots: 1981–2004', in *Rioting in the UK and France. A Comparative Analysis* (Cullompton: Willan Publishing, 2009), pp. 27–38.

8 Alec G. Hargreaves, *Voices from the North African Immigrant Community in France: Immigration and Identity in Beur Fiction* (New York, NY and Oxford, UK: Berg, 1991).

9 'Grand Urbanism' is a term coined by Theresa Enright to refer to 'a particular manner of governing bigness that relies on the use of megaprojects to restructure metropolitan political, economic, and social relations in the pursuit of speculative growth and generalized gentrification'. Theresa Enright, *The Making of Grand Paris: Metropolitan Urbanism in the Twenty-First Century* (Cambridge, MA and London, UK: MIT Press, 2016), p. 20.

10 For an early authoritative discussion on the media's construction of the 'banlieues', see Alec Hargreaves, 'A deviant construction: the French media and the 'banlieues', *Journal of Ethnic and Migration Studies*, 22 (1996), pp. 607–118. For a more recent discussion on the media's representation of urban violence in the banlieues, see Isabelle Garcin-Marrou, 'De l'exclusion à la "guerre" : les émeutes de 2005 et 2010 dans la presse française', in J. Carpenter and C. Horvath (eds.), *Regards Croisés sur la banlieue* (Brussels: Peter Lang, 2015), pp. 91–106.

11 Julia Kristeva, *Pouvoirs de l'horreur : Essai sur l'abjection* (Paris: Éditions du Seuil, 1980).

12 Colin McFarlane and Jonathan Rutherford, 'Political infrastructures: governing and experiencing the fabric of the city', *International Journal of Urban and Regional Research*, 32.2 (2008), pp. 363–374 (p. 364).

13 Author's emphasis. Jacques Rancière, 'Xénophobie et politique, entretien avec Jacques Rancière', in Florence Haegel, Henri Rey and Yves Sintomer (eds.), *La Xénophobie en banlieue, effets et expressions* (Paris: L'Harmattan, 2000), p. 215. Cited in Marc Angélil and Cary Siress, 'The Paris *Banlieue*: peripheries of inequity', *Journal of International Affairs*, 65.2 (2012), pp. 57–67 (p. 64).

14 In the context of Grand Paris, this 'common space' is most evident in the pervasive but non-critical use of terms such as 'mixité', 'renovation', 'attractivity' or 'creativity', and their application within grand urbanism's strategy to sell amenities associated with a global city, to solicit public support for its financing, and to financialize property markets.

15 Ash Amin, *Post-Fordism: A Reader* (Malden, MA: Wiley-Blackwell, 1995); Saskia Sassen, *The Global City: New York, London, Tokyo* (Princeton, NJ: Princeton University Press, 2001).

16 David Harvey, *A Brief History of Neoliberalism* (New York, NY: Oxford University Press, 2005); Leslie Sklair, 'The transnational capitalist class and contemporary architecture in globalizing cities', *International Journal of Urban and Regional Research*, 29.3 (2005), pp. 485–500.

17 See Michael Sheringham, *Everyday Life: Theories and Practices from Surrealism to the Present* (Oxford: Oxford University Press, 2006) for the tradition of 'proximite ethnography' in French writing. For a discussion on the 'postnational', see Jürgen Habermas, *The Postnational Constellation: Political Essays*, trans. Max Pensky (Cambridge, MA: MIT Press, 1998).

18 Didier Daeninckx, *Artana! Artana!* (Paris: Gallimard, 2018); Lydie Salvayre, *Les Belles Âmes* (Paris: Éditions du Seuil, 2000); Joy Sorman, *Gros Œuvre* (Paris: Gallimard, 2009). Given that the above works have yet to be translated into English, all translations of citations from the novels are the author's.

19 Slavoj Žižek, *Violence: Six Sideways Reflections* (New York, NY: Picador, 2008), pp. 10–11.

20 Galtung, 'Violence, peace, and peace research', pp. 167–191.

21 Ibid., p. 168. Italics in the original text.

22 Galtung, 'Violence, peace, and peace research', p. 171.

23 Ibid.

24 Akhil Gupta, *Red Tape: Bureaucracy, Structural Violence and Poverty in India* (Durham, NC: Duke University Press, 2012).

25 For a discussion on urbanism, neoliberalism and structural violence, see Martin F. Manalansan IV, 'Race, violence, and neoliberal spatial politics in the global city', *Social Text*, 84–85 (2005), pp. 141–156.

26 Lydie Salvayre, *Passage à l'ennemie* (Paris: Éditions du Seuil, 2003); Olivier Brunhes et al., *Des Nouvelles de la banlieue* (Paris: Éditions Textuel/Ivre d'images, 2008).

27 Salvayre, 'En français parfumé', in Brunhes et al., *Des Nouvelles de la banlieue*, p. 258.

28 On satire in Salvayre, see Warren F. Motte, 'Voices in her head', *SubStance*, 33.2 (2004), pp. 13–29.

29 Marie-Pascale Huglo, 'The Salvayre method', *SubStance*, 35.3 (2006), pp. 35–50 (p. 35).

30 Bourdieu discusses symbolic violence in a number of key texts. The following works have been useful for reading Salvayre: Pierre Bourdieu, *Ce que parler veut dire : L'Économie des échanges linguistiques* (Paris: A. Fayard, 1982);

Language and Symbolic Power, trans. John Thompson (Cambridge and Oxford: Polity Press, 1991) and Pierre Bourdieu, *Raisons Pratiques : Sur la Théorie de l'Action* (Paris: Éditions du Seuil, 1994); *Practical Reason Power*, trans. Randall Johnson (Cambridge and Oxford: Polity Press, 1998).

31 Laurent Dubreuil, 'Notes towards a poetics of *banlieue*', *Parallax*, 18.3 (2012), pp. 98–109 (p. 98).

32 Dubreuil, 'Notes towards a poetics of *banlieue*'.

33 Salvayre, *Les Belles Âmes*, p. 42.

34 For a concise definition of 'othering', see Jeremy Hawthorn, *A Concise Glossary of Contemporary Literary Theory* (2nd edn.) (London: Edward Arnold, 1994), p. 141.

35 Theresa Enright, *The Making of Grand Paris: Metropolitan Urbanism in the Twenty-First Century* (Cambridge, MA: MIT Press, 2016), p. 11.

36 For a key text in the field of dark tourism studies, see John Lennon and Malcolm Foley, *Dark Tourism: The Attraction of Death and Disaster* (London, UK and New York, NY: Continuum, 2000).

37 Salvayre, *Les Belles Âmes*, p. 42.

38 Ibid., p. 98.

39 Ibid., p. 99.

40 Ibid., p. 100.

41 Ibid., p. 51.

42 Ibid.

43 Ibid., p. 107.

44 Ibid., p. 112.

45 Jacques Lacan, 'Le Symbolique, l'imaginaire et le réel', conference paper given on 8 July 1953 at the Société française de Psychanalyse (online), http://ecole-lacanienne.net/wp-content/uploads/2016/04/1953-07-08.pdf, last accessed 16 November 2017.

46 Julia Kristeva, *Pouvoirs de l'horreur : Essai sur l'abjection* (Paris: Éditions du Seuil, 1980).

47 Joy Sorman, *L'Inhabitable* (Paris: Gallimard, 2016); *Gare du Nord* (Paris: Gallimard, 2011).

48 *Online Etymological Dictionary* (online), www.etymonline.com/word/inhabit#etymonline_v_9261, last accessed 12 July 2018.

49 Martin Heidegger, 'Building, dwelling, thinking', in M. Heidegger, *Poetry, Language, Thought*, trans. Albert Hofstader (New York, NY: Perennial Classics, 2001), pp. 141–160.

50 Sorman, *Gros Œuvre*, pp. 15–16.

51 Richard Sennett, *The Craftsman* (New Haven, CT: Yale University Press, 2008).

52 As such, her work chimes with feminist critiques of this conflation of dwelling, origin and stability. For some seminal work in this field, see Doreen Massey, 'A global sense of place', *Marxism Today*, 38 (1991), pp. 24–29; Gillian Rose, *Feminism and Geography: The Limits of Geographical Knowledge* (Cambridge: Polity Press, 1993).

53 For a fascinating cultural and ecological history of the beaver, see Rachel Poliquin, *Beaver* (London: Reaktion Books, 2015).

54 Sorman, *Gros Œuvre*, p. 49.

55 Ibid., p. 51.

56 Ibid., p. 52.

57 Jean-François Lyotard, *Discours, figure* (Paris: Klincksieck, 1971).

58 Lyotard, *Discours, figure*, pp. 379–382.

59 Michèle Gazier, 'Le roman francais : 2 ou 3 choses que je sais de lui', in Jean-Pierre Salgas et al. (ed.), *Le Roman français contemporain* (Paris: Ministère des affaires étrangères, 1993), pp. 55–69 (p. 60).

60 Stephen Steele, 'Daeninckx, quand le roman policier part en guerre', *French Studies Bulletin*, 71 (1999), pp. 9–10 (p. 9).

61 One character, Omar Belaïd, for example, has his father die in the 1961 Seine Massacre and later finds out that his mother is a child survivor of the Holocaust.

62 Daeninckx, *Artana ! Artana !*, p. 101.

63 The reader's attention is drawn to this ruse through the novel's reference to *La Princesse des Clèves* – an early example of the French *roman à clé* – and Daeninckx has also cited as the inspiration for the book the police seizure in 2013 of eleven kilogrammes of cocaine and firearms from the municipal Technical Centre. Nathalie Revenu, 'Aubervilliers : Daeninckx passe la ville au vitriol', *Le Parisien*, 5 June 2018, www.leparisien.fr/seine-saint-denis-93/aubervilliers-daeninckx-passe-la-ville-au-vitriol-05-06-2018-7754691.php, last accessed 10 July 2018. As Daeninckx observes, 'On s'est apercu qu'une partie de l'administration communale était entre les mains de voyous de haut vol. [...] C'était une nouveauté en Seine-Saint-Denis : il y avait des passerelles entre la voyoucratie, l'administration et le personnel politique.' / 'It became clear that part of the municipal council was being controlled by high-level gangsters. [...] There were clear channels connecting management and political personnel to yob rule; that was new for Seine-Saint-Denis.'

64 Daeninckx, *Écrire en contre : Entretiens avec Robert Deleuse, Christiane Cadet, Philippe Videlier, suivis de L'Écriture des abattoirs* (Vénissieux: Paroles d'Aube, 1997), p. 7.

65 Vaman Shivaram Apte, *The Practical Sanskrit-English Dictionary* (online), https://dsalsrv04.uchicago.edu/dictionaries/apte, last accessed 16 November 2018.

66 See Rosalyn Deutsche, ' "Chinatown," Part Four? What Jake forgets about downtown', *Assemblage*, 20 (1993), pp. 32–33.

67 For an excellent discussion of the 'knot' of memory, see Max Silverman, *Palimpsestic Memory: The Holocaust in French and Francophone Fiction and Film* (Oxford, UK and New York, NY: Berghahn Books, 2013).

68 See Charles Forsdick, ' "*Direction les oubliettes de l'histoire*": witnessing the past in the contemporary French *polar*', *French Cultural Studies*, 12 (2001), pp. 333–350.

69 Annie Fourcaut, Emmanuel Bellanger and Mathieu Flonneau, *Paris/Banlieues, Conflits et Solidarités : Historiographie, Anthologie, Chronologie 1788–2006* (Paris: Creaphis Éditions, 2007).
70 Daeninckx, *Artana ! Artana !*, p. 62.
71 Ibid.
72 Ibid., pp. 62–63.
73 Ibid., pp. 121–122.
74 Harvey, *A Brief History of Neoliberalism*, p. 159.
75 Ibid.
76 Lefebvre, *Le Droit à la ville suivi de Espace et Politique* (Paris: Anthropos 1972 [1968]).
77 Daeninckx, *Artana ! Artana !*, p. 101.
78 Deutsche, ' "Chinatown," Part Four?'
79 Daeninckx, *Artana ! Artana !*, p. 63.
80 Lefebvre, *La Production de l'espace* (Paris: Éditions Anthropos, 1974).

Chapter 12

1 This part of the debate may be viewed at www.dailymotion.com/video/x5kt7is, last accessed 19 July 2018.
2 'Discours du Président de la République au Parlement européen à Strasbourg', 17 April 2018, www.elysee.fr/emmanuel-macron/2018/04/17/discours-du-president-de-la-republique-au-parlement-europeen-a-strasbourg, last accessed 15 January 2019.
3 Ivan Rioufol, *La Guerre civile qui vient* (Paris: Pierre-Guillaume de Roux, 2016); David Djaïz, *La Guerre civile n'aura pas lieu* (Paris: Cerf, 2017).
4 Emile Chabal, *A Divided Republic: Nation, State and Citizenship in Comtemporary France* (Cambridge: Cambridge University Press, 2015). It is worth observing at this point the significant difference between the valency of the notion of 'secession' as it operates in the respective contexts of France and the United States. Whereas in the latter, it is identified primarily with right-wing libertarian hostility to and withdrawal from the state (a position which of course frequently self-identifies with the legacy of *the* Civil War), in the former, it features as either (i) a left-libertarian/anarchist or eco-localist strategy (as in the 'Zone à défendre' movement), (ii) a largely fantasmatic vision of already existing Islamist autonomy, or (iii) the invocation of a blank, undetermined site, the negative space exscribed by Republican saturation. (This third will be considered below.) Plainly, there is nothing symmetrical or complementary about this difference.
5 Jean-Pierre Azéma, Jean-Pierre Roux and Henry Rousso, 'Les guerres franco-françaises', *Vingtième siècle*, 5 (1985), pp. 3–5 (p. 3).
6 Chabal, *A Divided Republic*, p. 88. See also Andrew Hussey's reference to 'the unacknowledged civil war between France and its disturbed suburbs' (*The French Intifada: The Long War Between France and its Arabs* (London: Granta, 2014), p. 404.

7 See Fraser McQueen, 'France's "elites", Islamophobia, and communities of friendship in Sabri Louatah's *Les Sauvages*', *Modern & Contemporary France*, 26.1 (2017), pp. 77–90, doi: 10.1080/09639489.2017.1377693, last accessed 21 June 2018.

8 Laurent Obertone, *Guerilla* (Paris: Ring, 2016); Jean Rolin, *Les Événements* (Paris: P.O.L., 2015); Charles Robinson, *Fabrication de la guerre civile* (Paris: Éditions du Seuil, 2016).

9 See, for example, Homi K. Bhabha, *Nation and Narration* (London: Routledge, 1990); Ann Thompson and Vincent Newey, *Literature and Nationalism* (Liverpool: Liverpool University Press, 1991); Pericles Lewis, *Modernism, Nationalism and the Novel* (Cambridge: Cambridge University Press, 2000); Patrick Parrinder, *Nation and Novel: The English Novel from its Origins to the Present Day* (Oxford: Oxford University Press, 2008).

10 Jacques Derrida, *Passions* (Paris: Galilée, 1993), pp. 64–65.

11 Jacques Rancière, *Politique de la littérature* (Paris: Galilée, 2007), pp. 21–22, 30; *The Politics of Literature*, trans. Julie Rose (Malden, MA and Cambridge, UK: Polity, 2011), p. 21.

12 Rancière, *Politique de la littérature*, pp. 21–22, 30; *The Politics of Literature*, p. 21.

13 See Rancière, *La Mésentente : Politique et philosophie* (Paris: Galilée, 1995).

14 Chantal Mouffe, *Agonistics: Thinking the World Politically* (London: Verso, 2013), p. 8. See also Mouffe's earlier elaboration of this position, in her *Democratic Politics* (London: Verso, 2005), pp. 102–103.

15 Mouffe, *Agonistics*, p. 14.

16 Ibid., p. 79.

17 Mouffe, *The Democratic Paradox* (London: Verso, 2000), p. 13.

18 James's phrase comes from the preface to his *The Tragic Muse*. See www.online-literature.com/henry_james/tragic-muse/0, last accessed 19 July 2018.

19 In 2015, its second editor, Bernard Comment, described the series as 'un territoire d'accueil, d'audace, pour la littérature et la pensée en train de se faire' / 'a space that is open and auudacious for new literature and thought as it is emerging', www.fictionetcie.com/accueil, last accessed 8 June 2018.

20 Most prominently, work by such authors as Mehdi Charef or Faïza Guène; less prominently, work emerging from initiatives such as writing workshops. For an outstanding account of the debates around such literature, see Bruno Levasseur, 'Telling stories: narrating violence in the contemporary French *banlieues* (1992–2006)', *Modern & Contemporary France*, 24.4, pp. 395–410.

21 Charles Robinson, 'Fabrication de la guerre civile' (interview, 26 October 2016), www.youtube.com/watch?v=QBxWcXeBGpg, last accessed 16 May 2018.

22 Robinson, *Fabrication*, pp. 520–521.

23 Robinson, 'Fabrication de la guerre civile' (interview).

24 Ibid.

25 Ibid.

26 Robinson, *Fabrication*, p. 296.

27 Ibid., p. 168.
28 Ibid., pp. 166, 167.
29 For example, Robinson, *Fabrication*, p. 592.
30 Robinson, *Fabrication*, pp. 11, 317, 374.
31 Ibid., p. 376.
32 Ibid., p. 162.
33 Ibid., p. 63.
34 Ibid., p. 540.
35 Ibid., p. 625.
36 Ibid., p. 361.
37 Ibid., p. 292.
38 Ibid., p. 210.
39 Ibid., pp. 210–211.
40 Ibid., p. 247.
41 Ibid., pp. 117, 337, 377, 445.
42 Ibid., pp. 505–506.
43 Ibid., p. 551.
44 Ibid., p. 466.
45 Ibid., p. 518.
46 Ibid., p. 621.
47 Ibid., p. 622.
48 Giorgio Agamben, *The Coming Community*, trans. Michael Hardt (Minneapolis, MN: University of Minnesota Press, 1993), pp. 85–86; quoted in McQueen, 'France's "elites" '.
49 Robinson, *Fabrication*, p. 627.
50 On Finkielkraut, see Hussey, *The French Intifada*, pp. 11–12; and contrast Hussey's conclusion that: 'Most importantly, the rioters, wreckers, even the killers of the *banlieues* are not looking for reform or revolution. They are looking for revenge' (p. 404).
51 Robinson, *Fabrication*, p. 73.
52 For example, Robinson obliquely reconfigures a famous line from Baudelaire: 'luxe, calme et volupté' / 'luxury, calm and voluptuousness' becoming 'flux, calme et sécurité' / 'flow, calm and security', *Fabrication*, p. 71.
53 Robinson, *Fabrication*, p. 61.
54 Ibid., p. 270.
55 Ibid., pp. 516, 517, 521.
56 Robinson, 'Fabrication de la guerre civile' (interview). Author's emphasis in the French.
57 Robinson, *Fabrication*, p. 522.
58 Ibid., p. 520.
59 Ibid., p. 391.
60 Giorgio Agamben, *Stasis: Civil War as a Political Paradigm, Homo Sacer, II*, trans. Nicholas Heron (Edinburgh: Edinburgh University Press, 2015), unpaginated online version (essay 1, section 12).
61 Robinson, *Fabrication*, pp. 614, 616, 623.

62 Ibid., p. 364.

63 Ibid., p. 359.

64 Sylvain George, *Des Figures de guerre* (*Qu'ils reposent en révolte*, 2010; *Les Éclats*, 2011) (DVD) (Paris: Potemkine Films, 2016).

65 'If security forces and prison guards in Turkey, Libya, Mali and Sudan find themselves integrated into the EU's border regime, there has also been a multiplication of "deterritorialized" zones deep in the interior of the Union, where the rights guaranteed by the international conventions to which EU states subscribe no longer apply: detention centres close to airports and other points of passage; "temporary" camps, where conditions recall those in a war zone.' Stathis Kouvelakis, 'Borderland', NLR 110 (2018), pp. 5–33 (p. 12).

66 Chabal, *A Divided Republic*, p. 89.

Select Secondary Bibliography

Agamben, Giorgio, *What Is an Apparatus? And Other Essays*, trans. David Kishik and Stefan Pedatella (Stanford: Stanford University Press, 2009)

Amine, Leila, *Postcolonial Paris: Fictions of Intimacy in the City of Light* (Madison: University of Wisconsin Press, 2018)

Appadurai, Arjun, *Modernity at Large: Cultural Dimensions of Globalization* (Minneapolis: University of Minnesota Press, 1996)

Apter, Emily, *Against World Literature: On the Politics of Untranslatability* (London: Verso, 2013)

Arendt, Hannah, *Between Past and Future: Eight Exercises in Political Thought* (New York: Penguin, 1993)

Asibong, Andrew, *Marie N'Diaye: Blackness and Recognition* (Liverpool: Liverpool University Press, 2013)

Audet, René and Gefen, Alexandre (eds.), *Frontières de la fiction* (Quebec: Nota Bene, 2002)

Badiou, Alain, *Le Siècle* (Paris: Éditions du Seuil, 2005)

Barthes, Roland et al., *Littérature et réalité* (Paris: Éditions du Seuil, 1982)

    Préparation du roman : Cours au Collège de France, ed. Nathalie Léger (Paris: Éditions du Seuil, 2003)

    The Preparation of the Novel: Lecture Courses and Seminars at the Collège de France, trans. Kate Briggs (New York: Columbia University Press, 2010)

Baudrillard, Jean, *Baudrillard Live: Selected Interviews*, ed. Mike Gain (London: Routledge, 1993)

Bégaudeau, François (ed.), *Devenirs du roman* (Paris: Naïve, 2007)

Bensmaïa, Réda, *Experimental Nations* (Princeton: Princeton University Press, 2003)

Bessard-Blanquy, Olivier (ed.), *L'Édition littéraire aujourd'hui* (Bordeaux: Presses Universitaires de Bordeaux, 2006)

Best, Victoria and Crowley, Martin, *The New Pornographies* (Manchester: Manchester University Press, 2012)

Blanchot, Maurice, *L'Écriture du désastre* (Paris: Gallimard, 1980)

    The Writing of the Disaster, trans. Ann Smock (Lincoln: University of Nebraska Press, 1986)

Blanckeman, Bruno, *Les Fictions singulières* (Paris: Prétexte, 2002)

Blanckeman, Bruno, Millois, Jean-Christophe and Viart, Dominique, *Le roman français aujourd'hui : Transformations, perceptions, mythologies* (Paris: Prétexte, 2004)

Bornand, Marie, *Témoignage et fiction : Les récits de rescapés dans la littérature de la langue française, 1945–2000* (Paris: Librairie Droz, 2004)

Bourdieu, Pierre, *Les Règles de l'art : Genèse et structure du champ littéraire* (Paris: Éditions du Seuil, 1992)

    The Rules of Art: Genesis and Structure of the Literary Field, trans. Susan Emanuel (Cambridge, UK: Polity Press, 1996)

Cadiot, Olivier, *Histoire de la littérature récente*, tome I (Paris: P.O.L., 2016)

    Histoire de la littérature récente, tome II (Paris: P.O.L., 2018)

Camus, Audrey, 'Roman et antiroman' (pp. 92–104). *Littérature*, n° 180, December 2015

Casanova, Pascale, *The World Republic of Letters* (Cambridge, MA; London: Harvard University Press, 2007)

    La République mondiale des Lettres (Paris: Éditions du Seuil, 2008)

Citton, Yves, *Lire, interpreter, actualiser : Pourquoi les études littéraires ?* (Paris: Amsterdam, 2017)

Clarke, Robert (ed.), *The Cambridge Companion to Postcolonial Travel Writing* (Cambridge, UK: Cambridge University Press, 2017)

Compagnon, Antoine, *Le démon de la théorie : Littérature et sens commun* (Paris: Éditions du Seuil, 1998)

    La Littérature, pour quoi faire ? (Paris: Collège de France/Fayard, 2007)

Coquio, Catherine, *La Littérature en suspens. Écritures de la Shoah : Le témoignage et les œuvres* (Paris: L'Arachnéen, 2015)

Cusset, François, *La décennie : Le grand cauchemar des années quatre-vingt* (Paris: La Découverte, 2006)

Day, Loraine, *Writing Shame and Desire: The Work of Annie Ernaux* (Oxford: Peter Lang, 2007)

Derrida, Jacques, *Acts of Literature*, ed. Derek Attridge (New York: Routledge, 1992)

    Passions (Paris: Galilée, 1993)

Dion, Robert, *Des fictions sans fiction ou le partage du réel* (Montreal: Presses de l'Université de Montréal, 2018)

Doubrovsky, Serge, Lecarme, Jacques and Lejeune, Philippe (eds.), *Autofictions et cie.*, Cahiers du RITM, 6 (Nanterre: Université Paris X-Nanterre, 1993)

Dubois, Jacques, *Les romanciers du reel : De Balzac à Simenon* (Paris: Éditions du Seuil, 2000)

Ducas, Sylvie, *La Littérature à quel(s) prix ? Histoire des prix littéraires* (Paris: La Découverte, 2013)

Ducournau, Claire, *La Fabrique des classiques africains : Écrivains d'Afrique subsaharienne francophone 1960–2012* (Paris: CNRS 2017)

Duffy, Helena, Andreï *Makine's Historiographic Metafiction: No One is Forgotten, Nothing Is Forgotten* (Amsterdam: Brill, 2018).

Durand, Alain-Philippe and Mandel, Naomi (eds.), *Novels of the Contemporary Extreme* (London: Continuum, 2006)

Enright, Theresa, *The Making of Grand Paris: Metropolitan Urbanism in the Twenty-First Century* (Cambridge, MA; London: MIT Press, 2016)

Faerber, Johan, *Après la littérature : Écrire le contemporain* (Paris: Presses Universitaires de France, 2018)

Fanon, Frantz, *Les damnés de la terre* (Paris: Maspero, 1961)
　The Wretched of the Earth, trans. Richard Philcox (New York: Grove, [1963] 2004)

Fonkoua, Romuald, *Les Discours de voyages : Afrique-Antilles* (Paris: Karthala, 2001)

Forest, Philippe, *Le Roman, le réel* (Nantes: Pleins Feux, 1999)

Forsdick, Charles, *Travel in Twentieth-Century French and Francophone Cultures* (Oxford: Oxford University Press, 2005)

Forsdick, Charles and Murphy, David (eds.), *Francophone Postcolonial Studies: A Critical Introduction* (London: Arnold, 2003)

Fort, Louis and Houdart-Merot, Violaine, *Annie Ernaux : Un engagement d'écriture* (Paris: Presses de la Sorbonne Nouvelle, 2015)

Fourcaut, Annie, Bellanger, Emmanuel and Flonneau, Mathieu, *Paris/Banlieues. Conflits et solidarités : Historiographie, anthologie, chronologie 1788–2006* (Paris: Creaphis Éditions, 2007)

Franz, Anaïk and Maspero, François, *Les Passagers du Roissy-Express* (Paris: Éditions du Seuil, 1990)
　Roissy Express. A Journey through the Paris Suburbs, trans. Paul Jones (London: Verso, 1994)

Fumaroli, Marc, *L'État culturel. Une religion moderne* (Paris: Fallois, 1990)

Gefen, Alexandre, *Réparer le monde. La Littérature face au XXIᵉ siècle* (Paris: Corti, 2017)

Gefen, Alexandre and Samoyault, Thiphaine, *La taille des romans* (Paris: Classiques Garnier, 2012)

Genette, Gérard, *Fiction et diction* (Paris: Éditions du Seuil, 1991)

Grierson, Karla, *Discours d'Auschwitz : Littérarité, représentation, symbolisation* (Paris: Honoré Champion Editeur, 2003)

Grove, Laurence, *Comics in French* (Oxford; New York: Berghahn, 2013)

Hamon, Philippe, "Un discours contraint" in Roland Barthes et al., *Littérature et réalité* (pp. 119–181) (Paris, Éditions du Seuil, 1982)

Hargreaves, Alec, *Voices from the North African Immigrant Community in France: Immigration and Identity in Beur Fiction* (New York; Oxford: Berg, 1991)
　Post-colonial Cultures in France (London; New York: Routledge, 1997)

Hargreaves, Alec, Forsdick, Charles and Murphy, David, *Transnational French Studies: Postcolonialism and Littérature-Monde* (Liverpool: Liverpool University Press, 2012)

Henke, Suzette A., *Shattered Subjects: Trauma and Testimony in Women's Life-Writing* (New York: St Martin's Press, 1998)

Hiddleston, Jane, *Writing After Postcolonialism: Francophone North African Literature in Transition* (London: Bloomsbury, 2017)

Hilsum, Mireille, *Comment devient-on écrivain ? Sartre, Aragon, Perec et Modiano* (Paris: Kimé, 2012)

Hirsch, Marianne, *The Generation of Postmemory: Writing and Visual Culture After the Holocaust* (New York: Columbia University Press, 2012)

Hollier, Denis, *A New History of French Literature* (Cambridge, MA.: Harvard University Press, 1989)

Hollister, Lucas, *Beyond Return: Genre and Cultural Politics in Contemporary French Fiction* (Liverpool: Liverpool University Press, 2019)

Huggan, Graham, *The Postcolonial Exotic: Marketing the Margins* (London: Routledge, 2001)

Hutcheon, Linda, *A Theory of Adaptation* (New York: Routledge, 2006)

Jablonka, Ivan, *L'Histoire est une littérature contemporaine. Manifeste pour les sciences sociales* (Paris: Éditions du Seuil, coll. La Librairie du XXIᵉ siècle, 2018)

Jameson, Fredric, *Postmodernism, or, The Cultural Logic of Late Capitalism* (London: Verso, 1991)

Jordan, Shirley, *Marie Ndiaye: Inhospitable Fictions* (Oxford: Legenda, 2017)

Private Lives, Public Display: Intimacy and Excess in French Women's Self-Narrative Experiment (Liverpool: Liverpool University Press, 2019)

Jouanny, Sylvie and le Corre, Élisabeth, *Les Intermittences du sujet : Écritures de soi et discontinu* (Rennes: Presses Universitaires de Rennes, 2016)

Kemp, Simon, *Defective Inspectors* (Oxford: Legenda, 2006)

French Fiction into the Twenty-First Century (Cardiff: University of Wales Press, 2010)

Khanna, Ranjanna, *Algeria Cuts: Women and Representation, 1830 to the Present* (Stanford: Stanford University Press, 2008)

Khatibi, Abdelkebir, *Maghreb pluriel* (Paris: Denoël, 1983)

Figures de l'étranger dans la littérature française (Paris: Denoël, 1987)

Plural Maghreb. Writings on Postcolonialism, trans. P. Burcu Yalim (London: Bloomsbury Academic, 2019)

Kimyongur, Angela and Wigelsworth, Amy (eds.), *Rewriting Wrongs: French Crime Fiction and the Palimpsest* (Newcastle upon Tyne: Cambridge Scholars Publishing, 2014)

Krauss, Charlotte, *La Russie et les Russes dans la fiction française du XIXᵉ siècle (1812–1917)* (Amsterdam: Rodopi, 2007)

Kristeva, Julia, *Pouvoirs de l'horreur : Essai sur l'abjection* (Paris: Éditions du Seuil, 1980)

Langer, Lawrence, *Holocaust Testimonies: The Ruins of Memory* (New Haven: Yale University Press, 1991)

Lavocat, Françoise, *Fait et Fiction – Pour une frontière* (Paris: Éditions du Seuil, 2016)

Le Bris, Michel et al., *Pour une littérature voyageuse* (Brussels: Complexe, 1992)

et al., 'Pour une "littérature-monde" en français'. *Le Monde des livres*, March 2007. Available at: www.lemonde.fr/livres/article/2007/03/15/des-ecrivains-plaident-pour-un-roman-en-francais-ouvert-sur-le-monde_883572_3260.html

Le Bris, Michel and Rouaud, Jean (eds.), *Pour une littérature-monde* (Paris: Gallimard, 2007)

Lejeune, Philippe, *Le Pacte autobiographique* (Paris: Éditions du Seuil, 1975)

La mémoire et l'oblique : Georges Perec autobiographe (Paris: P.O.L., 1991)

Lévy, Clara, *Écritures de l'identité. Les écrivains juifs après la Shoah* (Paris: Presses Universitaires de France, 1998)

Lyons, John (ed.), *The Cambridge Companion to French Literature* (Cambridge, UK: Cambridge University Press, 2015)

Meizoz, Jérôme, *La Fabrique des singularités : Postures II* (Geneva: Slatkine, 2011)

La Littérature "en personne". Scène médiatique et formes d'incarnation (Geneva: Slatkine, 2016)

Morrey, Douglas, *Michel Houellebecq. Humanity and its Aftermath* (Liverpool: Liverpool University Press, 2013)

Motte, Warren, *Small Worlds: Minimalism in Contemporary French Literature* (Lincoln: University of Nebraska Press, 1999)

Neboit-Mombet, Janine, *L'Image de la Russie dans le roman français, 1859–1900* (Clermont-Ferrand: Presses Universitaires Blaise-Pascal, 2005)

Ní Loingsigh, Aedín, *Postcolonial Eyes: Intercontinental Travel in Francophone African Literature* (Liverpool: Liverpool University Press, 2009)

Nora, Pierre, *Les Lieux de Mémoire* (Paris: Gallimard, 1984–1992, 3 vols.)

Realms of Memory. Rethinking the French Past (New York: Columbia, 1996)

Panaïté, Oona, *The Colonial Fortune in Contemporary Fiction in French* (Liverpool: Liverpool University Press, 2017)

Rabaté, Dominique, *La Passion de l'impossible. Histoire du récit au XXe siècle* (Paris: Corti, 2018)

Rancière, Jacques, *Politique de la littérature* (Paris: Galilée, 2007)

The Politics of Literature, trans. Julie Rose (Malden, MA; Cambridge, UK: Polity, 2011)

Richard, Jean-Pierre, *Terrains de lecture* (Paris: Gallimard, 1996)

Ricœur, Paul, *La Mémoire, l'histoire, l'oubli* (Paris: Éditions du Seuil, 2000)

Rieffel, Rémy, *La Tribu des clercs : Les intellectuels sous la Ve République* (Paris: Calmann-Lévy/CNRS, 1993)

Robel, Léon, *Histoire de la neige : La Russie dans la littérature française* (Paris: Hatier, 1994)

Rolls, Alistair and Walker, Deborah, *French and American Noir* (London: Palgrave, 2009)

Rothberg, Michael, *Traumatic Realism: The Demands of Holocaust Representation* (Minneapolis: University of Minnesota Press, 2000)

Ruffel, Lionel, *Le dénouement* (Lagrasse: Verdier, 2005)

Brouhaha (Lagrasse: Verdier, 2016)

Ruszniewski-Dahan, Miriam, *Romanciers de la Shoah. Si l'Écho de leurs voix faiblit* (Paris: L'Harmattan, 1999)

Rye, Gill and Worton, Michael (eds.), *Women's Writing in Contemporary France. New Writers, New Literatures in the 1990s* (Manchester: Manchester University Press, 2002)

Samoyault, Tiphaine, *L'excès du roman* (Paris: Maurice Nadeau, 1999)

Samoyault, Tiphaine (ed.), 'Fictions contemporaines', *Littérature*, n° 151, September 2008

Sapiro, Gisèle (ed.), *Les contradictions de la globalisation éditoriale* (Paris: Nouveau Monde Éditions, 2009)

Sapiro, Gisèle and Rabot, Cécile (eds.), *Profession, écrivain?* (Paris: CNRS Éditions, 2017)

Sartre, Jean-Paul, *Qu'est-ce que la littérature?* (Paris: Gallimard, 1948)

Schaeffer, Jean-Marie, *Pourquoi la fiction?* (Paris: Seuil, 1999)

Sheringham, Michael, *French Autobiography: Devices and Desires* (Oxford: Oxford University Press, 1993)

   Everyday Life. Theories and Practices from Surrealism to the Present (Oxford: Oxford University Press, 2006)

Silverman, Max, *Palimpsestic Memory: The Holocaust in French and Francophone Fiction and Film* (Oxford; New York: Berghahn Books, 2013)

Suleiman, Susan Rubin, *Risking Who One Is: Encounters with Contemporary Art* (Cambridge, MA: Harvard University Press, 1994)

   Crises of Memory and the Second World War (Cambridge, MA: Harvard University Press, 2006)

   French Global. A New Approach to Literary History (New York: Columbia University Press, 2010)

Talbayev, Edwige Tamalet, *The Transcontinental Maghreb. Francophone Literature across the Mediterranean* (New York: Fordham University Press, 2017)

Todorov, Tzvetan, *La Littérature en péril* (Paris: Flammarion, 2007)

Viart, Dominique, *Anthologie de la littérature contemporaine française : romans et récits depuis 1980* (Paris: Armand Colin, 2013)

Viart, Dominique (ed.), *Ecritures contemporaines 1 – Mémoires du récit* (Paris: Lettres Modernes Minard, 1998)

Viart, Dominique and Baetens, Jan (eds.), *Ecritures comtemporaines 2 – États du roman contemporain* (Paris: Lettres Modernes Minard, 1999)

Viart, Dominique and Rabaté, Dominique (eds.), *Écritures blanches* (Saint-Étienne: Publication de l'Université de Saint-Étienne, 2009)

Viart, Dominique and Rubino, Gianfranco (eds.), *Écrire le présent* (Paris: Armand Colin, 2013)

Viart, Dominique and Vercier, Bruno, *La Littérature française au présent : Héritage, modernité, mutations* (Paris: Bordas, 2008)

Williams, Russell, *Pathos, Poetry and Politics in Michel Houellebecq's Fiction* (Leiden: Rodopi-Brill, 2019)

Xavier, Subha, *The Migrant Text. Making and Marketing a Global French Literature* (Montreal: McGill-Queens University Press, 2016)

Index

Abderrazak, Hakim, 185
Abouet, Aya Marguerite, 122
Académie française, 79, 82, 136
Agamben, Giorgio, 19–20, 32, 230, 233
Alexakis, Vassilis, 80, 82–83
Améro, Constant, 134
Amrani, Younès, 56
Angot, Christine, 51, 98, 153–154, 157
Angoulême, Festival, 118
Antelme, Robert, 167–169
Apter, Emily, 78
Armus, Seth, 100
Atwood, Margaret, 161
Azéma, Jean-Pierre, 220

Badiou, Alain, 4, 142
Bagieu, Pénélope, 127
Balzac, 35
Balzac, Honoré de, 81, 134
Barthes, Roland, 3, 7–10, 15, 141
Baudelaire, Charles, 104, 174
Beaud, Stéphane, 56
Beckett, Samuel, 7, 14
Bégaudeau, François, 54, 62–68
Beigbeder, Frédéric, 11, 34–36, 49, 97–98, 133
Bellos, David, 141
Ben Jelloun, Tahar, 10, 20, 31–33
Ben Mansour, Latifa, 155
Benjamin, Walter, 181
Bensmaïa, Réda, 29
Bernheim, Emmanuèle, 44
Besson, Luc, 42
Bilal et alii, 119
Binet, Laurent, 11, 46–48
Blanchot, Maurice, 189
Bon, François, 45–48
Boudjedra, Rachid, 74
Boudjellal, Farid, 122
Bourdieu, Pierre, 56, 65, 124, 201, 204
Bouvier, Nicholas, 73
Brachemi, Fawzi, 122

Brecht, Bertolt, 170
Bretécher, Claire, 119
Breton, André, 174
Busnel, François, 90
Butor, Michel, 50, 170

Cadiot, Olivier, 48
Calle, Sophie, 153
Camus, Albert, 43–44, 114–115
Cantet, Laurent, 62
Cappello, Mary, 152, 155–156
Carrère, Emmanuel, 133
Caruth, Cathy, 168
Casanova, Pascale, 6–10, 14
Cayrol, Jean, 170
Céline, Louis-Ferdinand, 100, 113
Cendrars, Blaise, 134
Césaire, Aimé, 179
Cestac, Florence, 119
Chabal, Emile, 220, 235
Chakir, 119
Chakrabarty, Dipesh, 9
Chambers, Iain, 18
Chamoiseau, Patrick, 73–74, 83–87
Chaplin, Charlie, 173
Charef, Mehdi, 199
Charlie Hebdo, 50, 109, 121, 125, 200
Chatrian, Alexandre, 134
Cheng, François, 82
Chevillard, Éric, 38–42, 51
Cinebook, 111
Cixous, Hélène, 154
Clifford, James, 8
Coen brothers, 42
Collège de France, 79
Compagnon, Antoine, 80
Confiant, Raphaël, 74
Conrad, Didier, 112–113
Conti, Anita, 73
Cooreman, Gaëlle, 186
Corominas, Enrique, 114

Coupey, Augusta, 134
Custine, Astolphe de, 134

Daeninckx, Didier, 12–13, 167, 175–179,
    200–201, 211–217
Daoud, Kamel, 43–44
Darrieussecq, Marie, 50, 97, 99
Daudet, Alphonse, 134
Delacroix, Eugène, 230
Delaume, Chloé, 153
Delbo, Charlotte, 12, 167–173
Denis, Claire, 97
Derrida, Jacques, 27, 221
Despentes, Virginie, 12, 91, 102–106, 108
Deutsche, Rosalyn, 215
Devi, Ananda, 81
Deville, Patrick, 133
Diouf, Abdou, 76
Djaïz, David, 219, 224, 233
Djavann, Chahdortt, 81
Djebar, Assia, 10, 20, 23–27, 48, 155
Djian, Philippe, 49, 105
Do, Tess, 195
Doubrovsky, Serge, 51, 152, 162
Doucet, Julie, 118
Dual, Alain, 115
Dubreuil, Laurent, 204
Dufourmantelle, Anne, 27
Dumas, Alexandre, 134
Dumont, Bruno, 97
Dupuis, Jacinthe, 103
Durand, Alain-Philippe, 97
Duras, Marguerite, 159, 170
Dworkin, Andrea, 150

Eakin, Paul John, 155
Echenoz, Jean, 11, 38, 42–43, 50–52, 93
Eco, Umberto, 123
El Nossery, Névine, 155
Ellis, Brett Easton, 98–99
Ellroy, James, 104
Énard, Mathias, 134
Erckmann, Émile, 134
Ernaux, Annie, 3, 11, 54–62, 64–65, 68–71, 154

Fabcaro, 128–131
Fanon, Frantz, 192, 194
Favier, Olivier, 88
Fellous, Colette, 10, 20, 27–30
Fernandez, Dominique, 134
Ferrandez, Jacques, 114, 122
Ferrante, Elena, 105
Ferri, Jean-Yves, 112–113
Finkielkraut, Alain, 230
Fizaine, Jean-Claude, 134

Flaubert, Gustave, 105
Fonkua, Romuald, 184
Forest, Jean-Claude, 110
Forest, Philippe, 153
Forsdick, Charles, 18, 184
Fumaroli, Marc, 4, 80

Gailly, Christian, 44
Gallimard, Éditions, 54, 77, 91, 93, 107, 122
Galtung, Johan, 201–202, 212
Garréta, Anne, 43–44
Gary, Romain, 35
George, Sylvain, 235
Germain, Sylvie, 134
Giguere, Noelle, 162
Glissant, Édouard, 85–87, 196
Goblet, Dominique, 116
Goldhammer, Arthur, 80
Goncourt des lycéens, Prix, 75
Goncourt, Prix, 36, 42, 44, 73, 75, 77, 80,
    101–102, 106, 161, 164
Goscinny, René, 112–113, 119
Grand Prix de la Ville d'Angoulême, 119
Grand Prix du roman de l'Académie française, 75
Grasset, Éditions, 102
Groensteen, Thierry, 124
Guène, Faïza, 11, 54–62, 65, 70
Gulliver, 72, 74
Gupta, Akhil, 202

Hamme, Jean Van, 111
Hanrahan, Mairéad, 154
Harvey, David, 215
Hawkins, Paula, 108
Heidegger, Martin, 209
Hewitt, Leah, 165
Hinant, Guy Marc, 116
Hirsch, Marianne, 171
Houellebecq, Michel, 11–12, 34–36, 49–52, 91,
    97–102, 106, 109–110, 115, 131, 220, 233
Huggan, Graham, 79, 82
Huston, Nancy, 13, 75, 81, 167, 179–183
Hutcheon, Linda, 148

Ionesco, Eugène, 82

Jablonka, Ivan, 8–10, 14
James, Alison, 156
James, E. L., 105
James, Henry, 223
Jameson, Fredric, 37, 41, 52, 91, 97
Jarry, Alfred, 170
Jauffret, Régis, 45–46
Jones-Gorlin, Nicholas, 98
Jonquet, Thierry, 102, 167, 175–179

Kaplan, Leslie, 11, 54, 68–71
Kassovitz, Mathieu, 59
Kebir, Benyoucef Abbas, 122
Kepel, Gilles, 219
Kerangal, Maylis de, 134
Khatibi, Abdelkebir, 10, 20–23
Krauss, Charlotte, 134
Kristeva, Julia, 200, 207
Kundera, Milan, 83
Kurmann, Alexandra, 195–196

Laâbi, Abdellatif, 74
Lacan, Jacques, 207
Lacarrière, Jacques, 73
Laferrière, Dany, 79
Lamothe, Alexandre de, 134
Lang, Jack, 3, 13
    loi Lang, 4
Laurens, Camille, 154
Le Bris, Michel, 72–74, 86
Le Brun, Annie, 150
Le Débat, 3, 8
Le Monde, 8
Le Pen, Marine, 219
Lê, Linda, 13, 184, 189–192
Lefebvre, Henri, 199
Lejeune, Philippe, 152
Leménager, Grégoire, 132
Lenoir, Hélène, 44
Liberati, Simon, 99
Lionnet, Françoise, 17
Littel, Jonathan, 75
Loichot, Valérie, 195
Loingsigh, Aedín Ní, 184
Louaath, Sabri, 106, 220, 233
Louis, Édouard, 11, 54, 62–68, 70
Lyotard, Jean-François, 142, 210

Mabanckou, Alain, 75, 79
Macron, Emmanuel, 90, 108, 219–220
Maillart, Ella, 73
Makine, Andreï, 12, 80, 82, 132–141, 147–151
Mallory, Daniel, 108
Mancas, Magdalena, 143
Manchette, Jean-Patrick, 76, 91–93, 101–103
Mandel, Naomi, 97
Marouane, Leïla, 155
Marx, Karl, 137, 220
Maspero, François, 74
Médicis, Prix, 42, 45
Mémoire d'encrier, 85
Meunier, Jacques, 72
Miano, Léonora, 75
Minuit, Éditions de, 34–36, 38–39, 42, 93–94
Miské, Karim, 84

Mizubayashi, Akira, 81
Modiano, Patrick, 12, 51, 167, 173–175, 177
Moebius, 76
Mokeddem, Malika, 155
Molnár, Katalin, 85
Monchoachi, 84
Montaigne, Michel de, 157
Montalbetti, Christine, 38, 41–44, 52
Montellier, Chantal, 120
Moréas, Jean, 80
Morin, Edgar, 123
Mouffe, Chantal, 221–223, 228
Munro, Martin, 189
Murphy, David, 18

Nancy, Jean-Luc, 53
NDiaye, 166
NDiaye, Marie, 12, 44, 52, 155, 161–165
Ndione, Abasse, 87, 185
Neaud, Fabrice, 115
Neboit-Mombet, Janine, 134
Noé, Gaspar, 97
Nora, Pierre, 3, 10, 80
Nothomb, Amélie, 44, 49, 99–100
nouveau roman, 34–37, 72, 142

Obertone, Laurent, 220
Ollivier, Émile, 13, 184, 186–189, 191
Ophuls, Marcel, 178
Otero, Nicola, 122
Oubrerie, Clément, 122
Oulipo, 15, 35–36, 43, 47, 142, 155–156, 160

P.O.L., Éditions, 38, 41, 54
Papon, Maurice, 175
Pellegrino, Bruno, 106
Perec, Georges, 12, 35–36, 47, 50, 142, 153,
    167–168, 171–174
Perna, Pat, 122
Pierre-Dahomey, Néhémey, 13, 184, 187,
    191–194
Pif, 109
Pilote, 110, 112, 119
Pireyre, Emmanuelle, 45–46
Pratt, Hugo, 76
Proust, Marcel, 43, 55–61, 69, 80, 100, 173–174

Quandt, James, 97
Queneau, Raymond, 123
Quignard, Pascal, 48–49

Radovic, Stanka, 83
Rahimi, Atiq, 81–82
Rancière, Jacques, 200, 221–223
Ren, Marietta, 126

Renaudot, Prix, 75
Resnais, Alain, 123, 170
Rimbaud, Arthur, 59, 65
Rioufol, Ivan, 219, 224, 233
Robbe-Grillet, Alain, 34–35, 50, 72, 170
Robinson, Charles, 220, 223–235
Rolin, Jean, 90, 134, 220
Rolin, Olivier, 46–48, 132
Rosello, Mireille, 182
Rothberg, Michael, 169
Roubaud, Alix Cléo, 15
Roubaud, Jacques, 12–13, 15, 155–161, 166
Rousset, David, 170
Rousso, Henry, 220
Roux, Jean-Pierre, 220
Rubin Suleiman, Susan, 19
Ruffel, Lionel, 143
Rullier, Jérôme, 88
Rushdie, Salman, 74, 76

Said, Edward, 78
Saldívar, José, 80
Sallenave, Danièle, 134
Salvayre, Lydie, 13, 200–201, 203–208
Samuel, Raphael, 176
Sand, George, 35, 134
Sansal, Boualem, 13, 167, 179–183
Sanyal, Debarati, 182
Sarr, Mohamed Mbougar, 89
Sarraute, Nathalie, 35
Sartre, Jean-Paul, 3, 10, 109, 114, 179
Satrapi, Marjane, 122–123
Sattouf, Riad, 120
Seigne, Aude, 106
Selao, Ching, 196
Sennett, Richard, 209
Seuil, Éditions du, 54, 223
Shemak, April, 185
Sheringham, Michael, 60, 172
Shimazaki, Aki, 81–82
Sijie, Dai, 81
Simon, Claude, 35, 132, 170
Singh, Kavita Ashana, 84
Slimani, Leïla, 12, 91, 106–108
Sorman, Joy, 13, 200–201, 208–211, 217
Soulès, Dominique, 150

Spivak, Gayatri, 78
Stassen, Jean-Philippe, 88
Stendhal, 134
Suleiman, Susan, 171
Surrealists, The, 35, 91

Tabary, 119
Takahashi, Rumiko, 119
Tardi, Jacques, 113
Tel Quel, 35
Theuriet, André, 134
Thompson, E. P., 176
Thúy, Kim, 13, 184, 192, 194–197
Tissot, Victor, 134
Todorov, Tzvetan, 79
Toussaint, Jean-Philippe, 11, 38–40, 42, 48–49, 51
Traoré, Mahmoud, 88
Troyat, Henri, 35, 80
Trump, Donald, 90

Uderzo, Albert, 112–113, 123
Urbain, Jean-Didier, 73

Vance, William, 111
Vargas, Fred, 51
Verne, Jules, 134
Viart, Dominique, 143, 151
Viel, Tanguy, 12, 91, 94–99, 101, 108
Vielé-Griffin, Francis, 80
Vigan, Delphine de, 51, 108
Volodine, Antoine, 12, 50, 132–135, 141–151
Vuataz, Daniel, 106

Wagneur, Jean-Didier, 142
White, Kenneth, 72
Wieviorka, Annette, 167
Wikipedia, 36, 50

Yourcenar, Marguerite, 35
YouTube, 1

Zep, 111
Žižek, Slavoj, 201–202
Zola, Émile, 100, 134
Zulma, Éditions, 85

Milton Keynes UK
Ingram Content Group UK Ltd.
UKHW022343200224
438080UK00012B/58